# www.wadsworth.com

*wadsworth.com* is the World Wide Web site for Wadsworth and is your direct source to dozens of online resources.

At *wadsworth.com* you can find out about supplements, demonstration software, and student resources. You can also send email to many of our authors and preview new publications and exciting new technologies.

**wadsworth.com**
Changing the way the world learns®

# From the Wadsworth Series in Mass Communication and Journalism

## General Mass Communication

Anokwa, Kwadwo, Carolyn Lin, and Michael Salwen, *International Communication: Concepts and Cases*

Biagi, Shirley, *Media/Impact: An Introduction to Mass Media,* 6th ed.

Bucy, Erik, *Living in the Information Age: A New Media Reader*

Craft, John, Frederic Leigh, and Donald Godfrey, *Electronic Media*

Day, Louis, *Ethics in Media Communications: Cases and Controversies,* 4th ed.

Dennis, Everette E., and John C. Merrill, *Media Debates: Great Issues for the Digital Age,* 4th ed.

Fortner, Robert S., *International Communications: History, Conflict, and Control of the Global Metropolis*

Gillmor, Donald, Jerome Barron, and Todd Simon, *Mass Communication Law: Cases and Comment,* 6th ed.

Gillmor, Donald, Jerome Barron, Todd Simon, and Herbert Terry, *Fundamentals of Mass Communication Law*

Hilmes, Michele, *Only Connect: A Cultural History of Broadcasting in the United States*

Hilmes, Michele, *Connections: A Broadcast History Reader*

Jamieson, Kathleen Hall, and Karlyn Kohrs Campbell, *The Interplay of Influence,* 5th ed.

Kamalipour, Yahya K., *Global Communication*

Lester, Paul, *Visual Communication,* 3rd ed.

Overbeck, Wayne, *Major Principles of Media Law,* 2003 Edition

Sparks, Glenn G., *Media Effects Research: A Basic Overview*

Straubhaar, Joseph, and Robert LaRose, *Media Now: Communications Media in the Information Age,* 3rd ed.

Whetmore, Edward Jay, *Mediamerica, Mediaworld,* Updated 5th ed.

Zelezny, John D., *Communications Law: Liberties, Restraints, and the Modern Media,* 3rd ed.

Zelezny, John D., *Cases in Communications Law,* 3rd ed.

## Journalism

Adams, Paul, *Writing Right for Today's Mass Media: A Textbook and Workbook with Language Exercises*

Anderson, Douglas, *Contemporary Sports Reporting,* 2nd ed.

Bowles, Dorothy, and Diane L. Borden, *Creative Editing,* 3rd ed.

Chance, Jean, and William McKeen, *Literary Journalism: A Reader*

Dorn, Raymond, *How to Design and Improve Magazine Layouts,* 2nd ed.

Fischer, Heintz-Dietrich, *Sports Journalism at Its Best: Pulitzer Prize–Winning Articles, Cartoons, and Photographs*

Fisher, Lionel, *The Craft of Corporate Journalism*

Gaines, William, *Investigative Reporting for Print and Broadcast,* 2nd ed.

Hilliard, Robert L., *Writing for Television, Radio, and New Media,* 7th ed.

Kessler, Lauren, and Duncan McDonald, *When Words Collide,* 5th ed.

Klement, Alice M., and Carolyn Burrows Matalene, *Telling Stories/Taking Risks: Journalism Writing at the Century's Edge*

Laakaniemi, Ray, *Newswriting in Transition*

Miller, Lisa, *Power Journalism: Computer-Assisted Reporting*

Rich, Carole, *Writing and Reporting News: A Coaching Method,* 4th ed.

Wilber, Rick, and Randy Miller, *Modern Media Writing*

## Photojournalism and Photography

Parrish, Fred S., *Photojournalism: An Introduction*

## Public Relations and Advertising

Hendrix, Jerry A., *Public Relations Cases,* 5th ed.

Hunt, Todd, Grunig, James, *Public Relations Techniques*

Jewler, Jerome A., and Bonnie L. Drewniany, *Creative Strategy in Advertising,* 7th ed.

Newsom, Doug, and Bob Carrell, *Public Relations Writing: Form and Style,* 6th ed.

Newsom, Doug, Judy VanSlyke Turk, and Dean Kruckeberg, *This Is PR: The Realities of Public Relations,* 7th ed.

Sivulka, Juliann, *Soap, Sex, and Cigarettes: A Cultural History of American Advertising*

Woods, Gail Baker, *Advertising and Marketing to the New Majority: A Case Study Approach*

## Research and Theory

Babbie, Earl, *The Practice of Social Research,* 8th ed.

Baran, Stanley, and Dennis Davis, *Mass Communication Theory: Foundations, Ferment, and Future,* 3rd ed.

Rubenstein, Sondra, *Surveying Public Opinion*

Rubin, Rebecca B., Alan M. Rubin, and Linda J. Piele, *Communication Research: Strategies and Sources,* 5th ed.

Wimmer, Roger D., and Joseph R. Dominick, *Mass Media Research: An Introduction,* 7th ed.

# International Communication

## CONCEPTS AND CASES

**Edited by**

**KWADWO ANOKWA**

Butler University

**CAROLYN A. LIN**

Cleveland State University

**MICHAEL B. SALWEN**

University of Miami

Australia • Canada • Mexico • Singapore • Spain
United Kingdom • United States

**THOMSON**
™
**WADSWORTH**

Publisher: Holly J. Allen
Assistant Editor: Nicole George
Editorial Assistant: Amber Fawson
Technology Project Manager: Jeanette Wiseman
Marketing Manager: Kimberly Russell
Marketing Assistant: Neena Chandra
Advertising Project Manager: Shemika Britt
Project Manager, Editorial Production: Paula Berman
Print/Media Buyer: Tandra Jorgensen
Permissions Editor: Joohee Lee
Production Service and Compositor: G&S Typesetters

Copy Editor: Mimi Braverman
Illustrator: Glenda Bender/G&S Typesetters
Cover Designer: Qin-Zhong Yu, QYA Design Studio
Foreground Cover Images: Detail of Tape Recorder/PhotoLink; Earth/StockTrek; Pyramids in Egypt/Glen Allison; The Great Wall of China/Glen Allison
Background Cover Images: Arthur S. Aubry, CMCD, Andy Sotiriou, Ryan McVay, PhotoLink
Text and Cover Printer: Transcontinental Printing, Louiseville

**Wadsworth / Thomson Learning**
**10 Davis Drive**
**Belmont, CA 94002-3098**
**USA**

**Asia**
Thomson Learning
5 Shenton Way #01-01
UIC Building
Singapore 068808

**Australia**
Nelson Thomson Learning
102 Dodds Street
South Melbourne, Victoria 3205
Australia

**Canada**
Nelson Thomson Learning
1120 Birchmount Road
Toronto, Ontario M1K 5G4
Canada

**Europe / Middle East / Africa**
Thomson Learning
High Holborn House
50/51 Bedford Row
London WC1R 4LR
United Kingdom

Library of Congress Control Number: 2002108254
ISBN 0-534-57519-6

# Contents

# Foreword

Several years ago, I concluded that international communication as an academic field was defined only by geography. It had no distinctive theories, research methods, or substance. The criterion for inclusion in a book with a title such as *International Communication* was that the research took place out of the country. It was a flimsy basis for arguing that international communication deserved recognition in curricula, professional associations, and research journals—and even less that a book should be devoted to it.

Curiously enough, the one factor that international communication could claim as its own was rarely addressed. One could find all sorts of studies addressing social and economic factors related to communication, particularly to aspects of mass media systems, but they were seldom invoked as explanations and were even more rarely tested systematically. All the factors that define a nation—culture, nationality, language, economic structure, political system, values—were pretty much ignored, as though communication was just another natural science governed by universal laws of human behavior. Physicists do not need to replicate their studies in different countries or invoke political or economic explanations for the phenomena they study. Physics, chemistry, and biology are pretty much the same in every part of the world. Communication must be the same.

At one point in my career I thought so. Twenty years ago we debated the influence of transnational corporations and argued about cultural imperialism (now we would call this globalization), but we rarely examined systematically the varieties of media systems or how they were influenced by economic, political, and geographic factors on the macrolevel or by individual-level characteristics that aggregate to define cultures on the microlevel. To me, at the time, people seemed similar all around the world and were steadily becoming more alike. Now my view of the world has changed.

The end of the cold war did not usher in the "end of history," as Fukuyama predicted, but the "clash of civilizations," as Huntington described it, and the speed with which old animosities resurfaced surprised everyone.[1] Depending on whose map of the post–cold war world you prefer, the fault lines form along the borders of Huntington's contentious civilizations or simply between the old/traditional and the new/modern, as represented by Friedman's *The Lexus and the Olive Tree* and Barber's *Jihad vs. McWorld*.[2] We all know the discomfort of finding that just about every place looks more and more like every other place,[3] but as a counterpoint to globalization, the world is becoming more fragmented, probably more culturally heterogeneous, and certainly more contentious. However you look at the world in the first years of the twenty-first century, culture, nationalism, language, geography, and conflict based on them play a big role. Whether we want it or not, international communication has found its place.

The various fiefdoms of communication that add the prefix *inter-, cross-, trans-,* or *multi-* to *culture* and *communication* constitute a boom industry. Look at the university programs, academic journals and associations, and, of course, the books that focus on them. If we are all American now, as journalists and academics around the world regularly lament, then we should also acknowledge that we are all multicultural, international, or simply global. Within that thin and superficial overlay of global culture, however, there is more diversity than ever before: more countries with flags and United Nations seats, more groups demanding independence and nationhood, more languages claiming legitimacy, more tribal associations asserting a separate identity and demanding respect. There is a lot out there to study.

The goals of international communication as a field are not different from the goals of the physical sciences, but the opportunities for study have increased. Physicists have to get outside the planet to see whether the rules of gravity are different elsewhere, and it is hard and expensive to do so. But the breakdown of old political and economic systems that stifled cultural variety and the emergence of all sorts of new and hybrid cultural entities constitute a laboratory that we can all take advantage of. The goal of research is still the same, and it is the same for all aca-

---

1. Francis Fukuyama, *The End of History and the Last Man* (New York: Free Press, 1992); Samuel P. Huntington, *The Clash of Civilization and the Remaking of World Order* (New York: Simon & Schuster, 1996).

2. Thomas L. Friedman, *The Lexus and the Olive Tree* (New York: Farrar, Strauss, Giroux, 1999); Benjamin R. Barber, *Jihad vs. McWorld* (New York: Times Books, 1995).

3. Pico Iyer, *The Global Soul: Jet Lag, Shopping Malls, and the Search for Home* (New York: Knopf, 2000).

demic fields. We seek description, explanation, and implication. In our own work and in evaluating the work of others, we want to describe what is happening, explain what is happening, and finally explore the implications of our findings for a larger understanding of our world. Questions that any research needs to answer are What? why? and so what?

In research terms description is necessary and useful, but its value is limited. The traditional tools of reliability, validity, and adequacy of evidence are even more important in international or intercultural settings because we need to be even more certain that others will observe what we observe, that we really are observing what we think we are observing, and that we have taken an adequate array of observations into account. Once we move from simple description (never easy and usually not simple when we cross cultural or national boundaries) to explanation and implication, then the opportunities for memorable research begin to emerge. Unfortunately, research in international communication that moves beyond description is rare. Too bad, because we miss a lot of opportunities to examine the influence of the one factor other than geography that belongs to us. Consider the following simple formulations:

1.  $A \rightarrow B$.
2.  $A \rightarrow B$ because of C.
3.  If $(A \rightarrow B$ because of C$)$, then D.

A lot of research in our field posits some relationship between variables (statement 1) but rarely specifies the explanation (statement 2). This means that the research will never be persuasive even if the evidence linking A and B is compiled with attention to reliability, validity, and adequacy. The explanatory factor, C, in most international communication research is somehow tied to the Western economic and political institutions, a product of the influence of European critical studies, where the tradition is to compile evidence to build a case rather than to derive a testable hypothesis and then to test it empirically (statement 3). "Empirical" in this sense is not necessarily quantitative but rather a dispassionate examination of the appropriate evidence with due regard for reliability, validity, and adequacy. It can be contrasted with "polemic," which is the amassing of evidence to support a particular position, usually without regard to these safeguards. It may also be a compilation of absolutely irrefutable "facts" that lead to a totally distorted descriptive summary and indefensible conclusion. International communication, it must be acknowledged, is particularly vulnerable to this problem.

If the C term (the explanation for the relationship between A and B) is something that exists on the cultural, national, or social level, then the first implication, D, is that the relationship between A and B will disappear in places where C is absent. In traditional social science we call this the null hypothesis. Rejection of the null hypothesis, of course, does not prove that A leads to (causes) B, but without some evidence of difference between countries with C and countries without C, the argument about the relationship between A and B because of C fails. If the ills of the world or parts of it are in some way related to the problems of late capitalism, then the evidence to demonstrate this lies in a comparison between countries or cultures. Even in the era of globalization, opportunities for comparison abound. Voila! International communication research that goes beyond geography.

Comparing two countries or cultures, one with C and one without C, does not give us the inferential power of a true experiment, but it is a good start—and one that is increasingly within the grasp of academic research, even if we do not have access to handsome research grants and a generous travel budget. The Internet itself and the globalization of academia put any researcher in touch with more and more of the increasingly varied cultures, nations, and media systems. Perhaps there are patterns to be discovered and new theories to be derived and tested. Even when research is description and categorization, it is important. I see international communication as a field operating something akin to chemistry a century ago and genetics now. Chemists first had to observe the elements, then categorize them. Later, a periodic table that explained how the physical world worked was put together, and it guided further exploration of the physical world. Something similar is happening as a new generation of explorers describes and categorizes the genetic codes that apparently control the biological world. We are a long way from extending the work to the level of individual consciousness and collective social behavior, and we may find that the rules are different when we move up the chain of complexity from atoms and cells to people and cultures. The promise of defining international communication as something more than geography is exciting, though, and it is likely to lead to more discovery.

I see this book as a good step in that direction. It assembles an outstanding team of scholars from various backgrounds and interests and invites them to present their research and speculation. It covers a wide range of concepts and case studies, theories and data, empirical observation and speculation. The editors usefully provide readers with a road map to each section but wisely let us pursue our own exploration and interpretation of the field. There is probably enough raw material here, from enough case studies in enough different parts of the world, to begin to construct the outlines of a periodic table for international communication. If we ever get even a cursory and tentative map of the field to guide further research, then, as in chemistry and genetics, progress in understanding the field will accelerate. And because the field is the world we now live in and the world the next generations will inherit, we have more than a dispassionate academic interest in joining the search. I hope readers will take up the challenge to use the material here to help define the field and guide exploration of it.

*Robert L. Stevenson*
Kenan Professor of Journalism and Mass Communication
University of North Carolina, Chapel Hill

# Preface

In this book we take a concept-case approach to the study of international communication, an area of communication study that communication scholar Robert L. Stevenson wrote has "no identifiable substance, body of theory, or specific research methods, only geography."* Not everyone agrees that international communication has no substance or theories. At the least, the field has the basic concepts that compose theories.

The concept-case approach involves elaborating some of the major concepts often used in international communication. Concepts, by their nature, are indistinct and ambiguous. The best way to understand them is through osmosis. To this end, most of the parts of this book offer chapters with pairs of case study examples written by leading scholars. One section has three chapters. The chapters take a variety of approaches and methods. Readers will find policy approaches, historical approaches, critical approaches, rhetorical approaches, and the like.

The book is designed to serve as a basic text for undergraduate and graduate college courses in international communication, political science and international

---

*Robert L. Stevenson, "International Communication," in Michael B. Salwen and Don W. Stacks, eds., *An Integrated Approach to Communication Theory and Research* (Mahwah, NJ: Lawrence Erlbaum Associates, 1996), 181.

relations, communication studies, and cultural studies and international business. Depending on the level of the course, instructors might adopt other books to supplement the text.

The first part examines the concept of press freedom. Robert G. Picard, of the Turku School of Economics in Finland, reviews press freedom in Europe (Chapter 2). In Chapter 3 Tsan-Kuo Chang and Zixue Tai, of the University of Minnesota, review press freedom in China. The vastly different cultural regions underscore major philosophical differences regarding press freedom. These two chapters drive home the point that peoples from different cultures see different things when they discuss the same concept of press freedom.

The second part examines the concept of propaganda. Antonio V. Menéndez Alarcón, of Butler University, describes propaganda techniques during political campaigns in Spain and France (Chapter 4). The next chapter, by John Spicer Nichols of the Pennsylvania State University, describes the ongoing propaganda battle between the United States and Cuba.

The third part describes the media gatekeeping concept. Jack Lule, of Lehigh University, describes how the prestigious *New York Times* drew on culturally shared myths to describe the recent flooding disaster in Central America (Chapter 6). In the next chapter, Heloiza Herscovitz, of Florida International University, describes how Brazilian media gatekeepers managed the news gates during different political periods.

In the fourth part we examine the related concepts of colonialism and mass media development. William W. Neher, of Butler University, deals with development support communication issues in Africa (Chapter 8). Michael B. Salwen, of the University of Miami, offers a historical example of colonialist press coverage of the Italo-Ethiopian War of 1935–1936 (Chapter 9).

The fifth part examines the trend of globalization. David J. Atkin, of Cleveland State University, describes the globalization of the film industry (Chapter 10), and Katherine T. Frith, of the Nanyang Technological University in Singapore, offers an Asian case study of the globalization of the advertising industry (Chapter 11). This section offers a third chapter that expands on Frith's chapter and examines the Asian situation more broadly. Thus in Chapter 12 four leading Asian media scholars (Penghwa Ang, Joseph Man Chan, Junhao Hong, and Jae-won Lee) offer a comparative study of globalization and media development in four fast-developing Asian countries, Asia's so-called tigers.

In the sixth part the important concept of culture is examined. In Chapter 13 Joseph D. Straubhaar, of the University of Texas in Austin, describes major theoretical approaches to understanding this nebulous concept. Douglas A. Boyd, of the University of Kentucky, provides a case study of media and culture in the Arab world (Chapter 14).

Finally, the last part examines the concept of news and information diffusion. A leading proponent of this approach, Everett M. Rogers of the University of New Mexico, describes this concept with particular attention to new media technologies (Chapter 15). In the final chapter, Joseph N. Pelton, of George Washington University, describes diffusion in the context of global telecommunications.

Our book does not pretend to be exhaustive. Rather, we selected what we believe are important and enduring concepts for the student of international communication.

We would like to give special thanks to our contributors for enhancing our knowledge and understanding of international communication.

We are grateful to the Wadsworth production staff, Nicole George in the editorial department, and especially to our publisher, Holly J. Allen, whose patience, cooperation, and leadership contributed to the successful completion of this book.

We also extend our appreciation to Robert L. Stevenson, University of North Carolina at Chapel Hill, for writing the foreword to this book.

We are deeply grateful to our families for their support and love.

Finally, we extend our thanks to the following scholars for their constructive and instructive critique of our manuscript: Craig Allen, Arizona State University; Mark Alleyne, University of Illinois at Champaign-Urbana; William Briggs, San Jose State University; Robert Finney, California State University, Long Beach; Ron Hull, University of Nebraska; Joel Kaplan, Syracuse University; Marilyn Matelski, Boston College; William H. Meyer, University of Delaware; Sandhya Rao, Southwest Texas State University; Churchill L. Roberts, University of Florida; and Douglas Starr, Texas A&M University.

*Kwadwo Anokwa*
Butler University

*Carolyn A. Lin*
Cleveland State University

*Michael B. Salwen*
University of Miami

# 1

# International Mass Communication from the Tower of Babel to the Babel Fish

### KWADWO ANOKWA
### CAROLYN A. LIN
### MICHAEL B. SALWEN

The Bible's book of Genesis (11:1–9) describes a time when "the whole earth had one language and few words." At this time the leader of a powerful tribe, in a "call to greatness," beseeched his people to erect a tower that reached to the heavens. It was as if humans aspired to be like God. God saw this as an insolent act by a prideful people.

So, God "confused the people" by making them speak in many tongues. They could not communicate with each other and, frustrated, they began to fight with each other and never built the tower.

The biblical story is instructive for more than its obvious moral message about the peril of vanity. It is also a metaphor for how, if we could only communicate with each other, we could accomplish great acts—great, not necessarily in the sense of good but (at least) in size and proportion. The acts may be arrogant, such as aspiring to be God; or they may be evil, such as building mighty weapons of war; or they may be noble, such as finding human unity and working for peace and understanding. This last aspect of greatness in the sense of goodness often resonates with idealistic students who want to make the world a better place. If we could only communicate, we could work together, solve our problems, and accomplish noble deeds.

Many students are instinctively attracted to the late Marshall McLuhan's belief in the 1960s that the proliferation of electronic communication media around the world would break down national and psychological borders that separate peoples and (in this way) create a global village. The global village, he predicted, would transform "the entire globe, and of the entire human family [make] a single consciousness."[1]

As with so many of McLuhan's predictions, he was partly prophetic and partly mistaken. The promise of the proliferation of electronic media of communication, even into some of the most remote villages on earth, is for the most part a reality. The human race probably knows more about how other peoples on the planet live and think than ever before. Yet the dream of shared consciousness and understanding remains elusive. Although McLuhan's protégés continue to argue for their hero's relevance,[2] signs indicate that the new media technologies may be contributing to keeping peoples apart rather than to bringing them into a global village. For example, the Internet has caused a breakdown in news media gatekeeping and agenda setting, processes whereby journalists select the news and set the agenda for the limited set of issues that most people think about. This may be causing groups to segment rather than to unite. Rather than segmenting along national lines or cultural lines, people are segmenting along lines of the Internet haves and have-nots.[3]

Not only McLuhan but also early mass communication researchers were mistaken about media's potential. Daniel Lerner's widely hailed *Passing of the Traditional Society* (1958) predicted that developing societies in the Middle East could jump start national development and achieve modernization by, among other means, adopting popular mass media:

> We speak, nowadays, of modernization. Whether from East or West, modernization poses the same basic challenge—the infusion of "a rationalist and positivist spirit" against which, scholars seem agreed, "Islam is absolutely defenseless." The phasing and modality of the process have changed, however, in the past decade. Where Europeanization once penetrated only the upper level of Middle East society, affecting mainly leisure-class fashions, modernization today diffuses among a wider population and touches public institutions as well as private aspirations with its disquieting "positivist spirit." Central to this change is the shift in modes of communicating ideas and attitudes—for spreading within a large public vivid images of its own New Ways is what modernization distinctly does. Not the class media of books and travel, but the mass media of tabloids, radio and movies, are now the dominant modes.[4]

Both McLuhan and Lerner recognized that the developing media of mass communication have the ability to extend communication messages across long distances, across nations. Their naïve hopes in the diffusion of more communication as a means of solving enduring societal problems warn us not to expect much from the idea of communication.[5] Today, many developing societies have well-developed mass media systems that reach large segments of their populations. Understandably, many import foreign media technologies and content (because producing original content is expensive), and at least the educated classes in these societies resent what they regard as the dumping of unwanted and culturally inappropriate mass communication messages into their countries as "media imperialism." As Indonesian President Sukarno, a Third World leader during the 1960s, declared, "You may not think of a refrigerator as a revolutionary weapon. But if a peasant woman sees one on TV in her village square and realizes what it could do for her and her family, the germ of revolt is planted."[6]

The difficulty with this communication-as-panacea approach is that sending messages is not the same as understanding messages, and understanding messages is not the same as caring about the messages. And language, in terms of meanings of the individual words, is not the only problem hindering effective communication between nations and peoples. The receiver of the message may understand the sender's words and content, but the sender's meaning and worldviews cannot be easily communicated. As critics often blithely note, what we need is not more communication but more effective communication. Achieving effective communication, however, even in national or culturally homogeneous settings, is difficult. Effective worldwide communication through impersonal mass communication channels requires an understanding of social psychology, history, political science, and other disciplines. It requires communication to overcome psychological barriers as well as national borders.

Perceptual theories of communication tell us that human information processing is not a simple matter of a source's creation of messages (encoding) and a receiver's reception (decoding) of the messages as intended by the source. Social psychologists and communication theorists who advance theories of selective perception remind us that human perception can be highly selective. It involves such processes as selective exposure (people's tendency to expose themselves to messages that are in agreement with their beliefs), selective attention (people's tendency to pay attention to messages that are in agreement with their beliefs), and selection retention (people's tendency to recall messages that are in agreement with their beliefs).[7] Many factors, including the elusive factor of culture, account for selective perception and explain why different peoples see a different world.

The theory of selective perception reminds us that we are attracted to culturally familiar messages. For example, research in binocular rivalry indicates that when people look into binocular-like devices with different images in each lens, they are more likely to see the culturally familiar image. Tests of binocular rivalry with American and Mexican subjects show that Americans are more likely to see the picture of the baseball game than the bullfight and that Mexicans are more likely to see the bullfight.[8] From binocular rivalry we can surmise that people see world events from their cultural perspectives. When they hear different messages, they are more likely to attune themselves to the more culturally familiar message.

Another instructive story that draws on the Tower of Babel parable sheds light on our inability to communicate. It comes from Douglas Adams's humorous science fiction series *The Hitchhiker's Guide to the Galaxy*. The books concern the story of Arthur Dent and his friend Ford Prefect. They escape Earth moments before an alien race destroys it to make way for a hypergalactic freeway. Together, Dent and Prefect hitch rides on alien vessels and travel through the galaxy. Unlike many other science fiction books, Adams explains how members of different alien races communicate with each other. Intergalactic communication is possible in Adams's universe because of a remarkable freak of nature (or act of God to confuse prideful humans?) called the Babel fish:

> The practical upshot of all this is that if you stick a Babel fish in your ear you can instantly understand anything said to you in any form of language. The speech patterns you actually hear decode the brain wave matrix which has been fed into your mind by your Babel fish. . . . [T]he poor Babel fish, by effectively removing all barriers of communication between different races and cultures, has caused more and bloodier wars than anything else in the history of creation.[9]

Adams's books underscore that there is more to effective international and intercultural communication than just exchanging messages. Part of the problem is that the exchange or flow of messages among nations and peoples is imbalanced, a one-way flow. But, as we have described, the problem of communication and understanding is more acute than the flow of messages. Although there is no simple answer to the problems in international communication, communication researchers have drawn from numerous disciplines and produced an impressive body of research that needs to be organized. The first step in creating models and eventual theories of international communication is to elaborate the major concepts in a field. Concepts are the building blocks of eventual theories.[10] We hope that this focus on important concepts will stimulate discussion and, perhaps with supplementary readings, lead to something more fruitful than the Babel among nations and different peoples.

## NOTES

1. McLuhan, *Understanding Media: The Extensions of Man* (New York: New American Library, 1964), 67.

2. Alexander Stille, "Marshall McLuhan Is Back from the Dustbin of History," *New York Times,* 14 October 2000, A17, A19.

3. Fred Tasker, "Home on the Net," *Miami Herald,* 10 November 2000, 1E, 6E. Also see E. Katz, "And Deliver Us from Segmentation," *Annals of the American Academy of Social Science* 456:22–33 (1996).

4. Daniel Lerner, *The Passing of Traditional Society: Modernizing the Middle East* (New York: The Free Press, 1958; second paperback printing, 1964), 45.

5. See John Durham Peters, *Speaking into the Air: A History of the Idea of Communication* (Chicago: University of Chicago Press, 1999); and Laurence D. Stifel and Ralph K. Davidson, eds., *Social Sciences and Public Policy in the Developing World* (Lexington, MA:

Lexington Books/D. C. Heath and Company, 1982).

6. Quoted in W. Manchester, "A World Lit Only by Change," *U.S. News and World Report,* 25 October 1993, 9.

7. Dolf Zillmann and Jennings Bryant, eds., *Selective Exposure to Communication* (Hillsdale, NJ: Lawrence Erlbaum Associates, 1985).

8. J. W. Bagby, "A Cross-Cultural Study of Perceptual Predominance in Binocular Rivalry," *Journal of Abnormal and Social Psychology* 54:331–334 (1957).

9. Douglas Adams, *The Hitchhiker's Guide to the Galaxy* (New York: Pocket Books, 1979), 59–61.

10. Werner J. Severin and James W. Tankard Jr., *Communication Theories: Origins, Methods, and Uses in the Mass Media,* 5th ed. (New York: Longman, 2001), 47–70.

# PART I

# Press Freedom

Press freedom is perhaps the most fundamental concept in international communication and is central to any discussion about the role of the press and democracy. An examination of this concept is thus a fitting starting point for this book. As the two chapters in this section make clear, the student should not take the term's meaning for granted. "Press freedom" is a culturally loaded term. The Western tradition regards press freedom as an individual freedom—freedom *from* external intervention, usually from the state. This is especially true in the United States.

Even what we call the Western tradition is not as widely shared as many students may think. The First Amendment, enshrined in the U.S. Bill of Rights, takes a libertarian approach in which the government is supposed to take a hands-off approach to press freedom. Many students know that many Third World nations and dictatorships do not share this view, believing that governments must intervene in press freedom for what they claim is the greater social good. Many students may be surprised, however, that democratic Western nations in Europe also do not share a libertarian, government hands-off approach to press freedom.

Western European cultures traditionally have not been so obsessed with state intervention and tolerate limited state intervention in press operations. Some non-Western conceptions of press freedom even view governments as potentially beneficial forces in promoting press freedom (e.g., communism). This last view should not be lightly dismissed as an excuse for dictatorships. Even in the United States, the Federal Communications Commission (FCC) imposes restrictions on broadcasting for the ostensible public good.

One thing is certain: The call for press freedom stirs emotions among peoples throughout the world. In Western societies paintings such as Eugène Delacroix's *Liberty Leading the People* (1830, in the Louvre in Paris) epitomize the empowering value of all basic freedoms, including freedom of the press. Non-Western societies, too, have similar symbols underscoring the attraction of basic freedoms. During the 1989 Tiananmen Square demonstrations in China, students exhibited a Goddess of Democracy monument that was remarkably (and not accidentally) similar to the Statue of Liberty. The Goddess symbolized the students' desire for fundamental freedoms in authoritarian China. Thus in this part case studies of the concept of press freedom in Europe and China are presented. These two radically different case studies accentuate cultural conceptions of press freedom.

The appeal of the concept of press freedom is that it offers citizens an opportunity to receive information about their societies. However, if press freedom is to be of any value to individuals and of consequence to societies, it must be more than simply the freedom to receive facts and opinions. It must also include the freedom to impart information and opinions. For the press to be truly free, it must be an open institution that, if for practical reasons most citizens cannot own a mass medium, provides citizens reasonable access to express their views.

In the first chapter of this part, Robert G. Picard, of the Turku School of Economics in Finland, provides an overview of press freedom in Europe. In so doing, he conjures the names of Western philosophers encountered by students in history, philosophy, and civics classes—Rousseau, Milton, Mill, Marx, and so forth. Picard relates these philosophers' ideas to concepts of free expression and press freedom. He also addresses how European democracies coped and still cope with troubling issues raised by press freedom, such as hate speech, secrecy, pornography, and libel.

It is important not to take a Western view about free expression and press freedom as the only view. University of Minnesota journalism professor Tsan-Kuo Chang and a Minnesota doctoral candidate, Zixue Tai, offer a chapter of extraordinary breadth on free expression and press freedom in China. Students in the United States and other Western countries may not find the ideas familiar, but these Eastern ideas about press freedom underscore that the West does not hold a monopoly on free expression and free press. As Chang and Tai note, although Western ideas (e.g., Marxism) have influenced Chinese ideas about press freedom, the Chinese have tailored these ideas to suit their conditions.

# 2

# Press Freedom in Europe

## ROBERT G. PICARD

As we enter a new millennium, public support for authoritarianism and communism is waning across the globe as social, economic, and political developments combine with the intrinsic appeal of individual liberties and democratic governance. Nearly everywhere, demands for greater personal freedoms and democratization are replacing authoritarianism. Freedom of expression, which subsumes press freedom, is playing a central role in this worldwide democratization, partly because modern communication technologies such as the Internet and the World Wide Web make it increasingly difficult for governments to control expression. In addition, freedom of expression appeals to people's desires to express their social and political opinions and receive others' opinions without governmental interference.

Most contemporary ideas about freedom of expression trace their roots to debates initiated by European philosophers during the last several centuries. Europeans and their descendants in their colonies implemented these ideas into political action, in the forms of policies and legislation designed to enhance individual liberties and democratic participation. These ideas have left an indelible imprint on Western culture and thought and are relevant for understanding today's global turmoil.

## BACKGROUND

European debates concerning freedom of expression occurred against the backdrop of the rebellion against the power of the Church that began with the Reformation and, later, as part of the wave of democratic revolutions that swept Europe during the 1700s and 1800s. As a result of these developments, Europe is where the earliest protections of individual rights and freedom of the press developed. Paradoxically, it is the location of some nations in which freedom of the press only recently emerged.

In 1766 Sweden enacted the first constitutional protection of press freedom anywhere in the world.[1] In 1789 the Declaration of the Rights of Man and Citizen was drafted in France, laying out the basic ideas of equality, protection against the acts of the state, and freedom of religion, speech, and the press. The Declaration became the preamble to the French constitution in 1791. Great Britain has never had a constitution, but it protected individual liberty through common law dating to the Magna Carta in 1215, when King John agreed to popular demands to establish the rule of law and granted citizens specific rights and freedoms.

To fully understand the development and current condition of press liberties in Europe, we must recall that Europe does not have the broad common historical and philosophical development that exists in the United States, Canada, and much of the British-influenced world. The British tradition is only one of several cultural and political traditions in Europe.

Broad and differing political and philosophical bases of society exist in Anglo, Franco, Germanic, Latin (southern European), and Nordic regions. Differences in legal systems, especially between statutory Franco legal systems, emerged from the French Code Napoléon and the common law traditions of the Anglo legal system.

These differences are compounded by historical factors, such as the rise of fascism in Germany, Italy, and Spain during the twentieth century, and the sublimation of Central and Eastern Europe into the Soviet bloc for 50 years during and following World War II. The result of these differences makes it impossible to consider the bases and contemporary conditions of press freedom in Europe in universal terms.

## WHAT IS EUROPE?

To begin a discussion of press freedom in Europe, we need a common framework of what "Europe" denotes. Clearly it includes the 15 nations of the European Union. That definition, however, excludes Norway and Switzerland, which are without doubt European but which have chosen to remain independent of the European Union for economic, social, and political reasons. To understand Europe, both Norway and Switzerland must be included in the area defined as Europe. The nations in this conception of Europe have the strongest and most numerous commonalities in approaches to human rights, including freedom of expression.

If we stop at this definition of Europe, however, we miss the historical heart of Europe that was once represented in cities such as Prague, Budapest, and Warsaw. These cities are now within the countries of the Czech Republic, Hungary, and Poland, respectively, and have an equal claim to being European and having European cultures.

The Baltic states of Lithuania, Latvia, and Estonia clearly have strong European backgrounds extending at least to the days of the Hanseatic League (fourteenth to seventeenth centuries).[2] They have been influenced by German, Polish, and Nordic cultures, although philosophically and culturally they have been more on Europe's edge. The Balkan states also exhibit traits that tend to make them less "European," but countries such as Slovenia have strong ties and have been influenced by European culture for many years. Turkey, which has historically leaned more toward the Middle East than toward Europe, is increasingly developing a European orientation and has aspirations to be included in a unified Europe in the years to come.

## THE CONCEPTS OF FREEDOM OF EXPRESSION AND PRESS FREEDOM

It is clear that there is no such thing as total freedom of expression or press freedom anywhere in the world. This occurs because communications are influenced by social, political, and economic factors that exert control over communication. Each factor is equally capable of controlling communication and limiting dissemination of ideas and information.

In Europe and in much of the developed world the first major controls were political and social. Monarchs, emperors, and other strong leaders exercised political (governmental) control to support their rule. Social control was exercised by religious and cultural organizations and from within society itself.

The Protestant Reformation that began in the sixteenth century broke much of the power of the Catholic Church in controlling communication, particularly in Central and Northern Europe.[3] The Reformation sparked then-radical new ideas that individuals could think for themselves, and it resulted in a breach of the tradition of Church operation of the printing press.

This ultimately led to an antimonarchy democracy movement that broke authoritarian political control and to the establishment of liberal democratic rule. These changes, however, did not end political and social controls but rather softened their application and made a broader spectrum of ideas and information possible.[4]

Among Western nations the concepts of freedom of expression and freedom of the press are applied differently. At the heart of discussions regarding freedom of expression are the concepts of *negative freedom* and *positive freedom*.

Negative freedom is freedom from something. Positive freedom is freedom to attain something. Some people ascribe only to the negative aspect that prohibits government actions that inhibit freedom. Others are willing to accept the notion

### Some Important Europeans and Their Contributions to the Philosophy of Press Freedom

**Jean Jacques Rousseau, Switzerland/France, 1712–1778**

A political theorist and philosopher, Rousseau was a major figure in the French Enlightenment. He argued for the equality of man. But he called also for a social compact between the people and the state, whereby individuals surrendered certain rights to receive the protection of the state. He argued that the institutions of government were not part of the social compact and that public opinion regarding them should not be constrained because they would lose the moral standing upon which they had been built.

Rousseau argued that the government could exercise censorship to serve the general will, but its use against the will of the people can cause censorship to lose its justification:

> As the law is the declaration of the general will, censorship is the declaration of the public judgement: public opinion is the form of law which the censor administers. . . . The censorial tribunal, so far from being the arbiter of the people's opinion, only declares it, and, as soon as the two part company, its decisions are null and void.[5]

**John Milton, England, 1608–1674**

A well-known poet, Milton was an active supporter of reform of the Church of England and wrote criticisms of the church and its structures.

When his and others' views were censored by acts of Parliament, he wrote an impassioned plea for press freedom in 1644 called *Areopagitica.* The essay established the argument that truth will emerge in free and open discussions:

> And though all the windes of doctrin were let loose to play upon the earth, so Truth be in the field, we do injuriously, by licensing and prohibiting to misdoubt her strength. Let her and Falshood grapple; who ever knew Truth put to the wors, in a free and open encounter. . . . How many other things might be tolerated in peace, and left to conscience, had we but charity, and were it not the chief strong hold of our hypocrisie to be ever judging one another. [in original seventeenth-century English][6]

**John Stuart Mill, England, 1806–1873**

A liberal political economist and philosopher, Mill wrote extensively on governance, empiricism, and a variety of social and economic issues. He articulated libertarian views toward free expression, arguing its centrality in democratic governance. Mill held that British laws on blasphemy and libel often inhibited expression in unwarranted fashion. Many of his ideas regarding speech were contained in his 1859 book *Essay on Liberty.* Although Mill's underlying views agree with Milton on the struggle between truth and

of positive freedom that government should act to make expression possible. Those who dislike positive freedom argue that if government promotes positive freedom, it will limit freedom. Those who dislike the idea of having only negative freedom argue that it places freedom under social and economic controls.

Americans, who tend to have strong antigovernment philosophical tendencies, embrace the negative view of freedom from something, most often from the government. In Western Europe government tends to be seen as less threatening and more responsive to social needs, so broader support for governmental activities promoting positive freedom activities exists.

In general, however, it can be said that European nations today embrace the same basic philosophies toward freedom of expression, freedom of the press, freedom of assembly, and freedom of religion that are found in the United States but that the processes and methods of dealing with disputes differ. Similarly, the kind of expression that induces limitations sometimes differs.

---

### Some Important Europeans and Their Contributions to the Philosophy of Press Freedom

falsity, he did not believe that truth always triumphed. In *Essay on Liberty* Mill argued that the only reason for government interference in the liberty of others was to prevent harm to other persons and that freedom of expression and disputes over ideas were helpful to society:

> I do not pretend that the most unlimited use of the freedom of enunciating all possible opinions would put an end to the evils of religious or philosophical sectarianism. . . . [I]t is not on the impassioned partisan, it is on the calmer and more disinterested bystander, that this collision of opinions works its salutary effect. Not the violent conflict between parts of the truth, but the quiet suppression of half of it, is the formidable evil: there is always hope when people are forced to listen to both sides; it is when they attend only to one that errors harden into prejudices, and truth itself ceases to have the effect of truth, by being exaggerated into falsehood.[7]

**Karl Marx, Germany, 1818–1883**
A political theorist most noted for fundamental contributions to the philosophy of socialism,

Marx is also considered the father of economic history and sociology. He provided explanations of the development of capital, wealth, property, and the workings of firms. In his philosophical writings Marx argued that liberty was infringed upon by social institutions under the control of the powerful. In terms of the press he advocated freedom of expression, perhaps because his own work was at times suppressed:

> A free press is everywhere the open eye of the national spirit, the embodied confidence of the people in itself, the verbal bond that ties the individual to the state and the world. . . . It is the spiritual mirror in which the people observe themselves, and self-observation is the first condition of wisdom. . . . Bear in mind that the advantages of freedom of the press cannot be enjoyed without toleration of its inconveniences. There are no roses without thorns.[8]

## EUROPEAN LEGAL SYSTEMS
## AND PROCESSES

Because of the structure of European governments—both domestic laws and processes and pan-European laws and processes—laws apply to conflicts involving rights for expression, but differences exist in the legal bases and processes for handling disputes. Some nations have prior restraint against disputed expression and some provide differing degrees of protection for individuals in libel actions.

The primary approach to expression and the press in pan-European law is laid out in the Convention on the Protection of Human Rights and Fundamental Freedoms (1950).[9] The convention and its rights to freedom of the press, assembly, religion, and other expression were incorporated into European Community law in the Treaty of the European Union (1957).[10]

In nearly every European nation constitutional protections for freedom of expression and press freedoms exist. The exceptions are the United Kingdom, which does not have a constitution, and France, where expression is protected by the 1789 Declaration of the Rights of Man and Citizen.

### Extracts from Two Important Documents Providing the Philosophical and Legal Bases for Freedom of Expression in Europe

**Declaration of the Rights of Man and Citizen, 26 August 1789**

The French people, as represented at the National Assembly, consider that the ignorance, disregard or contempt of human rights are the sole causes of the nation's misfortunes and of the corruption of governments and have resolved to state the natural, inalienable and sacred human rights. . . . Freedom is the power to do anything which does not harm another: therefore, the only limits to the exercise of each person's natural rights are those which ensure that the other members of the community enjoy those same rights. . . . No-one may be troubled due to his opinions, whether or not they are on religious issues provided that the expression of these opinions does not disturb the peace. . . . Free communication of ideas and opinions is one of the most precious human rights; all citizens may therefore speak, write and print freely, though they may be required to answer for abusing this right in cases specified by law.[11]

**European Convention on Human Rights, 4 November 1950**

Everyone has the right to freedom of thought, conscience and religion; this right includes freedom to change his religion or belief, and freedom, either alone or in community with others and in public or private, to manifest his religion or belief, in worship, teaching, practice and observance. . . . Everyone has the right to freedom of expression. This right shall include freedom to hold opinions and to receive and impart information and ideas without interference by public authority and regardless of frontiers. . . . The exercise of these freedoms, since it carries with it duties and responsibilities, may be subject to such formalities, conditions, restrictions or penalties as are prescribed by law and are necessary in a democratic society, in the interests of national security, territorial integrity or public safety, for the prevention of disorder or crime, for the protection of health or morals, for the protection of the reputation or the rights of others, for preventing the disclosure of information received in confidence, or for maintaining the authority and impartiality of the judiciary.[12]

Restrictions on expression and press freedom tend to be enacted in laws and involve issues of libel and privacy, reporting of certain criminal and court proceedings, state secrets or national security, pornography, and incitement of racism or hatred.[13]

National laws within European Union member states apply to domestic matters and the treaties, and regulations of the European Union apply to communication among states and stipulate basic requirements at the domestic level. The European-level judicial system also serves as a type of court of appeal in human rights matters (such as freedom of expression) resulting from domestic legal decisions.

In addition to European human rights tribunals, European nations typically recognize the authority of bodies such as the United Nations Human Rights Committee to determine the propriety of laws and regulations related to freedom of expression and other rights issues.

A European Union regulation relating to transborder communications and operations of domestic broadcasting provides some nations the right to regulate expression. The Television Without Frontiers Directive (1989) (89/522 EC) was designed to increase flow of programs, broadcasts, and cable and satellite materials among member states.[14] However, it provides nations the right to control broadcasts to protect minors from materials that could "seriously impair their physical, mental or moral development" and provides for the control of materials that incite hatred on the grounds of race, sex, religion, or nationality.

There are some specific differences in processes and approaches to laws within European nations.[15] In France and countries influenced by the French legal system, for example, the general approach asserts that whatever is not specifically forbidden is permissible. Another example of these differences is seen in the British law approach to libel, which differs significantly from the approach found in the United States and in some European nations. Under the British legal system, for example, defendants must essentially prove that they did not commit libel. Truth itself is not a full defense against libel damages.

As in the United States, expression that violates laws can be punished after the fact in all European nations. However, nations differ on whether and under what conditions speech can be halted beforehand.

# CONTEMPORARY FREEDOM
# OF EXPRESSION CONFLICTS

As is the case in the United States and in all nations, limits to freedom of expression in Europe and other nations arise in conflicts between media and governments and between individuals and governments.

In Europe these conflicts have tended to involve expression involving military matters, hate speech, intelligence services, pornography, and libel. These conflicts are discussed next, with a series of case studies to illustrate each.

## Limits to Expression During
## Military and Paramilitary Conflicts

Limits to expression related to issues involving security of military operations and state secrets during conflicts have produced few significant disputes in Europe because there is general agreement, as in the United States, about the need and the right of a government to limit expression to protect national security. Disputes have arisen, however, over restricting or halting expression that is not clearly threatening to security.

During the Gulf War, for example, journalists from many European nations reported conflicts with European and U.S. military personnel over access to battlefields, the ability to independently obtain information on operations, and delays in transmitting information. These disputes reflected similar problems in many conflicts over the rights and abilities of military personnel and government officials to control communications as a means of influencing public opinion about the action.

During the NATO-Yugoslavia war in 1999, military planners repeatedly targeted television and radio broadcasting facilities to reduce the ability of Slobodan Milosevic's government to communicate publicly. Spokespersons at NATO headquarters justified the actions by saying that they were designed to halt the flow of propaganda from the Milosevic government.

The efforts to halt Milosevic's communication ability were hampered, however, because Yugoslavia was a member of Eutelsat, an international satellite service provider operated by a consortium of European broadcasting systems. The Serbian government in Yugoslavia used the system to transmit satellite broadcast signals throughout the Balkans even when NATO bombing raids damaged its domestic broadcasting transmitters.

This situation prompted NATO and its allied governments to pressure the quasi-private Eutelsat to cut off the broadcasts. "It has been quite embarrassing to have a European satellite collaborating with Milosevic's propaganda machine while the European military was trying to destroy it," a NATO ambassador said.[16]

After two months of pressure, Eutelsat's governing board halted Serbian use of the system by expelling Yugoslavian television from the consortium, using a regulation prohibiting use of the system to distribute materials that would promote ethnic hatred. The delay in obtaining agreement was due, in part, to differing opinions among European nations about the desirability of restricting expression and the necessity of finding a basis for halting the communications with which a sufficient number of nations could agree.

Another example of a disputed restriction on expression resulted from the conflict in Northern Ireland. In the years before the government of the United Kingdom, the Irish Republican Army (IRA), and other parties began negotiations to settle disputes involving Northern Ireland, the British government employed the Prevention of Terrorism Act to control expression by members of the IRA, its political wing Sinn Fein, and supporters of the movement. Implementation of the control policy made it illegal for members or spokespersons of the IRA or Sinn Fein or even their supporters to speak on television and radio broadcasts in the United Kingdom.

This policy made it illegal for Sinn Fein spokesman Gerry Adams, who was also an elected member of the British Parliament, to speak on television broadcasts. This resulted in ridiculous situations in which video of Adams holding press conferences or being questioned by journalists would be broadcast but the audio of his answers would be turned off and the text of his words would be displayed on the screen or read aloud by a speaker.

The prohibitions against speech by supporters of the IRA or Sinn Fein made life difficult for radio call-in programs and even resulted in bans on the playing of some popular music groups on radio and television. For example, the ban included even the nonpolitical songs of the well-known group The Pogues because some of its members had expressed support for goals of the Sinn Fein and the IRA.

## Conflicts Involving Hate Speech, War Crimes, etc.

A number of European nations enforce prohibitions against inciting racial hatred, denying the Holocaust, or minimizing crimes committed during World War II. Notable in this regard are Belgium, Denmark, France, Germany, the Netherlands, and Spain. In some cases such acts are prohibited by national constitutions, and in other cases they are prohibited by laws. The philosophical and legal rationales for restricting these types of speech are based on the principle that they can incite hatred and lead to breaches of peace and violence.

European disputes over incitement of hatred and depictions of the Holocaust have been epitomized by conflicts involving Jean-Marie Le Pen, leader of the extreme-right National Front Party in France. His xenophobic and anti-Semitic party has for more than a decade averaged 15% of the vote in French national elections. Le Pen and his party advocate expelling all immigrants (including legal immigrants) and creating legal preferences in education, jobs, and state benefits for native-born French citizens.

Le Pen has been a center of continuing controversy and has used his positions on a French regional council and in the European Parliament as platforms to spread his views. In 1987 he called the Nazi gas chambers and concentration camps a mere detail of history and was prosecuted by the French government and fined 1.2 million francs ($200,000) for a violation of conventions against incitement of racism. In 1997 he accused French president Jacques Chirac of being controlled by the Jewish B'nai B'rith organization, accepting money to deliberately lose an election to avoid forming a coalition government with the National Front, and of publicly claiming that the races are not equal.

Le Pen repeated his statement that gas chambers were a mere detail of history during a visit to Munich, Germany. Because of his membership in the European Parliament, Le Pen had legislative immunity for making the statement. However, in 1998 the parliamentary immunity was removed by the European Parliament. German legal action against him is pending. (In 2002 Le Pen was soundly beaten by Chirac in the French presidential election. Many liberal French citizens were relieved by his sound defeat but were nonetheless shaken that the likes of Le Pen could even run for president.)

Similar actions against individuals have resulted in the destruction of printed materials. In 1998 a Spanish writer and bookshop owner, Pedro Varela, was sentenced to five years in prison for "Holocaust denial" and to three years for "spreading hatred and inciting violence." In addition, the Spanish court ordered that more than 20,000 books and videotapes belonging to Varela be burned.

Varela was convicted under a Spanish law forbidding the spread of ideas and doctrines that deny or justify the genocide against national, ethnic, racial, or religious groups and under a law against provoking discrimination or incitement of racial hatred against persons because of their religion.

In 1990 France enacted the loi Gayssot (90-615), which provides for one year's imprisonment for challenging the conclusions or verdicts of the International Military Tribunal at Nuremberg by denying the existence of crimes against humanity as defined for the Nuremberg trials after World War II. An impetus for the law was a number of anti-Semitic authors and lecturers who claimed that the Holocaust never happened or that some of the war crimes alleged were not proven.

Shortly after the law's enactment, a Holocaust denial writer, Robert Faurisson, argued that gas chambers did not exist in concentration camps and that it was a myth that there was a systematic extermination of Jews. Faurisson made his accusation in an interview in the magazine *Le Choc du Mois*. Faurisson and the editor of *Le Choc du Mois* were found guilty of violating the loi Gayssot and were ordered to pay 326,832 francs ($50,000) in fines and costs.

Faurisson appealed to the United Nations Human Rights Committee, which has jurisdiction because France is a signatory to relevant human rights protocols. He argued that his rights to free expression had been violated. The committee, however, ruled that the restriction was permissible under its rules providing for the ability to restrict speech that harmed the community as a whole, such as raising or strengthening anti-Semitic feelings. It ruled that the law under which he had been convicted served a necessary purpose of combating racism and anti-Semitism and therefore that the French law under which he had been prosecuted was proper.

In a related case the European Court of Human Rights in 1998 became the final arbiter of a dispute over an advertisement that appeared in the newspaper *Le Monde*. French courts ruled that the advertisement aided and abetted a public defense of the crimes of collaboration with the enemy. The law forbidding such expression carried penalties of five years in prison and a 300,000 franc ($45,000) fine. The French law was intent on halting expression designed to excuse or justify those who collaborated with Germany during World War II.

The case resulted from an advertisement placed by the Association for the Defense of the Memory of Marshal Philippe Pétain and the National Pétain-Verdun Association. Pétain was the leader of the pro-Nazi Vichy government after Germany defeated France in World War II. The advertisement carried passages about Pétain's contributions to France and how the country and its citizens benefited under his leadership as head of the Vichy government. Pétain was sentenced to death after the war for collusion with Germany. The associations, which included former members of the Vichy government and their supporters, published the ad with the intent of helping to revise historical interpretations of Marshal Pétain and seeking to reopen his case to overturn his conviction.

A *Le Monde* executive and those responsible for the advertisement's content were found guilty of the offense by French courts and fined 1 franc (15¢), a symbolic punishment, but they appealed to the European Court of Human Rights as a matter of principle. The court ruled that the criminal conviction was a disproportionate and unnecessary limitation on expression in a democratic society because it did not serve a pressing social need and that the conviction violated the Convention on Human Rights protection of freedom of expression. The court ordered the French government to pay the defendants 100,000 francs ($15,500) for costs and expenses.

Disputes over prosecutions of hate speech, Holocaust denial, and related expression are problematic across Europe because of the lack of agreement that expression in these areas can be restricted. Thus a speech, publication, or broadcast may be legal in one European nation but may become a crime if it crosses a border.

## Conflicts Involving Intelligence Services

A number of conflicts involving information about intelligence services have raised questions about the limits on free expression in European states. Intelligence services typically argue that disclosure of secrets or information about their operations should be limited because of the potential for harm to national security or because the disclosure can endanger the lives of personnel operating against other nations.

In the spring of 1999, for example, former British intelligence employee Richard Tomlinson began disclosing details of intelligence activities against other European Union nations, especially British foreign intelligence service MI-6's secrets about Germany and France. Tomlinson argued that the activities were illegal under European law and apparently unauthorized by Parliament. He called for investigations of the activities.

Tomlinson threatened to publish lists of MI-6 activities and names of MI-6 agents on an Internet site that he operated from Switzerland, where he resided. The British government obtained an injunction from the Swiss courts to stop him from carrying out his threat. The British government argued that it was necessary to restrain Tomlinson because he signed a secrecy agreement and because his threatened action would endanger the lives of agents who were exposed.

The government's response was similar to its efforts to halt distribution of Peter Wright's book, *Spycatcher: The Candid Autobiography of a Senior Intelligence Officer.* Wright was a former counterintelligence official with MI-5, the British domestic security agency. The book was published in the United States in 1987 and then in other countries, but its sale was banned in Britain for breaking secrecy laws. The government argued that in detailing the history of his own activities, Wright violated laws restricting discussions of past intelligence activities.

British newspapers and British citizens obtained copies of *Spycatcher* while abroad—and indeed there was no law forbidding British citizens from purchasing the book abroad and bringing it into Britain—but they were forbidden to publish extracts. A legal challenge to the ban was mounted, and in 1991 the European Court of Human Rights ruled that newspapers could publish extracts because the contents were no longer secret.

In 1998 the British government, using the Official Secrets Act, halted a broadcast by the BBC public affairs program *Panorama*. The government argued that the broadcast would carry details of a failed effort by MI-6 to assassinate Libyan leader Mu'ammar Gadhafi, including materials published in the *New York Times, The Guardian,* and other newspapers.

Thus, as in the United States, disputes over limits to communication about intelligence services and their activities are problematic because the limits of expression for national security can be used to hide problems or inappropriate activities by agencies as well as to protect legitimate secrets and activities.

## Conflicts Involving Pornography

Although Europeans tend to be more tolerant of nudity and depictions of sexual activity than Americans, disputes sometimes arise over the limits of acceptable pornography. Soft pornography magazines and videos are typically widely available in European kiosks and stores. Hard pornography is available in sex shops in which minors are not permitted. Broadcasts of erotic materials are not unusual, and television and cable television channels regularly carry programming that would not be broadcast in the United States. These range from nudity and depictions of sexual activity broadcast in prime time and other time slots to unedited scenes of vaginal penetration, ejaculation, and gay and lesbian sexual activities. Programs containing gay and lesbian sexual activities are typically broadcast late at night or on subscription channels to reduce their availability to minors.

Pornography is generally legal throughout Europe, but pornography involving minors is prohibited, as is bestiality in most nations. Despite the general tolerance toward various forms of pornography, there are conflicts over pornography within Europe, and the conflicts become especially contentious when pornography is deemed obscene and harmful.

A group of recent cases has pitted the British government against operators of pornographic cable and satellite channels in other nations. Arguing that it was trying to protect minors from materials that might corrupt them and that public morality should be protected, the British government banned channels such as Eurotica/Rendez-Vous, Satisfaction Club TV, Red-Hot Dutch, and Eros TV; these channels carried hard-core pornographic materials that required the use of decoders or smart cards for access. Because the government could not block satellite signals, it turned to such actions as forbidding advertising of the services and sales of smart cards to operate the services. The government argued that the broadcasts and cablecasts violated its Broadcasting Act (1990) and the Obscene Publications Act (1959), although they were permissible under European Community regulations.

Operators of erotic channels challenged the government's action in the British courts, where they lost. They then brought their case to the European Court of Justice. The European court ultimately ruled in favor of the British government in the Eurotica/Rendez-Vous case, indicating its policy to protect minors was narrowly within provisions of European law.

## Conflicts Involving Libel

Most European countries provide fewer protections to public figures, such as politicians and celebrities, than to private persons, as does the United States. The breadth of comment permissible under American law is much wider, however, particularly for speech about public officials and public figures. In the United States public officials must essentially show that the speaker knew the information was false, deliberately tried to harm the official, or made no effort to verify the questionable information.

Several nations still have rarely enforced laws that can be used against the libel of monarchs, a form of seditious libel that does not exist in the United States.

Many students wrongly believe that U.S. and British attitudes toward libel law are similar. Although the two nations shared common legal approaches until the eighteenth century and still have commonalities in legal traditions, their approaches to defamation differ today.

Under British law, for example, defendants must prove truth to reduce some damages, but proving truth is often difficult because journalists and others tend to get information secondhand. In the United States the most important Supreme Court case dealing with libel is without question *New York Times v. Sullivan* (1964). The case concerned a political advertisement purchased by a civil rights group that alleged that the Montgomery Police Department mistreated African Americans (and Montgomery Police Commissioner L. B. Sullivan maintained that, even though he was not named in the advertisement, he was libeled because he was in charge of the department). The court ruled in favor of the *New York Times*. The *Sullivan* case established the precedent that "public officials" (later cases extended libel law to "public figures") are different under the law of libel from private citizens. It ruled that public officials face more difficult (but not impossible) standards to sue the press for libel than private citizens. The case gave the American press great freedom to report about public officials and public figures without fear of libel. The American news media did not have to prove the truth of their allegedly libelous assertions. Rather, the case established that, to collect damages, plaintiffs (at least public officials and public figures) must prove that the media knowingly published false information or that they published the information with a reckless disregard for the truth. These are difficult standards for a plaintiff to establish, giving the press great freedom to report about public officials and public figures.

The situation is complicated in British law because the truthfulness of information can make the damages from libel even greater, especially in the case of information about personal lives. In a classic example of the problem this poses, the legal principle made it possible for the performer Liberace to collect damages when a British paper reported in the 1950s that he was gay.

Differences in libel laws among European Community member states have resulted in publishers' decisions not to export their products to some European nations, especially the United Kingdom. The movement of information across European borders becomes problematic with online publications that can be accessed from any member state.

In a recent case the British television news magazine *World in Action* carried a story revealing that clothing made in Morocco for the well-known retailer Marks & Spencer was made by children who worked as long as 49 hours a week for 10 pence (15¢) an hour. *World in Action* reported that the clothing articles were delivered to Marks & Spencer by a distributor bearing a label stating that they were made in the United Kingdom. The retailer sued, not contesting the facts presented but arguing that the program libeled it through an implication that it knew about the abuses, a fact that even the program's producers denied.

The jury decided that the "meaning" of the program was that Marks & Spencer knew of the abuses, and the broadcaster ultimately paid £50,000 ($80,000) in damages and costs totaling £1.3 million ($2.1 million), even though none of its actual words were found to be libelous.

Another interesting libel case in the United Kingdom during the 1990s pitted McDonald's against two activists of London's environmental Greenpeace movement, after the organization circulated a pamphlet criticizing the hamburger firm's business practices. Among other criticisms the pamphlet charged that the company destroyed rain forests, exploited its workers, and contributed to starvation in the Third World.

Under British law McDonald's did not have to show actual malice (knowledge of falsity or reckless disregard for the truth) on the part of the defendants. The burden of proving any truthfulness rested on the defendants. After the longest civil trial in English history, a British court ruled that most of the contested charges made in the publication were untrue and awarded £60,000 ($97,800) to the company.

## Conflicts Involving Advertising
## and Marketing

Rules regarding whether and how different types of products and services can be advertised are not consistent across Europe. This inconsistency creates conflicts when print, broadcast, or online materials are conveyed across European borders.

Regulatory differences exist involving advertising of alcohol, tobacco, over-the-counter and prescription drugs, financial services, and food products. Differences exist regarding the extent to which comparative advertising is permitted, the amount of advertising time and the number of advertising breaks permitted in television broadcasts, and a variety of other related matters.

Spain, for example, restricts advertising of over-the-counter drugs, but ads for these products are permitted in Portugal. Norway permits advertisements aimed at children, but such ads are banned in Sweden. Greece restricts religious advertising, but Germany does not.

Differences exist in terms of regulations affecting the marketing of products and services. These include rules covering discounting, when sales can be undertaken, whether premiums can be offered, and the extent to which such items can be promoted in advertising. These differences affect not only the ability of publishers and broadcasters to market their own products across national boundaries but also their ability to carry advertising and other marketing materials in their products and services on behalf of their clients. Most regulations are domestic, but conflicts involving these regulations are increasingly developing as materials cross national borders. The European Union has not yet solved problems regarding conflicting laws.

## Conflicts Involving the Internet

Some European governments' efforts to control the Internet during the last half of the 1990s sparked some contentious debates over freedom of expression and the nature of the new medium. These difficulties reflect the global debates over responsibility for material available on the Internet and the differences in the extent of protections of freedom of expression.

Probably no European nation typifies the conflict over the Internet better than Germany, which has one of the world's most active new media industries and high Internet use. As the Internet developed, it attracted the interest of legal authorities who attempted to regulate its content according to the same laws covering content in other mass media.

German efforts to halt the availability of illegal materials on the Internet produced one of the most contentious international debates over responsibility for material. That debate began in 1995 when prosecutors in Munich began investigating child pornography that had been obtained using CompuServe's German service. As a result of the inquiry, CompuServe corporate offices in the United States cut off access to more than 200 newsgroups, including many related to gay and lesbian groups and others that covered topics related to sex but were not pornographic.

In 1997 the director of the German CompuServe service was indicted on charges of allowing access to sexual and political materials that were illegal in Germany. It was believed to be the first case anywhere in which an Internet service provider (ISP) was charged with providing access to material available on the Internet rather than with producing illegal content.

The charges were brought as officials worldwide wrestled with how to regulate the Internet and whether the Internet should be considered a common carrier over which ISPs had no control or whether ISPs should be considered publishers responsible for the content they carry.

The German charges were brought under laws forbidding dissemination of obscene materials—charging the director of German CompuServe with distributing pictures portraying pedophilia, incest, and bestiality—and negligence in disseminating material morally harmful to youth, including charges that he permitted dissemination of violent games available online.

The director of German CompuServe was convicted in 1998 for complicity in 13 cases of distributing illegal materials. The conviction was reversed in 1999, primarily on the grounds that the director was not directly involved in the material and that there was no way to effectively block the material with technology. In a case of seeming déjà vu, Germany's largest Internet provider, Deutsche Telekom, cut access to 1,500 sites in 1996 after German prosecutors said they were considering indictments against the firm for assisting the distribution of neo-Nazi and Holocaust denial materials.

The debates sparked by these episodes ultimately led the German, Dutch, British, and other governments to conclude that policing the Internet through control of ISPs was difficult, if not inappropriate. Instead, these governments have redirected most of their attention to leading efforts to prosecute on the European level those people actually creating or providing illegal materials and to promoting or requiring that ISPs make filtering and blocking systems available to users. The result is that the European and the American approaches to the Internet are converging based on pragmatism and the understanding that ISPs cannot fully monitor materials sent over the Internet.

Enforcing national laws that regulate content throughout Europe is still difficult because these laws, relating to communication involving pornography, trafficking in human beings, racist materials, terrorism, and fraud, differ significantly from nation to nation. Although nations broadly agree on restrictions on pedophilia, far less agreement exists regarding other materials that are banned in only some nations. Because some acts are punishable in some countries but not in others, pan-European enforcement will continue to be problematic.

The European Commission has made significant studies of issues related to the Internet and enforcement of national laws. It recently issued a policy declaration that describes differences in national policy and legal approaches and technical difficulties in policing the Internet at the national and pan-European level.[17] The policy promotes action to develop and promote personal blocking software and increases efforts to coordinate pan-European enforcement of laws against child pornography. It notes, however, that there can be little pan-European enforcement against other types of content because of the differences in national regulation.

In implementing the approach, the European Union has moved to set up hot lines to report illegal materials, to promote the use of filters, and to have the industry engage in self-regulation.[18]

## SUMMARY

The European debates involving freedom of expression are quite similar to those occurring in the United States because of the basic support for freedoms and similar types of media and communications technologies. The latitude of freedom of expression differs, however, sometimes to a lesser or greater extent than in the United States, depending on the type of expression and the European nation involved.

Although Europe is in the process of continuing integration and is developing a stronger centralized European government, most regulation of expression remains national, somewhat analogous to the situation in the United States where most of the laws regulating communication are found at the state level rather than at the federal level. These differences make it impossible to speak of European press freedoms in absolute and universal terms but, in general, European nations are among those that provide the most liberty for expression worldwide.

## NOTES

1. Carter R. Bryan, "'Enlightenment of the People Without Hindrance': The Swedish Press Law of 1766," *Journalism Quarterly* 37 (summer 1960): 431–434.

2. The Hanseatic League was a league of merchant associations within the cities of northern Germany and the Baltic. They united to assure unfettered and safe trade by traveling together. This banding together of merchants on the road led to their alliances

at home as well and to agreements among city states.

3. Steven Ozment, *The Age of Reform: An Intellectual and Religious History of Late Medieval and Reformation Europe* (New Haven, CT: Yale University Press, 1986).

4. Robert Palmer, *Age of Democratic Revolution: A Political History of Europe and America, 1760–1800* (Princeton: Princeton University Press, 1959).

5. Jean Jacques Rousseau, *The Social Contract,* translated by Maurice Cranston (New York: Penguin Books, 1987).

6. John Milton, *Complete English Poems, of Education, Areopagitica,* edited by Gordon Campbell (New York: Everyman Paperback Classics, 1906; reissued, 1992).

7. John Stuart Mill, *On Liberty,* edited by Gertrude Himmelfarb (New York: Viking Press, 1982).

8. Karl Marx, *Rheinische Zeitung,* no. 135 (15 May 1842).

9. Council of Europe, "Convention for the Protection of Human Rights and Fundamental Freedoms (ETS 5)," Rome, 4 November 1950.

10. Treaty Establishing the European Community as Amended by Subsequent Treaties, Rome, 25 March 1957.

11. http://www.justice.gouv.fr/anglais/addhc.htm

12. Council of Europe, "Convention for the Protection of Human Rights and Fundamental Freedoms."

13. Manny E. Paraschos, *Media Law and Regulation in the European Union: National, Transnational, and U.S. Perspectives* (Ames: Iowa State University Press, 1997).

14. Commission of the European Communities, "Directives: 89/552 EC," *Official Journal* (Luxembourg: Office of Official Publications for the European Communities, 1989).

15. René David and John E. C. Brierley, *Major Legal Systems in the World Today,* 2d ed. (New York: Free Press, 1978).

16. Steven Pearlstein, "Europeans to Pull Plug on Serb TV Satellite Tie," *International Herald Tribune,* 22–23 May 1999, p. 1.

17. European Commission, *Illegal and Harmful Content on the Internet.* Communication to the European Parliament, the Council, the Economic and Social Committee, and the Committee of Regions, IP7977930, 16 October 1996.

18. European Commission, *Action Plan on Promotion of Safe Use of the Internet,* IP/97/10.

# 3

# Freedom of the Press in the Eyes of the Dragon

## A Matter of Chinese Relativism and Pragmatism

### TSAN-KUO CHANG AND ZIXUE TAI

During the U.S.-led North Atlantic Treaty Organization (NATO) attack against Serbia for its aggression in Kosovo, U.S. planes bombed the Chinese embassy in Belgrade, Yugoslavia, on 7 May 1999.[1] The Clinton administration later apologized. It claimed that the bombing was an embarrassing accident resulting from the military's reliance on outdated maps. The Chinese government refused to accept the U.S. explanation, insisting that the bombing was a calculated move designed to humiliate and intimidate China.

The potentially provocative international incident occurred during a particularly bad period in U.S.-China relations. China was incensed at the United States for what it perceived as Washington's support for Taiwan's independence. Taiwan is an island off the Chinese coast that China describes as a renegade province.[2] The United States was angry at China for Beijing's alleged spying activities and theft of U.S. nuclear secrets. Political posturing from both sides aside, the Belgrade bombing episode raised an important question concerning how the Chinese press reported the incident and what China thought was wrong with the American notion of press freedom. As will become clear in this chapter, this case represents contrasting and conflicting views of press freedom as a concept and its practices in cross-national settings.

After the Belgrade incident the *People's Daily,* the national mouthpiece of the Chinese Communist Party, published a critical commentary.[3] It contended that the

United States and other Western European countries exploited press freedom to advance their political aims and worldwide hegemony.[4] Well before the air attack against Yugoslavia, the commentary added, the United States and NATO circulated scurrilous lies about the Serbs in the world press to justify what the Chinese saw as American aggression. Western press freedom, the commentary concluded, was the freedom to lie, to spread rumors, and to engage in naked aggression against other countries.

For students unfamiliar with the Chinese idea of press freedom, these accusations may seem farfetched. From the Chinese point of view, however, the accusations were justifiable because the Chinese notion of press freedom is rooted in specific context and practical considerations. Our purpose in this chapter is to present the Chinese view of freedom of the press in historical, political, and social contexts. The Chinese viewpoint differs sharply from the Western theory described in chapter 2. Contrary to popular belief, China does not reject the notion and importance of press freedom. It simply looks at press freedom in relative and pragmatic terms.

The Chinese protest against Western press freedom did not end quickly. A week after the bombing the *People's Daily* reported that journalism students at major Chinese universities expressed their opinion about the true nature of the Western media system and their disillusionment with American-style press freedom. The paper quoted one student as saying that "press freedom only works for the Americans. For the voice of justice, the American press is not free at all."[5] Other students also condemned what they considered U.S. double standards. They declared their support for the Chinese conception of press freedom. Such sentiments were echoed throughout the news media in China. As the Chinese saw it, the Belgrade bombing was only the latest of many U.S. conspiracies to demonize China before the tenth anniversary of the 1989 Tiananmen Square crackdown.[6]

On 15 April 1989 hundreds of thousands of people gathered in Tiananmen Square in the heart of Beijing to commemorate the death of Hu Yaobang, former secretary general of the Chinese Communist Party and a reformist deposed in 1987 for his liberal ideas. The spontaneous gathering transformed into a nationwide student movement that called for democracy and free speech. During the demonstration, the student leadership succeeded in demanding a direct dialogue with the central authority, an unprecedented challenge to the Communists' power.

In Beijing various Chinese media defied official censorship by covering the confrontation faithfully and extensively. For the first time in Communist China journalists from major media organizations joined the student protest and openly demanded press freedom and an end to the official control of the media.[7] On 4 June 1989 the government ordered a heavy-handed military crackdown on the volatile democratic movement, killing hundreds, if not thousands, of students and other innocent people.

The gruesome pictures of the bloody aftermath carried by CNN and wire services shocked the whole world. Ever since, the Tiananmen Square suppression has been both a symbol and a thorny issue in Sino-American relations. The United States regarded the student movement as a democratic movement led by college students for greater freedoms and true democracy, including freedom of expression and freedom of the press. The students' quest for Western–style freedom and democracy was exemplified by the erection of a Goddess of Democracy monument in Tiananmen Square that remarkably and not coincidentally resembled the Statue of Liberty.

The Chinese government and its ideological media apparatus denounced the movement as counterrevolutionary, a seditious crime that warrants grave punishment. The government's subsequent manhunt forced many Chinese student leaders and journalists into exile overseas. The Tiananmen Square case represents the epitome of China's concerns over the ideas of press freedom, particularly those associated with the Western spirit and practices and the dangers they pose to the authority and legitimacy of the Communist Party.

The Chinese campaign against the Western press after the Belgrade incident further highlighted the fundamental political, social, and cultural differences between Western and Chinese conceptions of freedom of expression and the role of the news media in society. It signified Chinese leaders' uneasiness over the increasing demands for greater personal freedoms and political participation in China, including the freedom to criticize authority. Both the Communist Party and the government viewed, and still view, these demands as influenced by dangerous Western thoughts that enter China through foreign media, the Internet, Chinese overseas students, and Westerners. Notwithstanding, China continues to maintain its own version of press freedom and to resist any outside pressure to change.

Press freedom takes on a different hue in China. It is grounded in Chinese history and social structure. We briefly review the interplay between history and social structure later. Suffice it to say that there has never been press freedom in China in the Western sense. For a look into the Chinese concept of press freedom we can turn to a scholarly conception that is much in line with the Chinese official perspective.

According to the most authoritative dictionary of modern journalism in China,

> press freedom in any society is impossible to be absolute. Freedom is a right that is accompanied by responsibility. At no time should journalists be allowed to use press freedom to engage in any activities that may harm other people and society. Because the infringement of other people's rights through the abuse of press freedom occurs frequently in reality, the right and obligation of press freedom should be protected by law.[8]

Further, according to the dictionary, "press freedom in contemporary capitalist society carries great limitation and deception." This language is amazingly similar to the Chinese charge against American press freedom following the Belgrade incident. This consistency indicates an underlying principle that guides the Chinese approach to press freedom.

## THE CONCEPT OF PRESS FREEDOM

Because of historical traditions and contemporary political considerations, the notion of press freedom in China (and in most other Asian authoritarian nations as well) is quite different from that in the West. Although the dictionary definition

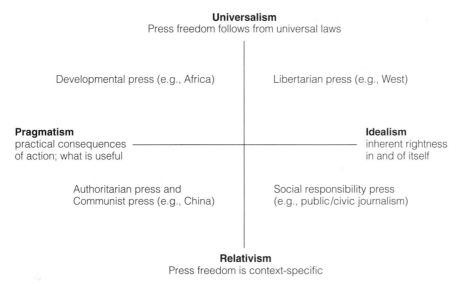

**FIGURE 3.1** Dimensions of Press Freedom

may be useful, it is too simplistic and one-dimensional. Chinese officials and journalists generally contend that there is press freedom in China in both the conceptual and the practical sense. Although it is impossible to provide a comprehensive analysis of the Chinese conception of press freedom, we try to tackle it through the two dimensions illustrated in Figure 3.1. You should keep in mind that there are other ways to conceive of press freedom under different dimensions.

As shown in Figure 3.1, one conceptual dimension deals with the origin of press freedom. At one end, press freedom is considered universal, regardless of the country or the political system (see top of figure). This position simply states that press freedom is press freedom, a similar concept no matter what the country or culture. According to this conception, there is no such thing as American or Chinese press freedom or press freedom unique to any country or society. At the other end, press freedom is believed to be context sensitive, subject to determinants of political and social conditions specific to each country. In this view press freedom is not absolute but relative. It is delimited by, among other things, social structure and national idiosyncrasies, such as historical experience, political philosophy, and institutional development.

Another dimension in Figure 3.1 involves the nature of press freedom itself. On one side, press freedom as an idea is deemed inherently right in and of itself, irrespective of the harm or costs it may bring. This idealistic view (see right-hand side of Figure 3.1) takes press freedom as a cornerstone of democracy. The press in a democratic society is free to pursue truth in any way possible, even though the uncovered truth may prove to be uncomfortable or costly to many people or institutions. The First Amendment to the U.S. Constitution invokes such idealism. The extensive or excessive coverage of the Clinton-Lewinsky scandal in 1999 is illustrative of this ideal form of journalism.

On the other side, press freedom is functional in that its practice has consequences for individuals, groups, or society as a whole because of sensationalism, invasion of privacy, unethical methods of news gathering, or violation of national secrecy. Because of the potential usefulness or harmfulness of press coverage, press freedom is thus judged not idealistically but pragmatically. It could be problematic and undesirable, depending on how press freedom can be used and what may come of its applications.

Because there are two dimensions with two basic positions, press freedom as practiced by countries around the world can be placed in four possible combinations. Within each quadrant there are degrees of variation among countries. In the upper right-hand cell is the *libertarian* press theory, in which freedom is conceived in the Western tradition, as it is exercised in the United States.[9] According to this view, at least in theory, the privately owned and operated press is independent of the government and is free to report as it pleases.

By acting as a watchdog over the government and without concern about government consequences and because the government cannot legally restrict the press, a free press will be able to expose and correct government abuses of power (e.g., Watergate) and wrongdoings (e.g., the Clinton sex scandal) through investigative reporting and critical commentary. Only through such unrestricted freedom can the press help create an informed citizenry with the ability to participate in democracy through voting, protesting, lobbying, or other means. Theoretically, the libertarian press sounds appealing. It certainly attracted the attention of the Chinese protesters at Tiananmen Square in 1989. The idea and ideal of the inherent rightness of press freedom are precisely what Chinese authorities and leaders in many authoritarian governments try to counter because of its potential to undermine the state's power over individual rights.

A variation of the libertarian theory is the *social responsibility* theory (lower right-hand quadrant of Figure 3.1). Social responsibility asserts the innate goodness of press freedom, but it emphasizes that freedom comes with responsibility and obligation. In addition to disseminating information, the press is responsible for public enlightenment, empowerment, and participation in civic society. A pure socially responsible press does not exist, but the recent interest in civic or public journalism in the United States may come close to the ideas of the social responsibility theory.

An alternative theory that more or less subscribes to the assumption of universal press freedom but leans heavily toward the pragmatic end is the *developmental* press theory (upper left-hand quadrant of Figure 3.1).[10] Many developing or underdeveloped countries in Africa, Southeast Asia, and Latin America normally recognize the value of press freedom. As a result of their colonial pasts, unstable social and political structures, and inadequate economic infrastructures, these developing nations stress that they cannot afford the luxury of Western-style press freedom. Their rationale is simple: If unchecked, press freedom tends to rock the boat, disrupt national harmony, or hinder economic development.

In other words, governmental restrictions on press freedom are needed because of the press's potential to impede national progress and social stability. In a developing nation the ostensibly laudable goals of national progress and social stability should have priority over all else, including the people's right to know and the media's access to information. More often than not, press freedom in countries that subscribe to the developmental perspective turns out to be lip service. Still, the developmental press theory differs in principle from the two systems in the lower left-hand quadrant: the *authoritarian* and the *Communist* press theories. This is where we find China on the conceptual map.

Press freedom in China is situated in the lower left-hand cell, at the intersection of pragmatism and relativism. It is worth noting that the Chinese conception of press freedom is the opposite of the Western libertarian press in the upper right-hand quadrant of Figure 3.1, at the intersection of universalism and idealism. On the one hand, China adamantly rejects universal or absolute standards of press freedom and insists on the internal criteria relative to a country's sociopolitical interests, historical development, or local context. Further, China shuns the idealistic assumption of press freedom as the quest for fundamental truth that is good in and of itself. Instead, China interprets press freedom in terms of its consequences or pragmatic outcomes.

In an interview with a German newspaper in 1998, for example, Li Peng, chairman of the National People's Congress, said that press freedom must be conducive to national development and social stability and cannot be used for unrealistic and distorted reports.[11] This position is deeply rooted in the history of press freedom, the relationship between the state and media, and contemporary social and political commitments in China. After we examine these aspects, it should become evident why China approaches the idea and practice of press freedom differently from the United States and other Western nations.

## THE PARADOX OF CHINA'S MODERNIZATION

Despite its enormous size, huge population, and military might, China has remained an economically weak—the politically incorrect term is "backwards"—and a relatively isolated nation since World War II. After the disastrous Cultural Revolution from 1966 to 1976, the late paramount leader Deng Xiaoping (1905–1997) initiated China's pursuit of modernization in 1978.[12] He took China on a long march to build the country into a world economic power, but this journey was fraught with problems.

To modernize, China had to open up to the outside world and establish close economic relations with other countries. It was necessary to allow foreigners with needed skills into China and to send Chinese students abroad for training in technology, economics, and other fields. The two-way street meant accepting not only the influx of foreigners but also the flow of alien ideas and the foreign press into China. In the course of opening up the nation many ideas deemed undesirable or dangerous by authorities reached and influenced the Chinese people. Thoughts, of course, breed actions. As the Chinese people became more exposed to the outside world and Western ideas, they demanded greater personal liberties and political participation. The 1989 Tiananmen Square movement was the most visible sign of this transformation. Whether by design or by default, China was forced to confront the paradox of economic development and social-political openness.

Samuel Huntington, a well-known American political scientist, argues that under certain conditions and in some cases over a fairly long period of time, an authoritarian country will promote economic growth at the expense of political reform.[13] This policy is a deliberate strategy to channel public attention and energy away from sensitive issues of governance into practical matters of everyday life. China and many other Third World countries fall into this pattern. Following its economic reforms and open-door policy, China succeeded in significant economic growth and improvement in living standards.

Authoritarianism can only be temporary, however. For China to continue its path to economic prosperity and maintain tight control over political and social life, it must strike a balance between progress and stability. The problem is how to maintain the equilibrium between progress and stability without disrupting either process. It has been documented that restructuring the political system and expanding public participation ultimately leads to democracy. South Korea, Taiwan, Spain, and Brazil are cases in point.[14] This is the dilemma China now faces.

Edward Friedman, another American political scientist, sees two possibilities for China. The deepening crisis of national identity in China may bring an end to the centralized regime established since 1949 and replace it with a democratic system. Then again, it may result in even more authoritarian policies detrimental to economic development.[15] Other scholars argue that the degree to which the economy is market oriented mediates the relationship between capitalism and democracy. A market economy, once institutionalized, is conducive to a stable liberal democracy, whereas substantial restrictions on the operation of market mechanisms generate obstacles to liberal democracy.[16]

Although China has been relatively open since the late 1970s, it is neither a capitalist society nor a democracy. China no longer adheres to the core ideas of a Communist utopia. Caught in a political quandary, its solution has been to take the pragmatic and relative approach of striking a balance between democratizing the state and modernizing the economy.

In the last two decades of the twentieth century the development of a market economy with Chinese characteristics whetted Chinese citizens' appetites for more individual and collective liberties, including freedom of speech and the press, freedom of assembly, and participation. To accommodate the changing mentality and behavioral aspiration among the citizens, the Chinese official response is to reshape the social and political system, at least in theory. For example, in 1997 the chief justice of the Chinese Supreme Court expressed China's desires to "build a socialist democracy based on the rule of law."[17] If China sticks to the rule of law, it eventually will have to address freedom of the press.

In the 1980s legal protection of press freedom in China, in the form of a formal press law, had been discussed somewhat. The 1989 Tiananmen Square crackdown and the subsequent purge of many liberal-minded journalists, however, halted the formulation of a press law. Renewed talk of the rule of law and possibly a press law will have profound implications for the news media in China. To put the issue into perspective, in the remaining sections we review the historical, ide-ological, economic, and contemporary policies and practices of Chinese press freedom.

## PRESS FREEDOM IN CHINESE HISTORY

Control over the mass media by means of censorship, suppression, and other types of restrictions is not peculiar to China. No media system is ever completely free from either governmental control or other forms of interference. The causes and consequences of controls vary greatly from country to country. In its long history of official regulation, repression, and manipulation over the media of mass com-munication, China has presented to the world a revealing saga in the fight for free-dom and democracy.

Throughout the process the press became both a tool and a symbol in the tus-sle for freedom of expression and publication against China's imperial and feudal systems. Extant historical records indicate that China invented movable type 500 years before Gutenberg in the West. China arguably also published the world's first newspaper, *Ti Pao* (literally "court gazette"), during the eighth century. Histori-ans regard *Ti Pao* as an official publication rather than as a general circulation newspaper because its circulation was restricted to bureaucrats and because it pub-lished only imperial edicts, memorials to the throne, and current reports on po-litical situations.[18]

When *Jing Pao* (*Beijing Gazette*) appeared in the sixteenth century, it was pub-licly available and carried diverse coverage of civil affairs and official announce-ments. The emperors and their puppet governments in feudal China never hesi-tated to regulate, restrict, and censor various publications for a variety of reasons. No press law was needed because the emperors' commands reigned supreme. Needless to say, rumors, sedition, criticism of the royal family, political dissension, and obscene or indecent literature were strictly prohibited.[19]

Not until the waning days of the Qing dynasty (1616–1911) did the first pub-lication law (the term "press law" was not used) emerge in China: the Special Stat-ute of the Great Qing Dynasty Governing Publications. As with other publication laws that followed, the 1906 statute gave the state an upper hand in dealing with the press. The statute established a bureau in Beijing to register and monitor pub-lishers and printed matter.

Among the punishable materials mentioned in the statute were libelous re-marks about the imperial household, comments on government policies, and in-formation about domestic and foreign affairs specifically forbidden by the author-ities.[20] Two years later the statute was replaced by the Press Law of the Great Qing Dynasty.[21] This was the first time the term "press law" appeared in a Chinese of-ficial legal ordinance.

The 1908 press law, consisting of 45 articles, was modeled after an antiquated Japanese law. The law again required that all newspapers and magazines be regis-

tered with the local government. Prior inspection of all publications was manda-
tory. Before any publication was printed, it had to be submitted to the police for
examination. A distinctive feature of the law was that it gave customs authorities
the power to ban the importation of undesirable materials, particularly revolutionary literature. At the time, during the waning years of the Qing dynasty, the
government was engaged in a futile campaign to curb an insurgent democratic
movement led by Dr. Sun Yat-sen.[22] Despite the imperial government's flagrant
and ruthless efforts to stifle the press, revolutionary ideas flourished.

In October 1911 Dr. Sun toppled the Qing dynasty and established the Republic of China in Nanjing. In March 1912 the new government adopted the Provisional Constitution of the New Chinese Republic. It would exert a lasting influence on the Chinese constitutions in both mainland China and Taiwan. For the
first time in China the Chinese people were constitutionally granted freedom of
speech, writing, publication, assembly, and association.[23] Nonetheless, the constitution specified that subsequent laws might curtail constitutional freedoms to promote public well-being or to maintain social order during a state emergency. The
constitution incorporated official concerns about the consequences of unchecked
freedom. This was no small point. It indicates that the seeds of pragmatism and
relativism were planted even after the birth of a democratic China.

In 1912 the Chinese republican government drafted the Provisional Press Law.
The press law had three articles concerning registration of publications, sedition,
and libel. Representatives of the press did not take these articles lightly. Because
the law was not enacted by the legislature, the National Press Association in
Shanghai challenged its constitutionality.[24] Afterward, the press law was rescinded.
The provisional government itself was short-lived, too.

An infamous warlord grabbed power and moved the central government to
Beijing to bring it under direct control. In May 1914 the warlord government
advanced a constitutional compact that substantially broadened the president's
power. Although the compact nominally guaranteed freedom of speech, writing,
and publication, it added an ominous qualifying clause: "within the scope of laws
and ordinances."[25]

The warlord government did not tolerate a free and critical press. A set of se-
vere press regulations similar to the 1908 press law soon accompanied the compact, including a law forbidding publications from criticizing the government.
These measures strictly censored and crushed any press criticism or defiance of authority. When needed, the government waged swift violence against the press. For
over a decade hundreds of publications were closed. Thousands of reporters and
publishers were arrested or killed.[26] The warlord's death did not spare the country from the sway of terror. His successors continued to suppress the press for years.

The Kuomingtang (KMT) (Nationalist Party) emerged in April 1927 as the
most powerful force in China. A year later, it unified the country, with Chiang
Kai-shek (1887–1975) as president of the central government. At the same time,
the rival Chinese Communist Party led by Mao Tse-Tung (1893–1976) began its
quest for power. During the bitter and destructive conflicts, the Nationalists ruthlessly suppressed the Communists. To quell public support of the Communists,
the KMT government recognized the importance and usefulness of the press.

In 1929 the KMT government announced six guiding principles for drafting laws to regulate publications. For the first time a Chinese publication law was designed with the stated goal of protecting press freedom. To safeguard press freedom, the press law paradoxically permitted the government to curb dangerous publications. Other than its rewording, the underlying mechanism in the 1929 law did not significantly deviate from the earlier conception of government control of the press, tipping practically in favor of the state's interests.

The publication law was proclaimed by the KMT in 1930.[27] Like its predecessors, the KMT ordered that all publications be registered with the Ministry of Interior and that copies of each issue be surrendered to specified government agencies before publication. The law forbade any publication to criticize the KMT, subvert the national government, damage the interests of China, or endanger domestic public peace or social order. Although not explicit, the prohibitions presumably applied to publications propagating Communist views.

More specifically, Article 21 stated, "In war, unrest, or in other times deemed fit, the publications shall obey the orders of the National Government to stop publishing articles relating to military and diplomatic affairs."[28] Within the next two years many regulations were drafted and enforced by the KMT government to restrict the distribution of newspapers, magazines, and books. A Censorship Commission was constituted in 1934 to censor the press.[29] The tacit thinking was that the unimpeded press would destabilize the social environment.

A few years later, in 1937, the KMT government passed the Revised Publication Law, a replication of the 1930 law with a few additions. During the following years and until the end of the Chinese Civil War in 1949, the Communists and their sympathizers were persecuted with a reign of terror on many fronts, including oppressive attacks against left-leaning newspapers. A leading Chinese journalist in the 1940s described censorship under the authoritarian Nationalists as harsher and more pervasive under the Nationalists than under the Communists.[30]

Still, the Nationalist campaigns against the Communists in both the military and the propaganda theaters failed to stop the Communists' ascent to power. The Nationalists eventually lost control of China to the Communists and fled to Taiwan. Under the official title of the Republic of China the rival KMT government continued its rule and exercised tight media suppression on the island.

For nearly four decades, before the democratization of Taiwan in the late 1980s, the KMT government insisted on its legitimacy as the sole ruler of not only Taiwan but also the Chinese mainland. It sustained its China claim by ironclad manipulation of the press system in Taiwan.[31] In addition to restricting the number of newspapers and the size of their pages, Taiwanese media owners and journalists with Communist connections—whether real or imagined—were purged or arrested during the 1950s and 1960s in what was later called the white terror.

The authoritarian rule of the KMT government ended when both martial law and the press ban were lifted in the late 1980s. Since then, press freedom has flourished in Taiwan.[32] On the Chinese mainland, meanwhile, the Communist government embarked on a new era of monopolistic control over the mass media. Its press philosophy was deeply grounded in the orthodox Marxist-Leninist conception of freedom of expression.

This historical review makes clear that even before the Chinese Communists came to power, the concept of press freedom never took root in China, at least not in the Western tradition that has become the backbone of the libertarian press theory. The various Chinese regimes in the twentieth century approached press freedom from such pragmatic considerations as social stability, national order, or economic progress, particularly when practical calculations might serve their vested interests. Nonetheless, the press was free from outright state control in both ownership and management before the Communist revolution.

The Chinese Communists changed the philosophical landscape when they took power. Press theory in Communist China has its origin in Marxist ideology. Since the collapse of the Soviet Union in 1991, China has become one of the last strongholds of Communism. How Marxism-Leninism has influenced the Chinese Communists and its impact on the press in China deserve closer attention.

## IDEOLOGICAL ORIGIN
## OF CHINESE PRESS THEORY

Other than John Stuart Mill, it has been argued that "Karl Marx (1818–1883) has had the greatest impact on 20th-century journalism and journalistic thinking of any 19th-century thinker." [33] Although Mill's idea of liberty ran deep in the Western libertarian journalistic practices, Marx and his collaborator, Friedrich Engels, greatly influenced the conceptual approach to politics and journalism in many Third World nations, including China.

Marx's ideas of press freedom centered on two aspects: total freedom of the press and the right of a newspaper to deal with questions of public interest. "Freedom is so much the essence of man," Marx wrote, "that even its opponents realize it in that they fight its reality. Every kind of freedom has therefore always existed, only at one time as a special privilege, another time as a universal right." [34] For Marx, journalism was a weapon to resist the ruling political forces. "We must not be afraid," he wrote in 1843, "to criticize the existing world ruthlessly. I mean ruthlessly in the sense that we must not be afraid of our own conclusions and equally unafraid of coming into conflict with the prevailing powers." [35]

In his youth the outspoken democratic Marx was convinced that free inquiry was beneficial to society and that censorship was not only evil and harmful but also counterproductive. [36] Marx's libertarian thought could be clearly seen in his critique of bourgeois society, in which the ruling elite mercilessly exploited the working class. Marx's conceptions of the press were sketchy at best and sometimes ambiguous. To Marx, press freedom was a means to an end rather than an end in itself. In the Communist utopia, Marx envisioned the press as simply serving the needs of proletariat revolution and the transformation to Communism. The press was the instrument of government and the Communist Party, which owned and directed their functionaries. Press criticism was tolerated so long as it did not threaten the basic ideology.

Freedom for Marx's socialist press was the freedom to support the system, to find and correct its flaws, and to protect and solidify the socialist ideology. Individuals and, for that matter, the mass media and other social institutions were subordinate to the state.[37] It should not be difficult to recognize the contradiction between Marx's early position in his campaigns against the bourgeois press and his later theory of press freedom in the Communist state. During his early years, Marx advocated an almost libertarian idea of complete press freedom. In his later years, however, he became more authoritarian. As in other Communist countries, China chose to refer to Marx's later writings. The Chinese Communists justified their authoritarian approach to press freedom in Marxism and Leninism.

Vladimir Ilyich Lenin (1870–1924), another influential activist in the Communist movement, saw the press as an effective instrument against entrenched power, in his case against Russian Czarist tyranny. In his fight against the Czarist regime, Lenin's two main objectives were "first, to unify the Russian Socialists under his leadership, and, second, to get a newspaper of his own."[38] The second objective underscored a fundamental conviction shared by the Communists about the power of the press to mold public ideologies.

This objective also provided the rationale for other Communist countries, through Communist parties, to own and operate all media. Lenin went about the task of unifying and manipulating the Communist Party by indoctrinating his followers with his concept of "democratic centralism."[39] Later, Stalin and Mao readily accepted the framework of democratic centralism in the Soviet Union and China, respectively.

In legitimizing the Communist Party's control over the media, Lenin asserted that a Socialist consciousness could not emerge spontaneously among the working class. Rather, correct consciousness had to be inculcated by the Communist Party, led by elite revolutionaries.[40] The party press could fulfill the roles of ideology education, policy direction, and mass mobilization. Furthermore, Lenin rejected absolute freedom of the press. He argued that the Communist Party, like other free political organizations, had the right to expel members who held dissenting opinions. Otherwise the party would disintegrate.[41]

After the proletariat revolution Lenin believed that the press should be used as an instrument by the state to suppress the antirevolutionaries and opposing ideas. The press thus took an active role in denouncing those regarded as antirevolutionaries. This conception of press freedom as relative to political circumstance and ideological unity laid the cornerstone for the Communist Party in the Soviet Union to solidify its grips on power and to justify its total domination of social and political life until the Soviet demise in 1991.

In sum, Marxism-Leninism maintains that only the proletariat class enjoys press freedom. Once an idea is branded as antiproletariat or bourgeois, it could and should be suppressed. Marxism-Leninism had a significant impact on the Chinese Communist revolution. The ideology guided all aspects of Chinese society and paved the groundwork for the relationship between the state and the mass media for nearly three decades.

The fanaticism of Marxism-Leninism was particularly evident during the 10-year Cultural Revolution (1966–1976) in China, when those who challenged or even mildly questioned the supremacy of Communist ideology were ruthlessly suppressed by the Communist Party through the militant Red Guards. Armed with their interpretations of Marxism-Leninism to advance their political purposes, Mao and the Communist Party launched a series of massive campaigns to repress press freedom in China.

## PRESS FREEDOM IN MAOIST CHINA

After the founding of the People's Republic of China in 1949, the Communist Party under Mao faced several daunting tasks: (1) to eradicate the economic and social consequences of the insufferable civil war; (2) to undo the damage of decades of foreign domination and exploitation, including the Japanese invasion in 1937 and the subsequent 8-year Sino-Japanese war; and, most important, (3) to win the trust and support of the people to overcome China's underdevelopment.

Taking power in China through the barrel of a gun is one thing; governing the world's most populous country and channeling the masses into a collective is another. To accomplish his goals, Mao had to rely on the press—what he called "the barrel of pens"—to wage never-ending campaigns against those regarded as anti-revolutionaries. The written press and later the broadcast media constituted the ideal means to mobilize the Chinese people.

Maoist China exhibits the major feature of a Leninist state: The Communist Party holds a monopoly over state power and national resources, including complete control of the mass media. No private ownership is allowed. In many aspects the influence of the Soviet model on the Chinese press is evident. The Communist Party uses mass media "as agitator, propagandist, organizer." [42] In the structure and processes of mass communication the media are tools of the party to integrate all sectors of society into toeing the party line.

Within the Chinese context, however, Mao realized that Marxist-Leninist teachings were not universal. They had to be modified to appeal to China's many ethnic groups and regions. [43] Mao's decision to revamp Marxist-Leninist guidance to fit the Chinese national setting caused, among other things, a political rift with the Soviet Union during the 1960s. It underlined Mao's rejection of a universal press theory and absolute press freedom.

In Mao's view the mass media were producers and molders of national consciousness. He justified Communist Party control of mass media by taking China's conditions into consideration. In Chinese agrarian society, where rural peasants were geographically and culturally secluded, Communist values and ideologies could be inculcated only through the party-run propaganda machines. The effective strategy was to employ both the gun and the pen in the Communist revolution. [44]

To solidify Communist rule, Mao instituted a series of campaigns during the early 1950s, using a remarkable system of mass communication to bring the people into direct contact with the central government. Never before in Chinese history did the leaders attempt to reach the people on such a large scale. The campaigns used all forms of communication, such as radio and newspapers, banner posters, posted announcements, study groups, and street lecturers, to indoctrinate the Chinese people in cities, towns, and the remote countryside. [45]

In the mid-1950s China's economy was experiencing rapid growth because of the rebuilding of the war-torn country. The economic turnaround and social stability strengthened the Communist Party's grasp on power. Despite and as a consequence of these positive developments, in Mao's calculation, the party was becoming alienated from the people and the Communist revolution was in danger of being undermined.

To ensure that the party did not become disconnected from the people, in 1956 Mao called for greater public criticism of the party to keep it vibrant: "Let a hundred flowers blossom, and let a hundred schools of thought contend." The party propaganda declared that "the Communist Party now stood for freedom of independent thinking, of debate, of creative work. It also supported freedom to criticize and to express opinions on questions of art, literature, or scientific research."[46]

This "two-hundred" movement represented a radical break from the past. It had significant, unexpected, and—from Mao's and the party's perspectives—undesirable social ramifications. From May 1956 to June 1957 China experienced greater intellectual activity, increased exchange of ideas, and often-fervent public criticisms of authority. The criticisms even went so far as to question whether China should be a socialist state and whether the Communist Party should share its power with other parties.

Social and political debates reverberated in media-related academic circles. In university journalism programs and scholarly mass communication journals, news values, press theories, and journalistic practices were debated in earnest.[47] The whole campaign, however, took on a momentum of its own and moved beyond what was intended. Mao initiated this form of freedom to revitalize the party and bring it closer to the people.[48] But he had seen enough and decided to curb the excessive freedom before it threatened the status quo and the Communist control of power.

In response, in June 1957 Mao launched what the government called an antirightist campaign to ferret out and punish anti-Communist revolutionaries. The campaign resulted in alarming academic, literary, and journalistic casualties. By one estimate, 10–30% of the journalists in China were branded "rightists" for their criticisms of the party.[49] The crackdown dealt a fatal blow to emerging democratic freedoms, including press freedom. After the Communist Party regained total ideological control over the media, dissemination of information was tightly regulated. News events that could lead the people to doubt the wisdom of the party were banned. As a result, stories about famine, starvation, and train and airplane accidents often went unreported.[50] Simply put, anything that might weaken the Communist authority or its image was forbidden.

The setback of the "two-hundred" policy and the ensuing expulsion of liberal-minded reformists from the Communist Party's rank and file and other walks of life were harbingers of Mao's penchant for extreme solutions to China's problems. Mao would allow unprecedented democracy and press freedom, only to mercilessly repress it later. More social and cultural destruction was to come. During the Cultural Revolution, mass media were forced to deify Mao and "Mao's thought" to the status of unchangeable and unquestionable dogma. Even the slightest criticism of Communist authority or disrespect for the "Great Chairman" invited harsh government and party retribution. For Mao's followers and the Red Guards, mass media were the means to repudiate the so-called revisionists and to humiliate intellectuals.

The "Ten Years of Turmoil," as the Communist Party itself later called the Cultural Revolution, came to an end only when both of the top two party leaders—Premier Zhou Enlai and Mao—died in 1976 and the reformists took control of the party. In April 1976 mass demonstrations led by students at Tiananmen Square paid their last respects to Zhou and denounced radical Maoist policies. The demonstration accentuated the disillusionment with Communist authoritarianism and the desire for greater personal freedom and less ideological command. After Mao died in September 1976, the members of the notorious Gang of Four, including Mao's widow, were arrested. The imprisonment of the Gang of Four marked the end of the Cultural Revolution.

Throughout the three decades of Maoist rule the Communist Party kept a tight rein on the press to eradicate undesirable elements in China. A Marxist-Leninist pragmatist, Mao never envisioned an absolute or universal application of press freedom. He tried to mold press freedom to suit his goals by exploiting Chinese conditions. His success not only silenced the press but also suffocated public expression. In 1977, when Deng Xiaoping resumed control of Mao's party and the government posts that had been stripped from him during the Cultural Revolution were restored, popular sentiment for a break from the radical disorder gained momentum. With Deng at the helm of Chinese economic reform and openness, China entered the reform era.

## PRESS FREEDOM IN THE REFORM ERA

In 1977, in the wake of the Cultural Revolution, the Chinese mass media spearheaded a crucial nationwide debate between the Maoists and the reformists over the country's ideological direction.[51] The Maoists were still in control of the Communist Party's propaganda department and stood firmly opposed to change. The reformists, led by Hu Yaobang, the future general secretary of the party whose death ignited the Tiananmen Square pro-democracy demonstrations, urged the party to use pragmatic criteria to evaluate Mao's policies and ideas. One argument was that, within the Communist structure, some form of democracy and openness was a prerequisite to economic reforms. It was the first time that a high Communist official critically challenged Mao's policies and ideology.

The debate sparked questions about the legitimacy of the Marxist-Leninist political system that failed to check the abuse of power by Mao and his followers. Democracy and press freedom again became the focus of growing aspirations among journalists and intellectuals. Some young reporters pointed to the absence of reliable organizations and systems to safeguard socialist democracy in China. They demanded press freedom to expose the defects and mistakes of party officials.[52]

A crucial turning point came in December 1977, when the party's Central Committee shifted its focus from ideological struggle to economic reform. Working with Deng and other reform-minded senior Communists, Hu Yaobang was appointed the party's general secretary. He was truly the first reformist leader in the Communist Party to advocate democratic rights, including press freedom. His efforts to draft a press law that would legalize journals and publications as well as his support for the Democracy Wall, where citizens could publicly post their criticism for all to read and discuss, were aborted by conservative senior party ideologues in the Politburo.[53]

When the Democracy Wall and various publications in 1977 went beyond criticizing the Cultural Revolution and Maoist policies by exposing the defects in Communist rule, it was more than Deng Xiaoping could tolerate. As the central figure in Chinese politics during the reform period, the newly reinstated Deng authorized tight control and regulations concerning discussions about democratic reforms.

In March 1977 Wei Jingsheng, who had written and posted many articles criticizing the Communist Party and the government on the Democracy Wall, was arrested and charged with planning to overthrow the government. He was imprisoned for more than 15 years, and, afterward, exiled to the United States. The Chinese Association of Human Rights was also suppressed. Such draconian measures have remained largely unchanged over the past two decades. In early 1999 the Chinese Supreme Court reiterated that anyone who published, printed, copied, or distributed anything intended to split the country would be deemed seditious.[54]

In November 1978 the Spring of Beijing democratic movement witnessed two mass demonstrations calling for democracy. The reforms continued, even if the pace slowed. The party's general secretary, Hu Yaobang, entrusted the editor-in-chief of the *People's Daily* with the responsibility of forming a task force to draft a Chinese press law. In 1983, Hu Jiwei, the editor-in-chief (no relation to the general secretary), began to formulate a press law until he was ousted after the 1989 Tiananmen Square student democratic movement. An ardent advocate of press reform and independent journalism, the editor-in-chief argued that press freedom was indispensable to China's modernization and continued national development.[55] Because his idea of press freedom was considered similar to that in the West, the *People's Daily* denounced it as "bourgeoisie press freedom."[56] Editor-in-chief Hu lost his job.

The top editor of the *People's Daily* was not alone in calling for greater press freedom. Debates about press freedom were heard throughout China during the early 1980s.[57] Press legislation was seen as a solution to many of the problems facing the state-media relationship. The pursuit of freedom of expression and freedom of the press alarmed many conservative party ideologues. The Maoist factions felt threatened by the widespread student demonstrations demanding democracy in 1986 and 1987.

Being a pragmatist, Deng joined the party's conservative forces to launch the anti-bourgeois-liberalization campaign. The media again became the target of the campaign, and some outspoken journalists were persecuted. General Secretary Hu's reluctance to suppress the student movements and his declining favor among party elders cost him his job as the party boss in 1987.

The attempt to institutionalize press freedom in China through legislation suffered another setback. Zhao Ziyang, the new general secretary and a liberal with reform ideas, announced in the 13th Party Congress that the Chinese press should perform three key functions: "to oversee public officials, to report on important events, and to reflect debate on key policy issues."[58] This pronouncement was an important departure from the traditional role of the press as the party organ. Whether and to what extent Zhao would have permitted greater press freedom is a matter of debate because he was ousted in 1989 by the party's conservative forces when public demands for democracy reached a zenith.

In the largest democratic movement in Chinese history, millions of students and citizens peacefully demonstrated for one and a half months—from late April to early June in 1989. Journalists openly sided with the demonstrators and departed from their official role as party mouthpieces. In May 1989 reporters and editors joined protesters in the streets and demanded press freedom and journalistic independence. According to one report, "journalists all over Beijing" were convinced "that an irrevocable step toward press freedom had been taken."[59] But it was an illusion.

The bloody government suppression of the student demonstration ordered by the paranoid Deng and the nervous hard-line Communists had turned the mood of buoyant optimism into despair. As noted earlier, the military crackdown ended as a massacre that frightened the Chinese and shocked the world. The suppression had an immediate consequence on the passage of a comprehensive law involving press rights and responsibilities. The Standing Committee of the National People's Congress, China's legislative body, was scheduled to review the press law, but the review never materialized.[60] The party instead resorted to media subjugation and suspended discussion of the press law. In late 1998 China hinted that it would follow legal procedure to formulate a press law suitable to the Chinese national setting.[61] The assumption, of course, is that press freedom is relative.

After mid-1989 Chinese journalists became cautious about criticizing authority. On the surface the press resumed its role as a party organ. Journalists who had tasted press freedom, however, resented their subjugation. A pervasive resistance to orthodox propaganda simmered beneath the veneer of compliance and conformity. Although the central authority continued to suppress newspapers that promoted "the ideas of bourgeoisie freedom,"[62] there could be no return to the rigid ideological straitjacket.

After the Tiananmen Square massacre, Deng's rival ideologues in the party stalled many of the economic reforms and tightened their political control. Officially retired from all his posts, Deng counterattacked in February 1992. He traveled through China's most prosperous economic regions and urged the people to support economic reform efforts. The nation rallied around his powerful speeches; so did the mass media.

The early 1990s was marked by increased commercialization of the Chinese media. Except for a few national organs, such as China Central Television, the

*People's Daily,* and the Xinhua News Agency, mass media no longer received state financial subsidies. Although the state still retains media ownership, the mass media must compete in the market for revenues and for their survival. In an effort to integrate themselves into the market economy, the media, particularly newspapers and magazines, experimented with more daring forms and content to entice viewers and readers. Before the press reform newspapers and magazines in China were dull in design and monotonous in content. Their political intonations and recitations of party shibboleths often jaded readers.

On 17 November 1992 the *Worker's Daily,* a widely read national newspaper, published a startling article touting the commercialization of Chinese newspapers.[63] Taking the cue, national and local newspapers expanded their number of pages and added special columns to cater to reader interests. As advertising revenue surged, an avalanche of weekend editions and tabloids became available.[64] The number of newspapers increased to a record high, from 1,534 in late June 1991 to 2,030 by the end of 1993.[65]

Meanwhile, radio and television competed for market share. Radio talk shows, Western-style soap operas, and audience hot line programs added to the variety of programming. The increasing commercialization of the media eroded the party's power to control and dominate the marketplace of ideas.[66] For example, the daily circulation of the *People's Daily,* the national mouthpiece of the Communist Party, dropped from 6 million in the early 1980s to fewer than 3 million in 1998. Along with these developments, debates were rekindled on issues such as the role of journalism in a "socialist market economy," press freedom, party-press relationships, and the like.[67]

Although the expectation that economic reforms and external openness might lead China to democratic modernization was dampened by the Tiananmen Square tragedy, the last decade of the twentieth century nevertheless witnessed a revival of Chinese interest in media reform. Although press freedom has yet to be protected, media commercialization has resulted in greater leeway for news content and journalistic practices. The success of the market economy has created an environment where once taboo topics such as press freedom and political participation have resurfaced in open discussion. The Chinese government's strategy seems intent on a cautious path that allows mass media to take on a commercial flavor so long as they function within the political scope sanctioned by the state. How this delicate balance can be maintained depends on the extent to which the reforms stay on course in the post-Deng era.

## WHITHER PRESS FREEDOM
## IN THE POST-DENG ERA

The death of Deng in 1997 raised new questions about the direction of Chinese press freedom. China has entered a stage in which no strongman with an iron rule is poised to emerge. No matter how appealing in politics, personal charisma had lost its place in the quest for economic reforms. The old system of a single leader has been replaced by collective leadership. The government and the party need to be more pragmatic to accommodate the fast-changing Chinese social structure to maintain their domination and control over the general population. Given the ubiquitous presence of Chinese mass media throughout the country, especially the greater importance of television and local newspapers,[68] the news media increasingly will assume a key role in China's sociopolitical development. China's success in moving from a rigid Communist system to a market-oriented system hinges largely on the degree of freedom that the mass media will enjoy.

The development of the socialist legal system in China since 1978 has inspired debate in and outside China.[69] A rule of law should be the first natural step in democratic China. With two decades of economic reform the Communist Party has begun a slow process of moving the Chinese legal system toward a genuine rule of law. In 1998 the Ninth National People's Congress endorsed the liberal-minded Zhu Rongji as the new premier.

The new leadership is widely expected to generate a fresh round of capitalist-style economic reforms. What impact it will have on Chinese democracy and press freedom has attracted global attention. It is believed that, whereas the Chinese economy during the earlier reform era could be characterized as restrictive, the future points to an open market-oriented economy. With the growth of market forces and the steady rise of a privatized economy, Chinese citizens have been afforded unprecedented freedom to choose where to live, where to work, what to buy, and increasingly what to think about.

The successful and intensified economic reforms initiated during the late 1970s have encouraged various sectors in China to explore more and wider changes. This "consumer revolution"[70] has significant implications for the cultural industry. Standing at the forefront to capture China's social change, the mass media cannot stay immune to the pressing structural demand for greater autonomy and independence. Their search for press freedom, unhindered by state interference, will increasingly nag at the central authority.

The Chinese government now finds itself in an uncomfortable position of encouraging people to reap the benefits of economic developments while refusing to grant greater personal freedoms. How long and to what extent can the Chinese government control the press in a totally new domestic and international environment remains to be seen. One thing is certain: China can no longer afford to shun the pressure from other countries when its economic success has been tied to the world at large.

China's agreements with the United States and other Western countries to enter the World Trade Organization (WTO) have obliged it to open its telecommunications market to worldwide competition. New communication technologies, such as the Internet, have shrunk the world and have been readily embraced by the Chinese.[71] These developments undoubtedly will serve as new catalysts for more press freedom and freedom of speech, which are antithetical to the Communist state in China.

Even on the bulletin board on the Web site of the tightly controlled *People's Daily,* it is not uncommon to find dissenting opinions that challenge the Communist Party. Regardless of their origin, the form and content of new communication technologies will have political repercussions. The global information environment and the commercial Chinese media market will foster the next important chapter in the struggle for press freedom in China.

Whether the Chinese government likes it or not, the burgeoning public awareness and demand for a free press, the commercialization and internationalization of the Chinese media, and the increasing pressure from the world community may make the next step—what to say and what to publish without fear of state interference—irreversible.

When and how that will happen, however, is still intricately debatable. The question remains: What will become of press freedom in China? If the history of Chinese press freedom is any indication, China is likely to continue to take a pragmatic and relative approach in its dealings with this touchy issue.

## NOTES

1. On Wednesday, 24 March 1999, U.S.-led NATO forces launched air strikes against Serbian military targets in Yugoslavia. The reason for the strikes was Serbian military actions against ethnic Albanians in Kosovo after Yugoslav authorities and Kosovar Albanian leaders failed to reach a peace deal. NATO suspended the bombing campaign on 8 June 1999, when Yugoslavia agreed to a full withdrawal from and a NATO presence in Kosovo. China and Russia, both permanent members of the United Nations Security Council, with veto powers, opposed NATO's attacks throughout the campaign.

2. China and Taiwan split in 1949 when the Communists defeated the Nationalists in the Chinese civil war.

3. Liu Zhuyu, "'Press Freedom' Is Not Merely a Fig Leaf," *People's Daily,* 18 May 1999 (Internet edition).

4. Hegemony is a key concept in world politics and international communication. It is often used by Third World countries to refer to the domination of international politics and intrusion into national affairs by the Western industrial powers, especially the United States, over other nations.

5. "The Awakening of University Students in Shanghai," *People's Daily,* 24 May 1999 (Internet edition).

6. "'Conspiracy Theory' Circulated in Beijing," *China Times,* 11 May 1999 (Internet edition).

7. Hsiao Ching-chang and Yang Mei-rong, "Don't Force Us to Lie": The Case of the *World Economic Herald,*" in Chin-Chuan Lee, ed. *Voices of China* (New York: Guilford Press, 1990), 111–121.

8. Xifen Gan, ed., *A Dictionary of Modern Journalism* (Henan, China: People's Publishing House, 1993), 30.

9. For a useful discussion of theories of the press, see Fred S. Siebert, Theodore Peterson, and Wilbur Schramm, *Four Theories of the Press* (Urbana: University of Illinois Press, 1956). This is a classic book. According to Siebert et al., there are four basic theories of the press: authoritarian, libertarian, social responsibility, and Soviet Communist. The last two theories are mere developments and modifications of the first two theories. In our discussion we add the developmental press concept because it is widely accepted by Third World countries. It is worth pointing out that within each of the concepts there are significant permutations and transformations of the basic principles in the world press systems we see today. However, for a critique of the typology of the four theories of the press, see John C. Nerone, ed., *Last Rights: Revisiting Four Theories of the Press* (Urbana: University of Illinois Press, 1995).

10. For a review of developmental press and other media system theories, see William A. Hatchen, *The World News Prism: Changing Media of International Communication* (Ames: Iowa State University Press, 1996).

11. "Mainland to Establish Press Law," *World Journal,* 2 December 1998, A7.

12. The Chinese put family names first. In this chapter, names of Chinese leaders are spelled the way they have been used in China.

13. Samuel P. Huntington and Joan M. Nelson, *No Easy Choice: Political Participation in Developing Countries* (Cambridge, MA: Harvard University Press, 1976); Samuel P. Huntington and Clement H. Moore, eds., *Authoritarian Politics in Modern Society: The Dynamics of Established One-Party System* (New York: Basic Books, 1970).

14. Larry Diamond, "Economic Development and Democracy Reconsidered," *American Behavioral Scientist* 35 (1992): 450–499. Chin-Chuan Lee, "Sparking a Fire: The Press and the Ferment of Democratic Change in Taiwan," in Chin-Chuan Lee, ed., *China's Media, Media's China* (Boulder, CO: Westview Press, 1992), 163–204.

15. Edward Friedman, *National Identity and Democratic Prospects in Socialist China* (Armonk, NY: M. E. Sharpe, 1995).

16. Carlos H. Waisman, "Capitalism, the Market, and Democracy," *American Behavioral Scientist* 35 (1992): 500–516.

17. "Hope for Rule of Law Stressed," Agence France-Presse news release (14 November 1997).

18. Many scholars, both Chinese and Western, believe that *Ti Pao* was the first newspaper in the world. See, for example, Fan Hanqi, *A History of Modern Chinese Press* (Shanxi, China: Shanxi People's Press, 1981) (in Chinese); and Liang Jialu et al., *A History of Chinese Journalism* (Guangxi, China: Guangxi People's Press, 1984) (in Chinese). Others dispute this claim. See Li Longmu, *A Historical Study of Chinese Journalism* (Shanghai, China: Shanghai People's Press, 1985) (in Chinese).

19. Lee-hsia Hsu Ting, *Government Control of the Press in Modern China* (Cambridge, MA: East Asian Research Center, Harvard University Press, 1974), 7–26.

20. Ge Gongzhen, *History of Chinese Press* (Shanghai, China: Sanlian Publishing House, 1955), 334–369.

21. Ting, *Government Control of the Press,* 11.

22. Hailed as the Father of the Republic of China, Sun was born into a poor family on 12 November 1866, in the southern Chinese province of Canton (Guangdong). Always a revolutionary ahead of his times, Sun left for Hawaii in 1879, where he studied at a missionary school and later at Oahu College. After graduating from Oahu, Sun returned to China and finished his studies as a medical doctor in Hong Kong in 1892. He then was actively involved in revolutionary activities at a time of domestic political unrest and humiliation by Western powers. He successfully led an uprising in October 1911 to overthrow the Qing dynasty and founded the Republic of China. Sun was president of the new republic for a short time. He died on 12 March 1925 and left a lasting legacy in the history of modern Chinese revolutions. Among his contributions are his three principles of the people in state building: nationalism, democracy, and social well-being.

23. Fang, *History of Modern Chinese Press,* 676–688.

24. Li, *Historical Study of Chinese Journalism,* 71–80.

25. Ting, *Government Control of the Press,* 11–12.

26. For a full discussion, see Li, *Historical Study of Chinese Journalism,* 80–91, and Fang, *History of Modern Chinese Press,* 682–688.

27. Thomas Ming-Heng Chao, *The Foreign Press in China* (Shanghai, China: China Institute of Pacific Relations, 1931), 107–114.

28. Ibid., 111.

29. Ting, *Government Control of the Press,* 17.

30. Lu Keng, "Press Control in 'New China' and 'Old China,'" in Chin-Chuan Lee, ed., *China's Media, Media's China* (Boulder, CO: Westview Press, 1994), 147–162.

31. Lee, "Sparking a Fire."

32. "IPI: Mainland Should Learn Press Freedom from Taiwan," *World Journal,* 17 May 1999, p. A5.

33. John C. Merrill, *Legacy of Wisdom: Great Thinkers and Journalism* (Ames: Iowa State University Press, 1994), 94.

34. Raya Dunayevskaya, *Marxism and Freedom from 1776 until Today* (New York: Columbia University Press, 1988), 53.

35. Ibid., 53.

36. J. Herbert Altschull, *From Milton to McLuhan: The Ideas Behind American Journalism* (New York: Longman, 1990), 119–126.

37. For some of Marx's most influential writings in press freedom, see relevant articles by Marx in *The Karl Marx Library,* v. 4, *On Freedom of the Press and Censorship,* Saul K. Padover, ed. and trans. (New York: McGraw-Hill, 1974).

38. John P. Roche, *The History and Impact of Marxist-Leninist Organizational Theory* (Washington, DC: Institute for Foreign Policy Analysis, 1984), 14.

39. Roche, *Marxist-Leninist Organizational Theory,* 15–16.

40. Li Shaojun, *Party and Reform* (Beijing, China: Chinese Academy of Social Sciences, 1988), 28 (in Chinese).

41. For a detailed discussion, see Chen Lidan, *Classical Journalistic Works in Marxism-Leninism* (Beijing, China: People's Publishing House, 1987), 241–242 (in Chinese). A discussion of Lenin's development of Marx's conceptions is available in David W. Lovell, *From Marx to Lenin: An Evaluation of Marx's Responsibility for Soviet Authoritarianism* (New York: Cambridge University Press, 1984).

42. Siebert et al., *Four Theories of the Press,* 124.

43. There are 56 ethnic groups in China, of which Han Chinese make up 91.9% of the population. Other nationalities, such as Zhuang, Uygur, Hui, Yi, Tibetan, Miao, Manchu, Mongol, Buyi, and Korean, constitute the rest. There is a long history of ethnic tension between the dominant Han and other minorities, most of whom live in the border areas of China.

44. Mao not only developed his own Communist theory of the press, but he also advocated a revised theory in his writings. In addition to his numerous poems, he wrote a few important editorials for the major party newspapers. See *Selected Works of Mao Tze-tung* (Beijing, China: Foreign Language Press, 1977 and 1986).

45. For a full discussion, see James W. Markham, *Voices of the Red Giants* (Ames: Iowa State University Press, 1967), 354–357.

46. Won Ho Chang, *Mass Media in China: The History and the Future* (Ames: Iowa State University Press, 1989), 37.

47. Jianhua Yu, "The Abortive 1956 Reform of Chinese Journalism," *Journalism Quarterly* 65 (1988): 328–334.

48. Lynn T. White III, "Local Newspapers and Community Change, 1949–1969," in Godwin C. Chu and Francis L. K. Hsu, eds., *Moving a Mountain* (Honolulu, HI: University Press of Hawaii, 1979), 76–112.

49. Liu Binyan, "Press Freedom: Particles in the Air," in Chin-Chuan Lee, ed., *Voices of China* (New York: Guilford Press, 1990), 132–139.

50. Ibid., 132–139.

51. Merle Goldman, "The Role of the Press in Post-Mao Political Struggles," in Chin-Chuan Lee, ed., *China's Media, Media's China* (Boulder, CO: Westview Press, 1992), 23–35.

52. Ibid., 24–28.

53. Ruan Ming, "Press Freedom and Neo-authoritarianism: A Reflection on China's Democracy Movement," in Chin-Chuan Lee, ed., *Voices of China* (New York: Guilford Press, 1990), 122–131.

54. "'Journalists Without Borders' Urged Beijing to Respect Press Freedom," *World Journal,* January 2, 1999, p. A7.

55. Allison Jernow, "The Press in the 1980s: Testing New Ground," in Orville Schell and David Shambaugh, eds., *The China Reader: The Reform Era* (New York: Vantage Books, 1999), 229–236.

56. "Former Head of People's Daily Hu Jiwei Criticized Chinese Communist Party's Authoritarian Regime," *Central Daily News,* 21 January 1993, p. 4.

57. For a summary of this debate, see Kenneth Starck and Xu Yu, "Loud Thunder, Small Raindrops: The Reform Movement and the Press in China," *Gazette* 42 (1988): 143–159.

58. Marlowe Hood, "The Use and Abuse of Mass Media by Chinese Leaders During the 1980s," in Chin-Chuan Lee, ed., *China's Media, Media's China* (Boulder, CO: Westview Press, 1992), 37–57.

59. Seth Faison, "The Press During the 1989 Demonstrations," in Orville Schell and David Shambaugh, eds., *The China Reader: The Reform Era* (New York: Vantage Books, 1999), 236–246.

60. Judy Polumbaum, "The Tribulations of China's Journalists after a Decade of Reform," in Chin-Chuan Lee, ed., *Voices of China* (New York: Guilford Press, 1990), 39.

61. "Mainland to Establish Press Law," *World Journal,* 2 December 1998, p. A7.

62. "Beijing Tightened Control, Two Newspapers in Guangdong Sanctioned," *World Journal,* 13 January 1999, p. A7.

63. Xu Yu, "Professionalization without Guarantees: Changes of the Chinese Press in Post-1989 Years," *Gazette* 53 (1994): 23–41.

64. *China News Analysis* (Hong Kong), 1 March 1994, pp. 1–9.

65. Yu, "Professionalization without Guarantees," 25.

66. For further discussion of the changes in the early 1990s, see Leonard L. Chu, "Continuity and Change in China's Media Reform," *Journal of Communication* 44 (1994):4–21; Joseph Man Chan, "Media Internationalization in China: Processes and Tensions," *Journal of Communication* 44 (1994): 70–88; Tsan-Kuo Chang, Jian Wang, and Chih-Hsien Chen, "News as Social Knowledge," unpublished manuscript, 52–69; and Paul Siu-nam Lee, "Mass Communication and National Development in China: Media Roles Reconsidered," *Journal of Communication* 44 (1994): 22–37.

67. Xifen Gan, "Debates Contribute to the Development of the Journalistic Science," *Journal of Communication* 44 (1994): 38–51.

68. "Local Newspapers Taking over Leading Position in the Press Industry," *World Journal,* 27 April 1999, p. A7.

69. Ronald C. Keith, *China's Struggle for the Rule of Law* (New York: Macmillan, 1994).

70. Debra Davis, *The Consumer Revolution in Urban China* (Berkeley: University of California Press, 2000).

71. Recent surveys predict that the Internet-connected population in China will surpass that in the United States by 2010. See a related report on the Nua Internet Survey Web site: "Computer Industry Almanac Inc.: Chinese Users to Outnumber U.S. Users by 2010," available at http://www.nua.ie/surveys/?f=VS&art_id=905355392&rel=true (5 December 1998). Meanwhile, the Chinese government has decided to open its Internet market to foreign investors. See the related story: "Associated Press: China to Open to Foreign Investment," available at http://www.nua.ie/surveys/?f=VS&art_id=905355413&rel=true (8 December 1999).

# PART II

# Propaganda

By the seventeenth century the widespread adoption of the printing press in Europe had made it possible for Martin Luther's adherents to communicate their anti-Rome messages to peoples throughout Europe on a mass scale, launching "the first propaganda war."[1] The Church responded with predictable censorship but also with its own propaganda in an attempt to counter what it regarded as heretical anti-Rome messages. Pope Gregory XV appointed a committee of cardinals, the Congregatio de Propaganda Fide (Congregation for the Propagation of the Faith), to challenge the subversive messages. Most scholars trace the first use of the term "propaganda" to this committee.

Thus, from its beginnings, dissidents used propaganda to communicate messages across national boundaries with the goal of undermining authority. Those in power—whether the church or the state—regarded the messages as threats to their authority and designed counterpropaganda campaigns. International propaganda predates the mass medium of the printing press. Before the printing press individuals traveling across borders propagated their ideas through the spoken word, but the mass media and advances in mass media have made international propaganda possible on a wide scale.

Until the twentieth century politicians and citizens used the term "propaganda" freely and loosely, and scholars gave little attention to analyzing propaganda or studying its effects. The seemingly widespread and coordinated use of propaganda by governments during World Wars I and II forced researchers to devote scholarly attention to propaganda. Great Britain and the United States coordinated effective propaganda campaigns to demonize Germans as baby killers and evil Huns. A popular approach by a leading scholar, Harold Lasswell, views propaganda as the technique of changing attitudes and behaviors by manipulating symbols.

Symbol manipulation proved to be especially fitting for World War I and II wartime propaganda analysis. Through radio, posters, film, and other mass media the British, Germans, Americans, and others appeared to effectively use propaganda to whip up domestic public support for their positions and to demonize their enemies. New media technologies, such as shortwave radio, made it possible for nations to transmit messages to foreign nations and enemy nations—even if the receiving nations regarded the messages as unwanted hostile propaganda. Thus propaganda served both domestic and international functions.

The chapters in this part highlight contemporary scholarly interest in propaganda. Antonio V. Menéndez Alarcón, of Butler University, provides case studies of propaganda during Spanish and French referendum campaigns. His analyses of the campaigns attempt to flesh out propagandists' underlying methods or techniques. To this end, Menéndez draws on the classic seven techniques for analyzing propaganda. Although scholars advanced these techniques more than 60 years ago, they are still useful for identifying and analyzing propaganda appeals. This chapter provides students with a useful critical tool for recognizing propaganda and the propagandist's motives.

John Spicer Nichols, in the journalism program at the Pennsylvania State University, offers a case study of America's propaganda war directed against Cuba, in the form of Television Martí. Nichols pulls no punches in arguing that the U.S.-government television station aimed at getting the Cuban people to overthrow their government is a failure. One reason is that most Cubans cannot receive the station, but even if they could, Nichols argues that the station still would not succeed. Why? As Nichols contends: "The overwhelming body of academic literature on international communication and political persuasion indicates that audience members select messages that conform to their preconceived notions and actively avoid, perceive, or twist messages that create inner tension or that place them in conflict with those around them." Despite the station's ineffectiveness in changing Cubans' opinions, Nichols notes that the station has had consequences for domestic U.S. politics and U.S.-Cuban political relations.

### NOTE

1. J. Burke, *The Day the Universe Changed* (Boston: Little, Brown, 1985), 118.

# 4

# Propaganda in Spanish and French Referendum Campaigns

## An Analysis of Propaganda Techniques

### ANTONIO V. MENÉNDEZ ALARCÓN

The most well-known political propaganda campaigns in twentieth-century Europe took place in Nazi Germany, Fascist Italy, and the Soviet Union (before and after the USSR's revolution). In these cases information and popular culture were under complete or nearly complete control of the governments. The mass media were largely propagandist instruments of their governments. In fact, many people tend to associate the term "propaganda" with totalitarian and authoritarian states. However, propaganda exists in every society and political system. In this chapter I address political propaganda in contemporary democratic Western Europe. France and Spain serve as the case studies. Two historical political referendums are analyzed: (1) NATO in Spain and (2) the Treaty on the European Union in France. These referendums are salient examples of modern propaganda in Europe. They underscore the dynamism, pervasiveness, and completeness of contemporary political propaganda.

The concept of propaganda, according to *Encyclopaedia Britannica*,[1] "is the more or less systematic effort to manipulate other people's beliefs, attitudes, or actions by means of symbols. Deliberateness and a relatively heavy emphasis on manipulation distinguish propaganda from casual conversation or the free and easy exchange of ideas. The propagandist has a specific goal or set of goals."[2] Although propaganda has existed since antiquity—ancient civilizations used impressive statues, temples, palaces, and sumptuous clothing to convince their subjects of the greatness of a particular king, noble, or priesthood[3]—the word "propaganda" first began to be used in the Renaissance. It derives from a Catholic organization founded in 1622 to carry on missionary work, the Congregatio de Propaganda Fide.

During the Industrial Revolution, a new type of propaganda developed, aimed at affecting the buying preferences of consumers through the use of mass marketing. Large sets of data on consumer attitudes, socioeconomic characteristics, and perceptions were compiled to influence consumer habits through mass media. These techniques were also adapted to politics.

It is with World War I that the term "propaganda" began to be widely used "to describe persuasion tactics" used by the parties at war.[4] Immediately after the war, propaganda was adopted to describe persuasion techniques used in political campaigns. By the end of the twentieth century propaganda had "become increasingly integral to our way of life, to the extent that as a form of communication it is now the model form of suasive learning, appropriate for and distinctive to the civilization in which we live. To live in contemporary times is to be showered with the seeds of suasive ideas."[5]

Although propaganda takes many forms, "it is almost always in some form of activated ideology."[6] There are three basic types of propaganda identified by researchers: (1) white propaganda, in which a source is identified properly and the message is close to being accurate, even though it is presented in a manner that attempts to convince the audience that the sender is the good person with the best ideas and political ideology; (2) gray propaganda, in which the source may or may not be identified and the accuracy of the information is uncertain; and (3) black propaganda, in which a false source is given and lies, fabrications, and deceptions are spread.[7] In the cases examined in this chapter white and gray propaganda were most often used.

The purpose of propaganda is to promote a partisan or competitive cause in the best interests of the propagandist.[8] To accomplish this, political propaganda is often simplistic and one-sided. As one master of propaganda, Joseph Goebbels (reichsminister for propaganda under Hitler's Germany), once said: "There is nothing that the masses hate more than two-sidedness, to be called upon to consider this as well as that. They think primitively. They love to generalize complicated situations and from their generalizations to draw clear and uncompromising solutions."[9] In the same tone propaganda offers logical and seemingly rational one-sided explanations to particular issues. Pratkanis and Aronson[10] proposed two overarching principles to describe these responses to propaganda: "We humans seek to conserve our cognitive energy by taking mental short-cuts whenever we can, and we attempt to rationalize our thoughts and behavior so that they appear reasonable to ourselves and others." Thus the propagandist tries to convince by a simple one-dimensional form of demonstration. This lesson has been learned by all contemporary politicians who use slogans, sound bites, and simplistic ideas to get their points across.

Another major principle of propaganda is the appeal to emotions. This appeal is rather pervasive in contemporary propaganda, as Combs and Nimmo demonstrated.[11] The use of emotions is tied to negative and positive reinforcement. For instance, "if you do not agree with my program, then chaos will ensue." Also, often it is suggested that the propositions of the opposition are adventurous and dangerous. We will see in the cases analyzed here how political propaganda created a particular meaning and identification reactions based on emotions, often using what Janis and Feshback labeled fear-arousing techniques.[12]

Propagandists also make extensive use of what Touraine called the principle of universality.[13] Most human beings in democratic societies agree on some basic values, such as democracy, human rights, the good of the nation, and self-determination. Thus, in order to persuade, political propagandists tap into those overarching ideals to attract support for their causes.

These theories and assumptions provide the basis for the development of propaganda campaigns and specific techniques of persuasion. Some of the most common propaganda techniques are analyzed in this chapter. Alfred McClung Lee and Elizabeth Briant Lee,[14] a husband and wife team of sociologists and members of the Institute for Propaganda, described seven devices (I prefer the term "techniques" and use it in this chapter) used by propagandists; they used the devices to analyze the speeches of fascist radio evangelist Father Charles Coughlin. These techniques were revisited recently by Severin and Tankard[15] in an analysis of propaganda in the United States. They identified seven propaganda techniques:

1. *Glittering generality*—"associating something with a virtue world—is used to make us accept and approve the thing without examining the evidence" (p. 96).

2. *Transfer* "carries the authority, sanction and prestige of something respected and revered over something else in order to make the latter more acceptable" (p. 98).

3. *Testimonial* "consists in having some respected or hated person say that a given idea or program or product or person is good or bad" (p. 99).

4. *Card stacking* "involves the selection and use of facts or falsehoods, illustrations, or distractions, and logical or illogical statements in order to give the best or worst possible case for an idea, program, person, or product" (p. 101); it implies one single-sided presentation of an issue.

5. *Bandwagon* means that the propagandist "attempts to convince us that all members of a group to which we belong accept his program and that we must therefore follow our crowd and jump on the 'bandwagon'" (p. 103).

6. *Name calling* is giving an idea or a person a bad label; it "is used to make us reject and condemn the idea without examining the evidence" (p. 93).

7. *Plain folks* "is the method by which a speaker attempts to convince his audience that he and his ideas are good because they 'are of the people,' the 'plain folks'" (p. 100).

All these techniques are not widely applied in all campaigns (bandwagon was used often in the Spanish case, whereas it was rarely used in the French case), and some of them might be applied simultaneously in the same slogan. For instance, one could find a card-stacking one-sided argument that also used name calling to promote or disqualify an idea. These propaganda techniques were originally conceived with catchy names to help the average citizen detect propaganda. They were commonly included in school curricula during the 1940s to help children identify propaganda.

Leonard Doob[16] criticized this approach for oversimplifying the propaganda process. Others consider it dated, and others have developed new techniques based on Lee and Lee's devices.[17] However, Severin and Tankard's[18] and Fleming's[19] analyses demonstrate that the Institute for Propaganda's classification of propaganda techniques still provides a useful typology to guide the examinations of political propaganda campaigns in contemporary society. This is specially so if the analyses go beyond simply identifying techniques to explain the context in which messages are produced.

In this chapter the analyses focus on four of the techniques listed because they were the most commonly used: glittering generality, card stacking, transfer, and testimonial.[20] The analyses concentrate on the main aspects of the message and, when required, indicate the dual use of these techniques within the same message. No assumptions were made that these techniques are absolutely effective. Research has shown that these techniques are indeed effective.[21] However, the four techniques examined here are the most commonly applied in political communication. The analyses center on the rhetoric used during the campaigns, as reported in newspapers and other political communication messages,[22] and on personal observations. The analyses are limited to the most recurrent arguments.

## THE CAMPAIGN ON THE NATO REFERENDUM IN SPAIN

The 12 March 1986 referendum on whether Spain should remain in NATO was the first referendum in history on a military alliance. Spain officially joined NATO on 30 May 1982 under the center-right government of Calvo Sotelo, who took office in February 1981. At that time all the parties on the political left, including the two most important ones, the Partido Socialista Obrero Español (PSOE) (Spanish Workers Socialist Party) and the Partido Comunista Español (PCE) (Spanish Communist Party), opposed Spain's membership in NATO.[23]

In June 1982, a month after Spain joined NATO, the PSOE won the general elections by a landslide. It soon became clear that, once in power, the main leaders of this party were changing their position on NATO. In a major speech in October 1984 the prime minister and leader of the PSOE, Felipe González, publicly declared his support for his country's membership in NATO.[24] Being in power had brought González and the PSOE to see NATO membership from a different perspective. As González said on the issue: "There is a conflict between the heart and reason, and the reason has to predominate."[25] Another socialist, Angel Viñas, advisor to the Foreign Ministry, explained this turnaround as follows: "We realized that you could not separate political and economic ties from security ties."[26]

Despite this about-face, the PSOE could not escape its campaign promise of holding a referendum on NATO membership. The leaders of the PSOE were well aware of the lack of popular support for NATO. In fact, they had been instrumental in creating opposition to NATO before their victory in the 1982 elections. They could not simply repudiate their past commitment without a major risk of political discredit. Furthermore, because there was considerable opposition to NATO membership in the PSOE, not to hold a referendum would have implied political unrest within the party.

The PSOE had the passive support on this issue of the main political party of the opposition, the Partido Popular (Popular Party), which was even more pro-NATO than the government.[27] Together, the PSOE and the Partido Popular controlled close to 80% of the Cortes (the Spanish parliament). However, even with this overwhelming support for NATO in the Cortes, the government had a difficult task in convincing the Spanish population to vote in favor of continuing NATO membership. Indeed, polls between 1981 and 1985 on Spanish attitudes on security and defense showed a Spanish population largely pacifist and less anti-Soviet and more anti-American than its European neighbors, consistently blaming the United States far more than the Soviet Union for fomenting international tensions.[28] About 70% of Spaniards wanted the U.S. bases in Spain dismantled, and 55% wanted to withdraw from NATO. In addition to these sentiments, a will to maintain the tradition of Spanish neutrality (which prevented Spain from participating in the two world wars of the twentieth century) and the aspiration to an independent Spain were widespread across the country, including people who traditionally voted conservatively.

Public opinion, however, changed considerably as the campaign progressed. Spaniards in favor of withdrawing from NATO went from a margin of 10–12% over those in favor of remaining in the alliance in early 1985 to a margin of only 4–6% in early 1986. The last four published polls before the referendum[29] coincided in giving a slight majority to the no vote, although these same polls showed a large number of people still undecided.

The propaganda campaign mounted by both sides involved the use of all the media, including the state-owned television and radio, billboards, and extensive reports in national newspapers and magazines with wide readership, such as *El País, Diario 16, La Vanguardia, ABC, Cambio 16,* and regional newspapers.

According to the Spanish laws regulating political campaigns, television (two state-sponsored networks) and radio time was allocated to the political parties in proportion to their share of parliamentary seats. This gave the pro-NATO group a considerable advantage, because the opposition to NATO was represented in the parliament by only a shrunken PCE. No commercial spots were permitted on television, although they were allowed on radio and in the printed press.

It is estimated that the PSOE spent close to $2 million (U.S. dollars) on press and radio advertising (which was a considerable amount at that time by Spanish standards). Originally, they were planning to spend $600,000.[30]

The pro-NATO leaders visited every urban center in Spain during the campaign. The ruling PSOE held 770 meetings throughout the country during the campaign, according to White.[31] In addition, 28 million letters were sent to the electorate from Prime Minister Felipe González, asking people to vote yes for Spain's membership in NATO.

After making official the call for a referendum, the PSOE leaders had to confront minority currents within the party that were opposed to NATO. Using a combination of repressive measures (dissidents were threatened with expulsion if they did not follow party discipline) and internal propaganda, González and his close associates imposed a relatively efficient party discipline. Thus by February 1986 most of the party, including the left-wing group Izquierda Socialista (Socialist Left) and the youth organization, agreed to the party line. A notable exception was the socialist labor union, Union General de Trabajadores (General Union of Workers), and its leader, Nicolas Redondo.

On the other side, the opposition to Spain's membership in NATO was organized by the PCE and a small group of leftist parties. These included the Trotskyist Liga Comunista Revolucionaria (Revolutionary Communist League), the Movimiento Comunista (Communist Movement) with tiny electoral support, and myriad human rights and pacifist groups, which included a considerable number of well-known intellectuals, such as Antonio Gala and Ramón Tamames. This side had the support of some dissenting socialist leaders and historical figures, such as Enrique Tierno Galván, mayor of Madrid. These groups formed a countrywide coordination committee, Coordinadora Estatal de Organizaciones Pacifistas, and an ad hoc Plataforma Cívica para la Salida de España de la OTAN (Civic Platform for the Withdrawal of Spain from NATO). Furthermore, the opposition to NATO also had the active support of the main unions of the country, the already mentioned Union General de Trabajadores, closely associated with the PSOE, and the Comisiones Obreras (Workers' Commissions), closely linked to the PCE.

The movement of opposition to NATO countered with a budget of $300,000.[32] Half of that money came from voluntary contributions, and the rest came from the constituent bodies (the PCE and the Comisiones Obreras were the biggest contributors). Because of limited resources and their tiny representation in the parliament, the anti-NATO movement could not use the media as much as the government. However, by staging massive demonstrations and lively rallies, they were able to attract some mainstream media coverage and disseminate arguments for a neutralist alternative. They practiced a great deal of what the late French philosopher Jacques Ellul called agitation propaganda. Persuasive messages were accompanied by public expressions of discontent in the streets. This type of propaganda "is always translated into reality by physical involvement in a tense and overexcited activity."[33]

This anti-NATO movement, which had been active during the debate on adhesion during the previous government of Calvo Sotelo in 1981, started to mobilize again in early 1984, when it became clear that Felipe González's government was not doing anything to withdraw from NATO. Large demonstrations and rallies in most large cities characterized the anti-NATO campaign. The anti-NATO demonstrations intensified during 1985 and continued up to three days before the referendum in March 1986. Together with traditional rallies, the anti-NATO demonstrators used song festivals to promote their cause. For instance, at the last meeting, close to 500,000 people joined in a rally where rock music and movie stars appeared.[34]

Let's turn now to the specific techniques of persuasion used by both sides during this campaign.

## Glittering Generality

Both camps used the glittering generality technique to convince people that they were struggling for the good of the Spanish nation. The campaign slogan of the PSOE read: "Referendum on the maintenance of Spain in the Atlantic Alliance—in the interests of Spain, vote yes."[35] This appeal appeared on about 2,000 billboards all over Spain and in radio jingles.

According to this line of thinking, the pro-NATO officials would say that they supported NATO because it was good for the national interests of Spain and its people. This declaration uttered by González at a rally in Jaén is an example of this recurring argument: "I am proud to be swimming against the current because it is in the interest of Spain."[36] Furthermore, in declarations on television and newspapers González's supporters presented him as a man that, for the good of the nation, was ready to sacrifice himself and his party.

On the other side, the forces opposing NATO argued that "the interest of the Spanish people was to remain neutral," and therefore Spain should withdraw from NATO: "Spain can only develop in peace and NATO implies war. It implies being a pawn of one superpower against another."[37] The anti-NATO side appealed to deep-seated Spanish desires for independence, modernization, development, and peace.

The anti-NATO campaign was strongly based on the Spanish popular perceptions of the United States as an imperialist country. This perception was reinforced at that time by the Reagan administration's actions in Latin America (support for the Contras in Nicaragua, the invasion of Grenada, support of the repressive government of El Salvador, etc.). The negative views of the United States were also due to the friendly attitude toward Franco's dictatorship by U.S. administrations after the Spanish civil war.[38]

## Card Stacking

The card-stacking technique of persuasion was often used in the NATO referendum debate. This technique involves a biased selection of facts and reasoning to support or to oppose NATO membership. Two major forms of the card-stacking technique were used: a general one-sided argument and a more specific one-sided assertion based on fear-arousing mechanisms.

To deflate the anti-U.S. sentiment, the pro-NATO forces argued that if Spain was not in NATO, it would be in a weaker position to negotiate on the question of U.S. military bases. Furthermore, it was argued, "as part of NATO, Spain might find European solidarity in its negotiation with the United States" and that within the alliance, Spain had equal rights to be heard and a voice of equal strength to that of the other members. González suggested that NATO rejection might mean more, not less, Spanish-U.S. defense cooperation. "Instead of discussing our defense with our European partners, we would be completely tied to the United States."[39]

The pro-NATO movement also used economic issues at length. In several television appearances the economic minister, Carlos Solchaga, tried to persuade voters of the economic advantages of NATO membership and "the risks of an economic crisis, with unpredictable consequences if Spain withdrew from NATO."[40] Following the same logic, another leader of the PSOE declared that "NATO ensures progress, democracy, and freedom. If Spain rejects the alliance, there would be an international crisis of confidence, and foreign investments would dry up. This will cause the loss of jobs for thousands."[41] Unemployment was a burning issue for the Spanish people because their country had the highest unemployment rate of Western Europe at the time.

The likelihood of reduced investment from abroad and its negative consequences on unemployment were echoed by the representatives of the big banks in newspapers and magazines, such as *El País, Cambio 16, La Vanguardia, ABC,* and others. The following quote is typical of declarations that were presented by the authors as objective and professional analysis: "There will be a considerable loss of confidence on Spanish stability if Spain withdraws from NATO. This will inevitably reduce investments and limit our prospects to create new jobs."[42]

In their propaganda the pro–NATO forces declared that Spain would be in chaos if it were not part of NATO. They affirmed that a vote against NATO would inevitably carry many administrative complications because there was not an established and valid mechanism to implement the actual withdrawal from NATO. This would bring turmoil to the country. On 8 March 1986, González labeled the no vote as a dead end and asked, "Who will manage the no vote?" implying the possibility that he would leave the government and call for early elections if the anti-NATO forces won. In an interview published in *El País,*[43] González alluded to the far left's influence on the anti-NATO forces, saying that "if the country voted to quit NATO, then think of who is going to carry out that policy." Here he was trying to scare political moderates and conservatives about the possibility of a takeover of the government by the left and the far left.

The government appealed to the fear of the army: "By being part of NATO, the armed forces will have a role to play outside the country, and this will keep them out of internal politics."[44] The threat of a military takeover was mentioned by analysts in newspapers[45] as a reason to remain in NATO and was very much in the minds of many people in Spain during that period.[46] I had conversations with people ambivalent about belonging to NATO who were nevertheless inclined to support Spain's membership on the basis of that argument alone.

In addition, the wording of the question for the referendum was an excellent example of the card-stacking technique. Aware of anti-U.S. sentiments among the population, the leaders of the PSOE tried to separate the question of NATO membership from anti-U.S. perceptions in their campaign, particularly in the question for the referendum. The question was phrased as follows: "Do you consider it in Spain's interests to remain in the Atlantic alliance on the terms agreed upon by the government?"[47] The terms were (1) the government will continue to keep Spain out of NATO's integrated military structure; (2) it will continue to bar nuclear weapons from Spanish soil (these two commitments were already in place when Spain joined); and (3) it will seek a reduction of the military presence in Spain. Furthermore, the words used were carefully chosen. By using the words "Atlantic alliance" instead of NATO they were using a term that had no negative meaning for Spaniards, whereas NATO had been a familiar target of Spanish politicians in the recent past, including the PSOE.

The government put to use here what Pratkanis and Aronson[48] called prepersuasion: "how the problem is structured and how the decision is framed. By establishing how an issue is defined, a communicator can influence cognitive responses and obtain consent without even appearing to be attempting to persuade us." As shown by poll results,[49] when the question was framed in straight yes or no terms, there was a large majority against remaining in NATO, but the margin was considerably reduced when the question was asked as phrased in the referendum ballot.

The opposition to NATO also extensively used the technique of card stacking combined with fear appeals. The anti-NATO forces focused on "the possibility of war if Spain continued membership in NATO." The argument went that stability and peace would happen for the Spanish people only "if they stay neutral and independent from the blocs."[50] A dominant slogan of the anti-NATO campaign was *Dejennos en paz* ("Leave us in peace"), which in Spanish also means "Leave us alone." Furthermore, in response to the government messages, the opposition often tried to separate the NATO issue from the European Community issue: "A vote against NATO does not mean a vote against Europe."[51]

## Transfer

The government presented membership in NATO as an extraordinary opportunity for Spain to benefit from technological and financial integration and "to modernize" in general. The idea was to tie NATO membership to a process by which Spain would definitely turn the page on its isolated and psychologically devastating Francoist period. The message of the PSOE was that if Spain had to withdraw from NATO, it would not be able to become a modern nation firmly inside the Western world.

The PSOE systematically and repeatedly associated NATO membership with membership in the European Community. In the closing of the campaign speech, González urged Spaniards "not to turn your backs on Europe."[52] To be part of the modern Western world was a strong aspiration of most Spanish people, and as part of this ideal, membership in the European Community had widespread support among the Spanish population. Furthermore, by continuing Spain's association with NATO, the government argued, "it may ease the way to an understanding with the United Kingdom over the question of Gibraltar."[53]

In addition, the referendum was presented in such a way that it was not only a vote for or against Spain's membership in NATO but also a vote about supporting the PSOE and the government. Even those opposed to NATO strongly supported the PSOE as the only viable political party to govern Spain at that time.

In other words, the PSOE and its leader González turned the referendum into a plebiscite. They knew that there was no real alternative to replacing the party in power. No party on the right or the left was in a position to seriously challenge the PSOE in the coming elections, which were scheduled for June of that same year.

The members of the anti-NATO campaign tried to link the referendum to what they described as "González's internal right-wing politics" associating the government with policies that inspired negative feelings among many Spaniards. The following statement by one of the main figures of the anti-NATO campaign, Ramón Tamames, shows this association: "This is a referendum on González. It is a vote against his Thatcher economics, his Reagan politics, and his Mitterrand militarism."[54] Another common proposition of the opposition was that "NATO was warlike and a tool of the United States"[55] The NATO issue was presented as a U.S. issue, which implied U.S. intervention in Spanish affairs. A common slogan in these rallies was "NATO no! Bases out!"

These arguments demonstrate how both sides used the technique of transfer. The government accomplished this as follows: First, NATO was associated with modernization—an objective highly desired by the Spanish population. Modernization implied not only technological modernization but also democracy and especially breaking with the Francoist past, which was viewed as backward by most Spaniards. Second, the government made a transfer connection from membership in NATO to membership in the European Community, which had widespread support among the Spanish populace. Third, NATO membership was linked to the question of Gibraltar, which still played an important role in the Spanish national imagination and pride. Many Spaniards considered the British occupation of this little island to the south of Spain an affront to Spanish national sovereignty. Fourth, voting yes to NATO was associated with stability and with the PSOE, which was the political choice of the majority of the Spanish people. The message was that if people wanted the PSOE to continue in power, they would have to vote in favor of the continuation of Spain's membership in NATO.

The opposition associated NATO with war and with the United States, with NATO being presented as an instrument of the U.S. domination of Spain and the world. As stated earlier, the Plataforma Cívica para la Salida de España de la OTAN based its campaign on the Spanish public's hostile feelings toward the United States. Furthermore, the Plataforma Cívica tried to link the NATO issue and the referendum with what it considered the conservative economic, political, and military policies of the government.

## Testimonial

The use of testimonials by socially recognized and respected figures to persuade voters was widespread in this campaign. The PSOE primarily used their main leaders and especially Felipe González, who was at that time by far the most popular politician in Spain. His continuous presence in the mass media was an effective weapon in favor of NATO membership. The final TV broadcast of the pro-NATO campaign was carefully staged to promote González's image as a great statesman, presenting him next to a Spanish flag, carefully adjusted to show the crown, and in film clips that showed him in conversations with European leaders. Many symbols were carefully arranged. There was a call for patriotism and pride, an association of the crown with González, and a projection of González as a European leader and through him an association of NATO with Europe.

*Cambio 16* (17 March 1986) described one of González's last appearances on TV as "Spain's great communicator," glorifying him with these words: "Felipe, simply by being there, with that voice of his that is sheer magic, sheer charisma, was probably a decisive factor in changing people's minds."

The government also had other important allies in its propaganda campaign: King Juan Carlos and Queen Sofia showed up to vote before television cameras. The king normally does not vote in elections or speak on public issues, and his appearance at the voting booth probably played an important role in bringing many people and particularly conservatives, who generally revere him, to the polls. Although the king did not say how he voted, most people assumed that he had voted in favor of continuing NATO membership.

The anti-NATO movement countered with testimonials by well-known intellectuals, such as Antonio Gala, Ramón Tamames, movie stars, artists, and respected political figures, such as Enrique Tierno Galván. Indeed, these personalities connected with the Spanish people well beyond the reach of the leftist parties that constituted the political leadership of the movement.

Next, we turn our attention to the propaganda campaign on the French referendum for the ratification of the Treaty on the European Union.

## FRENCH REFERENDUM
## ON THE MAASTRICHT TREATY

The campaign that developed before the referendum for the ratification of the Treaty on the European Union in France (also known as the Maastricht Treaty, from the name of the town in the Netherlands where the treaty was first agreed on by the European Council in December 1991) is another meaningful example of propaganda in Europe. This treaty, which was signed by the governments of the then 12 states of the European Community on 7 February 1992, implied further economic and political union.[56] In some countries, such as Denmark, Ireland, and France, the government was formally required to consult the populace before the final ratification. In this section I deal with the propaganda campaign that developed in France regarding the Treaty on the European Union.

The campaign for the referendum disrupted the traditional political oppositions; partisans and adversaries of the treaty were often members of the same party. The socialists in power were in favor of ratification. However, a small but relatively influential group within the governing party [Parti Socialiste Français (PSF) (French Socialist Party)] was against the treaty. The Gaullist Rassemblement pour la République (RPR) (Rally for the Republic) was even more divided. About half the party leadership was in favor of ratifying the treaty, and the other half was opposed.

The centrist Union Démocratique Française (UDF) (French Democratic Union) also contained a small group that opposed the treaty within an otherwise largely pro-European integration party. The only parties with some electoral weight that were not internally divided on this issue were the Parti Communiste Français (PCF) (Communist Party) and the Front National (National Front). The leadership of the PCF and the ultra-conservative Front National were vehemently against further integration and against the treaty. The division of French laypeople on the issue of European integration crossed party lines as well.

The small parties on the extreme left followed different paths: The Trotskyist Ligue Communiste Revolutionnaire campaigned against the treaty, whereas the Anarchist Federation and another Trotskyist organization, Lutte Ouvrière (LO) (Workers Struggle), proposed abstaining. In addition, the farmers, most of whom opposed the treaty because they perceived it as detrimental to their economic interests, created a group called Coordination Rurale (Rural Coordination) to campaign against the treaty.

The French referendum took place on 20 September 1992. The official campaign started on 7 September and ended at midnight on 19 September. Both sides, however, started to promote their point of view much earlier, in the spring.

Both sides developed a vast propaganda campaign that pervaded French public opinion. Newspaper articles (particularly in the widely respected newspaper *Le Monde*), radio and television appearances, street signs, and rallies were used extensively by both sides to promote their points of view. However, the campaign on television and radio was limited to declarations of politicians during the time allotted to them and to news coverage of rallies and events staged to promote their views. At the time, in France, as in Spain, it was illegal to broadcast commercial television spots for political purposes. Political party access to television and radio was rigorously controlled. Even the government could not use the media as it wished.[57]

Following the recommendations of the Conseil Supérieur de l'Audiovisuel (Superior Audiovisual Council), the government issued a decree allocating antenna time on television and radio to the different political parties participating in the campaign. The organizations that were represented in the parliament had two hours of television time and two hours of radio time that were divided among them in proportion to the number of seats they occupied in the parliament. In other words, the PSF had 47 minutes, the RPR 30 minutes, the UDF 37 minutes, and the PCF 6 minutes.[58] Each party was responsible for deciding how their time would be used. The PSF and the UDF did not give time to the opponents of the treaty within their own party. However, the RPR divided the time between party members who favored and those who opposed the treaty. This decree also allocated broadcast time to parties with no representation in the parliament, if they had received at least 5% of the total votes in previous elections. Therefore the right-wing Front National and the two environment parties, Les Verts (the Greens) and Génèration Ecologie (Ecology Generation) also had access to TV and radio.

**Table 4.1 Public Opinion Trends Regarding the Maastricht Treaty**[a]

| | FALL **1991** | | | SPRING **1992** | | | SUMMER **1992** | | | SPRING **1993** | | |
|---|---|---|---|---|---|---|---|---|---|---|---|---|
| | Pro | Con | DK/NA | Pro | Con | DK/NA | Pro | Con | DK/NA | Pro | Con | DK/NA |
| European Union | | | | | | | | | | | | |
| Support[b] | 59 | 4 | 37 | 55 | 8 | 37 | 55 | 9 | 37 | 57 | 16 | 27 |
| Maastricht[c] | | | | 42 | 26 | 32 | 42 | 42 | 16 | | | |
| Referendum | | | | | | | 51 | 49 | — | | | |

[a]Percentages in the table were derived in part from the table, data, and explanations provided in Mark Franklin, Michael Marsh, and Lauren McLaren, "Uncorking the Bottle: Popular Opposition to European Unification in the Wake of Maastricht," *Journal of Common Market Studies* 32, no. 4 (December 1994): 457.

[b]This typology was constructed from two answers: "Membership of the European Union is a good thing/a bad thing/neither good nor bad" and "Being for, against, or undecided about efforts to unify Western Europe," from Eurobarometers 36, 37, 38, and 40. Pro-Maastricht respondents are those who provide positive answers to both statements, and anti-Maastricht respondents are those who provide negative answers to both, with the remainder classified as "don't know" (DK) or "no answer" (NA).

[c]For or against ratifying the Maastricht Treaty in IFOP/*Le Figaro* poll (9 June 1962) and IFOP/*L'Express* poll (27 August–1 September 1992). IFOP, Institut Français d'Opinion Publique.

Table 4.1 reveals the trend of public opinion over the months between the agreement on the Maastricht Treaty in December 1991 and the referendum in 21 September 1992.

This table shows the dramatic change in opposition to the Maastricht Treaty after the propaganda campaign concerning the treaty was developed.[59] The data for fall 1991, when the Maastricht Treaty was approved by the heads of the then 12 state members of the European Community, to summer 1992, just before the French referendum, show that support for the Maastricht Treaty changed considerably (in spring 1992, 26% were against the treaty, but by the end of the summer the percentage opposing the treaty grew to 42%) and that support for a general idea of a united Europe did not change as much. The percentage of the population that opposed the European Union in general went from 4% in fall 1991 to 9% in summer 1992 and to 16% in spring 1993. The reason for this difference is that the idea of European unification in the abstract does not inspire as much negative response in the French populace as the Maastricht Treaty. There is a long-standing tradition in France of support for some loose form of international agreements. Aspects concerning the European Community were generally perceived as matters of foreign policy and as general agreements on tariffs and other international issues that had little effect on their lives. In fact, until this referendum European integration was largely a matter of debate among political and economic elites. The public at large did not know or care much about this process.

However, the Treaty on the European Union brought home more concrete measures that eventually attracted the French people's attention. Lindberg and Scheingold[60] suggested in 1970 that the positive response to European integration might not withstand a major increase in the scope or capacity of the European Community. The debate created by this referendum seems to have confirmed their predictions to a certain extent. When the European Community started to be presented in the media as an issue that would directly affect domestic policies, the reaction to further integration was more negative than previously thought. It led people, particularly those who had little prior information on or interest in the subject, to realize that the European Union was evolving in ways that they were not prepared to support. For example, many people were surprised to learn that the treaty could allow other European citizens to vote in French local elections.

As in the previous section about Spain, I now examine the four most common techniques of propaganda used by both sides in this referendum.

## Glittering Generality

Mitterrand and his followers within the PSF organized the campaign by relying extensively on the idea of the universal good. For instance, in a government document published in *Le Monde* they stated: "France united to her neighbors gives herself the means to be stronger and safer, and within a more democratic Community, the French and the Europeans will better control their future. In a world of uncertainty the European Union will be a pole of stability and peace."[61]

These references to peace, democracy, and political and economic stability were reinforced by appeals to the future of the children—an appeal that loomed large in people's consciousness as a virtue world—for example:

> The European Union constitutes a formidable enterprise for our generation and especially for our children.
> FRANÇOIS MITTERRAND, *French president on the television network TF1 on 3 September 1992*[62]

> A yes vote implies a response to the desire of young people to live free.
> GISCARD D'ESTAING, *leader of the UDF and former president of France*[63]

The campaign against the Maastricht Treaty also referred to universal values. The campaign organizers made use of powerful symbols relating to democracy, freedom, sovereignty, and workers' solidarity against the cold-blooded bureaucrats from Brussels and the transnational corporations who were controlling Europe. The campaign organizers consistently used "Brussels" instead of "European Community" to symbolize a foreign intervention in French internal affairs (The Commission of the European Community has its headquarters in Brussels, Belgium), as the following declarations reflect:

> The way in which Brussels wants to build Europe is destructive of the national democratic process. I am concerned about losing my condition as a French citizen of acting democratically.[64]
> MAX GALLO, *dissenting socialist leader on the TV program* L'Heure de Verité *(TV network Antenne 2), 26 April 1992*

> The treaty of Maastricht implies submission to Germany, alignment with the U.S.A., abandonment of the French state, which secures more equality, and prioritizing the wild economic liberalism.[65]

A recurrent slogan of the opposition on billboards all over the country said, "Liberté, je chèris ton non" ("Freedom, I value your no"), playing on a popular saying, "Liberté, je chèris ton nom" ("Liberty, I value your name").

These examples of glittering generality draw on accepted and widespread values such as freedom, peace, stability, the virtue world of democracy, and French national identity and sovereignty.

## Card Stacking

The propaganda campaign mounted by both sides sought to translate for mass consumption and according to their view a complex set of measures contained in the treaty. In translating this complex package, the propagandist in favor of the treaty simplified most issues and emphasized those aspects that seemed to have more public support, whereas those opposing the treaty emphasized the aspects of the treaty that arouse more opposition among the public.

Playing on people's fears using a one-sided card-stacking type of message was a common practice in the French campaign (as it was in the Spanish referendum). Mitterrand suggested in his speech on 14 July 1992 that "a no to Maastricht would break Europe apart and will have negative consequences on the economy." The same idea was echoed by other supporters of the pro–Maastricht Treaty forces:

If France votes no, Europe will disintegrate.
LAURENT FABIUS, *premier secretary of the PSF on the Television Network Antenne 2*[66]

To vote no to Maastricht is to take a considerable risk and to create trouble in Europe. France should not take the historic responsibility to undo what has been successful for so many years.
NICOLAS SARKOZY, *general secretaire adjoint of the RPR on a radio news program RTL*[67]

If the no wins, there would be a financial crisis, a crisis of confidence, a depressing feeling that will affect the markets.
JACK LANG, *coordinator of the government campaign for the yes vote*[68]

Voting yes will imply peace: We would no longer have to open military cemeteries or to build monuments to the dead. . . . If the no wins, it will be a disaster for France.
GISCARD D'ESTAING, *leader of the UDF*[69]

The appeals to fear were often complemented by the need for protecting Europe from economic competition. Mitterrand, in a 3 September 1992 appearance on the television network TF1, declared: "We need a strong France within a strong Europe, a pacified Europe capable of resisting aggressions from the exterior. . . . The European Union is a protection from the dangers of war, a protection from crime, and the economic competition."[70] One of the government billboards showed a world dominated by a U.S. wrestler and a Japanese sumo wrestler and suggested the need for the union of Europeans to confront those powers.

Besides politicians, economists attached to banks and large companies (French and other European companies) entered the debate by the end of August 1992, when the no vote started to gain favor steadily and continuously. The following statement by an official of the Credit Lyonnais Bank was typical of these analyses: "If the French people do not ratify the Treaty, there will be most likely a crisis of exchange in money markets and an increase of the interest rates in France and in many other countries of the EU."[71]

The opponents to the treaty also made extensive use of fear-arousing techniques. They assailed the economic and political crisis that, in their opinion, the Maastricht Treaty would create:

> Maastricht would imply more unemployment.
> PHILIPPE SÉGUIN *on Radio Monte Carlo, 12 September 1992*[72]

> There will be a monetary and social crisis because of the rigidity of the criteria for monetary integration.
> JEAN-PIERRE CHEVÈNEMENT[73]

> The adoption of the Maastricht Treaty, which demands that every country follow a strict monetarist discipline, would aggravate the crisis.
> ANDRE LAJONIE, *president of the PCF group in the French parliament*[74]

In addition, the opponents appealed to the traditional symbols of French national identity by denouncing the European Union encroachment on French national sovereignty and the alleged threat that it posed to French identity. They claimed that France would cease to exist if the European Union went forward, as the following statements reflect:

> Maastricht will create a free space for the circulation of immigrants, drugs, and criminals. To vote yes is to choose the abdication; it is to negate our flag.
> MICHEL PONIATOWSKI, *former minister of Internal Affairs*[75]

> If this treaty is ratified, we will no longer be able to eat Camembert. This is an example of how they are undermining our culture.[76]

By suggesting that the European Union will not allow the production and selling of nonpasteurized cheese (such as Camembert), the opponents of the treaty were able to attract the attention of many people. This type of issue was used to illustrate what they saw as the dangers of European Union regulations in interfering in French domestic affairs and undermining French culture and the French way of life. The campaign for those against the Maastricht Treaty was to show that Brussels was controlling French people's lives, and therefore the best alternative people had was to oppose the project of integration proposed in the Maastricht Treaty.

## Transfer

The logic of associating the union of Europe with the objectives that appeal to French people was largely part of the pro-Maastricht strategy: "The present monetary events require more stability, and more stability implies more Europe," said Laurent Fabius, premier secretary of the PSF on the radio network France Inter.[77] He was referring to the monetary crisis that happened that summer in Europe (some countries were forced to devalue their currencies beyond the accepted margins of the European Monetary System). The following statement of Jean Kasper, leader of the labor union Confederation Française Démocratique du Travail (French Democratic Confederation of Workers), illustrates the use of the transfer technique of propaganda to promote the cause of European integration: "The creation of a social Europe needs the help from Maastricht." He associates the Maastricht Treaty with the development of better social conditions for the workers.

The aspiration of French people to have good and peaceful relations with Germany was often associated with the ratification of the Maastricht Treaty: "Germany has made the biggest sacrifices at Maastricht in accepting the disappearance of the Deutsche mark. If Maastricht is not ratified, we will break the contract of intimacy and reciprocity that has linked France and Germany lately," declared Giscard d'Estaing, president of the UDF.[78]

On the other side, the opposition to the Maastricht Treaty focused on the virtues of French democracy and independence. "Democracy is inseparable from national sovereignty," said Philippe Séguin on the television network TF1 on 3 September 1992.[79] Alain Griotteray, UDF congressman, underscores the advantages of an independent French society by suggesting that the problems that the other countries of the community were experiencing would become French problems if the Maastricht Treaty were ratified: "Each country has problems to solve: reunification for Germany, the Mafia in Italy. An aggregate of problems has never produced wealth."[80]

An additional example of the use of transfer as a propaganda technique is the association of the treaty with aspects that most French people reject, such as bureaucracy, a totalitarian system, and foreign intervention in domestic affairs: "We should vote 'no' to a treaty that gives more power to the Commission in Brussels, which is becoming increasingly totalitarian and bureaucratic," argued the Coordination Rurale.[81]

The PCF used a play on words (which exemplifies the use of the name-calling technique associated with transfer) and produced the slogan "Non à Maasfric"; the last four letters, "fric," mean money in French argot. During the campaign, the PCF presented the Maastricht Treaty as a treaty in favor of the rich and against the working class. This argument resonated among the working class and in a considerable proportion of the middle class, associating European integration with the world of money and exploitation. The pro-Maastricht forces tried to associate the Maastricht Treaty with stability, with the development of a social Europe, and with a continued peaceful relation with Germany. These were things that every French person supported. Meanwhile, the opposition, by associating national sovereignty with democracy and the treaty with crisis and crime, was seeking to link the ratification of the treaty with concrete consequences that would affect people directly.

## Testimonial

The pro-Maastricht forces relied on testimonials from the chancellor of Germany, Helmut Kohl, who asked the French people to vote yes to Maastricht in a televised address, and from French president François Mitterrand, who seems to have played a major role in favor of the ratification of the treaty. A poll conducted the day after Mitterrand's 3 September 1992 television appearance favoring the treaty revealed that the yes vote increased from 47 to 55%. Those against the treaty went from 53 to 45%. The abstentions and invalid votes went from 40 to 33%.[82] Another poll published in the weekly magazine *Journal du Dimanche* on 6 September 1992 reported similar results. The president's persuasive abilities could not be separated from his position as leader of the country. The position of president was revered enough to allow the incumbent to persuade a significant number of previously undecided voters to support the Maastricht Treaty.

The opposition often referred in their campaign to respected and revered figures of the past, such as Charles de Gaulle. The following statements are examples of these testimonial techniques:

> All the Foreign Affairs ministers of General de Gaulle and Georges Pompidou [the two previous presidents of the French Republic members of the RPR] are against Maastricht.
> MAURICE SCHUMAN, *RPR senator and former minister of Foreign Affairs*[83]

> We are behind General de Gaulle, we should stay faithful to his teachings and struggle for the national interest.
> CHARLES PASQUA[84]

> General de Gaulle would never have signed a treaty whose main philosophy is to nullify France and, specifically, to deprive her of the right to prepare her national defense.
> MICHEL DEBRÉ, *RPR leader and former prime minister*[85]

With these statements the opposition to the treaty tried to gain support from the French people who still revered the legacy of former president Charles de Gaulle.


## CONCLUSION

The referendum in Spain was finally won by the government with 52.6% of the vote. The campaign was so effective that even a number of intellectuals and public figures who were publicly opposed to the referendum changed their minds and voted in favor of Spain's membership in NATO. The scare vote seems to have played an especially major role. People became convinced of the possible destabilizing consequences if Spain withdrew from the alliance. The vote of confidence on general government policy and the stability of the democratic regime was brought effectively to the forefront of public debate by the prime minister and his associates. Many supporters of the PSOE, although anti-NATO, still cast their vote in favor of membership, fearing that a defeat on the referendum might allow the political right to come back to power.

What happened to many people can be illustrated by the process experienced by a producer for Spanish television. Schumacher[86] reported that this producer was opposed out of principle to military blocks, but she was afraid that Prime Minister Felipe González might fall from power if he lost the referendum. She added that she had become half-convinced that NATO membership was better for Spain. Another example is offered by the declarations of the conservative sociologist Rafael López Pintor: "I wanted to vote no to a referendum on this question, no to the socialists, and no to González, but I closed my eyes and voted yes for Europe and yes for the West."[87]

The government campaign was comprehensive and all embracing. It addressed not only military concerns but also overall social, political, economic, and cultural issues, whereas the opposition, with a few exceptions, concentrated on military and peace issues. The anti-NATO movement was able to draw on deep-seated hostile feelings toward the United States to keep the results of the referendum undecided until the last day.

In France the government also ended up winning the referendum, although with a small majority, 50.6%. Analyses made public a few days after the referendum in *Le Monde* and *Le Nouvel Observateur*[88] suggested that the calls for political and economic stability had made a slight difference in favor of the ratification.

Opponents of European integration used easily identified and powerful nationalistic symbols, arguing that national sovereignty, national independence, and French national culture were under threat. National symbols are deeply rooted in the French people's consciousness. Those in favor could not use European symbols to rally people. Indeed as Smith[89] and others have pointed out, national symbols are more potent than European ones, which in fact are almost null, as my own research has shown.[90]

In the same vein the anti-Maastricht campaigners were effective in convincing people of the supposedly negative ramifications of the European Union legislation by focusing on the nonpasteurized cheese issue and the possibility that foreigners could vote in municipal elections. Such stories trivialized the treaty, but they had an important effect on bringing the debate closer to the people. With these details the opponents were showing the people concretely how French culture was under threat from the European Union. Furthermore, by emphasizing the negative effects for workers if the Maastricht Treaty were ratified, the PCF and other leftist parties were able to mobilize opposition among the working class.

Incumbency probably played a significant role in securing the yes vote in the case studies analyzed here. The incumbents had on their side a public image created by the media that was fixed in the public mind. In particular, the grace, charm, and charisma of González in Spain and the majestic and kinglike image of Mitterrand in France seem to have played a vital role in these referendums. We have seen the extensive use of fear in both campaigns. These fear appeals were particularly effective not only because they scared people but also because they offered specific recommendations for overcoming the fear-arousing threat.[91]

These two cases show that politicians in contemporary Europe are aware of the importance of mastering the techniques of propaganda to reach the feelings and minds of their populace. They are conscious that reality is perception and that perceptions can be shaped. As Combs and Nimmo wrote, for the propagandist "reality is an existential creation, a product of shared belief, rather than something that just is."[92] These examples of referendums in Spain and France reveal that the combination of knowledge of human behavior and the everyday and extensive use of the media has made propaganda a powerful and efficient language to change opinions on social issues. In addition, these examples also reflect that political propaganda in contemporary Europe is carefully coordinated and comprehensive.[93] They consistently rely on simple heuristics and emotions.

Finally, the cases studied here confirm Ellul's assertion[94] that contemporary propaganda, especially given the new electronic techniques available and the enormous amount of time that people are exposed to the media, might result in a form of totalitarianism, the ultimate goal being to manipulate people into believing that they want to do what politicians demand of them.

In both campaigns propagandists tapped into widely accepted values and the populations' desires and fears using one-sided messages and respected figures as well as negative and positive associations to promote their ideas and projects. These approaches reflect the use of the glittering generality, card-stacking, transfer, and testimonial techniques. The objective of this type of political propaganda was not to create new values or change people's behaviors for the long term but rather to draw on existing and widely accepted values to change opinions on the particular referendum issues in order to obtain the desired voter response.

## NOTES

1. *Encyclopaedia Britannica,* 15th ed. (Chicago: University of Chicago Press, 1998). Quote available at http://www.britannica.com/prop (2002).

2. Other definitions of propaganda include: "the deliberate and systematic attempt . . . to achieve a response that furthers the desired intent of the propagandist" [Garth S. Jowett and Victoria O'Donnell, *Propaganda and Persuasion* (Newbury Park, CA: Sage Publications, 1986), 16]; "any attempt to persuade anyone to a belief or to a form of action" [William Hummell and Keith Huntress, *The Analysis of Propaganda* (New York: Rinehart and Winston, 1949), 2]; and "the typical propaganda situation is that A by one method or another communicates with B so as to tend to affect B's behavior" [Malcolm G. Mitchell, *Propaganda, Polls, and Public Opinion: Are the People Manipulated?* (Englewood Cliffs, NJ: Prentice-Hall, 1970), 23].

3. *Encyclopaedia Britannica,* 15th ed.

4. Anthony Pratkanis and Elliot Aronson, *Age of Propaganda: The Everyday Use and Abuse of Persuasion* (New York: W. H. Freeman, 1991), 5.

5. James E. Combs and Dan Nimmo, *The New Propaganda: The Dictatorship of Palaver in Contemporary Politics* (New York: Longman, 1993), 15.

6. G. H. Szanto, *Theater and Propaganda* (Austin: University of Texas Press, 1978), 10.

7. Jowett and O'Donnell, *Propaganda and Persuasion,* 17–18.

8. Ibid., 23.

9. Combs and Nimmo, *The New Propaganda,* 70.

10. Pratkanis and Aronson, *Age of Propaganda,* 24.

11. Combs and Nimmo, *The New Propaganda,* 70.

12. The use of fear-arousing techniques was first analyzed by I. L. Janis and S. Feshback. This research [published in C. I. Hovland, I. L. Janis, and H. H. Kelley, *Communication and Persuasion* (New Haven, CT: Yale Uni-

versity Press, 1953)] was followed by many works, such as R. W. Rogers, "A Protection Motivation Theory of Fear Appeals and Attitude Change," *Journal of Psychology* 91 (1975): 92–105; and K. K. Reardon, "The Potential Role of Persuasion in Adolescent AIDS Prevention," in R. E. Rice and C. K. Atkins, eds., *Public Communication Campaigns,* 273–289 (Newbury Park, CA: Sage, 1988).

13. Alain Touraine, in his *La Production de la Société* (Paris: Seuil, 1974), developed this idea of universality in his analysis of social movements' actions.

14. Alfred M. Lee and Elizabeth B. Lee, *The Fine Art of Propaganda: A Study of Father Coughlin's Speeches* (New York: Harcourt, Brace, 1939).

15. Werner J. Severin and James W. Tankard Jr., *Communication Theories: Origins, Methods, and Uses in the Mass Media* (New York: Longman, 1992), 96–101.

16. Leonard W. Doob, *Public Opinion and Propaganda* (Handem, CT: Archon Books, 1966).

17. The work of Hugh Rank [*The Pep Talk* (Park Forest, IL: The Counter Propaganda Press, 1984)] is another notable effort to identify techniques used in propaganda. Most of Rank's categories are similar to the appeals identified by Lee and Lee in *The Fine Art of Propaganda* and by Severin and Tankard in *Communication Theories.* Regarding advertising, Rank presents a number of devices: attention-getting techniques, which appeal to senses and emotions; confidence-building techniques, which establish credibility of the source; urgency-stressing techniques, which appeal to do like the others; and response-seeking techniques, which tell people what to do to make things better for themselves. More specifically, to analyze the political discourse, Rank divides what he calls the pep talk into four stages: (1) "Look out!" which asserts the threat to attract people's attention; (2) "Get together!" which appeals to audiences to rally in unity to combat the threat; (3) "Do good!" which spells out the vision, the sacrifices that must be made, and the benefits that will be won; and (4) "Let's!" which encourages people to do something together to change things, vote, march, and so on. The classification

offered by Severin and Tankard seems more comprehensive to understand how propaganda works in contemporary political campaigns.

18. Severin and Tankard, *Communication Theories.*

19. Charles Fleming, "Understanding Propaganda from a General Semantics Perspective," *ETC: A Review of General Semantics* 5, no. 1 (1995): 3–10.

20. The plain folks technique was hardly used in the campaigns analyzed in this chapter. The bandwagon technique was used a few times by the pro-NATO forces in relation to the European Community. The message was that, because the other nations of the organization we want so badly to become associated with are members of NATO, we should also be members of NATO. Name calling was used during the French referendum by the leaders of the opposition to dismiss those in favor of the Maastricht Treaty. For instance, Michel Poniatowski (former minister of the Union Démocratique Française), called Jack Lang, the director of the campaign in favor of the ratification, a "distinguished clown," and Charles Pasqua, leader of the Rassemblement pour la République group in the Senate, called President Mitterrand "the merchant of illusions" (*Le Monde,* 11 September 1992, p. 6).

21. Roger Brown, *Words and Things* (New York: Free Press, 1958), 306.

22. The country's leading newspapers in those countries were *El País* in Spain and *Le Monde* in France.

23. In 1981 the centrist government of Calvo Sotelo negotiated Spain's rapid entry into NATO. As Sotelo's cabinet was pushing membership of NATO through the Cortes (Spanish parliament), the PSOE together with the Communists and other leftist parties launched a powerful campaign that helped to shift Spanish public opinion. Indeed, in 1979 polls showed that 58% of Spaniards had no definite view on the subject and only 15% were mildly or strongly against Spain's integration into NATO, but by September 1981, 52% of the population was against integration, according to polls conducted by Centro de Investigaciones Sociológicas and published in "La opinion

publica española ante la OTAN," *Revista española de investigaciones sociologicas* 22 (April–June 1983): 187–262.

24. Gary Provost, "Spain's NATO Choice," *World Today* 42 (1986): 129–132.

25. Stanley Meisler, "Anti-Americanism Clouds Spanish Vote," *Los Angeles Times,* 9 March 1986, p. 6.

26. Angel Viñas, "Coordenados de la Política de seguridad española," *Leviatán* 17 (autumn 1984): 13. All translations from Spanish and French sources are mine unless otherwise noted.

27. The Partido Popular leader, Fraga Iribarne, called for abstention because he believed that the PSOE should not have called for a referendum on the issue.

28. See opinion polls conducted by the Centro de Investigaciones Sociologicas from 1975 to 1983. These results were published in "La opinion publica espanola ante la OTAN." See also Charles Boix and James Alt, "Partisan Voting in the Spanish 1986 NATO Referendum: An Ecological Analysis," *Electoral Studies* 10, no. 1 (1991): 18–32.

29. *El País,* 4 March 1986; *La Vanguardia,* 2 March 1986; *Diario 16,* 2 March 1986; *El Periódico,* 28 February 1986. It was forbidden to publish poll results during the last seven days of the campaign.

30. "Spanish Socialists Launch NATO Campaign," *Financial Times,* 15 February 1986, p. 2.

31. David White, "Spain to Vote Today on NATO Membership," *Financial Times,* 12 March 1986.

32. David White, "Spain Anti-NATO Campaign Launch," *Financial Times,* 27 January 1986, p. 2.

33. Jacques Ellul, *Propaganda: The Formation of Men's Attitudes* (New York: Knopf, 1966), 71–72.

34. *El País,* 10 March 1986, p. 4.

35. Translated by the writers of "Spanish Socialists Launch NATO campaign," *Financial Times,* 15 February 1986, p. 2.

36. Tom Burns, "Spaniards Divided on Staying in NATO," *Washington Post,* 8 March 1986.

37. *El País,* 10 February 1986, p. 6.

38. At that time, Spaniards still nourished old grievances against the United States. The political right remembered America's humiliating victory over Spain in 1898 (Spain lost the last colonies in America: Philippines, Puerto Rico, and Cuba), and the left remembered U.S. support for Franco's dictatorship, symbolized by the 1953 treaty that established U.S. military bases in Spain. U.S. president Dwight D. Eisenhower, embracing Franco at the end of his official visit to Spain in 1959, symbolized the closeness of the United States with the Franco regime. This photograph was widely distributed by the anti-NATO campaign.

39. *Cambio 16,* 23 February 1986, p. 3.

40. *El País,* 8 March 1986.

41. *El País,* 9 March 1986.

42. *El País,* 24 February 1986.

43. *El País,* 9 March 1986.

44. *Diario 16,* 12 September 1985, p. 3.

45. *La Vanguardia,* 10 March 1986, p. 5.

46. On 23 February 1981 a number of military officers attempted a coup d'état. The coup failed, but it reminded the Spanish populace that the military did not yet fully support the democratic process.

47. Translated by the writers of "Spain and NATO," *The Economist,* 8 February 1986, p. 46. The opposition wanted the government to simply ask, "Do you want Spain to remain in NATO?"

48. Pratkanis and Aronson, *Age of Propaganda.*

49. *El País,* 18 February 1986.

50. *El País,* 2 March 1986.

51. This statement by Savater, one of the leaders of the anti-NATO camp, was recurrent during the campaign. Cited in *La Vanguardia,* 28 February 1986, p. 5.

52. *El País,* 12 March 1986, p. 3.

53. *La Vanguardia,* 20 February 1986.

54. William Echikson, "Spain Comes Unglued Over Vote," *Christian Science Monitor,* 12 March 1986.

55. *El País,* 3 March 1986, p. 6.

56. The basic argument for the treaty was that the single market was almost completed,

but to further advance the economic union, some form of political union was needed. For full details on the European Union treaty and discussions, see Alan Cafruny and Glenda Rosenthal, eds., *The State of the European Community,* vol. 2: *The Maastricht Debates and Beyond* (Boulder, CO: Lynne Rienner, 1993); Desmond Dinan, *Ever Closer Union? An Introduction to the European Community* (Boulder, CO: Lynne Rienner, 1994); Finn Laursen and Sophie Vanhoonacke, eds., *The Intergovernmental Conference on Political Union: Institutional Reforms, New Policies, and International Identity of the European Community* (Dordrecht, The Netherlands: M. Nijhoff, 1992); and John McCormick, *The European Union* (Boulder, CO: Westview Press, 1997).

57. In fact, a television campaign developed by the government with the purpose of informing the public about the treaty was canceled because it was perceived by the opposition as propaganda and not general information. The opposition accused the government of using public funds for partisan politics (Pascale Robert-Diard, "La préparation du reféréndum du 20 septembre," *Le Monde,* 28 July 1992). In France an independent organization, the Conseil Supérieur de l'Audiovisuel (Superior Audiovisual Council), oversees the programming of the audiovisual industry (especially the public networks and stations) to guarantee fairness, free speech, and the application of the laws. The law of 16 January 1990 forbade any propaganda spot with political goals on public television. The main French television networks at that time were public. There was a private cable network (Canal Plus), but it did not reach a large portion of the population, and in any case its programming was essentially entertainment.

58. *Journal Officiel,* 12 August 1992. The small parties did not like this arrangement and wanted to have more access to TV, as reported in "La campagne radiotélévisée, protestation des verts, du FN [Front National] et des communistes," *Le Monde,* 7 August 1992.

59. Other polls confirmed the continuous and steady progression of the votes against ratifying the Maastricht Treaty after the campaign started in spring 1992. According to an Institut Français d'Opinion Publique poll published by *Libération* on 4 August 1992, the yes vote for the referendum would have 57% and the no vote 43%. This poll showed a progression of the no vote in relation to another poll by the same company published in *Le Figaro* on 9 June 1992, which gave 62% to the yes vote and 38% to the no vote. The abstentions and the no-responses passed from one poll to the other from 32% to 22%. By the end of August those opposing the treaty had grown to 53%, whereas those in favor had decreased to 47%, according to the Conseil Supérieur de l'Audiovisuel and published in the newspaper *Le Parisien,* 28 August 1992. Two other polls published in *Le Monde* (27 August 1992) and *Le Point* (27 August 1992) indicated similar tendencies.

60. Leon N. Lindberg and Stuart A. Scheingold, *Europe's Would-Be Polity: Patterns of Change in the European Community* (Englewood Cliffs, NJ: Prentice-Hall, 1970), 277.

61. Christine Chombeau, "La campagne pour le référendum sur le traité de Maastricht," *Le Monde,* 14 September 1992.

62. Cited in "La campagne pour le référendum sur le traité de Maastricht: L'intervention de M. Mitterrand à l'émission Aujourd'hui l'Europe," *Le Monde,* 5 September 1992, available at http://web.lexis-nexis.com/univers.

63. Frederick Bobin, "La campagne pour le référendum du 20 septembre," *Le Monde,* 4 September 1992.

64. "Le débat sur la révision de la constitution et sur la ratification du Traité de l'Union Européenne," *Le Monde,* 28 April 1992.

65. *Le Monde,* 29 August 1992, available at http://web.lexis-nexis.com/univers.

66. *Le Monde,* 27 August 1992, available at http://web.lexis-nexis.com/univers.

67. *Le Figaro,* 29 September 1992, available at http://web.lexis-nexis.com/univers.

68. *Le Monde,* 20 August 1992, available at http://web.lexis-nexis.com/univers.

69. Pascale Robert-Diard, "L'UDF sous ses propres couleurs," *Le Monde,* 24 July 1992.

70. Patrick Jarreau, "La campagne pour le référendum sur le traité de Maastricht: L'in-

tervention de M. Mitterrand sur TF1," *Le Monde,* 5 September 1992.

71. *Le Monde,* 27 August 1992, available at http://web.lexis-nexis.com/univers.

72. Cited by Pierre Glachant, "Un non sans équivoque à Maastricht pour la fête annuelle du PCF," *Agence France Press,* 13 September 1992.

73. Jean-Pierre Chevènement, "Inventer une autre Europe," *Le Monde,* 9 July 1992, p. 2.

74. Patrick Jarreau, "Le référendum sur le traité de Maastricht: Changes et échanges," *Le Monde,* 19 September 1992.

75. Guy Porte, "La campagne pour le référendum sur le traité de Maastricht," *Le Monde,* 11 September 1992.

76. *Le Parisien,* 24 August 1992, available at http://web.lexis-nexis.com/univers.

77. Jarreau, "Le référendum sur le traité de Maastricht."

78. Frederic Bobin, "La campagne pour le référendum du 20 septembre," *Le Monde,* 4 September 1992.

79. "La campagne pour le référendum sur le traité de Maastricht: L'intervention de M. Mitterrand à l'émission aujourd'hui l'Europe," *Le Monde,* 5 September 1992, available at http://web.lexis-nexis.com/univers.

80. "La campagne du référendum du 20 septembre," *Le Monde,* 22 July 1992, available at http://web.lexis-nexis.com/univers.

81. "La préparation du référendum du 20 septembre," *Le Monde,* 1 August 1992.

82. *Le Parisien,* 5 September 1992, available at http://web.lexis-nexis.com/univers.

83. *Le Monde,* 28 August 1992, available at http://web.lexis-nexis.com/univers.

84. Guy Porte, "La campagne pour le référendum sur le traité de Maastricht," *Le Monde,* 11 September 1992.

85. "La campagne du référendum du 20 septembre," *Le Monde,* 22 July 1992, available at http://web.lexis-nexis.com/univers.

86. Edward Schumacher, "The Stakes Are High in Spain's NATO Vote," *New York Times,* 12 March 1986, p. 6.

87. William Echikson, "Surprise Win on NATO Strengthens González for the Next Election," *Christian Science Monitor,* 14 March 1986, p. 11.

88. *Le Monde,* 22 September 1992; *Le Nouvel Observateur,* 23 September 1992.

89. Anthony Smith, *National Identity* (Reno: University of Nevada Press, 1993).

90. Antonio V. Menéndez Alarcón, "National Identity, Nationalism, and the Organization of the European Union," *International Journal of Contemporary Sociology* 35 (1998): 57–74.

91. Pratkanis and Aronson, *Age of Propaganda.*

92. Combs and Nimmo, *The New Propaganda,* 79–80.

93. Ibid., 80.

94. Ellul, *Propaganda.*

# 5

# U.S.-Cuba Propaganda Wars

## The Case of Television Martí

### JOHN SPICER NICHOLS

Of all the weapons used by the U.S. government in its four-decade-long propaganda war with the Cuban regime of Fidel Castro, Television Martí is probably the most bizarre. Launched in 1990 to deliver television propaganda to Cuba, the station was intended to unseat the Castro government and bring democracy to the island. However, in its effort to achieve these goals, Television Martí had to resort to a peculiar and expensive transmission technology that was supposed to overcome the laws of physics as well as unconventional broadcasting practices aimed at circumventing the laws of nations. The result has been an embarrassing failure. Television Martí was and still is easily jammed by Cuban authorities and therefore cannot be seen by Cuban viewers. Furthermore, the station has been ruled in violation of international telecommunications regulations, which the United States is bound by treaty to uphold.

Despite this, the U.S. government has continued to operate Television Martí for over a decade at the cost of millions of dollars per year. Why? My purpose in this chapter is to explain this phenomenon using some basic concepts of international propaganda.

The United States and Cuba are separated by more than 90 miles of water. Because television signals travel in a straight line, potential audiences on the island are over the horizon and therefore outside the range of a normal land-based television transmitter in the United States. Consequently, to deliver a clear picture to Cuba, U.S. propagandists had to dramatically raise the line of sight over which the television signal travels. The solution was to mount Television Martí's transmitter and antenna on a U.S. military blimp (dubbed Fat Albert) and float them 10,000 feet above the Florida Keys, from where the signal could reach the island. However, the airborne transmitter could not be sent aloft during high winds, thunderstorms, and other bad weather that frequents the region. As a result, during its first few years of operation, Television Martí broadcast barely more than every other day, on average. On two occasions Fat Albert broke away from its mooring and crashed in the Everglades, leaving Television Martí out of commission for months.

Even when the weather cooperated, Television Martí still was on the air for only a few hours in the early morning when most Cubans were asleep. This odd airtime was intended to stave off enforcement of international broadcasting regulations that prohibit cross-border television broadcasts without prior agreement. The purpose of these regulations is to vest each nation with sovereign control over its own broadcasting system and to prevent disruption of domestic programming by stations from neighboring countries that operate on the same or adjacent channels. In a vain attempt to get around these rules, Television Martí broadcast only when Cuban television was off the air, and U.S. authorities could claim "no harm, no foul."[1] This is akin to a motorist driving an automobile at high speed down the wrong lane in the early morning hours when no oncoming traffic would be expected and later arguing before a judge that, because the driver did not cause a wreck, he or she should not be found guilty of a crime.

The International Telecommunications Union (ITU), the United Nations regulatory agency, would have none of it. Shortly after Television Martí went on the air, the ITU ruled that the station was in violation of international broadcast regulations and called on the United States to end its interference with the Cuban television system. The U.S. government simply ignored the ITU ruling. Since then, however, U.S. diplomats have been scrambling to explain why other countries should comply with important international agreements when the United States selectively chooses the agreements it wishes to obey. Television Martí has become a global symbol, especially in the Third World, of superpower arrogance and of the U.S. inclination to force its will on smaller, poorer countries regardless of its obligations under international law.

Television Martí's predawn schedule and the ITU ruling notwithstanding, the Castro government was furious over what it called American "television aggression." Claiming Cuba's "legitimate right to reject any action against its sovereignty," it immediately began jamming Television Martí.[2] Because television signals become weaker as they radiate farther from the transmitter, by the time Television Martí's signal had crossed the long stretch of water separating the two countries, it was fragile and easily susceptible to disruption. The Cuban government easily blocked the broadcasts by using low-tech, low-power equipment operated at only a tiny fraction of the cost of Television Martí.

The result, of course, was that the Cuban audience for Television Martí broadcasts was virtually nil. The station's proponents initially claimed that they had a large number of viewers on the island, but as evidence to the contrary mounted,

U.S. officials finally were forced to concede that almost nobody in Cuba could see more than a few wavy lines through the interference.

There were other important political costs, especially to the bilateral relations between the United States and Cuba and to the stated U.S. foreign policy goal of helping to bring democracy to the island. The already bad relations between the United States and Cuba deteriorated further. As long as Television Martí remained on the air, serious negotiations on other important matters of mutual concern, such as immigration, drug trafficking, telephone communication, and the environment, became difficult at best. The human rights situation in Cuba also deteriorated. Seemingly threatened by the propaganda broadcasts and other worrisome U.S. actions, the Castro regime circled the wagons. It cracked down on Cuba's tiny dissident movement, purged the university of reform-minded scholars, and pointedly rejected any suggestion from even friendly countries, such as Canada, about how to improve its human rights record. The Cuban congress passed a tough internal security law that, among other things, provided for 20-year jail terms for Cubans who sent information to foreign media outlets deemed hostile to Cuba or who otherwise distributed subversive material to Cuba's adversaries. Dissident journalists, particularly ones who filed reports for Television Martí and other U.S. media, were harassed or jailed on charges of consorting with the enemy. In other words, Television Martí probably exacerbated Cuba's serious human rights problem.

In any case there was no indication that Television Martí or any of the other U.S. propaganda broadcasts that have been a key part of U.S. policy toward Cuba for four decades were, in any way, achieving the goals of speeding Castro's departure and bringing a democratic government to Cuba. At this writing, Castro remains firmly entrenched in power, perhaps even more firmly than before Television Martí was launched.

"Unfortunately, American policy impedes the transformation we seek," wrote Elizardo Sanchez Santacruz, Cuba's leading human rights activist. Sanchez, a former university professor who himself served a lengthy jail term for distributing enemy propaganda, has long argued that pressure from the United States, if not a contributing factor in the regime's growing repression, is at least an excuse. "The vast majority of us on the island who oppose the government believe that a dialogue and relaxation of tensions between the United States and Cuba would better facilitate a transformation," he concluded.[3]

In addition to the political costs, Television Martí has significant financial costs. The United States spent nearly $8 million in start-up costs, not including the cost of using the blimp and other government equipment and services, to launch Television Martí in 1990. Through 1999 Congress had appropriated $120 million in annual operating costs.

In the ratings-driven real world of broadcasting, a television station with little or no audience certainly would be taken off the air, but not so for Television Martí. In this chapter I explain why the U.S. government continues to operate, at considerable financial and political costs, a station that has virtually no viewers or signs of success. I also explain why the Cuban government reacts so angrily to propaganda broadcasts that cannot be seen on the island and therefore cannot directly alter the attitudes of the Cuban people toward the Castro regime.

# FOUR PROPOSITIONS FOR UNDERSTANDING
# INTERNATIONAL PROPAGANDA

Although Television Martí is an extreme case among propaganda campaigns in general, even in the long history of U.S. efforts to unseat the Castro regime, it demonstrates the following four basic propositions for understanding international propaganda.

1. *Propaganda doesn't work very well.* Despite the fact that most governments of the world devote considerable resources and effort to international propaganda, there is little evidence that propaganda can easily manipulate the basic attitudes and behavior of target audiences or effectively communicate an alternative view of their own condition or the outside world.

Most propaganda campaigns are built on the dubious assumption that a message sent, especially messages sent by means of powerful transmitters or other high-tech means, is a message received, accepted, and acted on by the audience. Achieving a propaganda effect, it is widely believed, is as simple as shooting fish in a barrel. All the propagandist needs is a rifle, proper ammunition, and good aim. The foreign audience, like the fish, has little or nothing to say about it.

In fact, the opposite is true. The overwhelming body of academic literature on international communication and political persuasion indicates that audience members select messages that conform to their preconceived notions and actively avoid, perceive, or twist messages that create inner tension or that place them in conflict with those around them. Although media messages may have some marginal effects on low-involvement decisions (such as which brand of laundry soap to buy), they are notoriously ineffective in changing people's views on high-involvement matters (such as cultural values, nationalism, ideology, and basic interpretations of important issues or events).[4]

People tend to be highly nationalistic and deeply rooted in their culture; therefore most people, even those living under repressive regimes, strongly prefer their domestic media to foreign media, and they usually do not listen to foreign propaganda broadcasts. For example, during the 1999 war in Kosovo, forces of the North Atlantic Treaty Organization (NATO) dropped leaflets and broadcast television propaganda into the Serbian capital of Belgrade in hopes of countering the propaganda of the government of Slobodan Milosevic. Serbian university students, despite their sophisticated understanding of the sins of the Milosevic government and access to a variety of other media sources, told the *New York Times* that they strongly preferred the propaganda of their government and rejected that of NATO. "We hate Milosevic," one student said, "but at least he's ours."[5]

Even when people become seriously disaffected with their government or distrustful of their own media, they typically do not tune in the broadcasts of hostile nations. Rather, they tend to listen to more neutral or third-party sources of information. Therefore, to the extent that propagandists have a foreign audience, they are largely preaching to the converted. Dissidents usually become alienated from their government for political, economic, or personal reasons and afterward seek out foreign broadcasts that reinforce their new attitudes against the government. There is no evidence of the reverse: that foreign propaganda can convert a government supporter into a dissident.

This is not to say that all propaganda is ineffective all the time. Propaganda campaigns sometimes are successful in achieving noble goals, but the law of unintended consequences usually governs. Consider the case of Tokyo Rose, the notorious Japanese radio propagandist who sought to undermine the fighting effectiveness of U.S. troops in the Pacific arena during World War II. Attracted by her sultry voice and the American music she played on her program and with few entertainment alternatives, U.S. servicemen listened to her in large numbers. Late in the war, Rose explained over the air that U.S. bombing over Tokyo was limiting her supply of new jazz selections. Shortly after, U.S. warplanes not only delivered its usual load of bombs but also a package of recent records addressed to Tokyo Rose.[6] Clearly, that was not the effect the Japanese propagandist intended.

In sum, the effect of propaganda is ultimately determined in the minds of the audience; not in the content, channels, and methods of the propagandist. Consequently, significant changes in people's attitudes and behavior as a result of international propaganda campaigns are rare, and most official claims of propaganda successes are grossly overstated.

2. *The sender gets more than the receiver.* To the extent that propaganda does have an effect, it tends to be more on the sender of the message than on the target audience. Frequently, the domestic rewards of disseminating international propaganda are so great that the lack of a significant foreign audience or effect becomes largely irrelevant.

Much international propaganda is little more than ideological masturbation. Similar to the sexual act, propaganda may provide an internally satisfying release of tension even though it has little or no external effect; and although propaganda may be stimulated by external factors, its primary motivation is internal.

Starting a new international propaganda campaign often has proved to be satisfying to the U.S. domestic political system regardless of any foreign audience or effect. When politicians or policymakers are polarized over how to deal with external conflict, agreeing to an aggressive policy of propaganda often is a good compromise. Political hawks initially propose strategies of military force and confrontation in dealing with the foreign enemy. Doves gravitate toward strategies of avoidance, compromise, or even capitulation. Both of these extreme approaches, however, have great consequence: the hawk stance in loss of lives and expense of military force and the dove stance in loss of face for not standing up to the enemy. Although launching a propaganda campaign is far short of the more aggressive strategies proposed by hawks, it is at least some sort of action, and although far more than the doves advocated, a propaganda campaign is not lethal. This middle ground minimizes the costs to both sides.

In short, adopting the propaganda strategy—even if it is ineffective or counterproductive abroad—may help to reduce domestic political tensions over how best to respond to an external conflict and prevent turmoil at home during troubled times. This proposition—that there are important functions for the sender of a propaganda message irrespective of any audience effect—is well established in the academic literature, if not among government policymakers.[7]

3. *The receiver views propaganda as interference.* Even when there is little or no indication of an effect on the audience, the target government usually regards the propaganda as hostile interference in its domestic affairs and/or frequently reacts out of fear that the propaganda might be effective.

No government, even a democratic one, looks kindly on foreign interference in its domestic affairs. The United States is no exception. From its earliest history, the United States has vigorously resisted intrusion into internal matters, even from friendly nations. In 1793, for example, President George Washington demanded that France recall its ambassador, known as Citizen Genêt, for interfering in domestic U.S. politics. France, which aided the United States during the Revolutionary War, was itself at war with Great Britain. Most people in the United States, especially those in the ranks of Thomas Jefferson's Republican Party, were sympathetic to the French cause, but Washington and the Federalists strongly believed that an official policy of neutrality was the best course. When Citizen Genêt sought to reverse the policy by appealing directly to the U.S. public to support Jefferson's position instead of Washington's position, President Washington acted to remove the envoy. Even though most did not agree with Washington's neutrality policy, the U.S. public rallied to support his response to the French intrusion into the fledgling U.S. political system. Later, in his farewell address, Washington warned his new nation against "the insidious wiles of foreign influence . . . since history and experience prove that foreign influence is one of the most baneful foes of republican government."[8]

When the United Nations was created after World War II, the United States and its allies saw to it that nonintervention in the domestic affairs of other nations was a core principle of the new international order. It was roundly agreed that, to keep global conflict to a minimum, all nations must respect the sovereignty of other nations. Although never absolute and clearly eroded in the 1990s, the principle of state sovereignty remains an important component of the international order, especially for smaller, more vulnerable nations seeking protection from larger, more powerful ones.

Some international propaganda primarily seeks to explain the policies and perspectives of the sponsoring nation to other nations or to the rest of the world and therefore is usually not perceived as intervention in the domestic affairs of other nations. An example is the Voice of America, the official U.S. government overseas broadcasting service that explains U.S. policies and interpretations on current issues and events to global audiences. However, to the extent that broadcasts from the United States or any other country are intended to undermine the legitimacy of a foreign government or otherwise change another government's relationship with its own citizens, the broadcasts usually are seen as interference in the domestic affairs of the other nation and as a violation of its sovereign rights.

Governments tend to react to hostile foreign propaganda out of fear that it may be successful, although propaganda usually is not effective. This is a classic manifestation of the third-person effect, in which people exposed to a persuasive communication message in the media see the message as having a greater persuasive effect on others than on themselves. A classic example of the third-person effect took place during World War II when Japanese planes dropped propaganda leaflets over a sector of Iwo Jima Island where a U.S. military unit consisting of African American troops was positioned. The leaflets sought to drive a wedge between the African American soldiers and their white officers by characterizing the U.S. war effort as one against people of color. "Don't risk your life for the white man," the leaflets urged African American soldiers. "Give yourself up at the first opportunity." Although these African American troops had previously fought heroically against the Japanese and although there was no evidence that the propaganda had any effect on them, the white officers reshuffled personnel in the African American unit.[9]

In other words, one of the greatest effects of propaganda is not a change in the beliefs and behaviors of the target audience but rather the reaction of some third party that expects the propaganda messages to have a negative impact on others.

4. *Propaganda can make things worse.* Although propaganda rarely achieves its stated goal, it usually heightens tension between nations already in conflict and complicates efforts to resolve international problems.

For all the reasons previously discussed, international propaganda, especially that between countries already mired in conflict, is usually dysfunctional. Instead of resolving problems, propaganda tends to exacerbate and complicate conflict to the detriment of the sender, receiver, and entire international community. Once propaganda wars begin, the probability that disputes can be settled through negotiation or other peaceful means decreases and the probability of a shooting war increases.

Moreover, there is nothing like an external threat—real or perceived—to unify quarrelsome internal political factions of a troubled nation. During wartime or other foreign conflict, domestic dissent toward government policies usually dissipates. If a real external threat does not exist, national leaders often will manufacture one to reduce domestic divisions and to consolidate power. Consequently, foreign propaganda campaigns often have the opposite of the intended reaction. Instead of undermining a regime, they frequently bolster it.

In short, propaganda usually does more harm than good.[10]

These four propositions will be explored in more detail in the context of the troubled relations between the United States and Cuba.

## SHORT HISTORY OF THE
## U.S.-CUBA PROPAGANDA WAR

The U.S.-Cuba propaganda war is one of the longest and intensely fought in modern history. Television Martí is only the most recent addition to the U.S. arsenal in a massive propaganda campaign that began shortly after Fidel Castro overthrew a U.S.-backed dictator in 1959 and took control of the Cuban government. Among the top priorities for Castro's revolution was to extricate Cuba from U.S. economic control. U.S. investors owned nearly one-quarter of Cuban land. They dominated manufacturing, transportation, and utilities on the island and had a huge stake in the sugar industry, which was the largest sector in the Cuban economy. The revolutionary government immediately began confiscating U.S. properties. That action combined with Castro's embrace of communist principles to lift his country out of poverty and his alliance with the Soviet Union, the United States's cold war enemy, set off alarm bells in Washington.

At the end of his last term in office, President Dwight D. Eisenhower authorized a covert plan to overthrow Castro. Shortly after entering office, President John F. Kennedy implemented it. The central component of the plan was the so-called Bay of Pigs invasion, an amphibious landing on the island by a Cuban exile force trained, financed, and directed by the U.S. Central Intelligence Agency (CIA). To undermine Castro's popular support before the invasion, the CIA established Radio Swan, a clandestine radio station that spewed acidic criticism of the Communist regime. But neither the invasion nor the clandestine broadcasts were successful in sparking a popular uprising on the island. When the exile force landed on Cuba's southern coast in 1961, the Cuban army and civilian militia rallied behind the government and decisively defeated the invaders.

After the Bay of Pigs fiasco, an embarrassed Kennedy administration resorted to covert political operations in lieu of overt military action to topple the Cuban regime. Greatly expanded anti-Castro propaganda was central to the revised approach. This audible sign of continued U.S. hostility concerned not only the Cuban leadership but also its Soviet patrons. Fearing that the United States might again use military force against its Cuban outpost, the Soviets began to install nuclear missiles on the island as a show of its own force. The ensuing Cuban Missile Crisis is widely believed to be the closest the world has ever come to nuclear war. Part of the U.S. response was to further expand its propaganda bombardment of the island. U.S.-backed clandestine stations called on Cubans to burn crops, sabotage public utilities, and break beer bottles (in hopes of disrupting the beer supply on the island and thereby fomenting popular discontent). These messages were supplemented by more measured appeals over the Voice of America, the official U.S. overseas radio service. In addition, White House officials cobbled together an unprecedented network of high-powered commercial stations in the United States to broadcast government propaganda to Cuba during the emergency.[11]

The missile crisis was eventually resolved after the United States agreed, in part, to respect Cuba's territorial integrity in exchange for the Soviet removal of the missiles. Despite the agreement, the CIA continued—indeed, intensified—its covert operations against Cuba. The program, named Operation Mongoose, mixed some deadly serious actions (including numerous assassination attempts on Castro and sabotage of key installations) with downright goofy ones (such as trying to slip a chemical to Castro that would make his beard fall out and, the CIA believed, thereby distract from his charisma with the Cuban people). Every imaginable means of propaganda was employed: broadcasts from a ship and submarine in international waters, air drops of leaflets, rumor campaigns, and comic books. President Kennedy's point man in Operation Mongoose and infamous cold warrior, General Edward Lansdale, was a firm believer that propaganda and other covert political operations could spark a counterrevolution in Cuba. As one of Lansdale's co-workers later reported, he "really thought if you said something on the radio, people would believe it. . . . He thought one statement or blast could move people's minds, and it doesn't work that way."[12]

Although U.S. propagandists fired far more ammunition during this period than did the Cubans, the war of words was by no means one-sided. Cuba retaliated with massive quantities of inflammatory propaganda of its own. The official government station, Radio Havana Cuba (RHC), broadcast venomous anti-U.S. rhetoric in eight languages for hundreds of hours per week. At the height of U.S. involvement in Southeast Asia, the RHC transmitter relayed English-language "Voice of [North] Vietnam" programs on shortwave radio to audiences in North America. Another Cuban broadcast of the period, named Radio Free Dixie, urged African Americans in the southern United States to arm themselves, torch white-owned property, and commit other acts of violence.

As subsequent U.S. administrations focused their attention on the Vietnam War and other pressing foreign and domestic matters, the anti-Castro campaign waned and most of the propaganda programs were downsized or dismantled. President Jimmy Carter even made a short-lived attempt to normalize relations with Cuba. After Carter was defeated in his 1980 reelection bid by Ronald Reagan, the new president made ideological confrontation with the Soviet Union and its allies, especially Cuba, the heart of his foreign policy, and international propaganda was back in vogue.[13]

## BIRTH OF RADIO AND TELEVISION MARTÍ

Early in the Reagan administration, Charles Z. Wick, director of the U.S. Information Agency (USIA) and close friend and adviser of the president, went to the White House to pitch for more U.S. propaganda programs to support the more assertive foreign policy. Wick said that the additional funding would give the USIA "the velocity of a projectile" in combating adversaries abroad and would help rearm his agency to fight the international war of ideas. President Reagan, a former radio announcer and motion picture and television actor, was delighted with the proposal and told Wick: "Gee, Charlie, this could be the greatest weapon of all."[14]

Reagan presided over the largest expansion of U.S. international propaganda since the beginning of the cold war. His use of military metaphors reveals a Lansdale-style faith in propaganda's effectiveness. If only the United States had quantitative superiority in numbers of transmitters, wattage, and hours of programming for propagating its version of the truth, political change in unfriendly countries would surely follow. In the administration's view, counting the number of transmitters was not substantially different from counting cruise missiles or tank divisions as a measure of military strength. If the United States could mobilize enough propaganda resources aimed at Cuba, the Castro regime would eventually fall.

To help in this strategy, the right-wing faction of the Cuban exile community that assisted the United States in past anti-Cuban campaigns, including the Bay of

Pigs fiasco, was reenlisted. In 1981 Reagan's national security adviser urged the creation of a front organization that would lobby the press, Congress, and the public for additional funding for anti-Castro propaganda projects and help deliver the message to the island. The organization created was the Cuban American National Foundation (CANF). Its leader was Jorge Mas Canosa. A self-made multimillionaire with nearly unchallenged political clout in the South Florida exile community, Mas Canosa was ideal for the job. He had devoted his entire adult life to unseating Castro and harbored aspirations of becoming president of Cuba himself. Mas Canosa was a veteran of the Bay of Pigs, a broadcaster on the CIA's Radio Swan, and a longtime leader of political and paramilitary groups seeking to overthrow Castro's regime. In earlier years Mas Canosa had used armed violence to achieve his goal. There is evidence that he and/or other CANF officials might have secretly continued to direct and finance terrorist plots against Cuba while wielding political power in Washington.[15]

The centerpiece of the renewed anti-Castro campaign was to be Radio Martí. Mas Canosa pushed aggressively to establish a new propaganda station named for José Martí, the nineteenth-century Cuban patriot. The Cuban lobby's political action committee showered large contributions on the campaigns of legislators who supported appropriations for Radio Martí. Opponents were branded communist sympathizers or worse. In the end, Mas Canosa was successful. Congress authorized $14 million in start-up expenditures and $11 million in annual operating costs. In 1985 Radio Martí went on the air.

Nearly five years later, after more intense CANF lobbying, Congress authorized and President George Bush established Television Martí. "The only reason there is a TV Martí is because Jorge Mas twisted every political arm he could reach," said Richard Allen, the former national security advisor to President Reagan.[16] The White House rewarded Mas Canosa with an appointment to chair the President's Advisory Board for Cuba Broadcasting, the oversight panel for Radio and Television Martí. From that post, which he held until his death in 1997, Mas Canosa ran the stations as if they were his personal hacienda. He set broad policy and dictated specific editorial content, much of it flattering to him and the CANF. U.S. government–mandated editorial standards were ignored when they stood in the way of ever more strident attacks on Castro. Mas Canosa's stooges held key administrative positions at the stations and tyrannically repressed any dissent. Staff members who questioned the stations' direction or were otherwise suspected of disloyalty were forced out of their jobs, despite being government employees.

The Cuban leadership fully understood that the caudillo of Radio and Television Martí and his associates were the same people who sought to overthrow it through other, sometimes violent, means. The sponsorship of the stations and their hostile intent were even more troubling in Havana than any of the program content. An enraged Castro retaliated in a variety of ways, including counterpropaganda, interference with the transmissions of U.S. commercial radio stations, and suspension of an important immigration agreement with the United States. Although the Cuban government attempted to jam Radio Martí, radio signals are much more difficult to disrupt, and the station had significant listenership throughout the island.[17] In sum, Castro's government viewed Radio and Television Martí as voices of an enemy that would use any means to bring about the government's demise. Just tuning in to the station was deemed an act of political opposition hedging on collaboration with the enemy during wartime.

## LESSONS LEARNED FROM
## THE CASE OF TELEVISION MARTÍ

Despite the fact that Television Martí has virtually no audience in Cuba and may be undermining stated U.S. foreign policy goals, continuing to operate the station has great domestic political benefit. For decades, Congress has been badly divided over how best to deal with Cuba. A thin congressional majority has advocated aggressive tactics toward Castro; a large minority has favored rapprochement. Television Martí was a near perfect political compromise. After all, who could be opposed to broadcasting "the truth" to the repressed people of Cuba? Irrespective of any external audience or effects, Television Martí was useful for resolving internal conflict within the Washington political structure.

Furthermore, support for the station was a good vote-getting plank in the campaign platforms of both hawks and doves. This is especially true in presidential elections in which the Cuban Americans are key voting blocs in Florida and New Jersey, two states usually on the "must win" lists of both political parties. Republican and Democratic candidates alike could point to their support of the station as evidence of their anti-Castro bona fides. No matter that establishing Television Martí was largely a way of avoiding decisive action regarding the Cuba problem; voting for it was good politics.

In addition to reaping political benefits at the polls, many of those in Congress who backed Television Martí received large campaign contributions and political support from the network of wealthy and powerful Cuban exiles. In each election cycle the political action committee of the CANF lavished donations on friendly politicians. Presidents Reagan, Bush, and Clinton all supported U.S. government broadcasting to Cuba during their administrations, and all were generously funded by Cuban exile groups in their election or reelection bids. In turn, establishing Radio and Television Martí meant hundreds of million of dollars in federal funds were pumped into the Cuban American economy. Many Cuban exiles, often cronies of Mas Canosa, landed plum government jobs at the stations. And having achieved an important, if largely symbolic, victory in the national political arena, Mas Canosa greatly expanded his power as a wheeler-dealer within the exile community and parlayed that into even more influence in the corridors of power in Washington.

In this respect, Television Martí is a classic example of political pork barrel. In this time-honored tradition of U.S. politics, elected officials win a share of public funds for construction projects of questionable utility. The contractors, unions, and other beneficiaries of the publicly financed project, in turn, raise campaign contributions and deliver votes to send the politicians back to Washington for additional dips into the pork barrel. Whether these projects are in the best interests of the taxpayers who foot the bill is usually irrelevant in this self-sustaining political process.

Television Martí served an important domestic function in Cuba. According to one expert, by putting the station on the air, the U.S. government gave Castro a convenient tool for tapping Cuban nationalism, reducing domestic opposition, and mobilizing public opinion in favor of his regime. Ernesto Betancourt, the first director of Radio Martí, testified before a presidential commission:

> Fidel Castro was well aware of the limitations in the U.S. position and took advantage of them in the most dramatic and effective way from the propaganda viewpoint. Instead of using the cheapest answer to our broadcasts, . . . he militarized the issue by making use of Cuban army helicopters to block the TV Martí signal. He called this military display an "electronic war" and claimed—correctly unfortunately—that Cuba had won this war against the most technological power in the world. The signal has been blocked effectively ever since it went on the air. Instead of broadening the information base for the Cubans, TV Martí gave Castro a propaganda victory.[18]

Betancourt was ousted from his post in 1990 for questioning the technical and legal feasibility of the proposed Television Martí and for resisting the growing influence of the CANF and its leader, Mas Canosa, on the editorial content of Radio Martí. Betancourt subsequently charged that, because Mas Canosa lacked support among the Cuban people, the only way he could fulfill his dream of becoming the next president of Cuba was through U.S. military intervention. Television Martí was primarily intended to spark a confrontation that could lead to such an intervention, Betancourt asserted. Instead, the result was to consolidate support for the regime among the upper echelons of the Cuban military and political leadership who otherwise might have questioned Castro's continued rule. The Cuban elite, Betancourt wrote in the *New York Times,* was threatened by Mas Canosa and was guided, in part, by "fear of Cuba's losing its sovereignty after Mr. Castro falls." Therefore the political embrace of Mas Canosa and his agenda by U.S. presidents "has done nothing but coalesce the Cuban elite around Mr. Castro. . . . [T]hat may be good Florida politics," Betancourt concluded, "but it is certainly not in the best interests of our policy toward Cuba."[19]

Television Martí was supposed to pave the way for a peaceful transition to democracy in Cuba and help resolve the decades of conflict between the United States and the Castro government. Instead, it has prolonged Castro's repressive rule and increased the likelihood of violence and chaos when his regime falls. Although the U.S. government may view the propaganda station as a peaceful alternative to the use of force, the Cuban leadership and at least some of the Cuban public see it as a hostile intrusion into their domestic affairs. The broadcasts have served as a convenient excuse for the Castro government to crack down on the opposition movement on the island and to consolidate its power. In addition, rather than reducing tension and resolving the long-standing problems, the station has exacerbated and complicated the conflict between the two countries and made resolution of bilateral problems more difficult. In short, Television Martí has been counterproductive.

One of the more unsettling aspects of Television Martí is that top U.S. officials were fully aware that it was a political illusion. They knew, at the least, that the station would not be effective and probably would result in Cuban retaliation that could cause serious harm to U.S. domestic and foreign interests. Yet they put the station on the air anyway. Kenneth N. Skoug Jr., the coordinator of Cuban affairs at the U.S. Department of State at the time, reported in his memoirs that government studies clearly indicated that the proposed television station was seriously flawed. "The cost would be high in relation to any probable benefit because the signal could easily be jammed," he wrote. "Hence . . . it would probably not be an effective instrument." Also, based on the Cuban response to Radio Martí years earlier, the State Department anticipated that starting Television Martí would widen and complicate conflict between the two countries.

Skoug repeatedly warned his superiors that it was unwise to proceed under these circumstances. "Pressure for TV-Martí in an election year, however, prevailed," he wrote. In spring 1988, Vice President Bush, then running hard for the presidency, met with CANF officials and unequivocally endorsed Television Martí. Before the day was over, Skoug received his orders: "No excuses; full speed ahead."[20] The serious misgivings among broadcasting and foreign policy experts in the administration notwithstanding, plans for Television Martí were drawn up and Congress appropriated the funding within months.

Television Martí was not a serious miscalculation by an inept government. Rather, it was a willful act by political power brokers who knew full well that the broadcasts probably would not be seen in Cuba and could harm U.S. interests. But support for the station generated campaign contributions, votes, and other political benefits for them. The fact that the station was launched at all, let alone that it continued to operate for more than a decade, demonstrates the most important lessons of this chapter: Most international propaganda is driven more by the internal political dynamics of the propagandist's country than by the needs of the target audience or any other external reality. The losers in this equation are the vast majority of people in both countries: the U.S. taxpayers who pay for and suffer the effects of a foolish foreign policy and the Cuban people who have been denied political and economic advancement that otherwise might have been possible.

## NOTES

1. "President Pushes TV Martí; ITU Pushes Back," *Broadcasting,* 9 April 1990, pp. 37–38; "State Tells IFRB to Mind Its Own Business," *Broadcasting,* 7 May 1990, pp. 42–43. For further reading on the legal and policy dispute over Television Martí, see Laurien Alexandre, "Television Martí: 'Open Skies' Over the South," in Kaarle Nordenstreng and Herbert I. Schiller, eds., *Beyond National Sovereignty:* *International Communication in the 1990s* (Norwood, NJ: Ablex Publishing, 1993), 343–367; Stephen D. Bayer, "The Legal Aspects of TV Martí in Relation to the Law of Direct Broadcasting Satellites," *Emory Law Journal* 41 (spring 1992): 541–580; and Kyu Ho Youm, "The Radio and TV Martí Controversy: A Reexamination," *Gazette* 48, no. 2 (1991): 95–103.

2. "TV Martí Takes Off—But Will It Fly?" *Broadcasting,* 2 April 1990, p. 50.

3. Elizardo Sanchez Santacruz, "Cuba Can't Change on Its Own," *New York Times,* 27 April 1997, p. A23.

4. For example, see Irving L. Janis and M. Brewster Smith, "Effects of Education and Persuasion on National and International Images," in Herbert C. Kelman, ed., *International Behavior: A Social-Psychological Analysis* (New York: Holt, Rinehart and Winston, 1966), 190–235; Garth S. Jowett and Victoria O'Donnell, *Propaganda and Persuasion* (Newbury Park, CA: Sage Publications, 1992); William J. McGuire, "The Myth of Massive Media Impact," *Public Communication and Behavior* 1 (1986): 173–275; and K. Kyoon Hur, "International Mass Communication Research: A Critical Review of Theory and Methods," in Michael Burgoon, ed., *Communication Yearbook,* no. 6 (Beverly Hills, CA: Sage Publications, 1982), 531–554.

5. Carlotta Gall, "NATO TV Is Sent to Serbs, Who Are Harsh Critics," *New York Times,* 26 May 1999, p. A13.

6. Donald R. Browne, *International Radio Broadcasting* (New York: Praeger, 1982), 91.

7. Robert K. Merton, "Manifest and Latent Functions," in Robert K. Merton, ed., *Social Theory and Structure* (New York: Free Press, 1968), chap. 1; Lewis Coser, *The Functions of Social Conflict* (New York: Free Press, 1956), 104–110; John Spicer Nichols, "When Nobody Listens: Assessing the Political Success of Radio Martí," *Communication Research* 11 (April 1984): 281–304.

8. Howard F. Bremer, ed., *George Washington, 1732–1799: Chronology, Documents, Bibliographical Aids* (Dobbs Ferry, NY: Oceana Publishing, 1967), 77. Also see Alexander DeConde, *Entangling Alliances: Politics and Diplomacy of George Washington* (Durham, NC: Duke University Press, 1958); and Clyde Wilson, "Global Democracy and American Tradition," *Intercollegiate Review* 3 (fall 1988): 3–14.

9. W. Phillips Davison, "The Third-Person Effect in Communication," *Public Opinion Quarterly* 47 (spring 1983): 1–15. Davison suggests that in some cases the propagandist might intend to provoke a reaction by a third party rather than achieve an effect on the ostensible audience.

10. For further development of this point, see John Spicer Nichols, "Effects of Propaganda on U.S.-Cuban Relations," in Richard R. Cole, ed., *Communication in Latin America: Journalism, Mass Media, and Society* (Wilmington, DE: Scholarly Resources, 1996), 77–103.

11. John S. Nichols, "Institutionalization of Anti-Castro Radio Broadcasting," in Nancy Lynch Street and Marilyn J. Matelski, eds., *Messages from the Underground: Transnational Radio in Resistance and Solidarity* (Westport, CT: Praeger, 1997), 103–115.

12. Quoting Donald Wilson, deputy director of the U.S. Information Agency during Operation Mongoose. Quoted in Jon Elliston, *Psywar on Cuba: A Declassified History of U.S. Anti-Castro Propaganda* (New York: Ocean Press, 1999), 104. Elliston's documentary history is the single most important and complete source on the U.S. propaganda campaign against Cuba.

13. Wayne S. Smith, *The Closest of Enemies: A Personal and Diplomatic History of the Castro Years* (New York: Norton, 1987), 101–127. For further reading on U.S.-Cuba relations, see Thomas G. Patterson, *Contesting Castro: The United States and the Triumph of the Cuban Revolution* (New York: Oxford University Press, 1994).

14. Phil Gailey, "Voice of America Finds Its Words Are Weighed," *New York Times,* 5 October 1981, p. B10.

15. Ann Louise Bardach and Larry Rohter, "A Plot on Castro Spotlights a Powerful Group of Exiles," *New York Times,* 5 May 1998, p. A1; Bardach and Rohter, "Key Cuba Foe Claims Exiles' Backing," *New York Times,* 12 July 1998, p. A1; Bardach and Rohter, "Life in the Shadows, Trying to Bring Down Castro," *New York Times,* 13 July 1998, p. A1; and Rohter and Bardach, "Cuban Exile Leader Among 7 Accused of Plot on Castro," *New York Times,* 26 August 1998, p. A3. For further reading on Mas Canosa and the CANF, see Saul Landau, "No Mas Canosa," *Monthly Review* 50 (October 1999): 22–37.

16. Elliston, *Psywar on Cuba,* 241.

17. The exact size of Radio Martí's audience on the island is difficult to determine

without the cooperation of the Cuban government. In the same way that official estimates of the initial size of Television Martí's audience were wildly exaggerated, so too were the audience figures for Radio Martí. However, early claims by the President's Advisory Board for Cuba Broadcasting that "86% of all Cubans continue to tune into Radio Martí at least once weekly and the majority of these people tune in daily" were never credible. In contrast, a classified U.S. government study, the results of which were leaked to the press, reported that only 9% of those interviewed in four Cuban cities in 1998 tuned in to Radio Martí regularly. Regardless of the size of the audience, there was no evidence that Radio Martí listenership translated into specific changes in attitudes and behavior of the Cuban people.

18. Ernesto F. Betancourt, Statement before U.S. Advisory Panel on Radio Martí and TV Martí, 13 January 1994. The helicopters carried airborne jammers to block Television Martí's signal. As Betancourt pointed out, this method of jamming was highly inefficient and used primarily for show.

19. Ernesto F. Betancourt, "The Castro Alternative," *New York Times,* 9 September 1994, p. A27. See also, Elliston, *Psywar on Cuba,* 271–272.

20. Kenneth N. Skoug Jr., *The United States and Cuba under Reagan and Shultz: A Foreign Service Officer Reports* (Westport, CT: Praeger, 1996), 202.

# PART III

# Gatekeeping

Writing in 1922, the celebrated American journalist Walter Lippmann remarked that the mass media were coming to play an increasingly important role in shaping the collective "pictures in our heads" about "the world outside." To illustrate how people learned about and acted on events known not through direct experience but through media depictions, Lippmann related the story of English, German, and French citizens living peacefully on an island in 1914. Because of their isolation, they did not know about the outbreak of World War I until a mail steamer brought them old newspapers. With this news the islanders' social worlds turned upside down. For many islanders, old friends became enemies because their friends' countries were at war with their homelands, and people changed their social relationships accordingly.[1]

Lippmann was referring to the situation in America and in industrialized European countries. In his day many people living outside the industrialized world still knew about their environments through direct experience and personal communications with other people. Their knowledge of their world was limited to their experiences. By midcentury, however, even people in remote regions of the world had access to radio. With radio and other mass media, people once cut off from the outside world learned about and responded to events they never personally experienced.

Lippmann was interested in the effects of news media depictions on public knowledge and behaviors. Years later, scholars devoted their attention to how people working in the news media select and reject the stories that the news audience receives. This selection and rejection process is media gatekeeping. The metaphor suggests that the final news product involves the transmission of news through a series of gates by gatekeepers. At each gate in this process a gatekeeper has the power to stop, alter, or reshape the news that will affect millions of people's lives. Perhaps 90% of the news available to the news media fails to pass through all the gates and reach the public.

Oddly, gatekeeping research has been largely the domain of American and European scholars, who study gatekeeping in Western contexts. The gatekeeping process is relevant to international contexts. The two chapters in this part fill a gap in the literature by applying the gatekeeping concept to international communication, with interesting results.

Jack Lule, of Lehigh University, describes how the prestigious *New York Times* reported the devastating floods in Central America in late 1998. His deep readings of the stories show that the *Times*'s editors drew on cultural myths about floods to report the news. Working journalists think that they are just reporting the facts, and they might take issue with this controversial approach that cultural myths affect their reporting. However, facts cannot be separated from culture contexts, and Lule argues that all cultures have their myths that frame the facts and affect storytelling. Lule indicates that news stories about disasters unfold like mythic tales, and perhaps international stories are especially susceptible to such a storytelling style.

Heloiza Herscovitz, of the Florida International University, describes how, in Brazil, journalists' gatekeeping procedures changed as the society underwent transformation from an authoritarian to a democratic society. Her chapter underscores that gatekeeping procedures are not static and that they are a function not only of the cultural environment but also of the political and social environment.

## NOTE

1. Walter Lippmann, *Public Opinion* (New York: Harcourt, Brace, 1922), 3–4.

# 6

# Waters of Death in Central America

## News Values and Myth

### JACK LULE

**M**y purpose in this chapter is to study news coverage of the 1998 Central American floods through the framework of myth. I first discuss myth and archetypal stories. Myth can mean many things to many people, so we need a good definition of myth. Then, I briefly review the work of writers who have compared news and myth. The comparison might seem strange, but writers have considered news as myth for decades. After briefly looking at the myth of the flood, I explore ways that myth can provide insights into the *New York Times* coverage of the Central American disaster. I ask: To what extent can myth explain or illuminate news reporting of the floods? More broadly, what insights can archetypes and myth bring to the study of gatekeeping and news values?

**Case 1:** The Choctaw tribe of North America told of a time when total darkness covered the earth. Tribal leaders searched endlessly for daylight. Finally, a light was seen in the north. The tribe rejoiced, but a few wise families understood that danger could be found in the light as well as in the dark. The families built themselves a great raft. The rest of the tribe ignored the possible danger. The light was revealed to be the headwaters of a huge flood that carried off the tribe, except for the wise families on the raft, who created the tribe anew.

**Case 2:** Chief priests and elders of the Inca taught their people about the demise of the Pachachama era. It was a time of corruption and barbarity.

Only two humble shepherds and their families remained true to their gods. Llamas warned the shepherds that a great flood was approaching. The shepherds and their families sought refuge on the highest mountain. They watched as the world below was subsumed beneath the waters.

**Case 3:** Genesis tells the story of Noah and the ark. The Lord saw that wickedness and corruption were great on the earth, but Noah, a good man, found favor with the Lord. The Lord told Noah to build an ark and to fill the ark with living things. Then, the floodgates of the sky were opened and rain fell on the earth for 40 days and 40 nights. Only Noah, his family, and the animals living in the ark survived.

**Case 4:** The *New York Times* told how Central America was devastated in late 1998. Great poverty plagued many nations. Impoverished people erected poorly built homes in areas dangerously close to rivers or precariously perched on mountain slopes, areas forsaken by the wealthier classes and corporations. The nations' leaders looked away. A hurricane came from the east. Rain fell for days. Floods and great mountains of mud swept away entire villages. Thousands of people died. The scene was a vision out of Dante, a deluge of biblical proportions, the *Times* reported. "It's a punishment from God," said an elderly Honduran carpenter quoted on the front page of the *Times*.[1]

Tales of great floods have been told in many societies. The tales have a remarkable similarity across centuries, continents, and cultures. They are stories of birth and renewal, death and apocalypse. They portray people who have done grave wrong, people who have sinned against their gods, people who have strayed from the right path. They depict gods or fabulous forces of nature that punish and purify. They culminate, always, with the same image: the devastating, cleansing waters that sweep away a people.[2]

Our modern society describes the flood tale of ancient societies as myth. Our society calls the flood tale of the *New York Times* news. This chapter is about connections between news and myth. I suggest that similarities between flood myths and news stories are just one example of a much larger phenomenon. I suggest that myth has taken modern form in the news, that age-old tales and ageless archetypes live on in the stories of news. In addition, I suggest that U.S. journalists may make decisions regarding international news based on myth and guided by stories as old as humankind.

## FUNDAMENTAL STORIES

Storytelling is fundamental to human life. Every society has left evidence of stories. Humans apparently make sense of the world and their time in it through stories.

Some stories are fundamental to human life. Astonishingly similar folk tales, legends, and myths can be found across cultures and eras. Some anthropologists are convinced that direct connections among these stories can be traced. They argue that neighboring societies borrow ideas, custom, tools, and recipes—as well as stories—from one another. They point out that great cultural centers of the ancient world were often great trading centers. Stories, they say, were traded too. Stories were part of an overall process of diffusion of culture.[3]

Early psychiatrists and psychologists, however, argued differently. In particular, Sigmund Freud and Carl Jung noted similarities between folk tales, myths, and dreams. How could a 7-year-old girl, an unlikely candidate for cultural diffusion, have dreams with symbols and motifs taken from ancient stories? Jung was especially intrigued. He was, for a while, Freud's foremost student and colleague in the psychoanalysis of mentally disturbed individuals. Later, he broke with Freud and became more interested in a broader scope: the mental health of humankind. He pointed out that humans were born with bodily organs that had long evolutionary histories. He believed that the human mind also had its own evolutionary history. This collective unconscious, Jung said, contains powerful, primordial patterns—archetypes—that can lead to creations of universal symbols, characters, stories, and myths.[4]

Definitive answers about fundamental stories are not likely to be established by anthropologists or psychologists. Perhaps the best answer bears a bit of both. Some stories do seem to be fundamental to humans, probably based on the shared experiences of being human. People are born into an almost infinite variety of circumstances, yet we still share some experiences. We share birth, the entry into the world as small and helpless babies. We share infancy and hazy images from childhood. We often have families or relationships with mother figures and father figures. We have feelings of love, hate, anger, compassion, jealousy, and joy. We have bodily, natural sensations of hunger and thirst. We need to sleep. We need to move. We produce and understand, tell and retell, stories based on these experiences; and these stories sometimes are shared and spread across cultures and eras.

These stories can indeed be understood in terms of archetypes. We can use the word in its original broader meaning without the Jungian theory. Archetypes are original figures or frameworks, powerful patterns, models to imitate and adapt. The fundamental stories of humankind derive from archetypes and give form to the archetypes. The flood that destroys and cleanses human society is an archetypal story. The hero who sets out on a quest is an archetypal story. Born from universally understood archetypes, such stories could have had great emotional impact on listeners in ancient times—and on mass media audiences today.

Stories thus assert their own influence. Stories shape storytelling. As writers and societies attempt to understand and express their experience of the world, they sometimes consciously and unconsciously draw on the special stories, the commonly shared, universally understood stock of stories born from archetypes. They draw from within themselves and from within their societies. A person may never have been told or taught the story of the flood, but the person has experiences with the unpredictable forces of nature or with driving rain and wild winds or with sensations of being submerged in a bath or pool, lake, or ocean. And the person can be led by those experiences to understand and perhaps to tell the story of the flood.

## MYTH: SACRED AND SOCIAL STORIES

Not all archetypal stories are myths, however. Archetypes influence much story-telling, from the imaginative play of children to daydreams to romance novels to Shakespearean plays.[5] Myths are archetypal stories that play crucial social roles.

Storytelling seems fundamental to social life. Through stories, a group of people define themselves. They tell stories of their origins. They tell stories of what they believe and do not believe. They tell stories of evildoers who threaten the group. They draw from the archetypal stories to pass on to their children their ways of life, love, worship, and work. These societal stories attain sacred status. They become accepted and assumed. They narrate and illustrate shared beliefs, values, and ideals. They are myths. Myth has been classified and defined in numerous ways, but some basic principles can be established. For the purposes of this chapter, myth is defined as a sacred societal story that draws from archetypal figures and forms to offer exemplary models and meaning for human life.

Because myths draw on the archetypal stories of humankind and because myths are traded and diffused across cultures and eras, it is not surprising that similar myths recur in myriad societies. Indeed, some myths appear to be almost universally told. Myths of floods, heroes, good mothers, tyrannical fathers, and murdered children recur with amazing similarities across many societies and times.

For example, anthropologist Stith Thompson worked for decades on the wonderfully convoluted multivolume *Motif-Index of Folk-Literature,* first published in the 1930s.[6] The first section harbors hundreds of categories and thousands of myths. Bibliographical references point to published versions of a myth across cultures and centuries. For example, the first section classifies myths of the creator. The second identifies myths of gods and demigods. Another section contains myths of cosmogony and cosmology—the universe, heavens, and earth. Subcategories abound. For example, a large section classifies myths of world calamities. Beneath this are subcategories such as the flood, the flood from tears, and the flood as punishment—the very theme echoed by the *New York Times* in 1998 stories from Central America.

Other scholars have resisted the accounting attractions of such indexing, but they also have recognized and identified recurring myths. James Frazer compiled thousands of myths in *The Golden Bough.* Joseph Campbell analyzed the many appearances of the hero myth in *The Hero with a Thousand Faces.* Mircea Eliade studied stories of origins and creations in *Patterns in Comparative Religion.*[7] These compilations do not gather simple stock characters, such as the mother or the king. They do not gather narrative formulas, such as mother harms child or king kills rival. They compile myths: sacred stories that draw on the archetypal stories of humankind to offer models, morals, and meaning for their societies.

## NEWS: THE LATEST ECHO

The researchers agree: No society exists without myth. Our society is no different. Scholars have worked for decades to argue that news stories can be understood as the modern recurrence of myth. News, they say, is the latest echo of stories uttered long ago. Like myth tellers of every age, journalists draw from the archetypal stories of humankind to describe and make sense of the world. These myths are more than story structures and journalism conventions, such as inverted pyramid leads or formulas for writing speeches, fire stories, or obituaries.[8] They are sacred societal stories with shared values and beliefs, with lessons and themes, with exemplary models that instruct and inform.

Studies of news and myth have come from a varied, eclectic group of scholars.[9] Myth especially became an important conceptual element in American and British cultural studies during the 1970s and 1980s. Researchers have adopted myth to study news coverage of politics, terrorism, assassinations, labor disputes, social movements, South African elections, presidential addresses, the Titanic, modern films, and other topics.[10]

For example, in a recent study I showed that news coverage of baseball player Mark McGwire could be understood as portraying the myth of the hero.[11] The study looked at reporting of the St. Louis Cardinals first baseman during the 1998 season when he set the major league home run record (which has since been broken by Barry Bonds). Like Ulysses, Achilles, and other ancient heroes, McGwire was shown as coming from a humble background, undertaking a quest, enduring trials and tribulations, and succeeding in triumph. As with all heroes, McGwire was shown in the news to embody important social values, such as hard work and compassion. This study and others show that, consciously or unconsciously, journalists often cast modern experience in terms of myth.

There is no need to overstate the case for mythic stories in the news. Many news stories have no relation to myth. Many news stories are derived from simple narrative forms and professional conventions: Official gives speech; home team wins; fire destroys building. Freud warned against the danger of overanalyzing, of seeing symbolic content in every object. "Sometimes a cigar is just a cigar," Freud allegedly once said wryly. Well, sometimes a fire story is just a fire story. But sometimes, in describing some experience, in reporting some event, reporters and editors unconsciously draw on a fundamental story of earthly existence, a universal and shared story of humankind. Sometimes news becomes myth. But why? It is a process that arises from and exists in a particular social order.

## NEWS, MYTH, AND SOCIAL ORDER

Myth is vital to social order, the established ways of doing things and understanding things in a society. Myth defends a social order. Myth explains its origins. Myth dramatizes dominant values. Myth upholds and supports ideology and ideals. If we understand news as myth, we should understand the news story too as a fundamental story that helps shape and is shaped by social order.

The term "news story" is used often in newsrooms, classrooms, and living rooms. Some news is reported as bare information. Stock prices, sports scores, and vote tallies, for example, can be reported in tables, tickers, and boxes. Almost all other news, however, is presented as stories. A hero returns as an international success. The president battles Congress over the budget. An aging baseball player, facing the end of his career, finds the spirit and strength to succeed once more. An earthquake devastates a country.

Such stories do not arrive fully formed on the dusty computer screens of journalists, although journalists sometimes wish they would. Scholars and journalists have shown that many social forces shape news stories.[12] Editors and reporters make sure they have a mutual understanding of "the story." Colleagues may suggest their own interpretations. Expectations of the publisher may be well known in the newsroom. Previous stories found in databases or clippings files influence the way the story will be told. Conventions and traditions, such as inverted pyramid leads and codes of objectivity, guide research and writing. Sources have their own view of the story. Questions asked by competing reporters are noted. Expectations of the audience and long-term circulation goals can be considered.

Through all these forces the established social order shapes the news story. The established order provides the context in which the individual news story becomes myth. As myth, then, news can be understood as one of the important ways that social order is expressed and portrayed. As myth, news upholds a society's ideology and dramatizes its values. As myth, news often supports the established hierarchy and its authority. As myth, news usually accepts and maintains the status quo. Journalists draw on the fundamental stories, consciously and unconsciously, to sanction and support social order.

This perspective offers a broad view of news stories and social order. It does not offer news—or myth—in narrow political or ideological terms. With each election, for example, news coverage does not support social order by simply shifting support to whatever political party is in power. Social order is more deeply entrenched. For example, U.S. news can be expected to uphold the two-party system rather than specific parties. News can be expected to accept and assume a global free market system rather than particular monetary policies. News, as myth, supports the order of things.

This chapter might be understood as continuing the long, interesting discussion of news, myth, and social order. I look at news coverage of an event that seemed to resonate with mythic overtones: the 1998 Central American floods. Before turning to that news coverage, for background and context I turn first to the myth of the flood.

## THE FLOOD

As Thompson demonstrated in his motif index, the myth of the flood has appeared across centuries and cultures. Alan Dundes, who edited a book on the subject, argues that "the flood myth is one of the most widely diffused narratives known."[13] Many reasons have been put forth for this wide diffusion. Some writers argue that a real cataclysmic flood did occur on earth. They search still for Noah's ark. Others find in flood myths the human need to explain our origins. They say that humans are mostly water. We are born into the world on the waters of the womb. We need stories that dramatize and explain the life that flows within us. Other scholars find that the flood myth serves as the ultimate morality tale. They say that humans are warned to mend their ways or else the cleansing waters will come to vanquish the world. Freudian scholars see more fundamental drives. They attribute the prevalence of flood myths in every culture and time to the result of humans dreaming with full bladders.[14]

Although the flood myth has many interpretations and permutations, some basic characteristics or themes can be established:

1. Flood myths almost always are based on the premise that humankind has sinned or that people have erred or strayed from the path of righteousness.
2. The flood comes and is complete in its devastation. The flood does not discriminate or evaluate gradations of evil. Entire ways of life are destroyed.
3. Humans are helpless against the power of the flood.
4. Humankind, once purified, is regenerated and renewed. Some worthy or fortunate individuals rebuild, solemn and chastened in the wake of the flood.

Can these characteristics and themes be found in news coverage of the 1998 Central American floods? Did journalists unconsciously make decisions about the selection and presentation of news based on myth? In attempting to describe and explain the disaster, did news stories draw on the myth of the flood?

## MYTH IN THE *NEW YORK TIMES*

To study such questions, I looked at coverage by the *New York Times,* an elite and essential newspaper for study of news values and international reporting.[15] The time period was 26 October 1998, when the first reports on Hurricane Mitch, which spawned the floods, appeared in the *Times,* to 6 December 1998, when the cleanup was underway and the intense coverage waned. Every *Times* article, editorial, column, letter, and photograph was scrutinized—125 news items.

Hurricane Mitch was a particularly devastating storm. Spawned in the Gulf of Mexico in late October 1998, Mitch became a huge hurricane with wind speeds of 180 miles per hour. It was ranked as category 5, making it one of the top four storms of the twentieth century. Rather than moving swiftly over sea and land, the hurricane stalled off the Central American coast, adding to the devastation. The coastal area received days of misery and deluges of rain, which caused major mudslides and floods. In the span of a week more than 10,000 people were reported killed.

As will be shown in detail, I found that the myth of the flood could indeed be found in its entirety in the *Times*'s coverage. All four of the myth's primary themes played a dominant role in the *Times*'s reporting. Humans were shown to have erred and strayed from a right path. The flood came and was complete in its devastation. Human efforts and ingenuity were helpless in the face of the flood. And in the wake of the flood, people began the slow process of rebuilding.

The structure of the story, however, was somewhat different in the *Times*'s coverage. Myths often begin with the wrongdoing of the people. They show why the flood must come. In the *Times*'s coverage reports of the devastation came first. Humanity's futility then was shown. Survivors were found. Then, in the aftermath of the flood stories began to consider that the flood had come to those who had erred or strayed. The following sections follow that structure and demonstrate the ways in which the myth of the flood took modern form in the *New York Times*.

## COMPLETE DEVASTATION

A central aspect of the flood myth is that the flood's devastation is total and complete. Descriptions of the flood emphasize its enormity. This is not a serious storm: It is a catastrophe. Entire peoples are washed away. The earth is laid waste. During the first days of the hurricane, even before the full ravaging had occurred, the *Times* offered themes of widespread destruction. The hurricane paused off the Honduran coast. Floods washed out roads, downed bridges, overflowed rivers, and killed 32 people. The *Times* had not yet been able to get its own reporter to the scene, but the paper used an Associated Press report that gave its third paragraph to a quotation of ruination: "'The hurricane has destroyed almost everything,' said Mike Brown of Guanaja Island, who was within miles of the eye. 'Few houses have remained standing.'"[16]

The rains continued. Floods caused mudslides that added to the destruction. On 1 November 1998 the *Times* used another Associated Press account to report that mudslides had "buried several communities near Nicaragua's northwestern border with Honduras." The mayor told reporters that only 57 of the 2,500 people living in 10 communities at the foot of Caistas Volcano had been accounted for. "It is like a desert littered with buried bodies," he said.[17]

On 1 November 1998 the *Times* finally managed to get its reporter, Larry Rohter, to the scene. The next day, death and destruction became front-page news. "Intense and widespread flooding in the wake of Hurricane Mitch has killed more than a thousand people in Central America, with hundreds more still missing, their villages buried under huge mudslides," Rohter's report began.

Rohter's first quotation, in the fourth paragraph, emphasized the devastation. "Some communities were completely destroyed," said Leonora Rivera, a spokeswoman for the Nicaraguan Red Cross. She said that "the number of dead will increase considerably once it stops raining and we can get into isolated areas." General Rodolfo Pacheco, chief of the Honduran Air Force, was quoted at the end of Rohter's story as saying: "This is catastrophe beyond measure. It's incredible. The entire nation is in danger."[18]

On the following day the *Times* devoted much of its front page to the flood. A dramatic, 6 × 8 inch aerial color photograph blanketed four of the six columns above the fold. Taken from an aircraft, the photograph showed trapped residents on a tiny island of high land surrounded by muddy waters that had risen to the treetops. Rohter's report ran on the top right-hand column of the page. The second paragraph stated:

"There are corpses everywhere—victims of landslides or of the waters," Carlos Flores Facussé, the President of Honduras, said in a grim television address this afternoon that followed a thorough inspection tour of his stunned and beleaguered nation of four million people. "We have before us a panorama of death, desolation, and ruin throughout the entire country." [19]

The report directly drew on mythic references of destruction. It said, "Relief workers and evacuees, who were visibly disturbed over what they had seen, used phrases like a 'vision out of Dante' or 'a deluge of Biblical proportions' to describe the destruction." It concluded with the words of the Honduran president: "The floods and landslides have erased many villages and households from the map, as well as whole neighborhoods of cities. I ask the international community for human solidarity." [20]

Another front-page report by Rohter emphasized the decimation. "In one way or another, every part of Nicaragua has been devastated by the relentless floods and landslides that followed Hurricane Mitch," the story began. It went on to describe "a realm dominated by destruction and suffering." [21] Two days later, another front-page report continued the theme. The lead paragraph reported:

Where just a week ago there were fertile fields of corn, beans, and peanuts almost ready for harvest, there are now only discolored corpses, swelling grotesquely in the tropical sun. Where the simple thatched houses of peasants have always stood, all that remain are clusters of ripped and shredded clothing and a few scattered kitchen utensils.[22]

*Times* reports quoted U.S. officials, who attested to the destruction of Honduras and Nicaragua in particular. "'Those two nations have been wiped out,' said J. Brian Atwood, head of the United States Agency for International Development, which is overseeing the Administration's disaster relief effort in Central America." [23] Another source said, "It's total, pure devastation. I've never seen a human drama of that magnitude." [24]

## HUMANITY HUMBLED

The flood myth emphasizes that humans are helpless in the face of the flood. In society after society humans come to think that they have advanced beyond nature, that their knowledge, ingenuity, and technology have inured them to the earth's power. The flood sweeps away such hubris. Humanity is humbled. Similarly, early *Times* reports suggested the capitulation of humankind to nature's forces:

People fled coastal homes and the Honduran Government sent air force planes to pluck residents off remote Caribbean islands today in the face of the most powerful hurricane in a decade to threaten Central America. Thousands of people abandoned or were evacuated from coastal regions of Belize, Mexico, and Cuba.[25]

The *Times* offered numbers to attest to the immense power of the storm. It noted that wind speeds reached 180 miles per hour, that 20 inches of rain could fall in the mountains, and that the storm was listed as category 5, making it one of the top four storms of the twentieth century. In addition, the *Times* offered more descriptions of panicked humans fleeing towns and resorts:

> The rain and winds snapped trees and sent thousands of people fleeing for higher ground. . . . Most of the population of Belize City fled inland in cars and Government buses. In neighboring Mexico tourists rushed to leave the resorts of Cancún and Cozumel, where the hurricane, Mitch, is expected to hit by the end of the week.[26]

The report was accompanied by a two-column photograph of a crying Guatemalan child, wearing a bright, frilly dress, being lifted by firefighters from flood-waters. Two days later, the image was repeated. Another photograph showed rescuers pulling a woman from rising waters in La Ceiba, Honduras.[27]

Even the highest officials, stories said, were humbled by the flood's power. One *Times* report stated:

> "Not just this country, but all of Central America is cut off," President Arnoldo Alémán of Nicaragua said in a televised address to his nation in which he urged vulnerable citizens to seek shelter on higher ground. His Honduran counterpart, Carlos Flores, found himself trapped in San Pedro Sula, an industrial city of 500,000 people that was cut off from the capital by flooding.[28]

A week later Rohter interviewed Flores, who said, "In 72 hours we lost what we had built, little by little, in 50 years." Flores added, "In Honduras everything will be measured before and after" the floods.[29]

Witnesses testified to the enormity of the disaster. A *Times* story quoted a cleric: "I have seen earthquakes, droughts, two wars, cyclones, and tidal waves," said Miguel Cardinal Obando y Bravo, the Roman Catholic archbishop of Managua and the nation's senior religious figure, "but this is undoubtedly the worst thing that I have ever seen."[30]

A rescue worker emphasized the humbling powers of the flood. "'We could hear people buried in the debris imploring us to help them,' said one shaken resident-turned-rescue worker, who would give his name only as Nicolas. 'But there was nothing we could do for them. It was the most impotent I have ever felt in my life.'"[31]

The *Times* often portrayed relief efforts as futile. "Honduran authorities struggled today with meager resources to deal with catastrophic damage from torrential rains and floods," one report began. "Many families have been waiting for days on top of their houses or perching in trees without food or water," the officials said. "'The demand is so great and the equipment we have is so little that we feel impotent,' said the Army Chief of Staff, Gen. Mario Hung Pacheco."[32]

Humanity was left with prayer and beseechment. Rohter ended a "Week in Review" essay with the words of a survivor: "'We've lived through earthquakes, a pair of civil wars, volcanic eruptions, tidal waves, and now this, all in the last 25 years,' said Maria Lourdes Rodriguez, a peasant who lives north of here. 'When is God going to take pity on us?'"[33]

## REBUILDING IN THE WAKE

Although the devastation is complete, although humanity is humbled, the flood myth ends on notes of rebuilding and regeneration. The floodwaters are waters of birth as well as waters of death. Miraculous stories of survivors emerge, grieving and chastened.

The theme can be seen in numerous *Times* reports. One article, "1 House Left in Sea of Mud," began, "Of 164 houses in this northwestern Nicaraguan farming village, only one was standing today in a sea of mud that stretched as far as the eye could see."[34] Another item told the story of Laura Isabel Arriola de Guity, a teacher, who "reportedly drifted on a makeshift raft in the Caribbean for six days before her rescue. Her husband and three children died."[35] Another story began with the mythlike memories of one survivor who, using what sounded like a biblical phrase, saw the "earth open up" before him:

> Selvin Joynarid Perez was standing under the awning of his small house on a bluff overlooking the Choluteca River early Saturday morning, keeping an uneasy watch on the torrential rain and the rising waters below.
>
> Suddenly the earth trembled, he said. He turned to run into the house to wake his wife and 3-year-old daughter. He never made it.
>
> "When I tried to go into the room where my wife and child were sleeping, the earth opened up," he said.[36]

Other reports, too, focused on stunned survivors. Vicente Hernandez and his wife and brother were away visiting relatives when the flood and mudslides engulfed his village. "'We have been left with nothing but this,' he said, gesturing toward a small plastic bag containing a few items of donated clothing that was attached to the handlebars of a bicycle he was riding. 'Our family has been dispersed, and a great misfortune has fallen upon us.'" The same story ended with the words of another survivor, shocked but ready to move forward. Milton Juarez had his farm and livestock swept away. "'Everything I had is gone, and all we have been left with is rocks and stone,' he said as he sat on his bedraggled horse and surveyed the destruction here. 'I'm ready to plant, but somebody has to give me seeds. But so far, nobody has come here to help us, nobody.'"[37]

A story of a burial service offered the thoughts of a grandmother, stricken but resigned to go on. "'There were six in that family, and now only one remains, Isaac, the youngest son of my only daughter,' the boy's grandmother, Candida Morales Delgado, said tearfully as the coffin was lowered into the ground. 'We will care for him as best we can because he is all that we have left.'"[38]

More than a month after the storm, the *Times* suggested that survivors had begun the process of rebuilding. In a photo essay for the *New York Times Magazine*, Larry Towell captured the devastation—and regeneration:

> And yet, the floodwaters seem to have washed away something else—a lethargy induced by decades of foreign economic control, along with the humiliation of being used by the Nicaraguan contras in their war against the Sandinistas. Honduras has been energized by the sheer effort to survive as a nation. No matter where I look, I think I've seen the worst. But I am constantly surprised, not just by the destruction, but also by the will of the people to overcome it.[39]

## STRIKING THOSE WHO HAVE STRAYED

A primary characteristic of the flood myth is that devastation comes to a people who have done wrong. Detailing the wrong—defining the sins—is a crucial and socially specific aspect of the flood myth. Were people punished for hubris and pride? Did they erect other gods? Did men take wives for themselves, "whomever they chose," as in Genesis? As noted, myths often begin here. In the *Times*'s coverage this theme did not emerge until the aftermath. The *Times* first reported the disaster. Then, stories sought reasons or meanings behind the disaster. In *Times* reports the Central American people seemed to be punished for the sins of their nations and governments, for which the people were responsible. Corrupt leaders, petty politics, and backward economies explained the devastation. Such errors, the *Times* suggested implicitly and explicitly, would not bedevil U.S. society.

The theme first appeared more than a week into the coverage, at the end of a report on survivors returning to destroyed towns. Although the survivors blamed the river, the report suggested devastation had come because officials allowed houses to be built in illegal and unsafe areas.

> Several acknowledged that the houses that had rumbled down the bluff had been illegally built in a zone where construction is prohibited. "The reality of the thing is that it is not the Government's fault," said Florentino Sanchez, who had spent the day digging with his bare hands for the bodies of four children of his cousin. The mother's body was found on Tuesday.
> "We never believed the river would do this," he said.[40]

Soon after, in a "Week in Review" essay, the *Times* again suggested that the governments were at fault. Rohter used the governments' responses to the flood to draw comparisons among nations. His premise: A disaster "teaches a lot about the way a society does or does not work," and "the nations of the region always seem to respond in ways that illuminate their history and character." He continued:

> Nicaragua, for instance, is still grappling with many of the same problems it could not resolve in the 1980's, when the Sandinista National Liberation Front was trying to fend off American-backed contra rebels in a bloody civil

war. In that polarized political climate, the relief effort here last week was hampered by petty partisan squabbling; the conservative Government and the Sandinistas, who are now in opposition, even disagreed over whether it would be more appropriate to declare a "national disaster" or a "state of emergency."

Rohter compared the response with actions taken by a U.S. territory, Puerto Rico, during a previous hurricane, Georges. "In Puerto Rico, *an American possession*," Rohter said, with an important choice of words, the government leaped into action as soon as the first hurricane watch was issued."[41] Rohter was making a contrast between Nicaraguan and U.S. society that was damning of Nicaragua.

The *Times* returned to this theme in a 2,800-word, front-page story that looked back on how the hurricane caused so much grief. The report acknowledged that much of the destruction resulted because the storm moved slowly, allowing huge amounts of rain to fall. But the nations and people bore responsibility, the *Times* said.

> The freakish behavior of the storm is the major reason it caught governments and people off guard. But the high death toll also owes something to poverty and politics. Most working-class houses are poorly built, and many impoverished people erect their homes, often illegally but with a wink from local politicians, on marginal lands close to rivers or clinging to unstable mountain slopes that have been stripped of trees.[42]

In a bylined editorial, a *Times* editor, Tina Rosenberg, focused specifically on government policies of deforestation. "Five days of torrential rain would have caused damage anywhere, but there would have been fewer lethal mud slides if the land in Honduras and Nicaragua had been covered with trees," she wrote. "Trees hold the soil together and help it absorb rain. When the land is stripped of trees, heavy rains sweep mud and minerals into the rivers, swelling and clotting the water and increasing its power to destroy."[43]

A letter to the editor saw government capitulation to corporations as part of the problem, a theme not emphasized in *Times* coverage. It said:

> The infrastructure that was destroyed was often created to meet the needs of the military and the multinational organizations. In Honduras, which is an oligarchy, the poor, who took the brunt of the storm, had been forced to live on the edges of banana plantations in flood-plain shantytowns or on hillsides that were of no economic value to the landowners. While aid efforts should continue, this disaster provides an opportunity for issues of basic justice and land reform to be addressed.[44]

Finally, some stories raised the idea that the flood could be interpreted as a punishment from the heavens. For example, a report on survivors quoted survivors who explicitly offered the theme of punishment. One story quoted Jose Antonio Amaya Garcia of Honduras:

> "It's a punishment from God," Mr. Amaya, an elderly carpenter, said late last week as he searched under an avalanche for what was left of his house. He is

tiny and frail in his soiled shirt and pants, the last clothing he owns. "I am 73, and I've never seen a disaster like this."[45]

An essay on the *Times* op-ed page—"The Wrath of God?"—offered a similar theme. Arturo J. Cruz Jr., a Nicaraguan professor, said that in the seventeenth century the people of León, Nicaragua, left the original site of the city, "believing that they were being punished by God for the sins of their ancestors, conquerors from Spain whose treatment of the native population was barbarous. Since then, doom has remained an indelible component of the Nicaraguan worldview. To this day, many wonder if they have a pending 'bill' with God."[46]

## DISCUSSION: NEWS VALUES AND MYTH

On one level the retelling of the flood myth in the *Times* supports the work of those who argue that myth has taken modern form in the news. Scholars have affirmed that myth still plays an important role in our society through the news. *Times* reporting shows how naturally myth might take shape in the news. *Times* coverage seemed normal, traditional. It is only on close examination that we can see the comparison to myth. As the writer and philosopher Roland Barthes wrote at the beginning of his book *Mythologies:* "The starting point of these reflections was usually a feeling of impatience at the sight of the naturalness with which newspapers, art, and common sense constantly dress up a reality which, even though it is one we live in, is undoubtedly determined by history."[47]

On another level other insights can be gained into this mythic examination of *Times* coverage. For decades gatekeeping studies have shown that U.S. news coverage of international affairs is dominated by stories of coups, crises, and catastrophes.[48] In tending the gates, in deciding what is international news and how it should be covered, U.S. news media often give priority to calamity. Nations and peoples around the globe merit U.S. news coverage in times of earthquakes, train wrecks, tidal waves, airline crashes, famines, and floods.

Research has suggested why this is so. Scholars have argued persuasively that U.S. news media reaffirm U.S. superiority and authority on the global stage. International news coverage, they suggest, is dictated by U.S. foreign policy. Coverage legitimizes global inadequacies, defends U.S. action or inaction, explains U.S. positions, and degrades the positions of others. Areas of U.S. interest become areas of U.S. news coverage. Other areas become newsworthy only when they meet dramatic, attention-grabbing requisites: calamities. Even then, the portrayals of crises and catastrophes often can be understood to lay claim to U.S. superiority as they symbolically lay waste to a people or nation.[49]

Myth can provide an additional perspective to the distinguished literature on gatekeeping. International communication researchers perhaps have identified a mythic dimension to U.S. news coverage. As we have seen, myth has always affirmed the authority and superiority of the social order. Myth legitimizes and justifies positions. Myth celebrates dominant beliefs and values. Myth degrades and demeans other beliefs that do not align with those of the storyteller or, in the case of news, the reporting nation's cultural values. And myth has often fulfilled these roles through portrayals of disasters and calamities, such as the flood. The flood, again, can be seen as the ultimate morality tale. People who have done wrong or who have taken the wrong path or who have otherwise strayed are punished and swept away. The righteous are left, confirmed in their position and place. Societies around the world have told themselves stories of the flood to affirm their own status, to sanction their actions, to explain the fall of others, and to warn doubters and slackers.

In reporting global events, in tending the gates, perhaps U.S. news is doing what myth has always done. News is drawing on the archetypal stories of calamity and crisis to uphold the social order and to affirm the superiority of a way of life. *Times* coverage of the 1998 Central American floods can be understood as fulfilling this mythic role. Months can go by without *Times* stories from Guatemala, Honduras, or Nicaragua. With the onslaught of the hurricane and the resulting floods the *Times* published daily front-page stories chronicling the catastrophe and symbolically degrading the victims by suggesting that they were at fault.

The four themes of the flood myth were clear. As the myth suggested, *Times* coverage averred that Central Americans had made social and political mistakes; the devastation of the flood was in part the result of those mistakes. The flood was complete in its devastation; entire communities were ravaged. Humans were helpless against its power. Survivors were left to renew and rebuild. These things seem natural and logical in the *Times*'s coverage, but the naturalness—the structure and pattern and themes—derives from myth.

Journalists do not see themselves as telling and retelling ancient tales of humankind. Yet like myth tellers of every age, journalists draw from archetypal stories to make sense of events. They draw from sacred societal stories that celebrate shared values, counsel with lessons and themes, and instruct and inform with exemplary models.

Were the Central American floods too convenient, too easy as a case study of news values and gatekeeping? The analysis suggests precisely otherwise. The mythic structure and themes identified actually appear often in the news. International news coverage is replete with stories of calamities and catastrophes that are caused by the inadequacies of other nations, that are complete in their devastation, that humble humanity, and that leave chastened survivors to reflect and renew. Tales of floods, famines, tidal waves, plagues, volcanoes, and countless other disasters regularly tell us the same story again and again, a story told since stories were told. The stories of disaster brought to us in international news are drawn from the fundamental stories of humankind. The gatekeepers of U.S. news open the gates for myth.

## NOTES

1. James C. McKinley Jr. with William K. Stevens, "The Life of a Hurricane, the Death That It Caused," *New York Times,* 9 November 1998, pp. A1, A8.

2. Don Cameron Allen, *The Legend of Noah* (Urbana: University of Illinois Press, 1963); Alan Dundes, ed., *The Flood Myth* (Berkeley: University of California Press, 1988); J. F. Bierlein, *Parallel Myths* (New York: Ballantine Books, 1994), 121–135.

3. Martin S. Day, *The Many Meanings of Myth* (Lanham, MD: University Press of America, 1984), 1–32; see also Ivan Strenski, *Four Theories of Myth in Twentieth-Century History* (Iowa City: University of Iowa Press, 1987).

4. Carl G. Jung, *Archetypes and the Collective Unconscious,* R. F. C. Hull, trans. (New York: Pantheon, 1959); Carl G. Jung, ed., *Man and His Symbols* (New York: Dell, 1964); Carl G. Jung, *Symbols of Transformation,* 2d ed., R. F. C. Hull, trans. (Princeton, NJ: Princeton University Press, 1976).

5. Jung, *Archetypes and the Collective Unconscious;* Mircea Eliade, *Patterns in Comparative Religion,* Rosemary Sheed, trans. (New York: Sheed and Ward, 1958); Northrop Frye, "The Archetypes of Literature," *Kenyon Review* 12 (winter 1951): 92–110; Northrop Frye, *Anatomy of Criticism* (Princeton, NJ: Princeton University Press, 1957).

6. Stith Thompson, *Motif-Index of Folk-Literature* (Bloomington: Indiana University Press, 1955).

7. James Frazer, *The Golden Bough* (New York: Macmillan, 1951); Joseph Campbell, *The Hero with a Thousand Faces* (New York: Meridian, 1956); Eliade, *Patterns in Comparative Religion.*

8. Robert Darnton, "Writing News and Telling Stories," *Daedalus* 104 (spring 1975): 175–194; David L. Eason, "Telling Stories and Making Sense," *Journal of Popular Culture* 15 (fall 1981): 125–129; Michael Schudson, "The Politics of Narrative Form: The Emergence of News Conventions in Print and Television," *Daedalus* 111 (fall 1982): 97–112.

9. Roland Barthes, *Mythologies,* Annette Lavers, trans. (London: Jonathan Cape, 1972); Marshall McLuhan, "Myth and Mass Media," in Henry Murray, ed., *Myth and Mythmaking* (New York: George Braziller, 1960), 288–299 [originally published in *Daedalus* 88 (1958): 339–348]; Mircea Eliade, *The Sacred and the Profane,* Willard R. Trask, trans. (New York: Harcourt, Brace & World, 1959), 205.

10. See W. Lance Bennett, "Myth, Ritual, and Political Control," *Journal of Communication* 30 (autumn 1980): 166–179; S. Elizabeth Bird and Robert W. Dardenne, "Myth, Chronicle, and Story: Exploring the Narrative Qualities of News," in James W. Carey, ed., *Media, Myths, and Narratives* (Newbury Park, CA: Sage, 1988), 67–86; Myles Breen and Farrel Corcoran, "Myth in the Television Discourse," *Communication Monographs* 49 ( June 1982): 127–136; Richard Campbell, *60 Minutes and the News: A Mythology for Middle America* (Urbana: University of Illinois Press, 1991); James W. Carey, ed., *Media, Myths, and Narratives* (Newbury Park, CA: Sage, 1988); Howard Davis and Paul Walton, "Death of a Premier: Consensus and Closure in International News," in Howard Davis and Paul Walton, eds., *Language, Image, Media* (Oxford: Basil Blackwell, 1983), 8–49; Graham Knight and Tony Dean, "Myth and the Structure of News," *Journal of Communication* 32 (spring 1982): 144–158; John Lawrence and Bernard Timberg, "News and Mythic Selectivity," *Journal of American Culture* 2 (summer 1979): 321–330; David L. Paletz, John Z. Ayanian, and Peter A. Fozzard, "Terrorism on TV News: The IRA, the FALN, and the Red Brigades," in William C. Adams, ed., *Television Coverage of International Affairs* (Norwood, NJ: Ablex, 1982), 143–165; Robert Rutherford Smith, "Mythic Elements in Television News," *Journal of Communication* 29 (winter 1979): 75–82. See also Sarah R. Hankins, "Archetypal Alloy: Ronald Reagan's Rhetorical Image," *Central States Speech Journal* 34 (1983): 3–43; Paul Heyer, *Titanic Legacy: Disaster as Media Event and Myth* (Westport, CT: Praeger, 1995); Jack Lule, "The Myth of My Widow: A

Dramatistic Analysis of News Portrayals of a Terrorist Victim," in A. Odasuo Alali and Kenoye Kelvin Eke, eds., *Media Coverage of Terrorism* (Newbury Park, CA: Sage, 1991), 86–111; J. A. F. Van Zyl, *Media and Myth: The Construction of Television News* (Mowbray, South Africa: IDASA, 1991).

11. Jack Lule, "Myth, News, and Sport: Mark McGwire as Mythic Hero," paper presented at the 1999 International Communication Association annual conference, San Francisco, May 1999.

12. Some good examples of these newsmaking studies are Stanley Cohen and Jock Young, eds., *The Manufacture of News* (Beverly Hills, CA: Sage, 1973); Stanley Cohen and Jock Young, eds., *The Manufacture of News: Social Problems, Deviance, and the Mass Media* (Beverly Hills, CA: Sage, 1981); Mark Fishman, *Manufacturing the News* (Austin: University of Texas Press, 1980); Bernard Roshco, *Newsmaking* (Chicago: University of Chicago Press, 1975); Michael Schudson, "The Sociology of News Production," *Media, Culture, and Society* 2 (1989): 263–282; Leon Sigal, *Reporters and Officials: The Organization and Politics of Newsmaking* (Lexington: D. C. Heath, 1973); Gaye Tuchman, *Making News: A Study in the Construction of Reality* (New York: Free Press, 1978); and Jeremy Tunstall, *Journalists at Work* (Beverly Hills, CA: Sage, 1971).

13. Dundes, *The Flood Myth,* 2.

14. Allen, *The Legend of Noah;* Arthur C. Custance, *The Flood: Local or Global?* (Grand Rapids, MI: Zondervan, 1979); Leonard Woolley, "Stories of the Creation and the Flood," in Alan Dundes, ed., *The Flood Myth* (Berkeley: University of California Press, 1988), 89–100.

15. The influence of the *New York Times* on U.S. national and international affairs is discussed in the following works: J. Herbert Altschull, *Agents of Power: The Media and Public Policy,* 2d ed. (White Plains, NY: Longman, 1996); R. O. Blanchard, *Congress and the News Media* (New York: Hastings House, 1978); Stephen Hess, *The Government-Press Connection* (Washington, DC: Brookings, 1984); Martin Linsky, *Impact: How the Press Affects Federal Policy Making*

(New York: Norton, 1986); Michael Parenti, *Inventing Reality: The Politics of the News Media,* 2d ed. (New York: St. Martin's Press, 1993); Mark J. Rozell, *In Contempt of Congress: Postwar Press Coverage on Capitol Hill* (New York: Praeger, 1996); and Carol H. Weiss, "What America's Leaders Read," *Public Opinion Quarterly* 38 (1974): 1–22. One classic study that counted the number of times the *Times* was cited is Craig H. Grau, "What Publications Are Most Frequently Quoted in the Congressional Record?" *Journalism Quarterly* 53 (1976): 716–719. Also see Nicholas Berry, *Foreign Policy and the Press: An Analysis of The New York Times Coverage of U.S. Foreign Policy* (New York: Greenwood, 1990); Russ Braley, *Bad News: The Foreign Policy of the New York Times* (Chicago: Regnery Gateway, 1984); Edward Herman and Noam Chomsky, *Manufacturing Consent: The Political Economy of the Mass Media* (New York: Pantheon, 1988); Stephen Hess, *International News and Foreign Correspondents* (Washington, DC: Brookings, 1996); Jarol B. Manheim, *Strategic Public Diplomacy and American Foreign Policy* (New York: Oxford University Press, 1994); Patrick O'Heffernan, *Mass Media and American Foreign Policy* (Norwood, NJ: Ablex, 1991); and Philip Seib, *Headline Diplomacy: How News Coverage Affects Foreign Policy* (Westport, CT: Greenwood, 1996).

16. "32 Killed in Major Hurricane, Honduras Says," *New York Times,* 19 October 1998, p. A5.

17. "Death Toll from Storm Hits 450 after Mudslides in Nicaragua," *New York Times,* 1 November 1998, p. A6.

18. Larry Rohter, "Flood Toll Estimate Rises above 1,000 in Central America," *New York Times,* 2 November 1998, pp. A1, A6.

19. Larry Rohter, "Officials Predict Hurricane's Toll Will Exceed 7,000," *New York Times,* 3 November 1998, p. A1.

20. Rohter, "Officials Predict Hurricane's Toll Will Exceed 7,000."

21. Larry Rohter, "Nicaragua's Main Highway Is a Flow of Human Misery," *New York Times,* 4 November 1998, p. A1.

22. Larry Rohter, "For Nicaraguan Victims, Not Even a Grave," *New York Times,* 6 November 1998, p. A1.

23. Philip Shenon, "U.S. Says Storm Aid Could Cost Billions," *New York Times,* 7 November 1998, p. A3.

24. Mirta Ojito, "Central Americans in New York Scramble to Help Hurricane Victims," *New York Times,* 4 November 1998, p. D7.

25. "Hurricane Threatens 4 Caribbean Nations," *New York Times,* 27 October 1998, p. A14.

26. "Hurricane Hits Coasts of Honduras and Belize," *New York Times,* 28 October 1998, p. A11.

27. "Storm's Floods Rise in Honduras and Nicaragua," *New York Times,* 31 October 1998, p. A3.

28. Rohter, "Flood Toll Estimate Rises above 1,000 in Central America."

29. Larry Rohter, "Now Ruined Economies, Afflict Central America," *New York Times,* 13 November 1998, p. A12.

30. Rohter, "Officials Predict Hurricane's Toll Will Exceed 7,000."

31. Ibid.

32. James C. McKinley Jr., "Relief Effort in Honduras in Dire Need of Resources," *New York Times,* 4 November 1998, p. A6.

33. Larry Rohter, "How Nations Run: Disasters as a Guide," *New York Times,* 8 November 1998, p. K6.

34. "1 House Left in Sea of Mud," *New York Times,* 3 November 1998, p. A13.

35. "Leveled by Storm," *New York Times,* 10 November 1998, p. A16.

36. James C. McKinley Jr., "Honduras's Capital: City of the Dead and the Dazed," *New York Times,* 5 November 1998, p. A3.

37. Rohter, "Nicaragua's Main Highway Is a Flow of Human Misery."

38. Rohter, "For Nicaraguan Victims, Not Even a Grave."

39. Larry Towell, "Rebuilding Honduras," *New York Times Magazine,* 6 December 1998, p. 67.

40. McKinley, "Honduras's Capital: City of the Dead and the Dazed."

41. Rohter, "How Nations Run: Disasters as a Guide."

42. McKinley with Stevens, "The Life of a Hurricane, the Death That It Caused."

43. Tina Rosenberg, "Trees and the Roots of a Storm's Destruction," *New York Times,* 26 November 1998, p. A38.

44. Ronald Patterson, "Hurricane Relief Is Just a Band-Aid" [letter to the editor], *New York Times,* 14 November 1998, p. A12.

45. McKinley with Stevens, "The Life of a Hurricane, the Death That It Caused."

46. Arturo J. Cruz Jr., "The Wrath of God?" *New York Times,* 16 November 1998, p. A21.

47. Barthes, *Mythologies,* 11.

48. The gatekeeping literature is voluminous and includes Kurt Lewin, "Channels of Group Life: Social Planning and Action Research," *Human Relations* 1 (summer 1947): 145–146; David Manning White, "The 'Gate Keeper': A Case Study in the Selection of News," *Journalism Quarterly* 27 (fall 1950): 383–396; James W. Markham, "Foreign News in the United States and South American Press," *Public Opinion Quarterly* 25 (summer 1961): 249–262; Paul B. Snider, "Mr. Gates Revisited: A 1966 Version of the 1949 Case Study," *Journalism Quarterly* 44 (fall 1967): 419–427; John Dimmick, *The Gate-Keeper: An Uncertainty Theory,* Journalism Monograph 37 (Lexington, KY: Association for Education in Journalism, 1974); Sophie Peterson, "Foreign News Gatekeepers and Criteria of Newsworthiness," *Journalism Quarterly* 56 (spring 1979): 116–125; Richard M. Brown, "The Gatekeeper Reassessed: 'Keeping the Gates for Gatekeepers': The Effects of Wire News," *Journalism Quarterly* 5 (spring 1982): 60–65; Glen Bleske, "Ms. Gates Takes Over," *Newspaper Research Journal* 12 (1991): 88–97; Pamela Shoemaker, *Gatekeeping* (Newbury Park, CA: Sage, 1991).

49. See, for example, Bernard C. Cohen, *The Press and Foreign Policy* (Princeton, NJ: Princeton University Press, 1963); Johan Galtung and Mari Holmboe Ruge, "The Structure of Foreign News," *Journal of Peace Research* 2 (spring 1965): 64–91; Mort Rosenblum, *Coups and Earthquakes: Reporting the Third World for America* (New

York: Harper and Row, 1979); Annabelle Sreberny-Mohammadi, "The 'World of the News,'" *Journal of Communication* 34 (winter 1984): 121–134; Herman and Chomsky, *Manufacturing Consent;* Daniel C. Hallin, *We Keep America on Top of the World: Televi-sion Journalism and the Public Sphere* (London: Routledge, 1994); Altschull, *Agents of Power;* and Edward S. Herman and Robert W. Mc-Chesney, *The Global Media: The New Mis-sionaries of Global Capita.*

# 7

# Social and Institutional Influences on News Values and Routines in Brazil

## From Military Rule to Democracy

### HELOIZA HERSCOVITZ

Journalists around the world share some common values, roles, and routines that help them define what is news and how to collect and report the news. Too often journalism scholars and practitioners focus on the differences among journalists around the world and ignore the similarities. Some scholars, however, point to the evolving global culture of journalistic practices, influenced to a large extent by American journalistic practices.[1] In Brazil, the focus of this chapter, journalism was originally influenced by French literary style.[2] This resulted in an elaborate writing style and advocacy of political causes. Starting 40 years ago, however, American journalistic practices, such as the summary lead, the inverted pyramid lead, and the notion of objectivity, started to influence Brazilian journalism.[3] Whether this is for the better or the worse is debatable. What is perhaps more relevant is how these practices affect news reporting in different cultural environments. We know little about how these values, roles, and routines, which were transplanted from one culture to another, interact with domestic social and institutional forces and affect the final journalistic product.

The body of theory and the formal studies addressing the forces shaping the news are known as media sociology. Research in this tradition developed in the United States during the 1950s, with David Manning White's famous gatekeeping study, which examined how a single media gatekeeper—an anonymous newspaper editor described as Mr. Gates—decided the day's news stories. A subsequent study on social control in the newsroom, by Warren Breed, further described how the final news product was standardized and shaped to fit dominant social values of the culture.[4] The study by Breed, relevant to this chapter, explored how journalists learn implicit newsroom policy and how implicit policy is enforced in newsrooms. During the 1940s and in the 1950s, implicit policy in U.S. newsrooms meant that journalists had to learn how their news organizations expected certain sacred cows to be treated (e.g., political parties, labor, the Japanese, and minorities). Breed found that journalists learned policy by osmosis, that is, by socializing and learning the ropes as a neophyte in a subculture.

Breed blamed publishers for news biases and pointed to a struggle between journalists and their bosses.[5] Breed's notion of social control in the newsroom is relevant in Brazil. In Brazil journalism is a highly personalized business. The news media are controlled by a small group of families and their heirs who imprint their own characteristics, political views, and biases on the enterprise. Thus each news organization has its own sacred cows. As a result, Brazilian newspapers, newsmagazines, and television stations subtly—and sometimes not so subtly—see to it that their journalists learn their organizations' unstated sacred cows.

Since the classic studies of the 1950s, American research has focused mainly on a microlevel sphere of the individual journalist. Social control in the newsroom was seen as a reciprocal process between the employee-journalists and their employer-owners. This mode of research ignored questions concerning the power exerted by various social institutions and structures and the entire society itself. American research has been associated with a liberal-pluralist approach and is heavily grounded in empirical research involving systematic observation and the scientific method. European and Latin American media scholars have focused on social and institutional influences on the news media and questions involving the locus of power. These scholars take critical, cultural, and Marxist approaches to studying how social forces shape the news. The focus on larger structures allows a good deal of theoretical speculation.

Researchers in the two traditions (i.e., liberal-pluralist and critical) examined the media in different contexts with different theoretical interests and research methods that stemmed from cultural and historical differences. In the United States the American dream of equality and opportunity for all, the emphasis on individual initiative, the existence of a large middle class, and the absence of a strong labor movement have blurred the clash between antagonistic political forces. American research hardly takes into account the concept of social class at all. Usually, social divisions in American society are perceived in terms of ethnicity and race.[6] In contrast, class relationships and regional identities are at the core of social life in European and Latin American societies, in which opposed political options have always been present through organized movements involved in fighting social stratification.[7]

In Latin America scholars have usually followed European research trends for three major reasons. First, the region's Iberian and Hispanic cultural heritage followed later by English and French influences affected research practices. Second, Latin America's history of class relationships, political movements, poverty, and economic instability has strongly influenced the region's communication scholarship in favor of critical, cultural, and Marxist approaches. Third, media–government relations in Latin America have taken a path distinct from that in the United States because of cultural, economic, and historical reasons.[8]

In the end the difference comes down to this: The American liberal-pluralist tradition sees society as a complex of equivalent competing groups and interests. Media organizations are perceived as autonomous enterprises free from the state, political parties, and institutional pressures, and journalists enjoy great autonomy. European critical, cultural, and Marxist traditions see society dominated by an elite. Media organizations are perceived as part of the ideological arena that rules society. Journalists have the illusion of autonomy, but in fact they internalize the norms of the dominant culture and reproduce them at work.[9]

At one time the liberal-pluralist and critical perspectives seemed irreconcilable, and scholars from the two schools were often in conflict. Cutting across the conventional divisions of left and right, the liberal-pluralist and critical perspectives have moved to a new path in which they form a diverse coalition of intellectual positions that can complement each other.[10] Gurevitch, for example, wrote that they have generated a diverse set of research strands that can be divided into four main areas:

1. Institutional structures and role relationships, which include various gatekeeper studies and news flow studies.

2. The political economy of news organizations, which focuses on ownership and control.

3. Professional ideologies and work practices rooted in the sociology of the profession, which investigate journalism as an occupation with certain beliefs and values.

4. The interaction of media institutions with the social-political environment, which examines how political sources and the state interact with media organizations and media professionals.[11]

In this chapter I deal with the fourth research strand, which emphasizes how social and institutional forces influence the news-making process. Hirsch identified this strand as institutional analysis. He defined it as the study of the influence of transmitted content on the surrounding political and cultural environment, and vice versa. Institutional analysis also involves the economic and organizational interrelationships among the elites in mass media corporations and those at the top of other institutional sectors.[12]

I also address in this chapter the work practices of Brazilian gatekeepers, the political economy of news organizations, and the presence of ideological values in the media. I describe the forces that influenced news selection and reporting in Brazil when the social and institutional forces were quite different. I examine how journalists performed their jobs under the harsh censorship of military rulers during the 1960s and the 1970s and describe how journalists performed their jobs during a transitional period from dictatorship to democracy during the 1980s and early 1990s. This era is known as the New Republic, and it culminated in the impeachment of President Fernando Collor de Mello in 1992. The media played a central role in the impeachment. Finally, I explore the evolution of journalism in Brazil's democratic regime after the impeachment and discuss how changing social values and institutional processes affect journalism as an occupation.

## THE BRAZILIAN ENVIRONMENT

In size, Brazil is the fifth largest country in the world after Russia, Canada, China, and the United States. With a population of 157 million, it is the only Portuguese-speaking nation in Latin America. Eighty percent of the population lives in urban areas near the coast. São Paulo, the country's main financial and business center and the country's media hub, is the world's third largest megalopolis, with a population of 16.6 million.[13] Brazil's diverse ethnic makeup includes descendants from Portuguese settlers, Africans, and native Brazilians as well as those who have intermarried over the years. Other Europeans, Asians, and Middle Eastern immigrants later joined them.

Social and economic disparities prevail in Brazil. Income is highly stratified by class and region, and social mobility is low. The average income for the richest 10% of the Brazilian population is 30 times more than the average for the country's poorest 40%. Unemployment in São Paulo reached 20% in August 1999. Illiteracy is a problem and, as with the distribution of wealth, is stratified by class and region. Almost 29% of the population is illiterate in the impoverished northeast; in the wealthy southeast the rate is 8.7%.[14]

There are 300 newspapers in the country. Only four dailies, however, have the circulation and national clout to significantly influence national opinion and politics. They are *O Estado de S. Paulo, Folha de S. Paulo, Jornal do Brasil,* and *O Globo.* The country's elite and middle class read these newspapers, but most Brazilians get their news from television and radio. In addition, a few weekly newsmagazines, such as *Veja,* and especially the influential television network Globo play a significant role in national politics.

Today Brazil is a functioning democracy with freedom of the press. Although the blatant brute force of military government censorship no longer exists, a number of forces combine to constrain the press so that it limits its criticisms of the government. The nation's media are highly concentrated in private hands by entrepreneurs who, at least in theory, are free to report the news as they see fit. However, precisely because these entrepreneurs come from the wealthy class and consort with government officials, they are likely to sympathize with officials and restrict their criticisms. In addition, the government still exerts significant political influence on the media through such means as credit incentives, tax breaks, and government advertising. By providing the news media with such goodies, ostensibly to promote freedom of the press, the media may be cautious about too severely criticizing the government in power so as not to lose the financial rewards provided by the state. Broadcast licenses are among the goodies that can be awarded or taken away by the state. Licensing of radio and television stations is granted by the minister of communications, using procedures that are not always clearly specified or fair.[15]

## THE HARD YEARS

From 1964 to 1985 Brazilians suffered under the longest ruling military dictatorship in South America. It was the first of a series of military takeovers that spread throughout the region. Throughout Brazilian history the state has always controlled the nation's economic development, social organization, and cultural practices. In the early 1960s the nation was experiencing the peak of a political movement called populism, a reformist movement known as a third route (neither capitalist nor socialist) to assert Brazil's economic independence in the global economy. Populism promised to destroy local semifeudal structures that hindered economic development and social justice. To do this, under the banner of populism a benign, paternalistic, and compassionate state would expand into a powerful interventionist institution supposedly bringing social justice.[16]

Populism, as a third route, was seen as an alternative to liberalism, which emphasized self-interest and individualism. Populism was also seen as an alternative to socialism and communism, which stressed class conflict. Populism was conceived as an alternative that emphasized the role of a benevolent state as the provider of popular political participation to the masses. In addition, the state could prevent a popular revolution from below and control the nation's development.[17] Populism, as an ideology, fitted well with the region's authoritarian, Catholic, and paternalistic traditions, but it faced the opposition of regional political elites who governed the states, controlled weak political parties, and practiced clientelism (the distribution of state resources in exchange for political favors).[18]

Populism was already in practice when Vice President João Goulart, a former protégé of charismatic ex-dictator Getulio Vargas and one of Brazil's largest landowners, succeeded to the presidency after President Janio Quadros resigned in 1961. Quadros was an emotionally unstable politician who won the election by what was then the largest political margin. After serving only seven months, Quadros declared that he was "defeated by the blind forces." Goulart's policies of land expropriation and social reforms threatened the entrenched power of the nation's elites, angered vested foreign interests, and polarized the country.[19] Goulart was mistrusted by leftists, who perceived him as politically undecided, and by rightists, who thought he wanted to be a new caudillo (dictator). During this uncertain political period, the military ousted Goulart in a March 1964 coup that, by and large, enjoyed support from the nation's press.

Before the coup most of the press opposed Goulart's populist reforms. However, although they demanded Goulart's removal, most newspapers hoped he could be removed through constitutional means rather than with a coup. After the coup the military quickly seized control of the government and made clear that it would not operate under the Constitution. The military announced that it would expel members of Congress, the judiciary, and state and regional government offices suspected of being communists. It suspended the political rights of its opponents for 10 years and eliminated judicial immunity and academic tenure.[20]

The newspapers that originally applauded Goulart's removal by the military were harassed by the new regime. Many newspapers experienced censorship, confiscation, police occupations, arrests of personnel, and closures. The military secured its domination by dismantling political parties, professional associations, and trade unions. The military believed that subversives dominated these organizations. It suspected enemies of the state everywhere. Any form of opposition was punished. Journalists, known for holding political positions on the left of the political spectrum, became suspect.

The military rulers eliminated populist measures and implemented their own political and economic projects. Parts of the state considered vital to national security grew rapidly. These included the postal services, interstate highways, and satellite communications. Although military rule did not get much support from the print media, it secured the support of the broadcast system by controlling the airwaves and the distribution of television channels. Globo television network, which was born with the coup, became a powerful ally of the military during the dictatorship.

## Press Control

During the first four years of military rule, the news media learned how to survive under military control. They were deferential and uncritical in their coverage.[21] Coverage of national politics was conventional and unlikely to anger the military, focusing on ceremonial affairs. A few newspapers, such as *Correio da Manhã* of Rio de Janeiro, criticized the mass arrests, political repression, and torture. One of its editorials after the coup was titled "Enough and Out!"[22]

The press situation worsened in the following years. In 1967, three years after the military coup, the government imposed a tough press law that prohibited the publication or broadcast of any information it considered harmful to the state or national security. Because this could include any topic, the law gave the government broad and sweeping powers to silence a critical press. Journalists who violated the law faced up to four years in prison. The publishing of false or distorted news deemed to disturb public opinion or negatively affect government institutions could land journalists in jail for up to six months. Journalists were prevented from making any potentially damaging accusations or charges against the government or government officials, even if they had solid evidence to support their charges.[23]

Also in 1967 the military government introduced what was regarded as de facto licensing of journalists. Aspiring journalists were required to possess a university degree, proof of citizenship, and a letter from local authorities stating that the candidate had not faced judicial action under the national security law. Although not literally a license, the requirements were regarded as a de facto government license because they set government standards for who could and could not practice journalism and because they kept potential critics of the state from entering journalism.

By 1968 tensions between the civil society and the state intensified, and various sectors of Brazilian society demanded an end to military control. Even many elites who had at first supported or at least tolerated the coup as a means of bringing social order had grown frustrated with military rule. In addition, power struggles developed within military factions, making the military less able to maintain strict control. After the police killed a student during street protests in Rio de Janeiro, strikes spread to São Paulo's manufacturing plants, and hundreds of students were imprisoned. The simmering resentment against military rule culminated in the Congress refusing to follow the military's orders to remove a left-wing congressman from office.

The military responded to the increasing demands to reduce military control by cracking down harder on dissent. Hard-liners in the military usurped power from soft-liners and led what was called the coup within the coup. The hard-liners promulgated a decree granting themselves absolute power, even over the Congress and the courts. The military's decision to crack down even harder on calls for liberalization surprised journalists and media owners, who had expected the military to leave power after a short time. Military interventions in the 1930s had been short lived. In the past the military saw their role as restoring order only after social chaos set in and then giving up power and allowing civilian rule after order was restored. The 1964 coup, in which the military not only usurped power but also remained in power and administered policy, was an anomaly in Brazilian history.

During this period of frustration with the military and demands for a return to civilian rule, the military regime revealed a tremendous animosity toward the press. It blamed the press for popular discontent. Its strategy to control the print media consisted of two methods: indirect attack and direct attack. Indirect attacks on the press included economic sanctions, such as withholding government advertising, pressing private advertisers to cancel their ads, denying loans from state banks, denying licenses to import newsprint equipment, and canceling a publication's registration when it did not pay its taxes. Direct attacks included harassment of journalists and media owners, confiscation of publications, suspension of radio stations, and censorship. In 1968 a bomb exploded at *Correio da Manhã's* headquarters. The incident was thought to be the work of the government. The police arrested the newspaper's main editors and its owner, Niomar Bittencourt. She was held incommunicado for two months, sharing a cell with prostitutes and robbers.[24] The government in many other ways harassed the newspaper. These pressures took their toll. The newspaper was forced to close in 1968.

In 1972 bombs exploded at *O Estado de S. Paulo's* headquarters after it had carried editorials critical of the military. Radio stations were suspended for reporting the actions of guerrilla movements. *Veja,* a weekly newsmagazine, was twice confiscated for news reports critical of the military.[25] From 1968 to 1978 many journalists were arrested and prosecuted under the press law or the national security law. Many others were held incommunicado and were beaten and tortured.[26]

The military targeted small publications as well. Weekly and small monthly publications known as the alternative press saw their editions confiscated at newsstands. The alternative press carried few advertisements. Their revenues came from sales and fund-raisers. Part-time journalists who worked for the mainstream press edited them. Their content focused on politics (*Opinião, Movimento*), culture (*Versus, Ex*), humor (*Pasquim*), feminism (*Nós Mulheres, Brasil Mulher*), gay rights (*Lampião*), and community affairs (*Reporter*). *Pasquim,* the most successful alternative paper, saw its entire staff of humorists jailed for two months. At the same time, the government advised a major foreign company, Volkswagen, that if it continued placing its advertisements in *Pasquim,* the government would consider that action unfriendly to the regime.[27]

The military denied that it used press censorship in its attempt to gain political legitimacy. At the same time, it fashioned an efficient and organized form of direct press control that became part of the news media's daily routines and that forced almost total compliance from media owners and journalists who feared for their futures and their business. Three basic forms of censorship were used: prior restraint, post-publication censorship, and self-censorship.

Prior restraint involved the government's imposition of restrictions on media content *before* (hence the word "prior") the information ever left newsrooms. It was the most dangerous form of government censorship because the media's message could never reach the public. Its intent was to perpetuate the regime and to suppress debates about social problems concerning the government's economic policy. Prior restraint created a culture of fear and a climate of uncertainty and intimidation. Prior restraint was enforced by two simultaneous means: (1) telephoned and written orders from the government to the press that prohibited press treatment of certain issues and (2) government agents assigned to newsrooms to review page proofs and edit the materials before publication. Both systems of censorship were conducted from 1968 to 1978.[28]

Post-publication censorship refers to punishment taken against the press *after* the material has been published and has reached the public. In December 1968, after the government launched a decree granting itself absolute power, *Jornal do Brasil* put out an edition filled with apocalyptic metaphors. These even appeared in the classified ads. The weather section, for example, announced on a balmy summer day that "dark clouds stalk the country." Recognizing that it had been fooled, the next day the military sent five censors to control the paper's content.[29]

Self-censorship occurs when gatekeepers in news organizations—whether they are the owners, editors, or journalists—voluntarily withhold publishing news stories that they would otherwise publish for fear of government punishment after publication. As with prior restraint, self-censored information never reaches the public. Neither journalists nor media owners talked openly about self-censorship. It is known that news organizations that practiced self-censorship or openly supported the regime received ample state advertising, bank loans, and incentives to buy new printing machines and build modern headquarters. Journalists who cooperated with the regime took advantage of new job opportunities, such as becoming press advisers to politicians and government agencies, receiving special favors from local authorities, or receiving private loans from Banco do Brasil, the national state bank.[30]

The process whereby Brazilian journalists learned how to work under censorship was similar to Warren Breed's description of how American journalists learned their organizations' policies. The written orders were shared with the top editorial staff and never openly discussed with journalists. Although the journalists were not always aware of the orders or were only vaguely aware of them, management was able to communicate the gist of the orders to them and get them to act accordingly. The journalists learned how to report and write stories according to the orders through informal silent routines that were incorporated into their daily work as they learned what was acceptable and what was not.

Journalists working at *Jornal do Brasil* compiled a secret black book containing the general rules established by the federal police. The rules prohibited newspapers from publishing anything potentially critical of the government and limited government news to such matters as government ceremonies and official press releases.[31] Here is an example of a written order from the black book reproduced in Anne-Marie Smith's book: "The Inter American Press Association released a statement regarding restrictions upon the press in Brazil and four Latin American countries. By order of the Minister of Justice, it is prohibited to disseminate only the part of this statement concerning Brazil" (3 January 1973).[32]

## THE NEW REPUBLIC: A TRANSITION PERIOD

By the mid-1980s the collapse of the military regime was inevitable. The military was not succeeding in bringing social order. Inflation had reached 200%, and Brazil's foreign debt was close to $100 billion.[33] In 1984 *Folha de S. Paulo* actively supported the unsuccessful popular campaign to reinstate free presidential elections. Other news organizations soon followed *Folha de S. Paulo*'s lead. Even the Globo television network, which had always supported the military, started reporting the antigovernment rallies in the state capitals, indirectly encouraging people to join in the protests against the government. As one leading Latin American scholar wrote, public opinion sensed that the dictatorship was coming to an end and that the Globo network was not prepared to go down with the regime.[34] The military agreed to a moderate political opening and a negotiated transition.

There were no free presidential elections in 1984, but the military was willing to accept civilian rule the following year so long as the military could retain control of power. An indirect presidential election took place instead. An electoral college composed of national, state, and local politicians—and in which the government enjoyed a secure majority—elected Tancredo Neves president. A member of the traditional political elite for 30 years, Neves emerged as a conciliatory leader accepted by most of the military, the public, and the media. He allegedly made a pact with the military promising to overlook their abuses while in power;

he also put in writing that members of the political elite who backed him would be repaid with posts in the government.[35] Still, he was regarded as the nation's best hope for ending military rule and restoring democracy.

Neves fell ill before taking power, creating a climate of uncertainty. Most media, concerned about how Neves' death would affect the delicate political situation, were cautious in covering his condition. Only one newspaper, *Folha de S. Paulo,* published what was really happening with the president's health and disclosed his eventual death. Most of the media did not adequately report Neves' health, never explaining his dire situation, so the public was surprised when he died. The media were afraid to inform the public that their president, who might end military rule and restore democracy, was dying. The coverage devoted to Neves' funeral was even more emotional than that of his election. All day television showed images of thousands of people crying and waving before Neves' coffin as it crossed the busy streets of São Paulo. At the newsrooms, exhausted from the nonstop coverage, journalists hugged each other and cried. They feared that the democratization process was at risk.[36]

Vice President José Sarney, a member of the northeastern political elite, assumed the presidency. The route to democracy under Sarney was stable, although it looked more like a labyrinth than a straight line. The political transition was tightly controlled by the military. Social and political institutions accused of corruption remained intact. There was no radical transformation in the state bureaucracy, and there was no major change in journalism. Journalists, who had suffered during the military dictatorship and who had hoped to practice their craft under the Neves government, now hoped that with increasing democratization they could report critical news about the government. Apparently, news organizations did not feel as comfortable engaging in investigative reports during this period of political transition as journalists had hoped. Besides, investigative journalism was considered expensive by news organizations.[37]

Journalism in the 1980s was a mechanical task rather than creative work. It was not as exciting as most journalists hoped it would be with the restoration of press freedom. Brazilian journalists were urged by their employers concerned with cutting costs to rely on press releases and telephone interviews rather than on more extensive and expensive means. Stories became shorter. Journalists became discouraged and doubted that investigative journalism in Brazil could ever generate anything like Watergate in the United States. "There will never be a Watergate in Brazil because the nation has no moral principles," predicted journalist Bernardo Kucinski in 1986.[38] He could not be more wrong. Only six years later the Brazilian press would expose its own version of Watergate, known as Collorgate.

## COLLORGATE

Fernando Collor de Mello became president of Brazil in March 1990, after defeating Luís Inácio Lula da Silva of the left-leaning Workers Party. He was the first directly elected president in 29 years. Collor was young and elegant, was fluent in foreign languages, held degrees in political science and journalism, and had once been an editor at his family's newspaper—and Collor made history by being the first Brazilian president to be impeached. Accused of conducting illegal large-scale business deals two years after assuming power, Collor was indicted on criminal charges. He resigned from the presidency minutes after being convicted by the Senate on 29 December 1992.

Brazil's press helped make Collor. Later, it contributed to his downfall. In many ways Collorgate was remarkably similar to America's Watergate, and it is instructive to examine how news media routines and practices had evolved by the time of Collorgate to contribute to bringing down the president. In addition to being the first president to be impeached and convicted, Collor made history for being the first presidential candidate to use political marketing techniques to make himself attractive to the masses and to the elites. The media's fascination with Collor began when he launched his political campaign while the governor of the impoverished northeastern state of Alagoas, where his family controlled a media group.

Journalists were intrigued by Collor's character and style. He was smart, articulate, aggressive, and, at the same time, eccentric, impulsive, and authoritarian. Collor's advisers instructed him to say what the people and the media wanted to hear. This may not seem odd in the United States, where politicians are routinely accused of caving in to public opinion and ingratiating themselves with the public, but it was a new thing in Brazil. Collor launched a popular moral campaign against corruption in the state bureaucracy, starting with attacks on his own party. It was not only what Collor said that made him popular but also how he said it. His colorful rhetoric gave journalists ready-to-publish headlines and slogans, such as "It's now or never," "Tomorrow there will be something new: Prices will be lower," and "I was in the woods with only one bullet to kill the tiger and hit the bull's-eye." [39]

Although journalists were fascinated by Collor's character, as a group they did not support his political views. Then and now, Brazilian journalists held left-leaning political tendencies and consistently supported the Workers Party, the largest leftist political organization in Brazil. Media owners, however, who traditionally associated with the nation's wealthy classes, identified with Collor's agenda, which included administrative reform, privatization, trade liberalization, and deregulation of industry.

The political differences between the relatively liberal journalists and the conservative media owners underscores an important point in understanding the political role of the press in Brazil, the United States, and other democracies with press freedom. Although the press is accused of being either liberal or conservative depending on the country and the political situation, the matter is not that simple. With liberal journalists and wealthy media owners, who, with other wealthy entrepreneurs, tend to be politically conservative, what is the final journalistic product? Rather than simply saying the press is liberal or conservative, the theoretical concept of social and institutional influences on news values suggests that the news is a product of clashes and negotiations among journalists, media owners, and other parties (e.g., politicians, the business community, and public opinion).

The reporting of the Collorgate affair was largely the result of a series of these clashes and negotiations in the media. The initial news coverage of Collor was largely favorable, but the honeymoon between Collor and the media was short. A few days after taking power in March 1990, the president revealed his nonconciliatory, arrogant style. Annoyed by a story that disclosed financial irregularities in his presidential campaign, Collor authorized federal police officers to raid *Folha de S. Paulo*'s headquarters. It was a blatant attempt to intimidate the newspaper, much as had been done during the military rule, but the action was inappropriate and was not as passively accepted by the press in the promised new Brazilian democracy. Next, Collor sued four *Folha* journalists, including the owner's son, for libel. The journalists were acquitted in 1992. This episode was another blatant attempt to intimidate a critical press that raised questions about Collor's commitment to democracy.

Rather than intimidate or silence the press, Collor's hostile reactions to press criticism caused other newspapers to believe that he had something to hide. Newspapers and magazines undertook investigations of P. C. Farias, the most controversial figure in Collor's entourage. Farias was Collor's campaign fund manager during the presidential campaign and remained close to Collor after the election, even though he had no clear function in the cabinet. The press attained some documents about Farias that would soon become a major scandal. Newspapers learned that Farias was in charge of bank accounts and bogus companies that were front organizations for laundering money that had been given in return for government favors. Farias usually collected a 30% commission for every transaction, which he split with his partner, President Collor.[40]

As the press began disclosing documents pointing to bribes and embezzlement in government agencies, cabinet members started resigning. Even the first lady was charged with fraud and with receiving political favors while administering the nation's main charity organization. She resigned from the charity. The scandal known as Collorgate in Brazil, like America's Watergate, involved the disclosures of a slow accumulation of numerous scandals that brought down a presidency.

Brazil's once cowardly media were not intimidated by Collor's attempts to silence critical press coverage. Journalists and media owners were in agreement regarding the need to pursue Collor. The tone of the coverage had a direct link to the family-owned media style that prevails in Brazil. Throughout Brazilian political history newspaper owners did not bother to separate their personal opinions from editorial policy and the news. Furthermore, despite an appreciation for the importance of objectivity in journalism, the notion of objectivity was not ingrained in journalistic culture or always practiced. Whatever influence objectivity had on Brazilian journalism quickly dissipated during periods of political crises such as Collorgate.[41]

## Family Feud

The situation escalated dramatically when Pedro Collor de Mello, the president's brother, offered his dossier on the president's illegal activities to the media. In a long interview to *Veja,* the country's leading weekly newsmagazine, Pedro Collor accused President Collor of being involved in several of Farias's dishonest business deals. Pedro Collor said that his brother and Farias made extravagant trips to foreign countries, created ghost bank accounts under different names, engaged in questionable real estate transactions inside and outside Brazil, and participated in dozens of illegal activities, including possibly drug dealing.[42]

*Veja* exploited the most sensational aspects of Pedro Collor's revelations. Once described by the press as a smart, articulate, aggressive leader and later as an eccentric, impulsive, authoritarian president, President Collor was now depicted in the press as a hypocrite, villain, and drug and sex addict. The coverage lacked objectivity and impartiality, because the press actively sought to bring down the president. The testimony of the first source on the record about the case offered no substantial proof of the president's alleged wrongdoing, but that did not seem to matter to news organizations at that point. It seemed only a matter of time until a news organization would acquire documents proving the case against the president. Pedro Collor had his own agenda in his campaign against his brother. The president's brother offered information on the government's corruption to *Veja* after discovering that President Collor and Farias were planning to launch a rival newspaper and over a dozen radio stations to compete with the family-owned media conglomerate in northeast Brazil, controlled by Pedro Collor.

*Veja* depicted the unfolding scandal as a family drama, a war between the brothers. The story resembled Brazil's popular prime time television soap operas that rivet the attention of millions of Brazilians every day. Pedro Collor revealed more and more lurid accusations against his brother, even accusing him of trying to seduce his wife while a governor in Alagoas state.

The word "impeachment" started to crop up in the media and in conversations among Brazilians of all social classes. Soon, *Veja* found more reliable government sources to incriminate the president, increasing its coverage of the case. *Isto É,* then the second largest weekly newsmagazine, published an interview with Francisco Eriberto França, the chauffeur of Collor's private secretary, Ana Aciolly. In exchange for protection and a small amount of money asked for by his wife, França told *Isto É* that President Collor routinely received checks and cash from a company owned by Farias, called Brasil Jet. França later confirmed to the Congressional Commission what he said to *Isto É*. On the eve of Collor's impeachment, news organizations portrayed França as a national hero, Farias as a gangster, and the president as an arrogant, unstable ruler.

News values used by the press during the Collorgate scandal were modified to fit the news organizations' political agendas. There are three points worth noting to explain why the press aggressively pursued Collor. First, the news organizations advocated Collor's impeachment to send the state a message: that the news media in the new democratic Brazil was going to be a watchdog of government actions. Second, the media reaffirmed the return of press freedom by confronting the state in a democratic environment free from government censorship, confiscation, harassment, or prosecution. Third, the media viewed the Collorgate scandal as a successful marketing strategy for increasing circulation and advertising sales.

The Congress voted on impeachment on 29 December 1992 in an open session broadcast live on all television channels. The impeachment was approved by 441 to 38 votes. Instead of tearing the country apart, as many had predicted, the vote brought the country together and temporarily restored Brazilians' self-esteem. Despite the disgrace to Collor, the impeachment affirmed that Brazil was a functioning democracy where political problems could be corrected by legal, constitutional means and where the press could and indeed should contribute to this corrective process.

## JOURNALISM AFTER COLLORGATE

The Collorgate episode reinvigorated the media and empowered journalists. News organizations temporarily attained credibility in the eyes of the public. The impeachment was a turning point in Brazilian journalism. On the positive side it encouraged news organizations and journalists to overcome any lingering fear from the authoritarian tradition that had defined Brazilian politics for many decades. It consolidated the media's belief that it had a watchdog function to bark when it believed the political system was not functioning properly. On the negative side Collorgate developed the media's hunger for scandal to realms beyond national politics.[43] After Collorgate the media was accused of being superficial, aggressive, and pessimistic.[44]

## DISCUSSION

In this chapter I have provided an overview of how journalistic values, roles, and routines interact with social and institutional forces. The overview focused on the crucial relationship between the media and the state in Brazil during different political periods and on how the state helped define the news-making process during the different periods. If media-government relationships in Brazil bear some similarity to those in the United States, especially after the period of democratization and the Collorgate scandal, which was eerily similar to America's Watergate, this underscores the global journalistic culture. A global journalistic culture does not mean that the media operate the same everywhere, but it does highlight shared values that influence practices. To cite a few shared values, Brazilian journalists at least give lip service to notions of fairness, accuracy, objectivity, and the media's role in a democratic society. These values have been transplanted to Brazil in recent decades but have an ambivalent meaning there for several reasons: ideology, democratization, and the Brazilian media model. I discuss each reason in the following sections.

### Ideology

In the United States journalistic values are implicit and parallel the values held by American society. These values include belief in the capitalist system, private ownership, and the pursuit of profit and free markets.[45] Along with the Protestant work ethic and the emphasis on individual achievement, American society is both pragmatic (a "can do" society) and utilitarian (things are good if they are useful)—values inherited from British rationalists.[46] In Brazil transplanted American journalistic values coexist with Brazilian society's own values. These include the ancient Greek and Latin traditions of an abstract knowledge based on speculation and rhetoric. Following the Iberian colonial legacy, Brazilian society remains paternalistic, authoritarian, hierarchical, and elitist.[47] The nation's sociocultural tradition embodies archaic and repressive social relations that refuse to go away.[48]

## Democracy and Development

There is more than one route to democracy. Although Brazil has completed its transition from authoritarianism to political democracy, it is still far from achieving socioeconomic and cultural democratization. Political democracy was achieved with the election and subsequent reelection of President Fernando Henrique Cardoso, in power since 1994. However, political scientists point out that continuities from the old order and the old ways persist into the present. The state bureaucracy retains tremendous power over most aspects of social life. National cabinet posts are still awarded to satisfy state quotas and to gain supporters. Political parties are weak. In addition, underprivileged voters still solicit home repairs or lunch for their families as payment for their votes when approaching party candidates.[49]

Another continuity is the existence of a press law, the same one created by the military. The Congress has discussed a proposed new press law since 1991. Although the proposed new press law eliminates prison sentences for offenses, it proposes excessive compensations for libel. The excessive libel punishments could cause small news organizations to go bankrupt. This would allow the government, even in democratic Brazil, to harass and silence a critical press. Besides, the proposed new press law does not eliminate the possibility of confiscating editions and suspending broadcast transmissions in unspecified situations.[50]

Nonetheless, as long as Brazil advances the consolidation of democracy, press freedom can only advance. As press theorist John C. Merrill argued, "The journalism of a nation cannot lag far behind the general development and values of the society, nor can it exceed the limits permitted by the society."[51] Despite lip service to the importance of journalistic objectivity, Brazilian journalists are not convinced that journalism should be impartial. Brazilian journalists today tend to favor an interpretive-investigative role, according to a 1998 survey of 400 journalists in São Paulo.[52] Although 46.5% of the survey respondents strongly agree that they are more effective when they take an impartial view of events, almost 40% strongly agree that their role is to help to transform society and to participate directly in the democratic process.

Finally, Brazil needs to address how democracy can thrive in an environment where many people's most basic living needs are not met. Democratization is invisible to many Brazilians who live in poverty and lack access to education and the health system.

## Media Model

Although there are no fixed models of professional journalism, the Brazilian case suggests an intriguing combination of foreign journalistic influences and local cultural and social traditions. Journalist Mino Carta, who played a crucial role in the

Collorgate scandal as director of the weekly newsmagazine *Isto É,* believes that Brazil has developed a caricature of American journalism: "There has been a distortion of some American lessons. Our model is inspired [by] *USA Today,* a newspaper you read in airplanes, that does not really inform you. Newspapers such as the *New York Times* have little influence in Brazil. . . . There is a general misunderstanding about American concepts of journalism."[53]

Media critic Alberto Dines shares a similar opinion: "Journalism in Brazil is a caricature of the American model because it clones superficial aspects. In the past some papers cloned French newspapers, such as *Libération.* Today newspapers face an identity crisis. There is no diversity."[54] These opinions, formulated by two leading Brazilian journalists, indicate that media workers and owners have a lot of homework to do in order to build a unique and distinguishing journalism tradition.

In sum, the progression of Brazilian journalism is bound to the interaction of media institutions with the social-political environment. During military rule, the media were locked into the power structure. During the New Republic, culminating in Collorgate, the media evolved into a semi-independent power in dealing with other social and institutional forces, especially the state. A third stage, with the media enjoying a greater degree of autonomy from the state and other social institutions, may be achieved when Brazil becomes a fully democratic society, breaking away from the old authoritarian and hierarchical social structure. An independent, fair, and accurate journalism depends as well on the development of the nation both socially and economically. In the process of remaking itself, Brazil may be able to define its own media model and close the gap between transplanted journalistic values and routines and domestic social and institutional forces.

## NOTES

1. See Wei Wu, David Weaver, and Owen V. Johnson, "Professional Roles of Russian and U.S. Journalists: A Comparative Study," *Journalism and Mass Communication Quarterly* 73 (autumn 1996): 534–548; Jian-Hua Zhu, David Weaver, Ven-Hwei Lo, Chong-shan Chen, and Wei Wu, "Individual, Organizational, and Societal Influences on Media Role Perceptions: A Comparative Study of Journalists in China, Taiwan, and the United States," *Journalism and Mass Communication Quarterly* 74 (spring 1997): 84–96; and Heloiza G. Herscovitz and Adalberto Cardoso, "The Brazilian Journalist," in David Weaver, ed., *The Global Journalist* (Cresskill, NJ: Hampton Press, 1998), 417–432.

2. Danton Jobim, "French and U.S. Influences upon the Latin American Press," *Journalism Quarterly* 31 (1954): 61–66.

3. Heloiza G. Herscovitz, "Similarities in News Values Between U.S. and Latin American Mass Media Models," *International Communication Bulletin* 28 (fall 1993): 13–16.

4. David Manning White, "The Gatekeeper: A Case Study in the Selection of News," *Journalism Quarterly* 27 (summer 1950): 383–390. Warren Breed, "Social Control in the Newsroom," *Social Forces* 33 (May 1955): 326–335.

5. For a critique of Breed's study and an overview of media sociology, see Stephen D. Reese, Jane Ballinger, and Pamela Shoemaker, "The Roots of Media Sociology: Mr. Gates and Social Control in the Newsroom," paper presented at the annual meeting of the Association for Education in Journalism and Mass Communication, Kansas City, Mo., 1993.

6. James Curran, Michael Gurevitch, and Janet Woollacott, "The Study of the Media: Theoretical Approaches," in Michael Gurevitch, Tony Bennett, James Curran, and Janet Woollacott, eds., *Culture, Society, and the Media* (London: Methuen, 1982), 11–29.

7. For a detailed explanation, see Gurevitch et al., *Culture, Society, and the Media;* and Marjorie Ferguson and Peter Golding, *Cultural Studies in Question* (London: Sage, 1997).

8. See José Marques de Melo, "Communication Theory and Research in Latin America: A Preliminary Balance of the Past Twenty-Five Years," *Media, Culture, and Society* 10 (1988): 405–418; Jesus Martin-Barbero, "Communication from Culture: The Crisis of the National and the Emergence of the Popular," *Media, Culture, and Society* 10 (1988): 447–465; Steven H. Chaffee, Carlos Gomez-Palacio, and Everett M. Rogers, "Mass Communication Research in Latin America: Views from Here and There," *Journalism Quarterly* 67 (winter 1990): 1015–1024.

9. Gurevitch et al., *Culture, Society, and the Media,* 1–3.

10. To read about how intellectual positions can live in happy contradiction, see James W. Carey, "Reflections on the Project of American Cultural Studies," in Marjorie Ferguson and Peter Golding, eds., *Cultural Studies in Question* (London: Sage, 1997), 1–24.

11. Gurevitch et al., *Culture, Society, and the Media,* 11–29.

12. Paul M. Hirsch, "Occupational, Organizational, and Institutional Models in Mass Media Research: Toward an Integrated Framework," in Paul M. Hirsch, P. V. Miller, and F. G. Kline, eds., *Strategies for Communication Research* (Newbury Park, CA: Sage, 1977), 1–28.

13. Information provided by Empresa Metropolitana de Planejamento da Grande São Paulo (São Paulo Metropolitan Company of Planning, Emplasa), available at http://www.emplasa.sp.gov.br (September 1999).

14. Information provided by the Instituto Brasileiro de Geografia e Estatística (Brazilian Institute of Geography and Statistics;

IBGE), available at http://www.ibge.gov.br (September 1999).

15. Anne-Marie Smith, *A Forced Agreement: Press Acquiescence to Censorship in Brazil* (Pittsburgh, PA: University of Pittsburgh Press, 1997), 191.

16. James Malloy, "Authoritarianism and Corporatism in Latin America: The Modal Pattern," in Roderic Aí Camp, ed., *Democracy in Latin America* (Wilmington, DE: Scholarly Resources, 1996), 129.

17. For an explanation of Latin American politics, see James Malloy, "Authoritarianism and Corporatism in Latin America," 121–137. For a thorough overview of theories on development and politics in Latin America, see Peter F. Klarén, "Lost Promise: Explaining Latin American Underdevelopment," in Roderic Aí Camp, ed., *Democracy in Latin America* (Wilmington, DE: Scholarly Resources, 1996), 91–120.

18. Guillermo O'Donnell, "Transitions, Continuities, and Paradoxes," in Scott Mainwaring, Guillermo O'Donnell, and J. Samuel Valenzuela, eds., *Issues in Democratic Consolidation* (Notre Dame, IN: University of Notre Dame Press, 1992), 44.

19. Ruth B. Collier and David Collier, *Shaping the Political Arena: Critical Junctures, the Labor Movement, and Regime Dynamics in Latin America* (Princeton, NJ: Princeton University Press, 1991).

20. Smith, *A Forced Agreement.*

21. Ibid., 42.

22. Ibid., 22.

23. Jair Lot Vieira, ed., *Lei de Imprensa, Profissão de Jornalista* (São Paulo: Jalovi, 1989).

24. Fernando Jorge, *Cale a Boca Jornalista!* [Shut Your Mouth, Journalist!] (Petropolis, Brazil: Vozes, 1987), 98.

25. Jorge, *Cale a Boca Jornalista!* 109.

26. Ibid., 102. Jorge, a journalist himself, recounts many cases of journalists who suffered torture, such as that of reporter Antonio Carlos Fon, then working for *Jornal da Tarde.* Carlos Fon spent 17 days at a military facility in São Paulo, where he faced sessions of beating and electric shocks. The worse case of harassment by the military occurred in October 1975, when journalist Vladimir Herzog, who worked for a public

television station in São Paulo, died under torture. Officials claimed that Herzog had confessed to being a communist and then had committed suicide. However, the photo distributed by the police and further investigations indicated that Herzog did not hang himself. His funeral was attended by thousands of people in an event that marked a turning point in society's protest against the military.

27. Jorge, *Cale a Boca Jornalista!* 108.

28. Joan R. Dassin, "Press Censorship and the Military State in Brazil," in Jane Leftwich Curry and Joan R. Dassin, eds., *Press Control Around the World* (New York: Praeger, 1982), 149–185.

29. Alberto Dines, *O Papel do Jornal* [The Role of the Newspaper] (São Paulo: Summus, 1982), 135.

30. Smith, *A Forced Agreement,* 154–157.

31. Dines, *O Papel do Jornal,* 135–138. Topics under censorship included student protests, labor strikes, disputes between the military and the Catholic Church, living conditions, publicity about communist nations, foreign and domestic criticism of government, state treatment of indigenous populations, prison conditions and torture of political prisoners, and news about homosexuality, drugs, and prostitution.

32. Smith, *A Forced Agreement,* 138. The black book reproduces other written orders prohibiting news about torture, newspaper confiscations, certain Catholic bishops, outbreaks of hemorrhagic fever and meningitis, the quality of frozen meat, pipeline leaks, and even the adherence of Patricia Hearst to a terrorist group in the United States.

33. Elizabeth Fox, *Latin American Broadcasting: From Tango to Telenovela* (Luton, United Kingdom: University of Luton Press, 1997), 63.

34. Ibid., 63.

35. O'Donnell, "Transitions, Continuities, and Paradoxes"; Frances Hagopian, "The Compromised Consolidation: The Political Class in the Brazilian Transition," in Scott Mainwaring, Guillermo O'Donnell, and J. Samuel Valenzuela, eds., *Issues in Democratic Consolidation* (Notre Dame, IN: University of Notre Dame Press, 1992), 30, 259.

36. Personal recollection. I participated in the coverage of Neves' death for *O Estado de S. Paulo.*

37. Testimony of journalist José Hamilton Ribeiro, in Cremilda Medina, ed., *O Jornalismo na Nova República* [Journalism in the New Republic] (São Paulo: Summus, 1987), 140–146.

38. Carlos Eduardo Lins da Silva, *O Adiantado da Hora, A Influencia Americana Sobre o Jornalismo Brasileiro* [The American Influence on Brazilian Journalism] (São Paulo: Summus, 1991), 100.

39. Fernando Lattman-Weltman, José Alan Dias Carneiro, and Plínio de Abreu Ramos, *A Imprensa Faz e Desfaz Um Presidente* [The Press Create and Destroy a President] (Rio de Janeiro: Nova Fronteira, 1994), 53.

40. Tom Bosque, "Looking Back at Collor, Part II," available at http://www.brazil-brasil.com (October 1996).

41. That was the case in 1954, when President Getulio Vargas committed suicide amid a massive press campaign accusing him of corruption and power misuse; in 1964, when the press urged the military to overthrow President João Goulart; in 1994, during the campaign for direct presidential elections; and in 1992, when the press engendered its own Watergate. An example of the media's crusade was *Folha de S. Paulo's* open letter from publisher Otavio Frias Filho to President Collor on the paper's front page in April 1991 criticizing the president for

impoverishing the population, selling the illusion national problems would be solved instantly, violating the Constitution, humiliating the Congress, and throwing the country in deep recession. . . . *Folha* approved your policy against inflation. The newspaper agrees with your ideas about the privatization of public companies, the reduction of the role of the state, the fight against social inequities, . . . the integration of Brazil in the international market. Practically, there is more convergence than divergence between the newspaper's beliefs and yours. The problem is the gap between what you say and what your government does. (Lattman-Weltman et al., *A Imprensa Faz e Desfaz Um Presidente,* 84–85).

42. Tom Bosque, content available at http://www.brazil-brasil.com.

43. In March 1994 newspapers and TV stations reported that six people were accused of sexually abusing children at a private elementary school in a middle-class neighborhood of São Paulo. The press relied on the accusation brought by the mother of a child enrolled in the school. Before this, cases of sexual abuse were seldom reported in the media. The topic was long considered taboo among Brazilians. The case, known as Escola Base, was proved false. Medical exams revealed that the abuse never happened. The coverage of Escola Base was a major embarrassment for the press. It revealed the media's eagerness to act as a moral agent based on the slightest evidence. The case is recalled in a book by a journalist who covered it: Alex Ribeiro, *Caso Escola Base: Os Abusos da Imprensa* [The Base School: The Press Abuses] (São Paulo: Ática, 1995).

44. In a national poll of 790 Brazilians conducted by the Institute Vox Populi in November 1997, respondents pointed out several main problems with the media: (1) 57% said that the media make accusations without evidence; (2) 41% said that the media violate people's privacy; (3) 36% said that the media neglect important information in their stories; and (4) 35% accused the media of favoring issues according to the news organizations' own interests. Respondents ranked their degree of distrust regarding professional categories: 40% said they distrusted journalists along with judges, and 42% said they distrusted media owners. The degree of suspicion toward journalists and media owners is superseded by the respondents' distrust of Congress (92%), state secretaries (88%), and business owners (51%). Data from Federação Nacional dos Jornalistas (National Federation of Journalists; FENAJ), *Jornal do Jornalista,* available at http://www.fenaj.org.br./jornal (November 1997).

45. Pamela Shoemaker and Stephen D. Reese, *Mediating the Message: Theories of Influence on Mass Media Content* (New York: Longman, 1981), 184.

46. For an in-depth analysis of the philosophical roots of American journalism, see J. Herbert Altschull, *From Milton to McLuhan: The Ideas Behind American Journalism* (New York: Longman, 1990).

47. Robert N. Pierce, *Keeping the Flame: Media and Government in Latin America* (New York: Hastings House, 1979).

48. O'Donnell, "Transitions, Continuities, and Paradoxes," 42.

49. Hagopian, "The Compromised Consolidation," 280.

50. Luis F. Carvalho Filho, "Lei de Imprensa, Projeto é Inibidor, Mal Redigido e Corporativo" [Press Law: The Project Inhibits Bad Writing and Corporatism], *Folha de S. Paulo* (23 October 1997), available at http://www.uol.com.br/fsp/brasil/fc231031.htm.

51. John C. Merrill, *The Dialectic in Journalism: Toward a Responsible Use of Press Freedom* (Baton Rouge, LA: Louisiana State University Press, 1989).

52. Heloiza G. Herscovitz, "A Portrait of Journalists of São Paulo, Brazil: Who They Are and What They Think About Their Profession Compared to American and French Journalists," Ph.D. diss., University of Florida, 2000.

53. Interview with journalist Mino Carta (May 1998).

54. Interview with journalist Alberto Dines (May 1998).

# PART IV

# Colonialism and Mass
# Media Development

During the last years of the nineteenth century, the more powerful European nations, led by Great Britain and France, acquired many territories in Africa and Asia, making this period before World War I an age of imperialism. Although there are few colonies today, the colonial legacy still affects these countries' cultures. The territories thus acquired now comprise most of the areas of the world now thought of as the Third World, or developing countries. The two chapters in this part consider themes representative of this colonial legacy. Leaders and apologists for colonialism in Europe and the West justified their domination by referring to these African and Asian territories as backward and lacking in modern trappings of civilization. Such justifications often used, either openly or implicitly, racist or superior attitudes toward the peoples and cultures of these regions. World War II, however, brought a quick decline and end to the Great Power status of the dominant colonial states, and most of the colonies consequently were seen as on the road to eventual political independence.

The colonial legacy, represented by the early paradigm of development communication discussed in Chapter 8 and by the colonial discourse described in Chapter 9, continued to influence communication in Africa in particular. In short, such discourse assumes Western superiority and right to rule over "inferior" African peoples and institutions. Colonial discourse, as with colonialism in general, assumes that the standard to which all nations and civilizations aspire is the model of modern Western industrial democracies represented by Western Europe and the United States.

In the first chapter of this part William W. Neher, of Butler University, follows the development of attitudes concerning the role of mass communication in national development from an approach akin to colonial discourse to today's view, which is more decentralized and more non-Western. As the colonies of Africa neared independence following World War II, Western academics, development officials, and governments turned their attention more to the process of ameliorating economic, health, and social conditions. The colonial assumption, however, still held sway—that is, that education, health care, industrial development, and political institutions should follow Western models, especially models from the United States and Western Europe.

Western theorists assumed that modern media spurred development in Third World nations. Early works of development communication, represented by such theorists as Daniel Lerner and Wilbur Schramm, proclaimed that mass communication and the development of modern media could multiply the effects of economic development and allow the new nations of Africa to leapfrog the early stages of development, industrialization, and modernization. The use of these terms should be seen as indicative of the kinds of assumptions being made, that the Western or the modern ways were true ideals for the peoples of Africa.

Neher analyzes the disappointments that followed this early paradigm of development communication, touching on explanations of the difficulties of development communication and media use in Africa. Neher also considers the evolution of the concepts of development communication and Everett Rogers's theories concerning the diffusion of innovations. The failures of centralized media and communication programs to further development led to the creation of new paradigms emphasizing equity in the distribution of benefits of economic and communication development, "small media" (i.e., indigenous communication systems and traditional media of communication), and more recognition of the role of traditional leaders and institutions in decision making at the local level.

Neher also provides a brief summary and analysis of the state of traditional and mass media in Africa today. The hopes for and limitations on the use of radio and television are discussed. The last section deals with telematics, wireless or cellular communication systems (such as e-mail), database sharing, and similar electronic networks, given international legal and commercial restrictions.

In the second chapter of this part Michael B. Salwen, of the University of Miami, analyzes Western news coverage of the Italian invasion of Ethiopia in 1935, using the analytical tool of colonial discourse. Salwen uses the war reports of novelist Evelyn Waugh, who covered the Italian invasion as a correspondent for the London *Daily Mail,* to illustrate the meaning of colonial discourse. Salwen then turns to a contemporary example of this sort of discourse: Robert D. Kaplan's travel descriptions in his book, *The Ends of the Earth.* Although not racist, Kaplan's book still exhibits some of the basic assumptions of what Salwen characterizes as colonial discourse and underscores that colonial discourse often enters our modern journalistic parlance.

# 8

# Development Communication in Africa

## Concepts and Case Studies

WILLIAM W. NEHER

Development communication assumes that communication, especially mass communication, can assist in furthering a nation's economic and social growth, or national development. Examining this topic requires an understanding of what is meant by national development and the role of communication in development. In the first part of the chapter I deal with the evolution of the concept of development; in the second part I cover the changing paradigms of development communication; and in the third part I bring the discussion down to the level of existing problems and prospects of the communication media in Africa and their potential for bringing about national development. As the concepts about development changed, ideas about development communication also changed. The current state of affairs regarding mass communication in Africa is thus framed in terms of this changing paradigm of development communication.

Feeling the optimism of the era of independence for new sub-Saharan African states in the 1960s, many government leaders and experts assumed that mass communication, especially Western-style and electronic media, would hasten national development in the new states. That early hope was overly optimistic, even naive, as later events came to demonstrate. In fact, over the last 30 years, our understanding of what development even means and the role that the media play in furthering it have changed dramatically.

In its simplest terms the word "development" connotes modernization and progress and other such ostensibly desirable goals in developing nations. The concept is much more complex, however, as will be seen. In addition, development is not always as desirable as it at first appears. It is necessary to understand the meaning of "development" and the various connotations and ideological baggage associated with the term. Similarly, ideas concerning the ways that communication, especially the mass media, can assist development have changed over the years. Today, the proliferation of so-called new media, associated with computer-mediated communication and electronic and digitized telecommunication systems, has raised hopes again of a communication revolution that will accelerate national development in Africa. The combined effects of new media and globalization of communication systems and networks lead to a host of significant issues and controversies facing developing countries throughout the world but especially in Africa.

In this chapter I cover the following three themes in development communication: (1) the evolution of the meaning of national development, (2) the functions of communication in national development in Africa, and (3) the state of media and development communication systems in Africa.

## EVOLUTION OF THE
## MEANING OF NATIONAL DEVELOPMENT

The concept of development derives from the notion of the developed countries (such as the United States or countries in Western Europe) in contrast to the underdeveloped, or developing, nations, usually in Africa and parts of Asia and Latin America. Developed countries typically exhibit industrialized economies and infrastructures and democratic political systems. Underdeveloped countries, on the other hand, are poor, lack a modern infrastructure or economy, and usually do not have a democratic system. The use of the term "national development" assumes that progress is the natural state of affairs and that all nations are expected to follow a similar positive evolutionary path, allowing for potentially invidious comparisons and hidden value judgments about material wealth and cultural practices. At least in the Western world, these values and assumptions were taken for granted after World War II, when African leaders and Western academics and statesmen looked forward to new African nations that would emulate the industrialized American or European model.

The colonialist ideology had justified European control of African countries on the basis of this supposed ideal of Westernized development. A recent study of the nationalist movement in Kenya describes this colonialist mentality of development as justification for domination of African peoples:

> The general opinion of the colonial authorities continued to be that Africans were bound to benefit from colonial rule. Colonialism, so it was argued, had brought with it the benefits of education, religion, modern commerce, and

government, and it had rendered the invaluable service of drawing Africans into the mainstream of human civilization and away from the pervasive barbarism which had hitherto enveloped the African continent. So long as this line of argument was maintained, it was impossible for the colonial state to sanction the genuine legitimacy of African discontent or nationalistic stirrings.[1]

The key terms associated with this early model of development revolved around the following clusters of terms:

- Modernization, urbanization, industrialization, and Westernization; in short, progress.
- Economic development, economic growth.
- Nation building, national integration.
- Development as diffusion of innovations.

## Development as Modernization

The first cluster of terms—modernization, urbanization, industrialization, Westernization—suggests that it is desirable to be modern. The ideal modern consumers live in large cities, where the individuals are exposed to new products and new lifestyles and to more variety of stimulation. Cities provide a mass market to produce and consume the products of newly established industries. James S. Coleman, in an early influential work on modernization, sums up the intended outcome in the following way:

A modern society is characterized, among other things, by a comparatively high degree of urbanization, widespread literacy, comparatively high per capita income, extensive geographical and social mobility, a relatively high degree of commercialization and industrialization of the economy, an extensive and penetrative network of mass communication media, and, in general, by widespread participation and involvement by members of the society in modern social and economic processes.[2]

Many of the new cities of independent Africa did become sprawling urban areas, but the overcrowding and overwhelmed public services quickly undermined the hope that urbanization necessarily meant development or improved living standards. Later development efforts would even try to stem the flow of people from the countryside to the cities.

## Development as Economic Development

Economic development, the key term of the second cluster of terms, means industrialization and domestic heavy industry, such as steel making, heavy machinery manufacture, and mechanized agriculture. As early as the 1962 publication of René Dumont's famous and influential work *L'afrique noire est mal-partie* (translated as *False Start in Africa* when published in English in 1966), there was a growing realization that these goals were neither practical nor desirable. The model, based on the desirability of promoting heavy industry, led many African states and leaders down the path of dependence on Western suppliers and manufacturers. The huge amounts of capital necessary for such development required dependence on massive amounts of foreign aid from Western nations, mammoth borrowing from Western banks and investors, or both.

This notion of development as modernization and Westernization therefore pitted development against traditional ways of life, which were thought to be risk averse and overly conservative and hence a brake on progress.

## Development as Nation Building

The third set of terms focuses on nation building. This concept suggests a broader notion encompassing political unification and integration as part of national development. During the 1960s and 1970s, *Kujenga taifa* ("to build the nation," or nation building, in Ki Swahili), became a central unifying theme in political communication. The phrase was liberally sprinkled throughout speeches by Jomo Kenyatta (the first president of Kenya) and Julius Nyerere (the first president of Tanzania). Behind the idea of nation building is the idea that national progress requires the creation of a new national identity, in which people accustomed to thinking of themselves in terms of regional, ethnic, or local loyalties begin to think of themselves as Kenyans, Nigerians, or Cameroonians.

Closely related to this idea is the term "national integration," which suggests the overcoming of divisive tendencies of ethnic, religious, or regional identities (the negative term was "tribalism"). The nations of Africa, which received independence after World War II, inherited boundaries laid out usually in Europe following the Berlin Conference of 1884–1885 for the benefit or convenience of the colonial powers. The borders of these new nation-states consequently cut across ethnic groups and lumped together in an artificial political entity a variety of peoples and former nations.

"To build the nation" thus meant to manufacture a national legitimacy and to create a new national market and economy within former colonial boundaries. Clinging to traditional identities and loyalties undermined the creation of the new national patriotism.

## Development as Diffusion of Innovations

The idea of what development was about shifted toward diffusion of innovation. This approach assumes that certain products, techniques, ideas, or innovations introduced into the developing countries allow them to develop more prosperous economies and to improve public services. National or economic development is thus put in the context of a long line of historical diffusions of significant technologies and ideas. Western or modern is not necessarily better because it is Western or modern; rather, certain techniques are better because they allow people to live better lives.

Thus in African history diffusion of innovation and development in this sense are hardly new. One can trace the diffusion of agriculture, the adoption of certain crops, such as plantains or maize, or the diffusion of iron working in earlier historical epochs. These technologies allowed for a historical and African form of economic development and progress, and they proceeded in many different directions, even from Africa to areas now thought of as developed countries.

This notion of development as diffusion of innovations includes the hoped-for green revolution in agriculture as well as the contemporary hopes for new, computerized communication systems. Diffusionist theories have long been associated with the communication theories of Everett M. Rogers and hence are considered in more detail later in this chapter.

## Criticisms of the Standard View of Development

Theorists of national development, disillusioned by the results from attempts at industrialization and modernization, began to question the premises of the standard paradigm. Emphasis began to shift to the notion of sustainable development. The Western model could not be imported as easily or as painlessly as early development proponents had hoped. Now development focused on local grass-roots efforts. In this view equity becomes as important a criterion of progress as raw economic indicators. Development requires the amelioration of disease, ignorance, and poverty along with equitable distribution of material resources. This view of development envisions full political participation, allowing all people to live fuller, more productive lives. Small technologies, renewable resources, and local initiatives become central in the new paradigm of development. Local control becomes more important than national and centralized planning, which had led to an extremely lopsided distribution of wealth and continuing poverty and misery in both urban and rural areas.

The force antagonistic to national development was thus no longer seen as traditional society but rather the dependence on multinational corporations and Westernized elites. This more recent theory of development is closely related therefore to dependency theory, in which states are underdeveloped as a result of historical and current actions by forces at the core of the modern transnational capitalist complex.

# FUNCTIONS OF COMMUNICATION
# IN NATIONAL DEVELOPMENT IN AFRICA

The early paradigm of development communication assumed that mass communication would be a significant multiplier of effects, allowing so-called traditional societies to leapfrog from underdevelopment to development. This viewpoint was first forcefully presented by Daniel Lerner with the publication of his landmark 1958 book on communication and development in the Middle East, *The Passing of Traditional Society.*[3] Godwin C. Chu, former director of the Communications Institute of the East-West Center in Hawaii, describes the significance of this work, calling it a "milestone for the study of communication in development."[4] Lerner's observations in Turkey led him to believe that villagers who were exposed to or who exposed themselves to the messages of modern mass media quickly became dissatisfied with the traditional lifestyle, became more empathetic with a broader spectrum of people, and began to develop a desire for modern things. From a normative perspective Lerner believed that these effects were desirable.

Lerner's views fit comfortably with the early concept of development described in the previous section. He observed, "Increasing urbanization has tended to increase media exposure; increasing media exposure has 'gone with' wider economic participation (higher per capita income) and political participation (voting)."[5] A modern person, according to this view, was mobile and could readily identify with citizens beyond the village. "Empathy, to simplify the matter," Lerner explains, "is the capacity to see oneself in the other fellow's situation. This is an indispensable skill for people moving out of the traditional settings."[6] Mass media allow people to vicariously experience life as lived in cities and even in other nations. For these reasons Lerner posited a relationship between the development of mass media in a society and the modernization of that society. As he put it, a "communication system is both index and agent of change in a total social system."[7] The mass media, particularly radio for Lerner, disrupted traditional values because opinion leaders turned to the new media for their modernizing values.

Wilbur Schramm, a leading communication scholar whom many regard as the founder of the academic study of mass communication, furthered this paradigm of mass communication as a multiplier of national development. Schramm believed that the mass media were a necessary, although not a sufficient, condition for economic development. He referred to the mass media as the great multipliers, and they played the role in a communication revolution that had been played by machines in the Industrial Revolution.[8] Admittedly, other conditions must be present, Schramm pointed out: effective national leadership, sufficient resources, and capital among other things. Nevertheless, Schramm contended that "if the mass media or some equally potent and rapid means of information were not available, it would be utterly impossible to think of national economic and social development in terms of the timetables that are being attached to such development today."[9]

Schramm and Lerner and other influential theorists such as Lucien Pye and Ithiel de Sola Pool thus became the leading figures of the dominant paradigm of mass communication and development. The sequence of development assumed that the individual was influenced by the mass media to adopt certain new attitudes. Individuals who were heavy users of mass media would become opinion leaders and agents for change, influencing their more traditional fellow citizens to become discontented with the old way of doing things.

This dominant paradigm of development communication relied on a linear model of communication effects. Such a model describes the communication process as proceeding from a source encoding a message, which is then transmitted through a channel and received and decoded by some other person. The effectiveness of development communication depended on the careful formulation (encoding) of a message and its dissemination through the most appropriate channels to the receivers. Communication specialists hence were required to determine the ways to improve the capacity of communication channels or to increase their number and effectiveness. It was an easy leap to the conclusion that mass media channels would therefore almost ensure development. In other words, as some critics have pointed out, the Schramm model suggests no specific communication policies; rather, more media and more mass communication channels are good in and of themselves.[10]

In sum, this dominant paradigm of the mass media in development envisioned the media playing the role of facilitator and accelerator of development. This view of the magic multiplier effect of the media, however, was based on misguided notions regarding the meaning of development and the effectiveness of the mass media. One theorist summarized the weakness of this dominant paradigm in the following way:

> By the 1970s, it was clear that the vast majority of people in the developing countries were not benefiting from the numerous capital intensive, industrial growth–based, unilinear communication supported development programs executed in their communities. . . . In fact, the attempt at industrialization caused large-scale migration from the rural areas; technology fostered greater dependency rather than self-reliance; and Western values and behaviors (e.g., high degree of self-interest and individualism) successfully threatened indigenous cultures and social institutions. A simplistic approach to communication in support of development, which was a natural counterpart of the simplistic model of economic development that held sway in the 1960s, had failed.[11]

Disappointed with the results of this early paradigm of development communication, researchers have turned to other theories, such as the diffusion of innovations, an approach briefly mentioned earlier and now examined in more depth.

## Diffusion of Innovations

The diffusionist theories of development, as noted earlier, are associated with the work of Everett M. Rogers and grew out of agricultural extension programs in the United States. One of the earliest studies of diffusion of innovations concerned the adoption of hybrid seed corn by Iowa farmers. These and later studies described the typical S curve of such diffusion. In the early stage of diffusion the slope (indicating the number of people adopting the innovation) is relatively flat, as only the early adopters begin to use the new technology. The slope rapidly increases in the second stage as a majority of users become adopters of the innovation. The curve then begins to flatten out again at the top as the late adopters gradually begin to accept the new practice.

Rogers defined the process in the following way: "Diffusion is the process by which an innovation is communicated through certain channels over time among members of a social system."[12] Hence diffusion of innovation is fundamentally a process of social communication. Rejecting the linear model of communication effects, Rogers preferred the notion of communication as convergence: Two or more people exchange information with one another to come to a new and mutual understanding, especially to determine how the innovation might fit the social and economic fabric of the life and culture of potential adopters of the innovation. This depiction of the diffusion process moves away from the perspective that an outside expert persuades recalcitrant adopters, convincing them that the expert's knowledge is to be accepted wholesale.

Rogers presented several case studies from Africa to indicate the problems with the linear outside-expert view of diffusion communication. The first case described the results of an effort to introduce clean drinking water into villages in the Nile River delta of Egypt.[13] The advantages of clean drinking water seem so obvious that development planners might assume that people would readily take to this innovation. In fact, the new technology came into a system of already existing practices and expectations. First, the program was oversold by politicians who wished to direct the new water to all areas of the delta at once because of its political popularity; but the effort was beyond the country's financial and technical resources. Second, villagers preferred to leave the taps open to have access to constantly running water. The consequence of these factors was that water pressure could not be maintained; people had to stand in long lines to obtain sufficient water from the dripping faucets. The water was furthermore seen as a boon for religious purposes because of the Muslim injunction to perform ablutions before prayer with pure water, placing a further strain on the pressure problems. The village women, the main water gatherers, preferred to wash clothes and pots in the polluted canals because of the social enjoyment of being with other women. The technology for bringing drinking water to the villages, in other words, was not well adapted to the actual daily lives of the delta peoples.

Several recent tragedies in the Niger River delta region of Nigeria exhibit some similarities to this case. In one instance people gathered at certain points along a petroleum pipeline to siphon petrol for cooking fuel, motorbikes, and other uses. In more than one instance, in the chaos of people gathered around a spilling tap on the line (probably an illegal and unsafe tap), a fire was ignited, leading to an explosion and the deaths of hundreds of people. Although these disasters resulted from an unplanned innovation, they stemmed from people adopting new technologies that depended on the use of petrol in the absence of a workable system for providing the fuel.

A better-known case deals with the introduction of formula and bottle feeding into the Third World. This innovation was advertised in a way associating bottle feeding with modern sophistication (harking back to the theories of Lerner and Schramm). The problem, again, was that the innovation was introduced into an existing pattern of behavior and resources. Lacking safe drinking water, mothers would mix formula with polluted water from rivers or canals. They further lacked the resources for keeping the bottles antiseptic. The result was increased infant mortality from diarrhea and dehydration. Diffusion researchers had to turn to campaigns to persuade mothers to return to breast feeding.

These cases make Rogers's point that diffusion communication and hence development communication must be transactional rather than linear. Transactional communication implies a two-way give-and-take process of communication in which the proponent of an innovation or technology communicates with potential adopters to understand their real needs and the needs of the larger social system. Transactional communication implies that the two communicators mutually influence each other continually during the interaction.

## New Paradigm of Development Communication

The reformulation of a new paradigm of development communication should take account of the following considerations: equity in the distribution of the benefits of development, indigenous communication systems, and traditional roles of leadership.

**Equity in Distribution of the Benefits of Development**  In many countries members of the Westernized elites are often the main consumers of modern mass media. Their advantageous location in the social and political system allows them to benefit more quickly from development projects, thus widening rather than narrowing the gap between rich and poor. In the case of the effort to bring pure drinking water to the Nile delta, Rogers observed that the more wealthy members of the elite were able to purchase metered water service with pumps, allowing them to maintain sufficient water pressure in the lines for their own use. In the old paradigm of "more is better," planners could overlook the effects of development programs resulting in poor distribution, further exacerbating tensions in developing states.

**Indigenous Communication Systems**  Western experts naturally looked to forms of mass media that were familiar to them: radio, television, films, newspapers, magazines, and books. The Lerner-Schramm view particularly emphasized radio, which is a one-way top-down medium favoring centralized governmental control. Indigenous sources of development communication for, say, health matters could include midwives, herbalists, and traditional healers. Such traditional healers and herbalists play a particularly important role among the Shona people of Zimbabwe, for example. Credible local organizations, such as age sets or rites of passage groups, ancestor groups, or groups similar to *Asafo* (warrior) companies in Ghana, should be brought into the communication process concerning new technologies and their adaptations to local conditions. Such groups could use traditional media, such as plays, songs, drumming, proverbs, and stories, presented in marketplaces, shrines, or local gathering places.[14]

In Ghana, for example, various indigenous communication events can provide opportunities for interpersonal communication to further development projects and goals. The Akan language of Ghana even has a term for such settings, *gyeduase,* referring to the shade of a tree (a traditional meeting place for communication), a veranda, or an artisan's workshop. In addition, appropriate messages could be incorporated into ceremonies and celebrations, village games, and the singing that accompanies these occasions. Village dramas and dancing as well as traditional storytelling and poetry reciting provide similar opportunities.[15]

**Traditional Roles of Leadership**  Recall that in the original paradigms of both national development and development communication there was a dichotomy between the modern, meaning developed, and the traditional, implying backward. In fact, in many parts of Africa traditional leaders and rulers are in the forefront of efforts to develop locally based, small, but practicable development projects. In rural Ghana traditional rulers, such as the *Omanhene* of Obo-Kwahu in the eastern region of Ghana, stockpile building materials in their enclosures and palaces. Officials at the palace of the *Asantehene* in Kumasi, the traditional ruler of all the Asante of Ghana, clearly exhibit a real interest in viable development projects on a larger scale. Such traditional authorities and leaders are typically much closer to the rural people and have a more genuine interest in the welfare of local people than do highly trained experts in capital cities.

This new concept of development communication thus emphasizes localization, widened political participation, and community-level decision making. Communication planning would thus rely on both the mass media and localized, indigenous communication systems and locally credible sources.[16] Furthermore, earlier theories of development communication did not take into account more recent developments in telecommunications and in interactive computer-based communication technologies, which are discussed later in this chapter.

The shift from the older paradigm of development communication of the 1960s to the newer paradigm began with the approach presented in the discussion of development support communication, sometimes referred to as development journalism. The latter term suggests journalism that is allied with state objectives in promoting development projects sponsored by the government.

An obvious tension exists between this view of journalists as promoters and advocates for certain policies and the more typical role assigned to journalists in the West, that of watchdogs of authority and critics of state policies. The press and radio service in Kenya, for example, headlined stories extolling *harambee* projects throughout the country. *Harambee* ("Let us pull together" in Ki Swahili) was the slogan for nation building during the administration of President Kenyatta in the 1960s and 1970s, and *harambee* projects were local development efforts, such as drilling wells, building new schools, and constructing roads. Many of these news stories were therefore positive depictions of these projects. Traditionally trained journalists naturally expressed skepticism about whether such advocacy was a legitimate function of news media.

More broadly, development support communication has been defined as a planned change strategy using traditional communication and mass communication media in alleviating development problems in Africa and the Third World in general. Childers, following his experience with the United Nations Development Program, explicated the concept in this way:

> Development support communication is a discipline in development planning, an implementation in which more adequate account is taken of human behavioral factors in the design of development projects and their objectives. Then, on the basis of behavioral analysis and the development of a feasible design, the requirements for technical human communication are built into that project as part of its plan of operation and budget.[17]

Development support communication is thus part of the general development planning process. This view places development communication in a more specific, restricted role than the broader theories of mass media as multipliers, as presented in the theories of Lerner and Schramm.

## Summary of Changing Views
## of Development Communication

Twenty years after the publication of *Mass Media and National Development,* Schramm was asked to prepare a supplementary report for the MacBride Commission's work on communication and Third World development, a program sponsored by the United Nations Educational, Scientific, and Cultural Organization (UNESCO) in the late 1970s. Schramm realized that the earlier optimism about mass media as multipliers was overstated. He further acknowledged the new fundamental importance of local self-reliance and the value of preserving traditional cultural values in development programs. Small media, he recognized, could be more significant than national systems of mass media.[18] In the next section I turn to the question of the state of development of both small and mass media in Africa.

# MEDIA AND COMMUNICATION SYSTEMS
# IN AFRICA: PROBLEMS AND PROSPECTS

In this section I examine the current state of communication systems in Africa in view of what is in place to further the goals of development communication.

After World War II the United Nations, through its specialized agencies, took up the question of the development of information systems and media in the Third World. UNESCO was directed to study the communication needs of underdeveloped countries. In 1948 the organization began studying communication services in the Third World. The organization's first report to the General Assembly on the state of mass communication in underdeveloped nations, in 1961, gave a fairly clear idea of the state of development of the mass media in Africa and other areas of the Third World.[19]

UNESCO's surveys of the needs and the existing facilities for mass communication in Africa revealed, to no one's surprise, that the needs were great. In the 1970s some of the members of UNESCO became convinced that, beyond the need for technical assistance and training of journalists and communication specialists, the major problem was the imbalance in information flow and control between the industrialized West and the Third World. The concern over this imbalance led to calls for a new world information order, officially presented in the New World Information and Communication Order, which was based on an earlier call for a new world economic order. The UNESCO studies of mass communication in underdeveloped countries thus became politicized and led to controversy between UNESCO and, especially, the Reagan administration in the United States.

The UNESCO surveys concentrated on the traditional mass media of the press and broadcast media and set standards for developed communication systems in statistical terms, such as newspaper distribution and radio or television sets per capita. These standards included the following: 100 newspapers per 1,000 population, 50 radio receivers per 1,000 population, 20 cinema seats per 1,000 population, and 20 television sets per 1,000 population.

The term "media of communication" covers a much wider range, however. A catalog of media or communication systems in Africa includes traditional or indigenous media; the press, newspapers, and news agencies; postal systems; telephony, telecommunications, and fax capability; publishing; radio broadcasting and journalism; television; film and cinema; libraries; satellite broadcasting and reception and direct satellite television; reproduction technologies, reprography, and taping (audio and video); and computer-mediated communication [i.e., e-mail, Internet, and networks; electronic publishing and databases; and computerized data flow (for banking, insurance, and commercial transactions)].

A survey of the state of these media in each African state would far exceed the space allotted for this chapter. It is more feasible to highlight the condition of the major media systems in broad strokes, with an eye toward indicating the directions that need to be taken for furthering development objectives. To understand the media situation in Africa, it is probably most useful to concentrate on the following media:

1.  The influence of traditional modes of communication on modern communication.

2.  The role of the press and the broadcast mass media.

3.  The growing significance of telematics, that is, the convergence of telecommunications, computer networks, cable systems, and wireless systems.

## Traditional or Indigenous Media

One of the most comprehensive treatments of traditional media in Africa is the 1981 book by Leonard Doob, *Communication in Africa*.[20] This wide-ranging study attempted to delineate all the variables that have been relevant to communication among African peoples. Such variables, or media for communication, include body shape or appearance; changes effected on the body, such as scarification, piercing, or painting; uses of clothes, hair, ornamentation, and insignia; and dancing, drumming, singing, and storytelling.

In a more recent study of media in Africa, Bourgault includes precolonial media, emphasizing the oral nature of traditional African communications. Bourgault suggests that the oral tradition has significantly shaped modes of expression in modern media, so that speeches by government officials or press reports follow a conversational, oral pattern rather than the more formal patterns of expression characteristic of Western communications.[21]

Oral expression tends to be more redundant, given to tangential sidetracks, and dependent on stories, proverbs, and personal references compared with the more abstract, expository reporting and speaking style in the West. As the Igbo people of Nigeria say, "Proverbs are the palm oil with which words are eaten." Or, as the English say, "A spoonful of sugar helps the medicine go down." Among the Igbo the most effective speakers are those who can string together the largest number of appropriate proverbs and aphorisms. Effective development communication may need to adhere to such oral conventions and styles (or, at least, be aware of such conventions).

A second important element in understanding traditional media is the importance given to the source of the message. The words of certain people have more credibility than the words of others. In many parts of West Africa the role of intermediaries, praise singers, bards, and linguists, as they were traditionally called, are particularly important in transmitting important persons' words to general audiences. For example, among the Akan peoples of Ghana the prestige of a chief is revealed in the oratorical skills of his *Okyeame,* or linguist, through whom the messages of the chief or king are expressed. The *Jeli,* or bards, among the Mande-speaking peoples of West Africa not only keep alive oral traditions of peoples and great heroes but also communicate political messages for modern applications. Efforts at contemporary political or developmental communication need to take account of these traditional roles. Whether such communications are effective or not may depend on this sensitivity.

## Print and Broadcast Media

In many cases the press in Africa has been directly or indirectly controlled by governments that display a tendency to promote progovernment positions regarding development projects. Although there may not be official censorship, self-censorship takes place when privately owned newspapers try to avoid running afoul of the government. Still, there are numerous exceptions, such as the robust press of Nigeria and, occasionally, of South Africa.

Variables affecting the press in Africa include problems of literacy, language diversity, and cost of production. These factors, in turn, affect the circulation and penetration of the press and thus its usefulness for development support communication. Low rates of literacy, on average below 50% of the population,[22] would appear to be an obvious limiting factor. Still, newspapers are tangible objects that can be passed around and read aloud to families and other groups, so circulation figures may understate their influence.[23] Nonetheless, the ostensible limitation attributed to illiteracy accounts for why many early development experts touted the role of radio over the written media.

Language diversity affects many of the media in Africa. A few nations do have the luxury of widespread indigenous languages, such as Ki Swahili in East Africa, especially Tanzania, Somali in Somalia, and Arabic in the Saharan regions. Others have a few clearly dominant and widely understood languages, such as Shona and Ndebele in Zimbabwe; Yoruba, Hausa, and Igbo in Nigeria; and Akan (Twi) in Ghana. Still, national newspapers often must be in the languages of the former colonial rulers: English, French, Portuguese, and to a lesser extent, Spanish. When one speaks of literacy, therefore, language may be an important issue.

Costs are a further limiting factor on the role of the press in development. For example, newsprint is not readily available in Africa and must be imported. Newsprint is often subject to import licenses and fees that ensure some governmental control over newspaper access to this vital element of production. The capital necessary to start up and run a newspaper is often in short supply. For that reason Western companies or corporations are often dominated by larger newspapers, such as the Argus Group of Southern Africa and the Nation Group of newspapers in East Africa. Often, only the government or the government-subsidized ruling political party can be a competing source of capital for the press. Another sort of cost is the shortage of trained journalists or local institutions for providing such training.

**Radio and Television**   The advantages of radio as a mass medium led governments to maintain tight control over the new medium, usually restricting broadcasting to stations owned and operated by the government. If one visits both the headquarters of the Ghana Broadcasting Corporation and the national assembly, one is struck by how much tighter military security is at the former than at the latter.

Radio can be used in the format most familiar in the West, known as open broadcasting, in which messages are disseminated to a heterogeneous, dispersed audience. A second format, thought to be more useful for development purposes, involves targeted audiences, perhaps organized in local learning groups, who gather to listen to and discuss the information or "lessons."

Some problems have limited the effectiveness of radio in Africa. Most notable has been the problem of allocation of radio frequencies for developing countries. The usable radio spectrum is finite and not always sufficient for all the demands for its use. Nations in North America and Europe, naturally, were first to develop and expand radio stations using available frequencies. Countries that were late entrants in the race to develop radio, including African countries, have found it more difficult to obtain space on the radio spectrum. New technologies, such as spectrum compression and data compression techniques, do not necessarily solve the problem, because the demand for the creation of new services and technologies proliferates:

> Such services include emergency services, personal communications, worldwide paging, security monitoring, and the exchange of electronic data (EDI). For several new services new consumer electronics need to be manufactured, for example, for digital TV or for digital SBSS [sound broadcast satellite service]. In order to successfully market such equipment, it is critical to obtain world-wide frequency allocations. Also service providers have a vested interest in obtaining world-wide standardization of frequencies to service a global market.[24]

African states along with other countries of the Third World have argued for international conferences to reallocate frequencies, starting over with a clean slate in deciding how to allocate spectrum space (this is known as a priori distribution). However, the United States along with other developed nations has generally been successful in maintaining the rule of allocation on a first-come, first-served basis (known as a posteriori distribution), so that early developers of broadcast services and uses get to keep their spectrum allocations as they are. The globalization of markets, especially in information and communication services, has meant that communication development needs in specific regions may be subordinated to market forces. Eventually, one may argue, these global information networks will lead to economic growth in the affected regions, as more dynamic or interactive media replace radio as the medium of choice for development support.

The hopes for the multiplier or educational effects of radio have not always been fulfilled. As with the mass media in general, radio has not lived up to the expectations of the traditional paradigm of Lerner and Schramm. One problem is that people generally prefer to listen to entertainment programs and some news rather than to the development support communication messages (or educational programming). Studies have indicated that programming aimed at rural audiences concerning AIDS programs, for example, has been largely ineffective.[25]

On the other hand, radio has shown itself to be unexpectedly effective in service of some negative causes. Most notable in this regard was the impact of the propaganda and incitement by Radio Television Libre des Mille Collines (RTLMC) in Rwanda during the massacres of 1994 and 1995. Ostensibly an independent station, RTLMC became an effective voice for the extremists controlling the government:

> [RTLMC] knew how to use street slang, obscene jokes, and good music to push its racist message. During the genocide, it became what one listener at the time called 'a vampire radio' openly calling for more blood and massacre. Yet people went on listening to it with a kind of stupefied fascination, incredulous at the relaxed joking way it defied the most deeply cherished human values.[26]

RTLMC even became the source of information for the opponents or potential victims of the genocide, because they could get hints regarding the targets and timetables of the extremists. These people were convinced that the radio station was effective in mobilizing both the militants to carry out the massacres and the majority to acquiesce in them.[27] This cautionary example serves as a warning that development specialists with the best intentions may not be able to determine which messages will be acted on by people. This case further weakens the notion implied by Schramm that more mass media is good no matter what the message.

In summary, radio may be effective in reaching large numbers of people and in overcoming barriers such as low literacy or education levels, but the effects of specific messages or campaigns may be difficult to predict, let alone control.

Television has been thought to be a medium even more potent than radio. In Africa, however, television is too costly and too restricted to largely urban elite audiences to have a broad-based impact on development objectives. Equipment and programming must be imported from outside the continent. The values that are reinforced tend to be those associated with Western sitcoms, advertising, and CNN.

Televised news tends to be either rebroadcast from the BBC or CNN or locally produced. The local news tends to focus on government-sponsored or government-controlled development projects. As is the case with radio, television is usually owned and operated by the national government. For that reason much coverage is devoted to speeches by the head of state. In addition, this type of coverage is relatively inexpensive to produce.

Many development specialists and government officials have hoped that the broadcast media, especially television, will be able to foster national integration, a new national identity and culture. This hope has been stifled, however, by the dilemma over whether to broadcast in local languages, thereby seeming to perpetuate regional or ethnic loyalties, or in a single national language, thereby portraying a national ethos. The second choice may undercut cultural traditions and may further suggest reliance on a foreign colonial language.

In sum, although television is perhaps the most important mass medium in developed countries, so far it is of lesser importance in development communication in Africa. It may be that television coupled with satellite and digitized imaging will eventually become more significant in supporting development.

## Telematics, Telecommunications, and Computer Networks

In many parts of Africa the postal system was combined with telecommunications in a post, telephone, and telegraph government agency. Increasingly, the technologies of telecommunications are converging with computer networks and broadcast and cable modes of radio and television. This whole area of convergence is often referred to as telematics or informatics. These technologies can be significant for African economic development because of the quick and relatively inexpensive access these networks provide to data and expertise for otherwise isolated decision makers.[28]

Telematics depends on the infrastructure of the telephone network in a particular country, represented by public telecommunications operators (PTOs), which in many African states are government owned and operated. These PTOs provide the vital last mile in the dissemination of telematic communication, but in Africa this link tends to be by far the weakest. Africa clearly has the least developed telephone system in the world, with an average teledensity (number of phone lines per 100 inhabitants) of only 1.6 compared to a teledensity of 45 for Europe.[29] This average overstates the case, because it includes the more highly developed systems of Northern Africa and South Africa.[30]

Furthermore, information on the actual level of communication infrastructure in many parts of sub-Saharan Africa is generally insufficient.[31] In 1962 the International Telecommunication Union helped to establish the Pan-African Telecommunications Network (PANAFTEL) for 50 African nations. In turn, PANAFTEL aided in the institution of regional telephone exchange systems in North, West, Central, and Southern Africa.

Telephone service is generally much more reliable in large cities, especially capital cities, than in rural areas. Many African states have embarked on the process of introducing fiber optic and digitized service, but outside the capital cities copper wire or analog service is more the rule. The difference is roughly the difference between touch-tone service (digital) and rotary dial-tone service (analog).

The human element is ultimately the controlling variable in the development and use of telecommunications in Africa (and elsewhere). There must be people with the education and training to make use of information delivered by these networks as well as individuals who can build and maintain the networks. An inadequate number of experts poses a definite obstacle in developing and profiting from these networks. There is also the problem of political will. Some government bureaucrats and officials may profit from the establishment and importation of certain kinds of equipment to the exclusion of others. The result is that the best possible equipment and networks may be shut out. Beyond that, some politicians may actually fear the access and open communication represented by developed telecommunications (especially e-mail and fax capability), which have the potential for exposing corruption and undemocratic practices.[32]

The use of fax transmissions by Chinese students during the Tiananmen Square demonstrations in 1989 is a case in point. Also, there is always the opposite danger that technology will be imported for its novelty or prestige value, regardless of the usefulness of a particular technology in a specific setting. Finally, the use of wireless broadcast and communication systems, satellite transmission systems, and even cellular technologies can circumvent some of the restrictions of the low level of development of the phone line infrastructure. These possibilities are further explored in the following discussion of computer-based systems and networks, such as the Internet in Africa.

**Computerized Networks** Internet connectivity is expanding rapidly in Africa despite the underdeveloped telecommunications systems. By 1996, 33 of the 54 African nations had some form of e-mail service. Most capital cities now have some access to the Internet, whereas regions outside the large cities usually are not connected. South Africa, of course, continues to be an exception, as it is among the top 20 nations in the world in terms of number of Internet nodes.[33]

Most of the PTOs or public telecommunication providers have acted swiftly to provide Internet access, although occasionally at access charges beyond the reach of most people. Most recent estimates suggest that 40 African nations are fully connected to the Internet.[34] These connections tend to be on analog systems that operate at the relatively slow speed of 9.6 Kbps (kilobytes per second). This fact and the restrictions on availability of lines can mean long waits for connections and for downloading images and other information. In addition, users must expect problems associated with problems of electricity providers: blackouts or rolling brownouts and power surges. In addition, use of Internet service is restricted to a relative handful of people in Africa. As one study indicated,[35] some of these difficulties can be overcome, at least in part, by using new, somewhat inexpensive innovations.

Packet radio, which allows the direct connection of two computers by radio, coupled with connections to low east orbit satellites (LEOS) can provide for Internet access without relying on the regular telephone system.[36] Companies such as Motorola have shown interest in placing in orbit a large number of LEOS so that they can relay signals to virtually anywhere on the planet using cell phones.

Because of their low orbits, LEOS allow for faster relaying of messages or data compared with the geostationary satellites used for very small aperture terminals (VSATs), the current most popular form for satellite relayed communication. On the other hand, the use of LEOS tends to be much more expensive.[37]

The use of new communication technologies provides hope for progress in education, a necessary component in long-term, sustainable development. For example, connections to computer networks and databases would allow libraries in Africa to enhance their services. South African libraries can be accessed from Zimbabwe and other states in the southern region, easing interlibrary loans or database searches.

## CONCLUSION

Regardless of how controversies surrounding new technologies and traditional media may work out, the hoped-for leapfrog effect predicted in the 1960s by Schramm and other proponents of the traditional paradigm of mass communication and development remains elusive. International development and aid programs have been designed to build computer network capability in Africa. The United Nations and other major nongovernmental organizations have been major players in providing aid to develop networking infrastructure. For example, the International Development Research Centre of Canada has instituted an initiative called Capacity Building for Electronic Communications in Africa, which is aimed at developing a broad base of network users in each of 24 targeted countries.[38]

The United Nations Development Program has funded significant projects in Africa intended to enhance computer networking. UNESCO continues to fund training and education efforts to assist development of national and regional computer networks for science and technical education. The World Bank has supported programs intended to build up national telecommunications connections for the Internet in Africa.[39] In sum, there are international agencies endeavoring to improve Africa's capability to benefit from networked communication systems.

## SUMMARY

Since World War II, the former European colonies of Africa have become independent nation-states. Most African states are designated as part of the Third World, that is, as developing nations. These new nations have been striving over the past half-century for national or economic development to enhance their prosperity and the quality of life for their citizens. Many development experts and communication theorists believed that mass communication or the mass media would play a significant role in furthering this development, but most were disappointed by the results. First, the very definition of development—national or economic—evolved from an emphasis on Westernization, industrialization, or Western notions of progress.

The concept of development communication has undergone similar transformation. Instead of looking to the mass media to provide an almost automatic multiplier effect in modernization, experts now look to communication strategies that combine mass and interpersonal communication, modern and traditional media. The new emphasis is on equity, use of indigenous communication systems where possible, and reliance on traditional roles of leadership and expertise. There are real constraints on the potential of the press and broadcast media in African nations today because of cost, historical disadvantages in media distribution, and political, ethnic, and regional differences and levels of government control. Some of the new forms of computer-mediated communication systems hold out some promise for improving Africa's development communication, but these systems are subject to the constraints on the development of the infrastructure for telecommunications.

## NOTES

1. Wunyabari O. Maloba, *Mau Mau and Kenya: An Analysis of a Peasant Revolt* (Bloomington: Indiana University Press, 1988), 1.

2. James S. Coleman, "Conclusion: The Political Systems of the Developing Areas," in G. A. Almond and J. S. Coleman, eds., *The Politics of Developing Areas* (Princeton, NJ: Princeton University Press, 1960), 532.

3. Daniel Lerner, *The Passing of Traditional Society* (New York: Free Press, 1958).

4. Godwin C. Chu, "Communication and Development: Some Emerging Theoretical Perspectives," in A. A. Moemeka, ed., *Communication for Development* (Albany: State University of New York Press, 1994), 36.

5. Lerner, *The Passing of Traditional Society,* 46.

6. Ibid., 50.

7. Ibid., 56.

8. Wilbur Schramm, *Mass Media and National Development* (Stanford, CA: Stanford University Press, 1964), 90.

9. Schramm, *Mass Media and National Development,* 91.

10. Njoku Awa, "National Development," in M. K. Asante and W. B. Gudykunst, eds., *Handbook of International and Intercultural Communication* (Newbury Park, CA: Sage, 1989), 429–430.

11. Andrew A. Moemeka, ed., *Communication for Development* (Albany: State University of New York Press, 1994), 6.

12. Everett M. Rogers, *Diffusion of Innovations* (New York: Free Press, 1995), 5.

13. Ibid., 101–104.

14. See Njoku Awa, "Communication in Africa: Implications for Development Planning," *Howard Journal of Communications* 1 (1993): 131–144; and J. F. Morrison, "Communicating Healthcare Through Forum Theatre: Egalitarian Information Exchange in Burkina Faso," *Gazette* 52 (1993): 109–121.

15. A. Ansu-Kyeremeh, "Cultural Aspects of Constraints on Village Education Radio," *Media, Culture, and Society* 14 (1992): 111–128.

16. Louise M. Bourgault, *Mass Media in Sub-Saharan Africa* (Bloomington: Indiana University Press, 1995).

17. E. Childers, "Taking Humans into Account," *Media Asia* 3 (1976): 87.

18. Robert L. Stevenson, *Communication, Development, and the Third World* (New York: Longman Press, 1988), 73.

19. Cees J. Hamelink, *The Politics of World Communication* (London: Sage, 1994), 196–203.

20. Leornard Doob, *Communication in Africa* (New Haven: Yale University Press, 1961).

21. Bourgault, *Mass Media in Sub-Saharan Africa,* 7–20.

22. Oliver Coeur de Roy, "The African Challenge: Internet, Networking, and Connectivity Activities in a Developing Environment," *Third World Quarterly* 18 (1997): 890.

23. William W. Neher and John C. Condon, "The Mass Media and Nation-Building in Kenya and Tanzania," in D. R. Smock and K. Bentsi-Enchill, eds., *The Search for National Integration in Africa* (New York: Free Press, 1976).

24. Hamelink, *Politics of World Communication,* 81.

25. Moemeka, *Communication for Development,* 126.

26. Gerard Prunier, *The Rwanda Crisis: History of a Genocide* (New York: Columbia University Press, 1995), 189.

27. Philip Gourevitch, *We Wish to Inform You That Tomorrow We Will Be Killed with Our Families: Stories from Uganda* (New York: Farrar, Straus and Giroux, 1998).

28. Mike Jensen, *Telematics for Development: Discussion Paper* (Addis Ababa: International Telecommunications Union, UNESCO, and United Nations Economic Commission for Africa, 1995).

29. Coeur de Roy, "The African Challenge," 889.

30. Ibid., 889.

31. Jensen, *Telematics for Development.*

32. Coeur de Roy, "The African Challenge," 889.

33. Mike Jensen, "Bridging the Gaps in Internet Development in African," paper prepared for the International Development Research Centre, Canada, 1996; available at http://www.apc.org.

34. Coeur de Roy, "The African Challenge," 889.

35. Jensen, "Bridging the Gaps in Internet Development."

36. Coeur de Roy, "The African Challenge," 889.

37. Jensen, *Telematics for Development.*

38. Ibid.

39. Ibid.; and Jensen, "Bridging the Gaps in Internet Development."

# 9

# Dateline Addis Ababa

## Our Special Correspondent Evelyn Waugh Reports War Preparations with Italy, Vivid Colonial Discourse Used

### MICHAEL B. SALWEN

In mid-1935, Addis Ababa, the dilapidated capital of Ethiopia (then known to most of the world as Abyssinia),[1] was daily front-page news in European and American newspapers. Only a few months earlier most Europeans and Americans knew little or nothing about this mysterious landlocked East African republic whose leader claimed that he was descended from King Solomon and the Queen of Sheba.[2] However, after Ethiopian and Italian troops clashed in a border incident and after Fascist Italian dictator Benito Mussolini demanded the implementation of international treaties that he said granted Italy protectorate rights over Ethiopia, Europe was thrown into political upheaval and Addis Ababa suddenly became a familiar newspaper dateline. Mussolini declared that he was ready to use military force if necessary. Europeans feared that if Italy attacked Ethiopia, Great Britain and France in confederation with the League of Nations (the predecessor of the United Nations), would intercede to defend Ethiopia.[3] Just two decades earlier Europeans had experienced a devastating war (World War I), which began with the assassination of an obscure Balkan archduke in an obscure place called Sarajevo. They feared that Addis Ababa would become another Sarajevo.

Up to 250,000 Italian troops amassed along Ethiopia's borders from the Italian colonies of Eritrea and Italian Somaliland. At this time, another army descended on Addis Ababa: up to 130 newspaper and newsreel correspondents from around the world. The correspondents crowded into the few hotels, up to three in a room, and waited for news—waited for war. They had little to do but wait while the two countries' armies faced each other. The correspondents passed their time drinking, playing cards, employing young men from the bazaars as "spies" to obtain the latest gossip, wantonly spending their employers' money, enriching business owners, and triggering inflation.

Europe may have been on the brink of war, but most Ethiopians were indifferent. Evelyn Waugh, a famous novelist and the (London) *Daily Mail's* Addis Ababa correspondent, whose news stories about Ethiopia are analyzed in this chapter, wrote in his first news dispatch about the Italo-Ethiopian conflict,[4] "I arrived expecting to find a menaced capital in a fever of preparation. Instead I find life following its traditional course."[5]

Meanwhile, in Europe the leaders of Great Britain and France sought to placate domestic opinion by publicly condemning threatened Italian aggression. Most Europeans and Americans admired the African nation and its courageous, soft-spoken emperor. Behind the scenes pragmatic British and French leaders agreed that they would not risk European war over Ethiopia. Through private channels they communicated their desire for peace to Italy. These communications stiffened Mussolini's resolve to invade Ethiopia.[6] On 6 July 1935 Mussolini addressed a rally of supporters: "Abyssinia, which we are going to conquer, we shall have totally. We shall not be content with partial concessions, and if she dares resist our formidable strength, we shall put her to pillage and fire. . . . To those who may hope to stop us with documents or words, we shall give the answer with the heroic motto of our first storm troops: 'I don't give a damn.'"[7]

After Italian troops invaded Ethiopia on 3 October 1935, the world responded with condemnations and sanctions but no larger European conflict. A feared European war had been avoided. Ironically, once the Italo-Ethiopian War had begun, European and American public interest in Ethiopia waned. Without European war the Italo-European War was just a little colonial war. By December 1935 waves of frustrated correspondents, most of whom were unable to get to the front and never witnessed battle, started leaving the country en masse. For the Ethiopians the war had just begun. As many as 750,000 Ethiopians from a population of no more than 10 million died in the war (including deaths from starvation brought about by the war); yet many major battles occurred without a single correspondent present. To this day, many Ethiopians regard the Italian invasion as the Ethiopian Holocaust.

The correspondents went to Ethiopia to report the war for Europeans and Americans, so their stories often ignored Ethiopians' concerns and depicted Ethiopians—when they depicted them at all—in debasing ways.[8] Their lack of understanding of the culture was underscored by the surfeit of "eyewitness" books written by returning Addis Ababa correspondents quick to capture "a transient market."[9] As one critic wrote of these books: "The weakness about many of the correspondents, who were sent out hastily from Europe, was that they had no Eastern African background to their minds, and they described as peculiar to Abyssinia the kind of phenomena familiar to all who frequent the world which lies between Casablanca and Allahabad."[10]

The correspondents reported Ethiopia from a perspective that, according to the method used in this chapter, could be described as colonial. All of Africa, except for Ethiopia, was under the domination of a European power.[11] The correspondents thus thought of relations between African and European countries and peoples in power relation terms of "colonized" and "colonizing" nations and peoples. In this chapter I use a method called colonial discourse to examine how Waugh[12] reported news during the Italo-Ethiopian War.

Colonial discourse involves closely reading the news stories to ferret out various categories or modes of discourse used by Western correspondents reporting on non-Western countries. I use Waugh's correspondence as a case study. By discourse (or discursive practices) I refer not only to Waugh the individual and his writings but to how his writings were shaped by and shaped the social, political, and cultural institutions that he represented.[13]

To not leave the impression that colonial discourse is a method for analyzing only historical discourse in the news, after reviewing Waugh's reportage of Ethiopia, I apply colonial discourse to Robert Kaplan's *Ends of the Earth* (1996) to illustrate how modern colonial discourse differs from earlier discourse in both subtle and blatant ways.[14] Kaplan, a contributing editor at the *Atlantic Monthly,* chronicled his journey through shantytowns in neglected parts of Africa and Asia. With particular focus on Kaplan's journey through West Africa, in this chapter I examine modern transformations of colonial discourse.

## WAUGH: THE CORRESPONDENT

As a war correspondent, Waugh was a self-acknowledged failure. "I am a very bad journalist," he confessed in a private moment after one of several incidents when the other Addis Ababa correspondents scooped him in getting big news stories. "Well, only a shit could be good on this particular job."[15] However, Waugh's confinement in the dreary African capital with correspondents whom he detested provided him with material for his novel *Scoop,* in which Ethiopia became the fictional African nation of Ishmaelia.[16] The novel was an amusing but biting satire of the correspondents and was a critical and popular success. In *Scoop* the war was the butt of humor; readers had no idea that the real-world inspiration for *Scoop* was a land devastated by a holocaust. Waugh also wrote a nonfiction book about his Ethiopian assignment, immodestly titled *Waugh in Abyssinia.*[17] It was a critical and financial failure. Several chapters were blatant propaganda tracts that championed the Fascist Italian cause and European colonialism.

It was precisely because Waugh defended the colonialist cause that I analyze Waugh's reporting of Ethiopia as a case study of colonial discourse in journalism. Waugh's reporting was not typical of the colonial discourse used by the other correspondents. It was, however, particularly egregious, making it an excellent case to identify various modes of colonial discourse. Waugh had no experience as a war correspondent, but he had considerable experience observing and commenting on other cultures as a travel writer. He was among the vanguard of a new generation of travel writers who ventured to exotic lands and sought to be entertaining and audacious for their readers, often by poking fun at "uncivilized" peoples. One critic wrote that Waugh fitted the bill of the new generation travel writer; he had to have a perceptive eye, one that was "directed both outwards and inwards; and his comments on his own reactions [must] serve to establish the link between writer and reader which is the note of these new works."[18]

Waugh was not unique, however. Even the popular news media during this time exhibited colonial discourse. This example of *Time* magazine coverage of Ethiopia and its emperor illustrates that even leading news organizations treated Ethiopia in a submissive fashion, much as a colonialist occupier bureaucrat might treat a local servant:

> That a Negroid nation should be menaced by spectacular Dictator Benito Mussolini highly excited the world's Negroes last week. Not only Harlem but every other darktown was on *qui vive* at news from Rome that for three nights running Il Duce had sat up secretly with His Grand Council, contriving who knew what against the African Majesty of cocoa-buttered-colored Haile Selassie I (Power of Trinity). . . . If correspondents who sought to approach His Majesty Power of Trinity in blistering Addis Ababa last week expected to hear him exclaim "I is right glad to see you all! Now I is gwine tell you how this all is," they were abysmally mistaken. The sharp-featured, politically cunning ruler of between five and ten million savage and uncounted blacks is emphatically the suave cream in Africa's strong coffee.[19]

Waugh was hired as the London *Daily Mail*'s war correspondent from 20 August to 9 December 1935. The *Mail* hired Waugh because his books were widely read and because it hoped that his famous byline would attract readers. He was the author of several travelogues and acclaimed novels, such as *Decline and Fall* (1928), *Vile Bodies* (1930), and *A Handful of Dust* (1934). The *Mail*'s subeditor gave extensive play to Waugh's first dispatch from Ethiopia, a descriptive account of the crowded cities, homeless population, European expatriate population, and oppressive rain. It carried the headline "Evelyn Waugh's Vivid Addis Ababa Cable."

The *Mail* hired Waugh because he shared the *Mail*'s pro-Italian position and because the paper was in need of a correspondent; its star foreign correspondent, Sir Percival Phillips, one of the most famous war correspondents in his day, had recently resigned and gone to the competition. Perhaps the most important reason that the *Mail* hired Waugh, though, was it accepted Waugh's claim that he was an authority on Ethiopia. In 1930 Waugh had reported the coronation of Ras Tafari Makonnen (*ras* is a title equivalent to a provincial governor, warlord, or prince) as Emperor Haile Selassie I of the Empire of Ethiopia.

## THE CORONATION

Waugh's decision to first visit Ethiopia in 1930, at age 26, was done on a whim. He wanted to escape England's stifling atmosphere. On 23 August he was engaged in a conversation with a group of friends. He expressed his desire to travel somewhere exotic, perhaps to China or Japan. One member of the party, who had recently returned from Cairo, piqued Waugh's interest in Ethiopia by describing how the country's leader was planning to crown himself emperor. The conversation took on a facetious tone. Waugh was amused by the land where the people supposedly subsisted on raw meat and mead, dined while wearing bowler hats, and consecrated bishops by spitting on their heads.[20] "Everything I heard added to the glamour of this astonishing country," Waugh wrote.[21] He immediately contacted his literary agent to arrange for him to travel to Ethiopia to contribute articles for several periodicals. These arrangements were insufficient to cover his expenses, so he drew on his savings in hope that a novel or travel book would come from his journey. He wrote both a novel (*Black Mischief,* 1932) and a travel book (*Remote People,* 1931).

*Remote People* is especially relevant to this chapter. Waugh described his experiences at the coronation and on the subsequent trip he took to other parts of Africa. Before undertaking his journey to report the coronation, Waugh said he looked forward to the trip. He may have been setting readers up for his anticipated disappointment, to make his point that there is nothing charming about "uncivilized" cultures. Before departing, he wrote, "I can scarcely imagine any more romantic mission than to attend the coronation of the Emperor of Ethiopia, Conquering Lion of Judah, King of Kings, direct descendant of King Solomon and the Queen of Sheba."[22]

Almost immediately on entering Ethiopia, Waugh changed his tone. He expressed abhorrence with the country. Waugh said that Ethiopia was a barbaric land that put on a front of civilization in the well-planned coronation. In Waugh's historical overview of Ethiopia early in *Remote People,* Tafari is depicted as a wily politician with no rightful claim to power who "gradually built up and consolidated his supremacy."[23] Waugh said that Tafari traveled to Europe, learned about European politics, ingratiated himself with European leaders, and played on their rivalries. Tafari's final coup was obtaining membership in the League of Nations. In actuality, Waugh said, Tafari had a tenuous hold on his country.

In a prophetic freelance article about the coronation, Waugh wrote about the tendency in journalism for places in the news to burst on the world scene, only to be eclipsed by subsequent events: "For the first week in November, this remote and murky empire was a center of world-wide interest. . . . But that will all be forgotten and the English papers will not mention Abyssinia again until some startling political event—and Ethiopian history is full of such occurrences—brings it once more to the 'news.'"[24]

## COLONIAL DISCOURSE

Students have often heard their teachers ask them to critically read or analyze materials. To make critical analysis easier, it is useful to have a framework for critically dissecting materials. Colonial discourse analysis, as a framework, involves a qualitative reading of any material (not just journalism). Through a deep reading of the materials the analyst identifies modes that illustrate colonialist language. Identification of these modes allows analysts to bring to the surface the covert persuasive and socializing techniques of colonial discourse that appear in Western news reports about non-Western countries and cultures.

In most cases journalists and their audiences are not aware of their colonial discourse. When journalists report their news stories, they are steeped in the time and place of the colonial culture. For this reason, analyzing a historical case of colonial discourse has an advantage. Modern readers of news stories often find that they can discern colonial discourse written during an earlier time because they were not part of the culture when the stories were written. Still, it is important for students to be aware that modes of colonial discourse make their way into contemporary news reporting. That is why, after analyzing Waugh's colonial discourse on Ethiopia during the 1930s, I then review Kaplan's *Ends of the Earth*.

Colonial discourse about racial issues in Africa illustrates the value of analyzing materials from an earlier time. As students read this colonial discourse analysis of Waugh's news reports about Ethiopia, the reports will seem overtly racist. Students should be aware that in Waugh's time and culture the social discourse about race was characterized by racism, especially toward Africans. This does not make Waugh's racism any more justifiable, but it allows analysts to understand the cultural context of the news reports (which is central to discursive analysis). The modern reader can clearly see the colonial discourse on race as racist because the reader is not immersed in Waugh's time and culture. It is worth noting that in Waugh's day few commentators—even in enlightened, progressive circles—criticized Waugh's racism. Perhaps they did not recognize the racism or, more likely, perhaps they did not think such comments were unusual because racial stereotypes about Africans so permeated their culture. Sometimes Waugh's racism is transparent to the modern reader, as when he expressed his irritation with Ethiopians because they were not properly deferential to Europeans. In other words, he disliked the Ethiopians because they were "uppity" Africans:

> The essence of the offence was that the Abyssinians, in spite of being by any possible standard an inferior race, persisted in behaving as superiors; it was not that they were hostile, but contemptuous. The white man, accustomed to other parts of Africa, was disgusted to find the first-class carriages on the railway usurped by local dignitaries; he found himself subject to officials and villainous-looking men-at-arms whose language he did not know, who showed him no sort of preference on account of his colour, and he had not the smallest reluctance to using force on him if he became truculent.[25]

Although there are many possible colonial discourse modes, David Spurr, in *The Rhetoric of Empire: Colonial Discourse in Journalism, Travel Writing, and Imperial Administration,* identified 12 modes that commonly appear in the literature.[26] Because the last mode is relevant only to scholars analyzing their own work about discourse analysis, I examine the first 11 of Spurr's modes in this chapter: surveillance, appropriation, aestheticization, classification, debasement, negation, affirmation, idealization, insubstantialization, naturalization, and eroticization. Spurr offered a richly detailed chapter to illustrate each mode. The modes are only summarized in this chapter, and in this condensed form much detail is lost. Often only a single aspect pertaining to each mode was distilled from the chapters of Spurr's book that were thought to be applicable to a discourse analysis of journalism. Spurr claimed that scholars should analyze colonial discourse guided by the research question, "How does the Western writer construct a coherent representation out of the strange and (to the writer) often-incomprehensible realities confronted by the non-Western world?"[27]

## Surveillance

Surveillance involves descriptions of landscapes, interiors, and physical bodies. Landscape surveillance was a declaration of the colonial writer's power over the land and all it contained (including the populations that inhabited them). The writer's gaze and accompanying commentary on some object or landscape distinguish the mode.

Waugh returned to Ethiopia in August 1936, after the Italian victory and long after most of the correspondents had left and the world had forgotten Ethiopia, to chronicle Mussolini's victory for the last two chapters of *Waugh in Abyssinia*. Waugh exhibited surveillance mode in the last chapter, titled "The Road." He cast his gaze on a road being constructed by the victorious Italians. Waugh saw the road as a metaphor for European civilizing culture in an uncivilized land. It was "the supreme achievement of the Italian spirit."[28]

The closing lines of *Waugh in Abyssinia* epitomize the surveillance mode as a form of propaganda. Waugh saw in the road project a rebirth of the Holy Roman Empire. To the modern reader the lines may seem heavy-handed, but to Italy's supporters they heralded Italy's coming-of-age as an imperial empire. No matter how iniquitous Waugh's views, no one can deny his craftsmanship with words:

> And from Dessye new roads will be radiating to all points of the compass, and along the roads will pass the eagles of ancient Rome, as they came to our savage ancestors in France and Britain and Germany, bringing some rubbish and some mischief; a good deal of vulgar talk and some sharp misfortunes for individual opponents; but above and beyond and entirely predominating, the inestimable gifts of fine workmanship and clear judgment—the two determining qualities of the human spirit, by which alone, under God, man grows and flourishes.[29]

## Appropriation

Appropriation refers to discourse in which the colonizer makes claim to the land and its natural resources. Through such rationales as civilization and mankind the colonizer declares a right to govern.

Waugh defended Italy's legal and moral rights to rule Ethiopia. To make his case, he described Ethiopia's wanton disregard for international law in excruciating detail in the first chapter of *Waugh in Abyssinia*. The chapter, which feigned to be an objective historical overview, was patronizingly titled "The Intelligent Woman's Guide to the Ethiopian Question." Waugh said that Ethiopians entered into international arrangements with no intentions of fulfilling their promises: "Tricking the European was a national craft; evading issues, promising without the intent of fulfillment, tricking the paid foreign advisers, tricking the legations, tricking the visiting international committees—these were the ways by which Abyssinia had survived and prospered."[30]

To illustrate this point, Waugh noted how Ethiopia repeatedly violated its 1928 Treaty of Friendship with Italy. The pay for this violation, Waugh said, Ethiopia must make its natural resources available to the colonialist world:

> The Abyssinians had no intention of maintaining the spirit of that treaty. Italy had expected tangible commercial advantages. . . . Abyssinia could not claim recognition on equal terms by the civilised nations and at the same time maintain her barbarous isolation; she must put her natural resources at the disposal of the world; since she was obviously unable to develop them herself, it must be done for her, to their [Ethiopia's and Italy's] mutual benefit, by a more advanced Power.[31]

## Aestheticization

Aestheticization is especially appropriate to journalism and other forms of popular writing. Among other things aestheticization deals with the changing nature of the news and the clash of events competing for reader attention. "Thus," Spurr writes, "the press presents a dynamic image of the world that is curiously both volatile and stable, in which periodic explosions into disorder are always brought somehow back under control."[32]

Lord Copper, the fictional pompous publisher of the *Daily Beast* in *Scoop,* gave his foreign correspondent advice before traveling to Ishmaelia to report the imminent civil war. Lord Copper had the entire story for the war decided before any fighting began. In line with aestheticization, it is preordained that this war must end with a resolution satisfying to the British reading public:

> What the British public wants first, last and all the time is News. Remember that the Patriots are in the right and are going to win. The *Beast* stands by them four-square. But they must win quickly. The British public has no interest in a war which drags on indecisively. A few sharp victories, some conspicuous acts of personal bravery on the Patriot side, and a colourful entry into the capital. That is the *Beast* policy for the war.[33]

## Classification

Classification refers to descriptions of humans in a "hierarchical classification of humanity along a series of gradations ranged between the two poles of civilization and savagery."[34] By classifying humanity, the writer or reporter makes the point that not all humans are equal and that the European races are superior to the colonized races.

The classification mode of discourse is pertinent to the race-conscious Waugh. Although Waugh frequently referred to Jews, Americans, French, and even the "Wop" Italians in derogatory terms, he particularly despised Africans. He admired

Muslim culture, though; and when Muslim and African cultures came into conflict in Africa, as they did in Ethiopia, he thought the Muslims were a culturally superior race.

In August 1935 Waugh and another correspondent left Addis Ababa to visit Harar and other Ethiopian towns in search of news. For Waugh, Harar was a chance to reminisce about a people he loved. He had visited the Muslim town of Harar in 1930 while reporting the emperor's coronation: "The Harari people spoke their own language, wore a distinctive costume, and exhibited a very high standard of culture in comparison with their rough neighbors."[35] Compared with his visit to Harar five years later, however, Waugh professed some disappointment. He attributed the decline to Ethiopian rule, which he said stifled Harari culture.

In chapter 5 of *Waugh in Abyssinia,* titled "Anticlimax," after the initial Italian attack and the following long lull before victory, Waugh described how one of the sheiks in Harar secretly arranged to meet with him in a mosque. The sheik believed that Waugh was an emissary from the British government, despite Waugh's protestations to the contrary. The sheik wanted the British to know that his people would welcome Harar's absorption as a British protectorate, and he even preferred an Italian victory over continued Ethiopian rule. Although the Hararis had many complaints about the Ethiopians, the chief complaint concerned excessive taxation that lined bureaucrats' pockets and did nothing for the Hararis. As the furtive conversation continued, Waugh said that he suspected a "higher thing" in the Hararis' complaints: "the destruction of their culture."[36]

When Waugh visited Harar again in 1936, after the Italian victory, he was delighted by the improvements. The Italians had lifted many of the burdensome taxes, he said, and were providing needed social services. Also, the Hararis were again able to openly practice their culture. "The Hararis had come back in crowds; their gay costume filled the streets. The market, which had been almost squeezed out of existence by Abyssinian impositions, was now going merrily. Merrily was the word. There could be no two opinions about whether the Hararis liked the change."[37]

## Debasement

Conceding that debasement is not entirely distinct from classification (a form of racial debasement), the mode of debasement occurs when the colonialist writer, in often contemptuous terms, explicitly blames an indigenous people for their problems.

Using the language of debasement, Waugh blamed the Ethiopians for failing to bring civilization to their empire:

> The Abyssinians had nothing to give to their subject peoples, nothing to teach them. They brought no crafts or knowledge, no new system of agriculture, drainage or roadmaking, no medicine or hygiene, no higher political organisation, no superiority except their magazine rifles and belts of cartridges. They built nothing; they squatted in the villages in thatched huts of the conquered people, dirty, idle and domineering, burning the timber, devouring the crops, taxing the meagre stream of commerce that seeped from the outside, enslaving the people.[38]

## Negation

Negation refers to colonized peoples "as absence, emptiness, nothingness, or death."[39] Spurr notes that the language of negation, of nonexistence, is epitomized by explorer H. M. Stanley's often-cited description of Africa as a "wide enormous blank." Discourse that relies on negation declares that whatever people inhabit the colonized land, they are worthless.

In a sense, all the Western correspondents engaged in negation because they reported the war for Western audiences. They were unconcerned about the Ethiopian people, who for the most part did not exist in their reports. Waugh felt compelled to mention how few Ethiopians the Addis Ababa correspondents came into contact with as business proprietors. To Waugh their nonpresence in positions of business illustrated that they were incapable of running the financial and commercial affairs of their country:

> I do not think there was a single shop or office managed by an Abyssinian. The artisans were Arab and Sikh. Even the porters on the railway were Arabs. There was no Abyssinian middle class. The lowest manual labour and the highest administrative posts were reserved for them; bullying and being bullied. They had no crafts. It was extraordinary to find a people with an ancient and continuous habit of life who had produced so little. They built nothing; they made no gardens; they could not dance. . . . To lounge at the door of his hut counting his cartridges, to indulge in an occasional change of wife, to have a slaveboy in attendance to trot behind his mule carrying his cheap Belgian rifle, to be entertained, now and then, by his chief to a surfeit of raw beef and red pepper and damp grey bread, to boast in his cups of his own bravery and the inferiority of all other races, white, black, yellow, and brown—after these centuries of self-development were the characteristic pleasures of the Abyssinian.[40]

On the larger national scale of negation, Waugh said that Ethiopia was not a united empire, as it claimed. The emperor held a tenuous grip on the land and the people he ruled. This led Waugh to derisively characterize Ethiopia's claim to empire:

> She was a member of the League of Nations, admitted on equal terms to the councils of the world, her territory guaranteed absolutely and explicitly; that vast and obscure agglomeration of feudal fiefs, occupied military provinces, tributary sultanates, trackless no-man's-lands roamed by homicidal nomads; undefined in extent, unmapped, unexplored, in part left without law, in part grossly subjugated; the brightly coloured patch in the schoolroom atlas marked, for want of a more exact system of terminology, "Ethiopian Empire," had been recognized as a single state whose integrity was the concern of the world.[41]

## Affirmation

Although news of the Third World often focuses on "chaos and disorganization," underlying such images are uplifting messages of affirmation, of "a governing ideology and the need for institutions for order."[42] Interestingly, the only place in his book where Spurr makes reference to Waugh's writings is in the context of affirmation. Spurr saw Waugh as a defender of an "aristocratic nostalgia" during the "twilight revival of aristocratic values which otherwise exist only in racial memory."[43] It was not surprising that Spurr referred to Waugh in the context of affirmation. No matter where Waugh traveled, he saw the world through European eyes, constantly affirming Europeans values in contrast to the barbarity and backwardness of non-Western nations.

In addition to his novels, Waugh was famous for his travel books. Travel for cultural experience, enlightenment, or self-growth was the farthest thing from Waugh's mind. Indeed, in his many travel books—whether it was to British Guiana and Brazil, Mexico, or Africa—Waugh brought his English values with him and allowed them to prejudice his interpretations of foreign cultures. He rarely interacted with the indigenous peoples. He spent most of his time with the colonists and other Europeans living abroad. A recent convert to Catholicism, Waugh saw the Church as a place of refuge, of Western civilization in the wilderness. When he recounted his visit to Uganda in *Remote People,* he described a convent operated by native women as a "heroic outpost" of civilization:

> At the convent they manage a small farm and hospital, and in recreation time do skilled needlework. It does not sound very remarkable to a reader in Europe; it is astounding in Central Africa—this little island of order and sweetness in an ocean of rank barbarity; all round it for hundreds of miles lie gross jungle, bush, forest, haunted by devils and the fear of darkness, where human life merges into the cruel, automatic life of animals; here they were singing the offices just as they had sung in Europe when the missions were little radiant points of learning and decency in a pagan wilderness.[44]

With all the strife, chaos, daily indignities, and just plain boredom in Africa, a reader might close *Remote People* asking, "Why travel at all?" Indeed, Waugh himself asked this question in the book's concluding lines. Back in London—the "centre of the Empire"—dining with friends and learning about all the exciting things he had missed during his African journey, Waugh asked, "Why go abroad?" Reaffirming his faith in English civilization, he continued, "See England first. Just watch London knock spots off the dark continent."[45]

## Idealization

Unlike the preceding seven modes, idealization involves an avowedly positive portrayal of indigenous peoples. Colonialist writers using this mode to reflect on what Europeans lost in their pursuit of progress—freedom, innocence, and the like. Idealization is the opposite of affirmation. In affirmation the colonialist looks at the "savage" and, in so doing, affirms what is good in Western culture. In idealization the colonizer looks at the "noble" savage and bemoans a better life that was lost.

Waugh experienced no moments of doubt about the superiority of European culture over native cultures, but he was aware of the tendency in European society during his day to idealize indigenous peoples, and he sought to counter the social liberals who "deplored all European influence in Africa":

[They] rejoiced to find an "unspoiled" area; [they] would have liked to preserve Ethiopia, in the way that national parks are isolated and preserved for
animals, as a sanctuary for savages; extreme lovers of the picturesque who
fostered lepers and eunuchs and brigand chiefs, as their milder brothers encouraged sulky yokels in England to perform folk dances on the village
green.[46]

## Insubstantialization

Insubstantialization refers to the Western writer's inner journey. The writer's self-
indulgence relegates the colonial nation and its people to "a backdrop of baseless
fabric against which is played the drama of the writer's self."[47] This mode reflects
an egotistical form of discourse because the colonized people are treated merely
as props for the colonialist writer's world.

Waugh was a supreme egotist, so naturally this mode is relevant to his writings. He engaged in insubstantialization in many of his travel books. He was
among a vanguard of writers who developed a new form of travel writing befitting
the post-Victorian era; in this new form the writer's expression of boredom was
raised to an art form. Readers were apparently amused by the writer in an exotic
land jaded by the bizarre sights and cultures and longing to be back home. This
new form of travel writing required the writer to be entertaining, sophisticated,
"even malicious; but above all the new-style travel-book had to be bright. If anyone was to be bored, it had to be the traveler, not the reader. Journeys might—
indeed they had better—begin, continue, and end with a fair dash of pointless-
ness, boredom, discomfort, that form a heroic hardship in a minor key which is
most attuned to subsequent relaxation in an armchair."[48]

In Waugh's travel writings the entire colonial culture was a backdrop for him
to express his boredom with travel. He did so with great élan in *Remote People,*
when after missing his train he was forced to spend four days in the Ethiopian
town of Dirre Dowa. "I am constitutionally a martyr to boredom," Waugh wrote,
"but never in Europe have I been so desperately and degradingly bored as I was
during the next four days; they were as black and timeless as Damnation."[49]

*Remote People* was Waugh's second travel book. His first described a Mediterranean cruise during 1929–1930 that resulted in *Labels* (1930). With each suc-
cessive travelogue Waugh became more adept at expressing his boredom. In 1933
Waugh journeyed to South America on a whim, just as he had selected Ethiopia
for *Remote People.* His book from the South American journey, *Ninety-Two Days,*
recounted the ennui of exotic travel. The very title of the book, one biographer
noted, "[sounds] as if the sufferer had been counting off the hours and minutes
as well as the days."[50] Waugh complained about the food, the insects, the heat, the
seasickness, the facilities, the smells, and, of course, the unbearable natives. The
review of the book in the London *Times Literary Supplement* aptly summarized
Waugh's many refrains of weariness:

A time comes when the club pessimist gets a laugh when he makes his
moan; and in this book the reader comes to reckon that Mr. Waugh is not
playing the part adequately unless he produces some such phrase as "De-

pression deepened"; "As depressing a time as I have known in adult life"; "Monotonous vegetable walls on either bank"; "It would be tedious to record . . ."; "I was to grow to hate it" [a river]; "But there were only two more days to Bon Success, where I should be leaving all three of them"; "At last that day, like all others, came to an end"; "My enthusiasm had already cooled considerably . . ."; "The mist of frustration still hung about us"; "Our camp was the least attractive we had yet made."[51]

## Naturalization

The mode of naturalization conjures up contradictory views regarding conceptions of nature. On the one hand, nature refers to colonial peoples' natural rights to their land. On the other hand, nature is antagonistic to modernity and civilization, which colonizers view as beneficial for them and colonized peoples. Spurr argues that writers naturalize the process of colonial domination by arguing "a natural justification for the conquest of nature and the primitive peoples, those children of nature." In this framework history is seen as "a great struggle between the opposing forces of nature and culture, instinct and reason."[52]

After having spent two weeks in Ethiopia to report Ras Tafari's coronation, Waugh traveled through the region, gathering material for *Remote People*. In Kenya he admired the quixotic British settlers who established "the traditional life of the English squirearchy" in remote Africa. Waugh argued against the popular view in Great Britain that the Kenyan settlers were "a gang of rapacious adventurers."[53] He put forward his philosophy that the settlers were part of the circle of nature:

> There is in existence a body of serious opinion in England which holds that in the past, the Africans have been unjustly exploited by European commercial interests, and is anxious to prevent this in the future. . . . There is one general principle which one may accept; that the whole of history from the earliest times until to-day, has been determined by the movements of peoples about the earth's surface; migratory tribes settled and adapted their cultures to new conditions; conquest, colonisation, commercial penetration, religious proselytising, topographical changes, land becoming worked out, pastures disappearing, harbours silting up—have preserved a constant fluidity of population. . . . The process will go on, because it is an organic process in human life.[54]

## Eroticization

By eroticization Spurr refers to the discourse of sexuality, in which the colonized world is approached as decidedly feminine (mysterious, alluring, treacherous). The "eroticization of the colonized" relies on the use of metaphors, seductive fantasies, and expressions of sexuality.[55] Eroticization includes "erotically charged language [that] . . . marks the entrance of the colonizer, with his penetrating and controlling power, as a natural union with the subject nation."[56]

Waugh did not use the eroticization mode in referring to the Ethiopians. He saw nothing mysterious or alluring about them. Although perhaps not qualifying as eroticization mode, Waugh wrote of his beloved Harar and the Harari people in terms of feminine beauty, if not sex. To Waugh, Harar was a bastion of Muslim civilization in black Africa. His racial comparison of Hararis and Ethiopians indicated the mode of classification, but here we concern ourselves with Waugh's sexual comparisons between the peoples that connote eroticization. To Waugh, even the women of Harar were beautiful compared with Ethiopian women:

> The beauty of the women was dazzling—far exceeding anything I had expected. The native women I had seen at Addis Ababa had been far from attractive; their faces had been plump and smug, their hair unbecoming heaped up in a black, fuzzy mass, glittering with melted butter, their figures swollen grotesquely with a surfeit of petticoats. The women of Harar are slender and very upright; they carry themselves with all the grace of the Somalis, but, instead of their monkey-like faces and sooty complexions, they had golden brown skins and features of the utmost fineness.[57]

## CONTEMPORARY COLONIAL DISCOURSE

Colonial discourse in the news is not confined to the past. Even today, modes of colonial discourse creep into news reports. Contemporary colonial discourse, however, is bound to be different today from in the past. Confounding colonial discourse analysis today, we may no longer be living in a colonial era. Since the 1960s many writers have noted that we are living in the "post-colonial era."[58] Although the colonial era may no longer exist, it lives on as a mindset, as a way of seeing and reporting the world. We now shift to an example of colonial discourse in the news today. To this end I examine Robert D. Kaplan's *Ends of the Earth*.

The most apparent difference that separates contemporary Western journalists writing about non-Western cultures from journalists in the past, such as Waugh, is that today's journalists are more understanding of colonial cultures and their problems. Some modern writers who come from a "critical" left-wing tradition even harshly criticize colonialism for creating the problems in Third World countries. Kaplan, however, represents a politically moderate and mainstream view. He acknowledges the role of colonialism as a wound hindering development in Third World countries, but he offers some tough-love advice, blaming Third World countries themselves for many of their problems.

One of Kaplan's points about West African countries was that, in a sense, they were not countries at all with centralized leadership. To foreigners the capitals of West African nations might give a semblance of a state apparatus, but the governments exert little control over the shantytowns and villages that most foreigners never see. Kaplan writes in the mode of negation, of nonexistence. The countries in this part of Africa, at least as Westerners conceive of countries, do not exist. For example, of Sierra Leone Kaplan wrote, "Social dissolution was all around. The government, as either a moral force or an organizing factor of public life, simply did not exist."[59] Of Togo he wrote, "I had come by airplane from Freetown to Lome, the capital of Togo, a country that may be less fact than fiction."[60]

Waugh referred to Ethiopia's lack of political control to underscore the nonexistence of the state. Waugh's purpose in negation was to suggest that in the absence of a central state a European power such as Italy had a right, even a moral duty, to assert authority over the land and its people. From his European colonialist perspective, without state authority there would be chaos and anarchy. Kaplan's purpose in describing negation is unclear, other than to point to the existence of the problem. As an illustration of the modern transformation of the negation mode, Kaplan's negation mode is neutral and at times even sympathetic. Kaplan questioned whether the Western notion of a state is appropriate in the African context: "The 'state' is a purely Western notion, one that until the twentieth century described countries covering only a small part of the land's area. Nor is there evidence compelling that the state, as a governing ideal, can be successfully transported to areas outside the industrialized world." [61]

Kaplan frequently used the surveillance mode. In several places—whether in the lush "botanical paradise" of Freetown in Sierra Leone or the splendid tourist-filled beaches along Togo's narrow coast—Kaplan focused his gaze on the beauty of the land. This was similar to Waugh's surveillance of the road being built by the Italian victors in Ethiopia. Recall that Waugh's surveillance had the underlying purpose of extolling what he believed was Italy's benign colonialism. Kaplan's observations were brief and quickly rebutted, because he, too, had an underlying purpose to his surveillance: to show the ugly truth that masked the pleasant facades. "Freetown was an easy place to fall in love with," he wrote, "a place about which you could easily suspend judgment for a few moments. I wish I had been younger and more naïve, and that I was not addicted to political analysis." [62] And then, as promised, Kaplan provided a list of the problems facing Sierra Leone. [63]

Kaplan's list of problems illustrates a point about contemporary colonial discourse in journalism. Kaplan offered no solutions. His purpose, in line with modern journalism, was to report what he saw. Another obvious point is that Kaplan's colonial discourse is bereft of blatant racism, although a reader might interpret racism between the lines. Modern writers employed by mainstream media, such as Kaplan, do not engage in brute racism, as Waugh did.

An observer might see racism in the classification mode. Among Spurr's modes classification has a racial component. Kaplan's book did depict a form of classification where at least cultures, if not races, were compared and contrasted in terms of desirable and undesirable qualities. Like Waugh, Kaplan admired the civilizing nature of Islamic culture in societies such as Turkey and Iran. Perhaps to the surprise of many readers who think of Iran in terms of stereotypes, Kaplan described Iran in favorable cultural, although not political, terms. He noted the lack of crime in Iran and how money changers operating on the streets during the early morning hours would stack their wads of U.S. dollars weighted down by rocks: "The sight of stacks of U.S. dollars piled up on the street, in no danger of being stolen, supported my initial views. Here was a society, like Turkey's, with a strong social mortar, a society that you needn't feel sorry for." [64]

Kaplan wrote that Islamic culture never took hold in West Africa. As a result, there was rampant crime. He repeatedly stated his fear of walking after dark in many parts of Africa. Kaplan commented that there was a loose sexual ethic in

West Africa, where prostitution was common and where he observed a woman in the Ivory Coast urinating in the street, oblivious to the crowds. While Kaplan admitted that inadequate housing and the tropical heat might have "helped defeat attempts at decorum," he added, "The immodesty might also have indicated how Islam had been weakened in the course of its arduous journey across the Sahara."[65] So here we see an example of modern classification. The upright moral standards of Islamic Iran were compared with the immoral standards of West Africa, where civilizing Islam never took hold. Unlike Waugh, Kaplan suggested no racial overtones. Rather, the classification mode is based on cultural-religious roots.

Kaplan's partiality to Islamic culture led him to exhibit a touch of the eroticization mode, when he commented on how Iran's veiled women occasionally flashed a peek of hair, lipstick, earrings, and knowing smiles from behind their chadors. It was arousing. His favorable disposition to Iran led him to write in the idealization mode, where the colonizer admires the colonized people for holding on to their values in the face of the modern world's cultural onslaught. In a political discussion with an Iranian woman Kaplan conceded her point about how the high rate of crime in the United States represented a breakdown of moral culture: "In some ways [Iran] was far more civil than my own [country]; where in 1994 the statistical chance of being a victim of violence was probably small compared to America."[66]

## DISCUSSION AND CONCLUSION

In this chapter I have provided students with a means for identifying modes of colonial discourse in journalism. I did this by using as a case study Evelyn Waugh's news reporting of the Italo-Ethiopian conflict and later war. It should come as no surprise that colonial discourse filters its way into Western reporting about non-Western nations. Colonial discourse analysis provides students with a system to identify various aspects of colonial discourse. Colonial discourse in journalism still exists but in a more subtle form than in the past. The subsequent analysis of Kaplan's *Ends of the Earth* illustrated the subtle form that colonial discourse in journalism takes today.

Several factors make analyzing contemporary colonial discourse in journalism challenging. For one thing, modern writers adhere to objectivity in journalism. Unlike Waugh and many writers in Waugh's day, Western journalists claim not to take sides or express opinions about controversial issues; rather, they simply provide readers or viewers with facts and then let them decide what these facts mean. Thus, with Kaplan the reader gets a numbing account of conditions in Africa with few or no suggestions for how to correct the problems.

The modern quest for objectivity sometimes confounds discourse analysis because it is not clear when the writer is expressing a certain mode or only reporting what some source is expressing. For example, although Kaplan described a personal account of his journey, he still sometimes wrote as an objective journalist. Without comment he quoted others as making disparaging and even racist comments about other cultures. In an earlier age the journalist might have either endorsed or rejected the comments or might even have directly stated such comments. Kaplan let the quoted comments stand by themselves, forcing readers to try to understand the African situation.

Further complicating the assignment of modes to Kaplan's reporting is that he wrote as an academic and as a journalist, frequently citing scholarly sources. This is an extension of objectivity. Kaplan's academic references exacerbate the job of the colonial discourse analyst trying to separate the writer's opinions from the scholarly references. For example, Kaplan cited scholars who said that the European slave trade had little impact on Africa's political and social development, noting that slavery existed in Africa before the Europeans arrived. On the other hand, Kaplan quoted other scholars who claimed that European slavery was more inhumane than African slavery and that the European slave trade arrested African development. This journalistic one-side-says-this-but-the-other-side-says-that approach, without a firm statement of Kaplan's position, makes it difficult for colonial discourse analysts to determine the writer's views.

Armed with the tool of colonial discourse analysis, it is worth warning students to not get too enamored with it. Colonial discourse in journalism may not manifest itself in every Western news story about non-Western nations. Colonial discourse is a tool that can be useful, but it also can be abused. The science philosopher Abraham Kaplan made the point about the excessive overuse of research tools when he related the story of the boy with a hammer: "Give a small boy a hammer, and he will find that everything he encounters needs pounding."[67] In other words, the student should not try to apply colonial discourse to every news story.

Colonial discourse is more likely to manifest itself in books and extended magazine articles and in some lengthy broadcast stories, where journalists have more space and time to comment. Colonial discourse might manifest itself in editorials in print media and in so-called pundit programs on television and radio, where journalists and other authorities analyze the news and expound their views. In these sorts of extended news reports the journalists might not be as restrained by the code of objectivity as they are with breaking news reports.

### NOTES

1. During the years under investigation in this chapter, Ethiopia was commonly called Abyssinia in Europe and the United States. The Ethiopians preferred the name Ethiopia, which referred to a territory that encompassed an empire of territories.

2. The Ethiopian constitution of 1955 stated that emperors were descendants of the House of David. "The imperial dignity

shall remain perpetually attached . . . to the line which descends without interruption from . . . the Queen of Sheba and King Solomon of Jerusalem" [James Dugan and Laurence Lafore, *Days of Emperor and Clown* (Garden City, NY: Doubleday, 1973), 11].

3. It was unlikely that the United States would enter such a war. There was an unofficial policy of isolationism regarding in-

volvement in European affairs. The United States was not a member of the League of Nations.

4. Also known as the Ethiopian War or the Abyssinian War.

5. Evelyn Waugh, "Evelyn Waugh's Vivid Addis Ababa Cable," *Daily Mail,* 24 September 1935, p. 9.

6. Dugan and Lafore, *Days of Emperor and Clown,* 108.

7. Ibid., 131.

8. For a readable and romanticized historical overview of war correspondence, see Phillip Knightley, *The First Casualty: From Crimea to Vietnam—The War Correspondent as Hero, Propagandist, and Myth Maker* (New York: Harcourt Brace Jovanovich, 1975).

9. G. T. Garratt, "News-Hunting in Ethiopia," *New Statesman and Nation* 11 (14 March 1936): 378–379; quote on p. 378.

10. Ibid., 378.

11. Until it was occupied by the Italians, Ethiopia had never been a European colony. Liberia was nominally independent, although the United Stated exercised so much influence on the West African nation that it was not truly independent.

12. For an excellent recent biography of Waugh, see Selina Hastings, *Evelyn Waugh: A Biography* (Boston: Houghton Mifflin, 1994).

13. Michel Foucault, *L'Ordre du Discours* (Paris: Gallimard, 1971).

14. Robert D. Kaplan, *The Ends of the Earth: A Journey at the Dawn of the 21st Century* (New York: Random House, 1996).

15. Letter to Penelope Betjeman, Dessye, Ethiopia (November 1935), in Mark Amory, ed., *The Letters of Evelyn Waugh* (New Haven: Ticknor & Fields, 1980), 102.

16. All references to *Scoop* refer to the widely available paperback edition (Boston: Little, Brown, 1937).

17. Evelyn Waugh, *Waugh in Abyssinia* (London: Longmans, Green, 1936). In fairness, the original planned title was *A Disappointing War,* inspired by a cable from the *Daily Mail*'s editor terminating Waugh's employment. The publisher, fearing disappointing sales, preferred *Waugh in Abyssinia* (Hastings, *Evelyn Waugh,* 344).

18. Frederick J. Stopp, *Evelyn Waugh: Portrait of an Artist* (Boston: Little, Brown, 1958), 24.

19. "Negroes v. Blackshirts," *Time* 25 (25 February 1935): 18.

20. These examples that amused Waugh illustrate how colonizers can twist facts to depict colonized peoples in demeaning ways. The Ethiopians did indeed have a *gebbur* ceremony where they feasted on raw meat. This was a cultural ceremony steeped in tradition with traditional signification and performed on special occasions, not daily eating. As for wearing bowler hats during dinner, Waugh's guest was probably witnessing Ethiopian officials confused about Western dining habits. They were likely trying to be gracious guests by wearing Western clothing. It is not clear where the story of spitting on bishops' heads comes from.

21. Evelyn Waugh, *Remote People* (London: Duckworth, 1931), 14.

22. Evelyn Waugh, "A Journey to Abyssinia," *Graphic,* 22 November 1930, p. 350.

23. Waugh, *Remote People,* 32.

24. Evelyn Waugh, "Champagne for Breakfast: A Journey to Abyssinia," *Graphic,* 20 December 1930, p. 544.

25. Waugh, *Waugh in Abyssinia,* 35.

26. David Spurr, *The Rhetoric of Empire: Colonial Discourse in Journalism, Travel Writing, and Imperial Administration* (Durham, NC: Duke University Press, 1993).

27. Spurr, *The Rhetoric of Empire,* 2.

28. Ibid., 243.

29. Ibid., 253.

30. Ibid., 27.

31. Ibid., 40–41.

32. Spurr, *The Rhetoric of Empire,* 44.

33. Waugh, *Scoop,* 56.

34. Spurr, *The Rhetoric of Empire,* 67.

35. Waugh, *Waugh in Abyssinia,* 85–86.

36. Ibid., 180.

37. Ibid., 223.

38. Ibid., 25–26.

39. Spurr, *The Rhetoric of Empire*, 92.

40. Waugh, *Waugh in Abyssinia*, 63–64.

41. Ibid., 11–12.

42. Spurr, *The Rhetoric of Empire*, 109.

43. Ibid., 116.

44. Waugh, *Remote People*, 207.

45. Ibid., 240.

46. Waugh, *Waugh in Abyssinia*, 33.

47. Spurr, *The Rhetoric of Empire*, 142.

48. Stopp, *Evelyn Waugh*, 23.

49. Waugh, *Remote People*, 116.

50. Hastings, *Evelyn Waugh*, 270.

51. "Ninety-Two Days," *Times Literary Supplement*, 15 March 1934, p. 178.

52. Spurr, *The Rhetoric of Empire*, 160.

53. Waugh, *Remote People*, 179.

54. Ibid., 180–181.

55. Spurr, *The Rhetoric of Empire*, 170.

56. Ibid., 172.

57. Waugh, *Remote People*, 100–101.

58. See Alastair Pennycock, *English and the Discourses of Colonialism* (London: Routledge, 1998), 16–17.

59. Kaplan, *The Ends of the Earth*, 64.

60. Ibid., 70.

61. Ibid., 83.

62. Ibid., 43.

63. Ibid.; see pp. 45–46 for the list.

64. Ibid., 185. Kaplan's admiration of Islamic culture was somewhat ironic because he had earlier written a book [*The Arabists* (New York: Free Press, 1995)] about how U.S. government officials were "Arabists" who overly romanticized and sympathized with Arab and Islamic cultures, as if they were modern-day Lawrence of Arabias.

65. Ibid., 15.

66. Ibid., 226.

67. Abraham Kaplan, *The Conduct of Social Inquiry: Methodology for Behavioral Science* (San Francisco: Chandler, 1964), 28.

# PART V

# Globalization

It is perhaps not uncommon for the following scenario to occur in Hong Kong. A group of youths in their 20s goes shopping and buys some Levi's Jeans, Nike shoes, and Calvin Klein cologne before having a meal at McDonald's, followed by a visit to the nearby Baskin-Robbins. The group then sees the most recent American action-adventure film while sipping Coke and chewing on M & M's in the theater. After the movie the group goes home and watches *Friends* together while eating a pizza ordered from Pizza Hut and drinking Budweiser beer purchased from the corner 7-11 store.

This scenario illustrates the globalization dimension of media and consumer products. The pervasiveness of Western media and Western consumer products in the world market is primarily a result of historical Western domination in the world's culture, economics, and politics. Yet the popularity of these products is primarily due to their quality and modern appeal. U.S. films, for example, cultivate and meet public taste by offering the most technically and artistically sophisticated products, satisfying a set of universal needs for seeing human spirit triumph over obstacles or evils.

On the other hand, U.S. multinational corporations have the financial means to build a global distribution and marketing network, using sophisticated advertising and marketing techniques to build brand image and loyalty as well as market share overseas.

Despite Western and particularly American dominance in the film industry, some developing nations (e.g., India) or newly developed regions (e.g., Singapore) have established either a solid film industry or a rudimentary modern advertising industry. In so doing, they have managed to market their own cultural and consumer products to compete alongside Western imports.

In the first chapter of this section, David J. Atkin, of Cleveland State University, explains the success of Hollywood media products by examining its history, financial structure, creative process, technological developments, and competitive edge. He traces Hollywood's success to such factors as a libertarian media system and a capitalist economy—as well as vibrant immigrant and ethnic cultures—that help shape diverse, interesting human conditions and social commentaries on screen. Atkin then outlines how Hollywood is the only entity that can produce and market entertainment products with a multimillion-dollar budget (e.g., the $200 million price of *Titanic*). No other entity can possibly compete with such deep pockets that lead to world media domination. Naturally, this domination has led to concerns about American media imperialism, even though much of the world audience appears to enjoy "all things American."

In the second chapter of this section, Katherine T. Frith, of Nanyang Technological University in Singapore, examines the global advertising phenomenon by contrasting the values of the standardized advertising approach and the specialized advertising approach. Although the standardized advertising approach claims that a standardized campaign strategy is the most efficient and effective mode of global advertising, the specialized advertising approach suggests the opposite. Frith then reviews three Asian countries (Japan, Malaysia, and Vietnam), which represent the social responsibility, authoritarian, and totalitarian media systems, respectively, as case studies for exploring whether a standardized or a specialized advertising strategy is more useful. Because each of these countries shows either self-imposed cultural restrictions or government-mandated cultural regulations on advertising practice, it appears that a specialized rather than a standardized approach to advertising is both more practical and more viable.

In the third chapter of this part, four leading Asian media scholars examine globalization and media development in Asia's four tigers: Singapore, Hong Kong, Taiwan, and South Korea. The scholars describe how global factors, cultural factors, and domestic mass media contributed to the four tigers' extraordinary growth and development.

# 10

# The Americanization of Global Film

## DAVID J. ATKIN

Although Americans tend to think of movie viewing as an occasional leisure activity, the industry is now in the vanguard of an intellectual copyright sector that represents America's leading export commodity. According to a 1998 report by the International Intellectual Property Alliance, the core copyright industries recently eclipsed America's perennial export leaders: agriculture, aerospace, and automobiles.[1] Citing U.S. Commerce Department data and industry figures, the report also showed that the copyright industries, which include recording, publishing, and software in addition to film, experienced annual growth rates of more than 5% during the late 1990s. This pace is more than twice the rate of inflation, and it places American film among the fastest growing sectors in the U.S. economy.

Thus, at the dawn of a new millennium, the United States stands poised to dominate global cultural affairs as no other nation has in history. Although ancient Rome controlled cultural development in Western Europe and the Mediterranean 2,000 years ago and although China was a dominant cultural force at the turn of the first millennium, no nation has possessed the influence over global culture that the United States now enjoys. What is different about this American cultural empire? The answer can be found through an examination of the Hollywood motion picture industry, the preeminent storyteller of our time.

Some critics argue that Hollywood's influence stems from a unique set of cultural conditions that help create transparent texts, or narratives, whose structure encourages diverse populations to accept Hollywood's cultural values as their own.[2] That is, these narratives are readily assimilated into different cultures because they allow global audiences to project their own values and meanings onto a given television or movie product. In this way Hollywood's messages carry universal appeal, enabling its media messages to be accepted as if they were home-grown productions throughout the world. This process helps to explain how, by the 1970s, most countries imported most of their film and television programming from the United States.[3] The resulting uneven exchange in media flows has been termed media imperialism,[4] which is explored more fully in Chapter 13.

Hollywood's emerging film infrastructure helps account for America's entry into the twenty-first century in a position of "unrivaled dominance that surpasses anything it experienced in the 20th century,"[5] when the country faced threats to its ideology and security.[6] Rosencrance concludes that the United States is "now controlling the essential language in which the basic formulas for the future are being worked out."[7] In this chapter I explore the root causes and cultural implications of this global fascination with all (celluloid) things American. In particular, I explore dominant forms of American film's influence around the world in light of a media systems paradigm, which states that the relation between a country and its media system is reciprocal.[8]

## BACKGROUND

### Media Systems Paradigm

We can gain a better understanding of the relationship between a country and its media system by considering Siebert, Peterson, and Schramm's classic four theories of the press.[9]

Although formulated at the height of the cold war and offering a biased view of Soviet communist theory, this model provides a sound foundation for understanding media systems in terms of political philosophy, media freedom (or control), and media ownership. Of particular importance to the present discussion is the freest system, termed the libertarian theory, which can be applied only to the American press system and film industry. The American press system (especially the print press system) rejects government involvement or interference in its affairs. Other industrialized democratic nations typically operate their press system under the social responsibility theory (e.g., Japan and Western European nations such as Great Britain), which is also relatively free but is chiefly distinguished from the libertarian approach by a slightly higher level of public interest–based government regulation (e.g., content regulations for broadcasting).

The libertarian and social responsibility theories, or systems, are juxtaposed against less expressive theories, including (1) the authoritarian system, wherein the press is charged with supporting the central state authority (as in many African, South American, Arab, and Southeast Asian countries), and (2) the communist system, in which the press is theoretically owned by the people but is in practice subject to strict government controls (e.g., Cuba and the People's Republic of China). Although other conceptions of press control have been introduced,[10] the authoritarian-libertarian continuum remains useful. Clearly, countries in the libertarian camp have had more successful media industries. This is probably because freedom of thought is the lifeblood of creativity. No clearer personification of libertarian ideals can be found than in the example of Hollywood.

In the United States films are produced, distributed, and exhibited primarily by for-profit entities. In contrast, in authoritarian nations and especially in communist nations government authorities make the bulk of those decisions, because film is often harnessed to promote the interests of the state (e.g., propaganda, socialist ideology, and artistic movements related to the revolution). As Gomery notes, these state interests are often served by stressing reality, whereas in America fictional forms (i.e., theme feature films) have dominated.[11] In fact, scholars have predicted or explained the fall of authoritarian regimes (and communism) based on the preeminence of Western media and loss of control over mass media.[12] For instance, Taiwan's mass media system was liberated to become an entity for free speech, which parallels the political development that turned its neo–authoritarian political system into a true democracy.

Of course, a nation's media output stems from a complex nexus of factors that extend beyond the level of artistic freedom. The media systems paradigm explains the reciprocal relations between a country and its media system; the paradigm contains three circles representing

> (1) social factors or natural forces essential to the creation of (2) media institutions . . . that (3) perform certain functions for the society (news and information, analysis and interpretation, education and socialization, persuasion and public relations, sales and advertising, and entertainment).[13]

The first element in this paradigm includes economic conditions, technological competencies, physical and geographic characteristics, cultural traits, and media qualities. I review each of these elements, particularly in the context of film and its entertainment function, to gain a better understanding of the distinctive evolution of Hollywood film. In the next section I outline the role that these social factors play in shaping the distinctive evolution of American film as an institution.

## HOLLYWOOD AS A CASE STUDY

### History

Before reviewing the history of America's ascendance as an entertainment capital, I should note that the film industry capitalized on a strong domestic media infrastructure that has its roots in the First Amendment to the U.S. Constitution.[14] During the 1920s, the United States took the lead in developing lengthy feature films (i.e., those two hours or more in length). American studios also distinguished themselves by actively promoting their actors as part of a star system, placing them along with directors and other artists under exclusive contracts. For instance, actor-directors such as Buster Keaton made great contributions to the slapstick comedy genre, and romantic films were invigorated by the popularity of such stars as Rudolph Valentino. Hollywood became dominant at this time, controlling 85% of the screen time in the English markets of Canada, Great Britain, and Australia and dominating a surprisingly large two-thirds of screen time in such non-English-language markets as France, Hungary, Poland, Romania, Yugoslavia, and South America.[15]

The medium was invigorated by America's contribution to genre and technology as well. For instance, the Western film, with its distinctive packaging of the mythology of American cowboy frontier culture, quickly established itself as a genre with international appeal. As with any genre, the Western can be defined by distinctive plots (e.g., good cavalry versus evil Indians), characters (e.g., the sheriff who is an independent man of action), settings (e.g., wooden storefronts in a Western desert), and iconography (e.g., distrust of sophistication and intellectualism). The genre also became heavily identified with particular actors, such as John Wayne, who once noted that "I play John Wayne in every part regardless of the character, and I've been doing okay, haven't I?"[16]

In the late 1930s advances in color technology (e.g., Technicolor) enhanced the production value of Hollywood fare, enriching the escapist themes embedded in such genres as the musical (e.g., MGM's *Wizard of Oz*). Wide screens were among the more successful Hollywood innovations of the 1950s, emphasizing film's competitive advantage over television's small screen. More recently, new distribution channels such as cable television, satellite television, and home video have extended Hollywood's reach.

Film also played an important role as a transmission belt for propaganda during World War II. Evidence of the cultural transparency of Hollywood texts was apparent at this time, with Hitler once remarking that, if given access to the resources of Hollywood, he could control the world.[17] Initially designed to underscore the superiority of Western democracy over fascism, Hollywood productions also played an important role in maintaining Western ideological cohesion during the cold war.

After World War II film fell off its perch as the dominant entertainment forum in the United States, buffeted by competition from television and a growing outdoor leisure industry. Domestic box office attendance fell from more than 90 million per week in 1946 to a low of 17.5 million in 1969, remaining in the 20 million range for the last quarter-century.[18] More than half of the U.S. population attended a movie every week in 1928. That proportion fell to one-tenth by the late 1990s.

After trying to outclass television with ever more spectacular visual effects (e.g., Cinemascope, 3-D) through the 1950s, the motion picture industry eventually began working with the nascent television medium. In particular, the studios began to produce movies and series for television while selling broadcast rights to their film libraries. Changing demographic and leisure patterns forced

Hollywood to refocus its product during the 1960s. In particular, more films were targeted for the under-30 demographic, which made up 75% of audiences by the mid-1980s.

Themes popular with this market segment—perseverance in the face of adversity, sex, violence, and opposition to authority—pervaded the more successful releases after 1970. These elements, combined with artful special effects, helped the *Star Wars* trilogy set box office records. The primacy of visual elements in science fiction and action-adventure genres enhanced the appeal of Hollywood productions in the global marketplace, insofar as their consumption was no longer contingent on a high level of fluency in English. Action and adventure with hand-to-hand fighting and car wrecks and other carnage flow well from one culture to another.

Relaxation of studio ownership restrictions under President Reagan in the 1980s enabled the major studios to increase their investment in exhibition chains. This sector is representative of several areas of the film industry that have undergone rapid consolidation since that time. The top 3% of the nation's theater owners controlled 61% of the nation's 34,000 screens (e.g., Universal Studios, a division of Canada's Seagram Inc., owns a 26% stake in Loews Cineplex).[19] Theater chains have invested extensively in the construction of multiplexes (i.e., multi-screen theater complexes) containing a dozen or more screens to increase the frequency of showings that maximize box office receipts.

Yet, rather than expanding content diversity by means of growth in the number of venues for movie screenings, this construction boom seems to be crushing independent distributors. This, in turn, exerts a homogenizing influence on movie production. As one film editor recently observed, "The middle-class $25 million movie doesn't exist anymore. Now the budgets are either $2 million or $100 million."[20] These centripetal forces are squeezing out feature-length projects for audience subsets that may not travel well abroad (e.g., films about African American women). Even with these rising costs, however, the number of films released in Hollywood soared to 171 in 1996, a 13% increase over the previous year.

## Global Dominance of Hollywood Film

American films are now earning nearly one dollar abroad for each dollar that they make in the domestic market, deriving a larger share of their income from the exhibition sector. Thus Hollywood has been breaking new box office records each year through the mid-1990s, reaching a domestic gross of $7.4 billion in 1999 and exceeding $8 billion in 2001.[21]

Although Hollywood initially feared the competitive prospects presented by premium cable television and home video, these and other new media quickly established themselves as lucrative revenue streams that supplement box office income. Global receipts for each of these secondary movie distribution platforms now surpass the domestic box office receipts for Hollywood releases. In video the major Hollywood movie studios account for 75% of the foreign market, reaping revenues totaling $4.1 billion in 1997 (including $1.4 billion in rentals and

$2.7 billion in videocassette sales); meanwhile, the domestic video business garnered $5.8 billion in the same year. The video release for the movie *Titanic* alone earned $480 million with sales of 32 million copies.

In fact, global box office receipts are projected to grow 34%, to $24 billion, from 1998 to 2008 as a result of rising ticket prices and worldwide multiplex theater proliferation.[22] The United States has the best developed cinema infrastructure in the world, possessing 30% of the world's screens, with a global box office share of 37%. These proportions are each expected to decline by 3% by 2007, as film industries in other territories start to catch up. In particular, box office growth is expected to be strongest in Europe and Latin America, but screen count increases will be fastest in Indonesia, Japan, Brazil, and South Korea.

As Farhi and Rosenfeld[23] note, U.S. products enjoy the competitive advantage of being created in English, the first or second language of choice for the developed and much of the developing world: "Today's young people have passports to two different worlds—their own culture and to ours." Farhi and Rosenfeld suggest that films produced in English annually command 60–65% of the global box office. The United States accounts for half of global ticket sales, followed by the United Kingdom, Canada, and Australia. During the 1990s, representative proportions of the U.S. share of domestic box office receipts were as follows: France (59%), Italy (85%), Germany (85%), and the United Kingdom (89%).

The media imperialism that the United States enjoys throughout the world contributes $60 billion to an otherwise bleak balance of trade. American entertainment media productions thus account for the bulk of the $1 trillion global entertainment industry, which is quickly merging with the communication and information industries (see Chapter 16 by Pelton). This expansion marks a new communication age, just as steam technology heralded the industrial age 300 years ago.

### Interpreting American Media Imperialism

The basic technology and economics of film influence society, and the social history of film flows from its economic status.[24] Jack Valenti, president of the Motion Picture Association of America, notes that, when it comes to intellectual property, "We dominate the world and nobody is even close to us. . . . This valuable prize has to be protected."[25]

Of course, as other chapters in this book detail, this new American empire or neocolonialism by means of media has not been welcomed in much of the world. Dupagne and Waterman detail how critical scholars subscribe to a notion of cultural imperialism that calls into question the motives of U.S. international distributors who sell films outside the United States.[26] Although some critics of "American hegemony" are Marxists,[27] others outline conspiratorial notions, asserting that "U.S. multinational corporations wittingly quench local cultures and implant their own cultural products in order to stimulate consumption of U.S. goods and services."[28]

In particular, Herbert Schiller provocatively suggests that the ascendance of Hollywood film is part of a coordinated effort, led by the U.S. military industrial complex, to project American influence and a homogenized American commercial culture.[29] Polities that were once hostile to America's ways of doing business or indifferent to its exports could thus be pushed to adopt consumer-driven market economies. Still others lament this growing American influence because it saturates the world with such untenable American values as materialism and devaluation of the public sphere in favor of privatization.[30]

Another leading critical scholar, Joseph Turow, outlines a less deterministic conception of this influence, one that frames the issue in terms of the comparative advantage that the United States enjoys in international trade.[31] Turow, citing Collins et al., suggests that America possesses advantages in terms of

(1) language (English is the most commonly known language across nations); (2) the large size and competitive structure of the U.S. domestic markets (it encourages the creation of a lot of products aimed at broad audience tastes); (3) the availability of a critical mass of competent creative personnel (this allows the United States a predictable flow of product); (4) the availability of financial services and manufacturers of necessary equipment (which gives U.S. media producers the basic material resources to sustain their output).[32]

Others see a softening in the American hegemony as nondomestic owners increase their purchases of American studios. Chan-Olmsted found that by 1990 half the major studios were owned by foreign companies.[33]

On the other hand, some American political conservatives laud Hollywood's domination of global entertainment markets.[34] This new brand of American triumphalism touts the benefits of peacefully expanding the core Western values—benevolent capitalism, altruistic democracy, upward mobility, etc.—in a way that prevents the rise of oppositionary discourses (e.g., communism). To wit, America recently triumphed in a prolonged clash of ideals embodied by the cold war, expanding its influence using the carrot of entertainment rather than the time-honored stick of military conquest. Economic historian Nathan Rosenberg notes that it is difficult to find another moment in history when a single nation so dominated world affairs, saying "There has never been anything quite like this state of the world."[35]

Although scholars[36] express concern that this cultural domination might represent media imperialism, recent trends in coproduction and national production suggest a need to consider more complex conceptualizations.[37] Other important outlets for national cinema include such countries as India, which produces more films than any other country. Hong Kong and Mexico are leading producers in their respective regions, and the Western European powers have also reestablished their film industry during the postmodern era.

As Schiller notes, "The domination that exists today, though still bearing a marked American imprint, is better understood as 'transnational corporate cultural domination.' Philips of the Netherlands . . . and Sony of Japan, along with some few thousand other companies, are now the major players in the international market."[38] In this regard, globalization and new distribution technologies may undermine the validity of such concepts as nationhood and media imperialism (see Chapter 13 by Straubhaar). Newscorp, with holdings ranging from Australia to the United Kingdom and the United States, was founded by Australian-turned-American Rupert Murdoch.

Yet, even as such movies as *Titanic* reflect both the lure and the economic necessity of international collaboration, including English and American talent, the film also illustrates the formidable allure of Anglo-American fare.[39] As Gomery notes, other countries have fought back at Hollywood with government prohibitions against imported films and subsidies to help native filmmakers.[40] In France, for instance, programmers adhere to strict quotas on the amount of English content that can be played in film houses or on radio and television. It is illegal to use English when promoting a product, aside from mentioning the product name itself.[41]

Although France has stood in opposition to creeping Americanization in many respects, Paris plays host to a theme park based on the output of a major American film studio: Euro Disney. This Disneyland spin-off, which opened in the 1990s, has already become the most popular tourist attraction in France. This seems somewhat ironic, given that the park embodies the American cultural ethos through its film and character-based merchandising.

Yet even when peoples in countries such as France or Russia disagree with America politically, they seem to put those differences aside and express a fascination with all things American. What factors are fueling this global fascination with Americana? To be sure, the recent lifting of the iron curtain has opened new markets around the world to American film and television distributors. Commerce data suggest that since 1991 total exports of intellectual property from the United States have risen 94% in dollar terms (losses to piracy notwithstanding).[42] Farhi and Rosenfeld echo Gitlin's observation that American popular culture is "the latest in a long succession of bidders for global unification. It succeeds the Latin imposed by the Roman Empire and the Catholic Church, and Marxist Leninism imposed by Communist governments."[43]

Indeed, even in the former Soviet Union, the record for ticket sales was set by a three-month run of *Titanic,* just one of several American pictures that dominate the schedule.[44] Aside from the pro-Western ideological implications of this arrangement, American content traditionally could be found only in places with the economic means to buy it and the exhibition technology to show it. As Farhi and Rosenfeld note, "Now, even in tiny Bhutan, a Himalayan nation so isolated that fewer than 5,000 people visit it a year, street peddlers offer illegally copied videos of Hollywood's latest blockbusters."[45]

Perhaps more than any other medium, film has contributed to the ascendancy of English as the dominant world language, now spoken by nearly 1 billion people. What's more, there are roughly as many people who speak English as a second language as there are native speakers. This upward spiral in English usage primes the market for further American media products.

Barriers to the diffusion of English-language content have fallen, sometimes dramatically, alongside evolving media systems. As scholars[46] note, this transition has been driven by changes in technologies, political climate, and national leadership, all of which were facilitated by (1) the distribution of new technologies (e.g., satellites, fiber optic cable, VCRs), (2) increasingly effective uses of public relations (weakening the control of a central authority), and (3) global media companies, nine of which dominate media distribution and are Anglo-American in orientation.[47]

## Economic and Cultural Polysemy

Hollywood is the only privately operated institution that can afford to invest tens of millions of dollars to make a film, $200 million in the case of *Titanic.* This hefty financial investment enables Hollywood to assemble the largest group of talented actors, directors, producers, and production technicians from around the world, as it has for most of the century. As *Titanic* demonstrates, the result can be a potent mix of special effects, quality acting, romantic story lines, and American dream themes (e.g., immigration, freedom, class mobility).

Moreover, anticipated receipts from the domestic market for any film are projected to cover the film's production costs, so the marginal costs of engaging in global distribution are negligible. Thus, as Turow notes, "When the Americans come to the international marketplace, most, if not all, of the costs of creating the public goods have already been made back through their domestic sales."[48] This American advantage enables Hollywood producers to offer lavish fare "at prices that are difficult to refuse."[49]

Some of the luster of American film stems from another advantage that Hollywood enjoys: access to new technology. As we enter an era of digital technology, Hollywood's proximity to California's Silicon Valley has aided its ability to capitalize on emerging digital technologies (e.g., computer animation). One need only look to the incredible digital animation technology displayed in recent Hollywood films, such as *Terminator 2, The Matrix,* and the *Toy Story* series to see the important role that computer technology plays in helping America to continually define the state of the art. These examples underscore the importance of time and technology in the motion picture diffusion process.

Film scholars maintain that American cinema has dominated world cinema for so long in terms of economic power, technological change, aesthetic standards, and social impact "that it provides *the* benchmark by which other means of filmmaking have to be evaluated."[50] The dominant aesthetic mode in the United States, which has defined American film since the late 1910s, is termed the classic Hollywood narrative style. Gianetti[51] defines classical cinema as a

> (a) movie strong in story, star, and production values, with (b) a high level of technical achievement, and edited according to conventions of classical cutting. The visual style is (c) functional and rarely distracts from the characters in action. Movies in this form are structured narratively, with a clearly defined conflict, complications that intensify to a rising climax, and a resolution that emphasizes formal closure.[52]

It is useful to explore dimensions of the classic Hollywood style, including the socioeconomic inputs that help it to travel so well across countries and cultures. As suggested at the onset, Hollywood's dominance can be traced to the charmed position that the U.S. economy has enjoyed in the global economy. In addition to its position as the 500-pound gorilla in global entertainment markets, Hollywood was aided in its development by the affluence of the U.S. economy through the twentieth century, one that ensured a steady stream of production capital and audience leisure.

Moreover, the cultural transparency of Hollywood's output was informed by the diverse human capital inputs that have proven so central to the film industry. America's relatively open culture and ethnic diversity in the early twentieth century served as a magnet for diverse groups, particularly religious and ethnic minorities, from across the globe. Gabler notes that Eastern European Jews (e.g., the Warner brothers, Sam Goldwyn) found the American entertainment industry to be much more hospitable than their native climes and endeavored to build an empire of their own within the studio system.[53] Directors such as Frank Capra, a Sicilian immigrant, captured the inspirational tones of upward mobility and belief in the American dream in such films as *Mr. Smith Goes to Washington* and *It's a Wonderful Life*.

Recent émigré directors, for example, Wayne Wang (*Joy Luck Club*), John Wu (*Face-Off*), and Ang Lee (*Crouching Tiger, Hidden Dragon*) are doing the same with their Asian American experience. The most recent examples of ethnic minority film development involve the fusion of American Indian and Hispanic minorities' creative talents; respective efforts from these groups can be found in *Smoke Signals* and *Mi Familia*. Perhaps the greatest progress during the last decade has been made by African American directors eager to reconstruct a market that once thrived in the 1930s and 1940s, only to disappear during the quarter-century to follow. Assuming the vanguard of this movement are such directors as Spike Lee (*Do the Right Thing*) and John Singleton (*Colors*). In an industry where 90% or more of the top executives are males, female directors such as Penny Marshall (*A League of Their Own*) have established a presence of their own since 1980.

Part of the polysemy of Hollywood's texts stems from the fact that America is a universal nation, that is, a nation whose inhabitants come from many different cultures. This dynamic melting pot in turn provides the potency for American culture to resonate that universality everywhere. Although the present patchwork of American immigrants may be different from that of 1900, encompassing new arrivals from Asia and Latin America, the United States remains a composite of different cultures and nationalities. It is this foreign-driven dynamic that explains Hollywood's success in making universal movies, because the producers had to communicate with Jews, Irish, Italians, and so forth.

These potent Hollywood images exert an influence that extends beyond the box office. For instance, Disney's creators emerged at a key time in America's economic domination in the world. When viewing a Disney film or theme park, global audiences are expressing a fascination with the energy, classlessness, and meritocracy of American society projected through film. This includes a belief that, to a much greater extent than in Europe, it is not one's background or alma mater that determines one's life chances. One of the more enduring myths suggests that in America anything is possible. This sentiment is projected in American films, which often portray a classless society with remarkable energy and universal themes, in a presentation that is enhanced through strong production values.

In general, then, it is Hollywood's ability to draw on the experiences of immigrant groups and racial or other ethnic minorities that helps imbue its goods with a universal human quality that is readily exportable to global audiences. In fact, at the confluence of economic and cultural influences we see that Hollywood now treats the domestic theatrical market as a mere first step in the global film distribution cycle, because more money is now made in international theatrical release and video distribution realms. A deeper cause of Hollywood's exportability can be found in the tone of its cultural outputs. Compared with national cinema in Europe, for instance, Hollywood's films are noted for being driven by plot (as opposed to character); that is, American movies focus on the question of how, in contrast to more cerebral European narratives, which typically focus on the question of why.[54] Thus European critics often dismiss Hollywood fare as overly dependent on a simplified, formulaic diet of sex and violence, symptomatic of an industry that has become "fat, happy, and stupid."[55]

This lowest common denominator orientation is further encouraged by America's capitalist-industrial structure. As a part of this commercial structure, American media offer low-brow mass entertainment fare (e.g., *Dumb and Dumber*) as part of a strategy to maximize audiences (and revenues) by offering programming with maximum audience appeal. This reinforces a certain mass production aspect that discourages provocative fare that might potentially challenge the intellect or taste of some segment of the audience, leaving a bland, lowest common denominator product. (Note Frith's discussion in Chapter 11 of a similar homogenizing influence of global advertising.)

A century and a half earlier another European critic, Alexis de Tocqueville, cited a deeper cause for this apparent low-brow appeal of Americana. He maintained that, as a relatively new nation in the world, America has not known the exclusive aristocratic circles that were so central to the perpetuation of high culture in Europe (e.g., wealthy patrons for composers and artists). As a nation forged instead with a democratic ideal, geared against aristocracy and favoring equality, the United States is predisposed to expressions that favor the egalitarianism of the common man. Hollywood film is no exception to this rule, championing such everyman heroes as the cowboy or the private detective. Of course, the glamour of Hollywood film is tempered by the glitz and opulence of the star system itself; the mythology of stardom often incorporates this "rags-to-riches-motif."[56]

Fortunately for Hollywood, in targeting the widest possible domestic audiences, American movies are remarkably appealing to the largest number of international audiences.

The fact that many big budget American films emphasize action over dialogue, for instance, helps make them readily transferable media commodities in countries where English is not a primary language. As movie mogul Sam Goldwyn purportedly instructed his writers and directors, "If you want to send a message, call Western Union."[57] This market-based orientation can explain the appeal of notably non-Shakespearean actors such as Arnold Schwarzenegger and Sylvester Stallone!

## SUMMARY

In this chapter I examined Hollywood's unique position in the global entertainment industry. As commentators such as Mast suggest, Hollywood's popularity stems in large measure from its big stars, lavish production values, special effects techniques and technology, action, and universal themes (e.g., upward mobility). As a result of Hollywood's emergence as the global standard for mass-appeal film in the last century, America's culture, symbols, and way of life are known around the world. For example, the recent success of the movie *American Beauty,* which provides a glimpse of suburban malaise, provides an interesting case study.

The classic style of Hollywood storytelling travels well around the world because, among other reasons, America perhaps represents the closest thing to a microcosm of the world. The question remains as to whether now, as the world turns into a communication network, we are seeing the growth of an American-dominated monoculture around the globe. Scholars such as Schiller see the ready availability of American film, dubbed into local languages, as a force that weakens indigenous cultures. Others see this Americanization of global tastes in a more benign light, perhaps reflective of the country's relative advantage in the film industry.

According to this view, countries become great because they influence the world. As Schiller and others point out, Americans are more vigorous than most in displaying a missionary streak that reflects the root of the country's foreign policy. Hollywood fits nicely in this tradition, assuming the vanguard in helping America influence global conditions in such a way that its ideas are unopposed and able to take root.

Of course, the pervasiveness of American values is not solely attributable to the ascendance of American film, nor are they limited to the realm of politics and economics. However, although critics of American media imperialism may see the country's dominance simply as the triumph of money leading to one-way media flows, this critique fails to explain the cultural dimension of Hollywood's appeal. The ideas underpinning this potent American fare do not exist in a vacuum; they flow from a unique nexus of economic, political, and multiethnic inputs that help define American film and culture.

I have outlined the formulas and values embedded in classic Hollywood narrative, a style that stresses a unique way of life focusing on values that are compatible with the capitalist-industrial state: upward mobility, individualism, and pluralism. As scholars (e.g., Turow) have noted, these were revolutionary notions in many parts of the world during the twentieth century, particularly in authoritarian countries, and they continue to solidify America's status as the dominant world power.

In sum, American film is influential because it represents a universal nation. The nation is universal because it is influential. In that regard, as presidential candidate John McCain noted, "The U.S. is the greatest enemy of tyranny," and Hollywood may prove to be one of the country's most potent weapons.[58]

## NOTES

1. Christopher Stern, "U.S. Ideas Top Export Biz," *Variety,* 11–17 May 1998, p. 56.

2. See, for example, Scott Olson, *Hollywood Planet* (Mahwah, NJ: Lawrence Erlbaum Associates, 1999).

3. See Kaarle Nordenstreng and Tapio Varis, *Television Traffic: A One-Way Street* (Paris: UNESCO, 1974); Tapio Varis, *International Flow of Television Programs* (Paris: UNESCO, 1985); Joseph Straubhaar, "International Satellite Networks: Gazing at the Global Village," in Carolyn Lin and David Atkin, eds., *Communication Technology and Society* (Cresskill, NJ: Hampton, 2002); and Joseph Turow, *Media Systems in Society* (New York: Longman, 1997). Turow notes that in the 1990s U.S. mass media accounted for 75% of broadcast and basic cable TV revenues and 85% of pay-TV revenues worldwide.

4. Oliver Boyd-Barrett, "Media Imperialism: Towards an International Framework for the Analysis of Media Systems," in James Curran, Michael Gurevitch, and Janet Woolacott, eds., *Mass Communication and Society* (Beverly Hills, CA: Sage, 1977); Chin-Chuan Lee, *Media Imperialism Reconsidered: The Homogenizing of Television Culture* (Beverly Hills, CA: Sage, 1980); Jeremy Tunstall, *The Media Are Anglo-American* (New York: Columbia, 1977).

5. Richard Rosencrance, "The American Century: Is It Coming or Going," *Wall Street Journal,* 21 January 2000, p. A1. As other contributors to this book detail, this influence extends to advertising (see Chapter 11 by Frith) and telecommunications (see Chapter 16 by Pelton), as the United States outdistances its rivals in military, economic, and especially (popular) cultural affairs.

6. Turow, *Media Systems in Society.* Drawing on Herbert Schiller's influential *Mass Communication and the American Empire* (New York: Kelly, 1969, 1992), Turow suggests that this empire is uniquely different from all those that came before it: Other empires have imposed and maintained their authority mainly through military force, subduing the locals and establishing armed outposts throughout their colonies. By contrast, the American empire projects its influence primarily not by the sword but through mass communication (p. 210).

7. Rosencrance, "The American Century"; Richard Rosencrance, "The Rise of the Virtual State," in Dale Neef, ed., *The Knowledge Economy* (Boston: Butterworth-Heinemann, 1998), 35–46.

8. Frederick Siebert, Theodore Peterson, and Wilbur Schramm, *Four Theories of the Press* (New York: Seven Stories, 1963); Ray Hiebert and Sheila Gibbons, *Exploring Mass Media for a Changing World* (Mahwah, NJ: Lawrence Erlbaum Associates, 2000).

9. Siebert et al., *Four Theories of the Press.*

10. Carolyn A. Lin and Michael Salwen, "Three Press Systems View Sino-U.S. Normalization," *Journalism Quarterly* 63 (summer 1986): 360–362.

11. Douglas Gomery, *Movie History: A Survey* (Belmont, CA: Wadsworth, 1991).

12. William Hachten with Havra Hachten, *The World News Prism,* 3d ed. (Ames: Iowa State University Press, 1992); Leo W. Jeffres, *Mass Media Effects* (Prospect Heights, IL: Waveland Press, 1997); R. Malik, "Communism vs. the Computer: Can the Soviet Union Survive Information Technology?" *InterMedia* 12 (May 1984): 10–23.

13. Hiebert and Gibbons, *Exploring Mass Media for a Changing World,* 43.

14. Gomery, *Movie History.* Gomery notes that Hollywood established an era of global dominance in film during the early 1910s—

ushered in by big budget features and rising production standards—forcing native industries to respond to this invasion and constant presence.

15. Ibid.

16. Cited in Louis Gianetti, *Understanding Movies* (Englewood Cliffs, NJ: Prentice Hall, 1990), 268.

17. This patriotic wartime output marked the beginning of an extraordinary amount of collaboration between Hollywood and the U.S. government, one that helped lay the groundwork for America's dominance in film for the next half-century. In addition to making narrative and documentary films about the war, Hollywood filmmakers produced several newsreels for exhibition in areas that had been occupied by the Nazis. One film, *Mrs. Miniver,* featured a portrayal of working-class British resistance to the Nazis that was so compelling that Franklin Roosevelt had it dropped by airships in occupied Europe; Winston Churchill termed it "propaganda worth a 100 battleships." See Hiebert and Gibbons, *Exploring Mass Media for a Changing World,* 194.

18. Ibid., 194.

19. Ibid. Meanwhile, with competing European cinema industries left in shambles by World War II, Hollywood again emerged as the unrivaled world leader in film. Concerned over the market dominance of the major studios, the Supreme Court in 1948 ordered them to divest themselves of one of the three sectors of their industry: production, distribution, or exhibition. Most studios parted with the exhibition sector, selling off their theater chains.

20. John Madigan, "H'wood Fights the Jitters," *Variety,* 1 February 1999, p. 178. Costs for producing an average, traditional live movie rose from $11 million in 1980 to $60 million by 1996.

21. Ibid. Ticket sales fell from roughly 4 billion to 1.3 billion during that time.

22. Andrew Hindes, "Study Sees Global B.O. Boost," *Variety,* 28 September 1998, p. 25.

23. Paul Farhi and Megan Rosenfeld, "Exporting America: From Films to Language to Bart Simpson, Our Power Is Felt the World Over," *Washington Post Weekly Edition,* 30 November 1998, p. 6.

24. Gomery, *Movie History.*

25. Stern, "U.S. Ideas Top Export Biz," 56.

26. Michel Dupagne and David Waterman, "Determinants of U.S. Television Fiction Imports in Western Europe," *Journal of Broadcasting and Electronic Media* 42 (spring 1988): 208–220; see also Boyd-Barrett, "Media Imperialism," 116–145; Cees Hamelink, *Cultural Autonomy in Global Communications* (New York: Longman, 1983); Thomas McPhail, *Electronic Colonialism* (Newbury Park, CA: Sage, 1989); and Schiller, *Mass Communication and the American Empire.*

27. G. John Ikenberry, "Rethinking the Origins of American Hegemony," *Political Science Quarterly* 104 (fall 1989): 375–400.

28. Dupagne and Waterman, "Determinants of U.S. Television Fiction Imports," 209.

29. Herbert Schiller, *Communication and Cultural Dominion* (New York: International Arts and Sciences Press, 1976).

30. Arthur Dorfman and A. Matellart, *How to Read Donald Duck: Imperialist Ideology in the Disney Comic* (New York: International General, 1975).

31. Turow, *Media Systems in Society.*

32. Richard Collins, Nicholas Garnham, and Gareth Locksley, *The Economics of Television* (London: Sage, 1988); cited in Turow, *Media Systems in Society,* 213.

33. Sylvia Chan-Olmsted, "A Structural Analysis of Market Competition in the U.S. TV Syndication Industry, 1981–1990," *Journal of Media Economics* 4 (fall 1991): 9–28.

34. See Rosencrance, *The Rise of the Virtual State.*

35. Rosencrance, "The American Century."

36. Lee, *Media Imperialism Reconsidered.*

37. Joe Straubhaar, "Beyond Media Imperialism: Asymmetrical Interdependence and Cultural Proximity," *Critical Studies in Mass Communication* 8 (spring 1991): 39–59.

38. Schiller, *Mass Communications and the American Empire,* 15.

39. Tunstall, *The Media Are Anglo-American.*

40. Gomery, *Movie History.*

41. Farhi and Rosenfeld, "Exporting America."

42. Ibid.

43. Ibid., 6.

44. Thomas Birchenough, "Russians Ready Screen Rush," *Variety,* 28 September 1998.

45. Farhi and Rosenfeld, "Exporting America," 6.

46. Hiebert and Gibbons, *Exploring Mass Media for a Changing World.*

47. Robert McChesney, *Corporate Media and the Threat to Democracy* (New York: Seven Stories Press, 1997).

48. Turow, *Media Systems in Society,* 213.

49. Ibid., 214.

50. Gomery, *Movie History,* xiii.

51. Gianetti, *Understanding Movies,* 442.

52. Gianetti (ibid.) further defines classical cutting as "a style of editing developed by D. W. Griffith, in which a sequence of shots is determined by a scene's dramatic and emotional emphases rather than by physical action. The sequence of shots represents the breakdown of the event into its psychological as well as logical components."

53. Neal Gabler, *An Empire of Their Own: How the Jews Invented Hollywood* (New York: Crown, 1988).

54. Gerald Mast and Bruce F. Kawin, *A Short History of the Movies,* 7th ed. (Boston: Allyn and Bacon, 2000).

55. Todd Gitlin, *Watching Television* (New York: Pantheon Books, 1987).

56. Gianetti, *Understanding Movies,* 230.

57. See George Melloan, "Don't Take Hollywood's Cultural Exports Too Seriously," *Wall Street Journal,* 15 February 2000, p. A27.

58. Ibid.

# 11

# International Advertising and Global Consumer Culture

### KATHERINE T. FRITH

## GLOBALIZATION OF U.S. ADVERTISING AGENCIES

As we enter the twenty-first century, we are finding that the distance between cultures is shrinking at an incredible rate. Two of the major forces shaping these changes are globalization and advertising. Today, American products are sold all over the world, and more and more foreign products, services, and ideas are available in the United States. The messages about these products and services are brought to us, for the most part, by advertisements. In this chapter I examine the history of the globalization of American advertising agencies, define the linkages between advertising and the homogenization of worldwide cultures, and describe how the regulation of advertising in many parts of the world has developed, largely in response to globalization.

Historically, the move toward globalization began in the late 1800s, when American businesses first started to seek markets outside the United States. By the early 1900s firms such as Ford, Singer, and Gillette had expanded abroad, and American advertising agencies followed their clients into the international marketplace.[1] The J. Walter Thompson advertising agency opened its first foreign office in Great

Britain in 1899. By the 1950s J. Walter Thompson had 15 foreign agencies.[2] The Standard Oil and Coca-Cola accounts took the McCann-Erickson advertising agency into Europe in the 1920s. Although the trend toward globalization slowed from 1920 to 1940 because of the two world wars, it picked up again in 1945 and has proceeded unabated since then.

The 1960s marked a major decade of international expansion of many multinational corporations and their advertising agencies. *Advertising Age* called 1960 "a year of decision—the decision to enter into the international field."[3] It was during this phase of agency expansion abroad that the international billings of the major U.S. advertising agencies first began to outstrip the growth of domestic billings.[4] By moving abroad, U.S. advertising agencies could not only service their multinational clients but also compete for the accounts of firms that were operating abroad. Thus, as the domestic advertising business began to level off in the United States in the 1960s and 1970s, foreign markets began to look more appealing to multinational advertising agencies.

The first phase of agency expansion focused mainly on Europe. During the 1960s, many U.S. transnational corporations opened subsidiaries in Europe, with most of them opening their headquarters in England. By the end of the decade U.S.-based transnational advertising agencies dominated the British scene, operating 6 of the top 10 agencies in London.[5] Likewise, in Latin America U.S. agencies dominated the market during the 1970s. For example, in 1977 the total billings of advertising agencies in Latin America reached $686 million, and transnational agencies accounted for 67% of this total. Of the 10 largest agencies in Latin America in the 1970s, the 5 largest were all based in the United States: J. Walter Thompson, McCann-Erickson, Kenyon and Eckhardt, Leo Burnett, and Grey Advertising.[6] As a consequence of global expansion, the international billings of U.S. agencies with foreign offices doubled during the decade. International billings of the top 25 U.S. advertising firms accounted for 40% of their total business; for the top 10 largest agencies this figure jumped to 46% of their total business.[7]

The second phase of international expansion by U.S. advertising agencies occurred during the 1980s, the decade of megamergers. These mergers involved a handful of large, highly profitable ad agencies operating on a global level. For instance, in 1986 BBDO International, Doyle Dane Bernbach, and Needham Harper Worldwide announced a three-way merger to create the world's largest advertising firm, Omnicom Group. Several weeks later, Saatchi & Saatchi PLC bought out Ted Bates Worldwide and immediately surpassed Omnicom in size and billings, with 150 offices in 50 countries. Next, J. Walter Thompson, the oldest U.S. advertising agency, was acquired by the British WPP Group. Although the United States is no longer the only major player on the global advertising scene (see Table 11.1), the influence of U.S.-style advertising continues to have a major impact on much of the world.

**Table 11.1  World's Top Ten Agencies in 2001**

| RANK | ORGANIZATION | HEADQUARTERS |
| --- | --- | --- |
| 1 | WPP Group | London, United Kingdom |
| 2 | Interpublic Group of Companies | New York, United States |
| 3 | Omnicom Group Inc. | New York, United States |
| 4 | Publicis Group (includes Bcom3 Group) | Paris, France |
| 5 | Dentsu Inc. | Tokyo, Japan |
| 6 | Havas Advertising | Levallois-Perret, France |
| 7 | Grey Global Group | New York, United States |
| 8 | Cordiant Communications Group | London, United Kingdom |
| 9 | Hakuhodo | Tokyo, Japan |
| 10 | Asatsi-DK | Tokyo, Japan |

Source: Ad Age Interactive, 2001.

# ADVERTISING AND
# GLOBALIZATION THEORY

The spread of advertising throughout the world has had a major impact on global culture. Theorists have noted that globalization has caused the distance between cultures to shrink.[8] Scholars such as Peter Drucker, John Naisbitt, and Joel Kotkin point out that globalization tends to bring homogeneity to cultures across the globe.[9] In conjunction with new forms of communications technology, advertising has contributed to a form of global consumer culture. As the language of consumption, advertising transcends national borders. Moreover, because advertising is primarily a visual language, it can overcome illiteracy and effectively communicate messages about products, such as soda pop and blue jeans, to even the remotest villages and towns around the world. Although the primary purpose of advertising is to transmit messages about goods and services, through its use of images advertising carries secondary messages about lifestyles, values, and consumption. These secondary messages have had a powerful impact on creating a worldwide or global consumption culture.[10]

Although mass communication researchers became interested in the theory of globalization in the late 1980s, globalization had been an important aspect of the advertising industry as early as the 1960s.[11] In 1967 Arthur Fatt, one of the founders of Grey Advertising, published an article in the *Journal of Marketing* stating, "A growing school of thought holds that even different peoples are basically the same and that an international advertising campaign with a truly universal appeal can be effective in any market."[12]

As the CEO of a successful multinational advertising agency, Fatt's words had a strong impact on the international advertising industry. He promised, perhaps even foretold, that advertising could help "to break down national economic boundaries. . . ."[13] He also contended that people everywhere, from Argentina to Zanzibar, wanted a better way of life for themselves and for their families. He suggested that there was a set of universal human characteristics: "The desire to be beautiful is universal. Such appeals as 'mother and child,' 'freedom from pain,' and the 'glow of health,' know no boundaries."[14]

Fatt advocated that advertisers and their agencies use these universal appeals, and he promised that global campaigns would lead to more effective planning and would save corporations huge amounts of money. He also warned that changing appeals to suit a localized market was not only unnecessary and expensive but also suicidal.[15]

Although the founder of Grey Advertising did not intend to suggest that the advertising industry set a course to create one homogeneous, universal culture, he nonetheless noted that teenagers all over the world were beginning to look alike. One can assume that was because as early as the 1960s all these teenagers were happily wearing Levi's jeans and drinking Coca-Cola.

## STANDARDIZATION OF VALUES

The issue of whether advertising campaigns should express local values or universal themes has also been debated by governments, consumer advocates, and academics who are concerned with the impact of consumer culture on indigenous cultures.[16] From the advertising practitioner's perspective the prospect of running a single advertising campaign translated into many languages offers great economic appeal. Standardized advertising campaigns offer the advertiser greater control over content, because only one creative campaign needs to be designed and produced. This commercial can then be run worldwide (with a sound track that has been translated into various languages). In addition, standardized campaigns allow advertisers to have one unified brand image worldwide (e.g., Marlboro = cowboys), and thus an agency does not have to pay multiple foreign employees to conceive unique local strategies.[17] For many years standardized campaigns were looked on as the ideal type of international campaign.

In the early 1980s Theodore Levitt published an article in the *Harvard Business Review* recommending that multinational advertisers minimize cultural differences and treat the world as if it were one homogeneous market.[18] He coined the term "standardized advertising," meaning one standard campaign that could run in all countries with minimal translations. Levitt wrote: "Companies must learn to operate as if the world were one large market—ignoring superficial regional and national differences."[19] He admonished corporations doing business abroad to operate with resolute constancy—to sell the "same thing, in the same way, everywhere"—and pointed to the worldwide success of McDonald's, Coca-Cola, Levi's jeans, and Hollywood movies.[20] To the movers and shakers who read the *Harvard Business Review,* Levitt predicted that "different cultural preferences, national tastes and standards, and business institutions are vestiges of the past."[21]

My point in reviewing all the conventional wisdom that has guided international advertising over the last half-century is to emphasize that the theories put forth by such people as Fatt and Levitt have been wildly successful. They made Marlboro the best-selling cigarette in the world, *Titanic* the largest box-office movie in history, and Coca-Cola a drink that is available in every tiny town or village in even the remotest corners of the world. These theories have been behind the successful launch of billions of pieces of Kentucky Fried Chicken and McDonald's burgers and fries. From an American point of view this all might seem like it has been a rather good idea. The problem, of course, is that in their eagerness to provide a better way of life to the peoples of the world, advertisers have not been terribly concerned about whether the lifestyle of consumption was what *all* the peoples of the world really wanted.

## HOMOGENIZATION OF VALUES

Some governments and consumerists have argued against the cola colonialism and McDonaldization of the world by way of American advertising, pointing out that Western advertising is based on a set of unchallenged beliefs and practices about communication and consumer behavior.[22] In Asia a debate has raged about the differing goals of communication and cultural values in the East and the West. For example, language, a major aspect of communication, differs in the East and the West. European languages tend to be low context. This means that the words are explicit. Most Asian languages are high context, meaning that less information resides in the actual words and that a listener must understand the context, the setting, the associations, and often the status of the speaker to properly decode the message.[23] In a high-context culture, for example, a headline might be indirect and open to a number of interpretations. As John Sherry points out, a can of beer in Japan carries the slogan, "May Your Life Be Marvelous."[24] The slogan does not necessarily relate to product features or the unique selling points for the beer but rather to the context of enjoyment. In a low-context culture such as the United States, we might expect the slogan to be more direct: "Budweiser— The King of Beers." This slogan is more resonant with the American penchant for directness and assertiveness.

Another area of cultural difference involves social orientation. Western nations tend to place high value on individualism and self-reliance, whereas most Asian nations value collectivism or group orientation. The Marlboro cowboy, alone on the range with his horse and a pack of cigarettes, seems quite normal to an American consumer. However, advertising in Asia generally features groups of people rather than individuals.[25] For the same campaign to be resonant in Indonesia, it might need to feature a group of cowboys riding together.

## ADVERTISING AND
## CULTURAL REGULATION IN ASIA

Global advertising, with its universal appeals, has generated a great deal of advertising in Asia and has been viewed with a strong degree of suspicion. Although proponents of globalization in the United States and Europe see the world through the lens of the homogenization of cultures, this vision is not shared in much of Asia. In fact, most Asian nations have only recently gained independence from Western colonial rulers. For this reason, validating the local or national culture and identity is far more important to them than glamorizing Western values and life-styles, as is often found in standardized ad campaigns. The three case studies used in this chapter demonstrate how cultural regulation operates in the Far East and how various nations view advertising.[26]

It is interesting to note that today only 25% of the people in the world watch the mass media free of direct government control and intervention.[27] Five main political-economic systems operate in the world. Each has different policies and structures for dealing with the media: (1) libertarian-capitalist (e.g., the United States), (2) socialist-capitalist (e.g., Great Britain), (3) authoritarian-capitalist (e.g., Brazil, Thailand, and Malaysia), (4) sectarian-authoritarian-capitalist (e.g., Saudi Arabia and Iran), and (5) totalitarian-semicapitalist (e.g., Vietnam and China). A country's advertising regulatory structure is a part of its overall political/economic system.

The only libertarian-capitalist system—the United States—regulates the advertising industry only in the areas of deceptive advertising and illegal product advertising. In this system industry self-regulation is typically the norm.

The socialist-capitalist system (e.g., Western Europe, Japan, Canada, Australia, and New Zealand) emphasizes a standard of social responsibility. Hence the countries often have stricter rules for advertising that they deem socially irresponsible. Industry self-regulation is typically the norm in these countries, even though there might be some advertising code established by the government. In Australia, for instance, beer advertising cannot feature people doing adventurous sports, such as car racing or boating, because this would imply that one could drink and drive.

The authoritarian-capitalist states (e.g., Malaysia, Brazil, Mexico, Thailand) often impose a tight grip on how the advertising industry should conduct itself to conform to the sociocultural and political order in the country. For example, in Thailand advertisers cannot show kissing, because public displays of emotion are considered unacceptable in this culture.

Almost all sectarian states are authoritarian by nature (e.g., Saudi Arabia and Iran). They enforce strict social controls on cultural and religious rules that are observed by the media as well as the advertising industry. Freedom of speech exists according to the rules set by political rulers and defined by religious beliefs. Strict religious rules are followed in the portrayals of women in media and in advertising.

In a communist totalitarian system advertising is generally not allowed, at least not in theory. However, both China and Vietnam permitted advertisements in the 1980s. Still, the advertising industry is heavily regulated.

In the following sections I examine the regulation of advertising in three Asian countries: Japan, Malaysia, and Vietnam. Japan is considered a developed country, and Malaysia and Vietnam, which are part of the Association of Southeast Asian Nations (ASEAN), are developing countries. ASEAN is a group of disparate nations, including one Islamic state (Malaysia), one Buddhist kingdom (Thailand), one Communist state (Vietnam), and one Confucian-based state (Singapore). Although all the ASEAN countries are geographically close neighbors, each state has its own ideological, political, economic, and multicultural uniqueness. This is not to say that the region is not a participant in what Ulf Hannerz dubs "the global homogenization scenario."[28] Rather, the developing nations of ASEAN are still actively engaged in the process of nation building. In many ways this goal flies in the face of all that globalization has come to mean.

In the ASEAN countries the mechanism most used to preserve cultural identity and cultural conservation is cultural regulation.[29] Thompson defines cultural regulation as

> the regulatory policies in various fields of culture and leisure activities, whether conceived by public or private agencies, [that] aim to foster or control practices in these fields and so have an important influence on the behavior of members of society.[30]

Thompson notes that regulation theory represents an effort by nations to escape the idea that capitalism is the single inevitable logic of development. The consumption lifestyle is highly valued in capitalist systems; however, consumption is often viewed as an individualistic endeavor that counters the collective efforts toward nation building.

Although Western-based multinational advertisers and their agencies have often found it most efficient to create global campaigns that reflect Western values and lifestyles, critics in Southeast Asia have argued that campaigns should be tailored to the particular local culture. The proponents of localization point out that most global campaigns are actually based on "an unexamined complex of Western values and practices and ignorance of the host culture."[31] Although multinational corporations find it far more expedient to think in terms of global or regional strategies rather than in terms of country-by-country strategies, the governments within ASEAN have historically used advertising regulation to protect cultures and to slow down the rate of homogenization.

## ADVERTISING REGULATION: THREE CASE STUDIES

### Japan

Over the past 50 years the Japanese have been successful in their efforts to transform Japan into one of the most affluent countries in the world. Although facing the same economic slowdown that has troubled much of Asia, most foreign economists agree that Japan is Asia's main economic force.

Japan's economic strength is to some extent due to the influence of the United States on its economic system. During the immediate post–World War II period, Japan's economic policies were influenced by the U.S. occupation forces that gave basic guidance to the postwar Japanese economy. Under the guidance of the United States the Japanese established a free trade system and enacted a series of measures, including an antimonopoly act, that promoted fair and free competition by excluding monopolies and unfair business practices. By the mid-1960s Japan had attained one of the highest economic growth rates in the world. By 1968 it had the second largest gross national product in the free world.

Foreign-based advertising agencies started their operations in Japan in the late 1950s. In 1956 J. Walter Thompson was the first to open a Japanese branch, followed by McCann-Erickson, Grey Advertising, BBDO, and Young & Rubicam.[32] These agencies joined the major Japanese agencies, such as Dentsu, Hakuhodo, and Asatsu.[33]

Today, Japan is the second largest consumer market, second only to the United States in total advertising expenditures. According to a Ministry of International Trade and Industry survey, 4,898 advertising agencies were operating in Japan as of 1992; however, their combined billings for the top five agencies (Dentsu, Hakuhodo, Tokyo Agency, Daiko, and Asatsu) accounted for nearly half of the total Japanese expenditures.[34] In terms of worldwide advertising billings both Dentsu and Hakuhodo have been among the top-ranking agencies worldwide for the past 10 years.

**Advertising Regulation**  Because of America's postwar influence on Japan, advertising regulation in Japan is similar to that in the United States. It is based on the Anti-Monopoly Act and the Act Against Unjust Premiums and Misleading Representations. These laws prohibit misleading or false indications in advertising. The Ministry of International Trade and Industry and the Japan Fair Trade Commission are the major authorities concerned with the advertising industry, and these bodies are responsible for enforcing the Act Against Unfair Advertising Practices. These two bodies act in much the same way as the Federal Trade Commission does in the United States; that is, they do not censor or review advertising but act on complaints brought by competitors and staff members. These agencies have broad powers to pursue suspected violators and to demand information substantiating their claims, endorsements, product warnings, and limitations.

As in the United States, complaints brought by consumers about individual advertisements are generally referred to a self-regulatory board. The Japanese self-regulatory organization that reviews consumer complaints is the Japan Advertising Review Organization (JARO). JARO consists of representatives from advertising agencies, the media, and advertisers. Their activities include (1) receiving and processing inquiries and complaints concerning advertisements and representations; (2) monitoring and giving guidance on advertisements and representations; (3) compiling standards for advertisements and representations; (4) promoting cooperation and linkages between advertisers, media, and advertising agencies; (5) working with consumer groups and administrative offices; (6) coordinating education and public relations activities for companies and consumers; and (7) establishing a role as an information center.[35]

Although freedom of speech and expression are guaranteed by the Japanese constitution, there is no established precedent that says this freedom is applicable to advertising. Aside from some legal restrictions, advertising is constrained by various customs and unwritten rules based on cultural values that are observed by most Japanese. These include regulations on indirect speech, the use of words or expressions that have positive connotations, and the avoidance of words with negative connotations.[36]

As noted earlier, the Japanese tend to use indirect speech rather than straightforward statements, even when they have distinct opinions about something. They will use indirect phrases or euphemisms. These roundabout ways of expression are generally considered more appropriate for polite conversation. The same holds true for advertising. The so-called soft-sell approach is more common than a direct appeal to reason.

Comparative advertising, which is common in the United States, has only recently been legally allowed in Japan because of the cultural value of indirectness. To criticize a competitor in public has long been considered inappropriate. As Inoue notes, "The Japanese believe it is better for advertisers to be modest and cautious, so that their advertisements are not regarded as slanderous to their competitors."[37] The Japanese prefer emotional and ambiguous expressions, and advertisers demonstrate their comparative advantages in humorous or roundabout ways instead of identifying their competitors directly.[38]

In sum, unlike many of the developing countries in Asia, Japan does not use censorship to control advertising content. The Japanese prefer to let the industry regulate itself. Both the United States and Japan are similar in this regard. The government agencies that deal with advertising are not set up to censor or review individual advertisements but rather to investigate major concerns against corporations.

## Vietnam

In a free market society such as the United States advertising is seen as an essential tool for a healthy economy.[39] However, the history and political ideology of Vietnam have shaped a different perspective on advertising. The government's stated political mission is:

> To build a socialist state of the people, by the people, and for the people, with the alliance of the working class, the peasantry, and the intelligentsia as the foundation and the Communist Party as the leadership. To fully observe the right of the people to be the master, strictly maintain social discipline, exercise dictatorship toward all infringements upon the interest of the Homeland and the people.[40]

Although Vietnam has begun to allow some aspects of capitalism to enter its economy through its policy of *doi moi* (economic reform), the Vietnamese nonetheless hold advertising in low regard. At the Eighth Congress of the Communist Party in 1996, speaker after speaker "warned against the capitalistic 'social evils' threatening Vietnamese society and the need to stamp out all manifestations of 'fanatic democratism' and multi-party politics."[41] Among the so-called social evils identified by the government were prostitution, gambling, illicit drugs, and the Western-based practice of advertising.[42]

**Government Policies Toward Advertising** Today, 18 international advertising companies have offices in Vietnam, and there are 84 Vietnamese advertising companies.[43] Multinational firms are allowed to do business only if they have formed an alliance with a Vietnamese firm. International advertising agencies have petitioned the Vietnamese government to establish joint ventures or branch offices to legitimize their business operations. So far, however, they have been unsuccessful.

Advertising in the mass media was banned in Vietnam before *doi moi*.[44] When advertisements first began to appear around 1990, the government initially took a liberal attitude toward them. In December 1994, however, the government published the first set of directives for the advertising industry. The regulations were essentially designed to protect the national language and culture. Although some areas of advertising regulation remain vague and difficult to enforce, others, such as the use of the Vietnamese language, are strictly enforced. In fact, the *New York Times* reported that "on storefronts and billboards all over the country neat swatches of paint have recently been applied, under government orders, to blot out the [English] brand name of foreign consumer products."[45]

All advertisements that appear in Vietnam must be in the Vietnamese language and must abide by the public morals and customs of the Vietnamese. If an ad needs to use some English, then it must also show the Vietnamese words at the top and the English at the bottom (or risk having the English words painted over by the government). Ads using any portrayal of European or American lifestyles are prohibited. In addition, the following items or practices are prohibited in all advertising: leotards, bikinis, kissing between adults, kissing between children, encouragement of gambling, and tobacco and alcohol (except beer).

Advertising executives complain that there is no centralized censorship body to approve advertising concepts in advance. This means that advertisers have to spend the money to produce the ads first and only later find out if the ads can be used. Television stations and print media are all government controlled, and they can directly censor the ads they carry if they are unsure of an ad's suitability.[46]

Like China, its communist neighbor to the north, Vietnam is in the process of experimenting with advertising and is wary of allowing this capitalist tool to spread too rapidly. The population of Vietnam is one of the fastest growing in the world. Coupled with China, these two emerging markets contain over 1 billion people. These two governments' determination to regulate the cultural content and expression of capitalism by controlling advertising practices could create a major barrier to the growth of capitalism in the region.

## Malaysia

**Cultural Context**  Malaysia is a multicultural, multiethnic society that consists of 56% indigenous Malays, 34% Chinese, and 10% Indians. Malaysia's current multiethnic character stems primarily from its days as a colony. When the country was a colony of England, the indigenous Malays were largely passed over in the development and modernization of the economy. During the late 1800s, Chinese and Indian laborers were imported for positions in the civil service and business. By 1911 the Malay population of the peninsula stood at only 59% of the population of 2.3 million.[47]

Malaysia peacefully gained its independence from the British on 31 August 1957. In 1963 the nation of Malaysia was formed and Islam was established as the official religion, because most of the indigenous Malays are Muslim. Under the administration of Tunku Abdul Rahman, the first prime minister, the country underwent significant development and enjoyed relative peace until the outbreak of race riots in May 1969. One major cause cited for the riots was the income inequality between the two major ethnic groups: the Malays (who held political power) and the Chinese (who wielded significant economic power). As a result of the riots, during which hundreds of Chinese were killed, the government's economic policy over the ensuing 30 years has been to maintain harmony by enabling the Malays to more significantly participate in the country's economic wealth. Today, Malaysia is a free market economy in which international advertising agencies are allowed to do business. However, because of Malaysia's history of ethnic friction, the advertising industry has to walk a tightrope to produce ads that are both creative and sensitive to the cultural values of each ethnic group.

**Government Policies Toward the Cultural Regulation of Advertising**
The need for advertising to fit within the cultural framework of Malaysia is reflected in the advertising code issued by the Ministry of Information.[48] For example, the code states that

> advertisements must project the Malaysian culture and identity, reflect the multi-racial character of the population, and advocate the philosophy of *"Rukunegara"* (the national ideology), which reads as follows: Belief in God; Loyalty to the King and country; Upholding the Constitution; Rule of law; Good behavior and morality.[49]

In addition to being "legal, decent, honest, and truthful," the Ministry of Information also requires that advertisements take into account the fact that Malaysia is a young nation striving to build a national identity and culture from a diverse population.[50] Thus the Ministry's advertising code explicitly warns against using foreign cultural values or symbols in advertising:

> [Ads may not contain an] adaptation or projection of foreign culture that is not acceptable to a cross section of the major communities of the Malaysian society either in the form of words, slogans, clothing, activity, or behavior.[51]

In addition, ads that depict "ways of life that are against or totally different from the ways of life followed by Malaysian Society," are not allowed.[52]

Because Malaysia is primarily a Muslim country, commercials for pork and pork products and liquor and alcoholic beverages are not permitted on Malaysian television. The law also prohibits intimate scenes. These include kissing between adults, silhouettes of people dressing or undressing, naked or scantily clothed models, and any other physically provocative type of visual.[53]

In addition to overt symbols of Westernization, even subtle things can, on occasion, offend religious sensitivities. In the 1980s the Seiko watch company ran a global advertising campaign using the theme "Man Invented Time, Seiko Perfected It." The Ministry of Information received a number of complaints from concerned Muslims saying that God, not man, had invented time. Seiko was required to withdraw or revise the campaign for Malaysia. The company came up with a new campaign that read: "Man Invented Timekeeping, Seiko Perfected It."

This slogan was deemed acceptable within the framework of the Islamic value system and was allowed.[54]

In an effort to further reduce the elements of foreign culture being shown in advertisements, the Ministry of Information also requires that all advertisements shown in Malaysia be filmed in the country. This is known as the made-in-Malaysia rule. Not only does the commercial have to be produced in the country, but it also must feature Malaysian actors. To conform to this requirement, multinational advertisers often filmed commercials in Malaysia that were later run in other nations in Asia. As a result, these advertisers used models that had a pan-Asian look, so that the models did not appear to be country specific. In general, these models were of mixed European and Asian ancestry. In the 1990s the Ministry of Information put a stop to this practice, pointing out that these models set an "unattainable" beauty standard for the people of Malaysia. Today, the models who are used in the ads must be from one of the identifiable ethnic groups in the country: Malay, Chinese, or Indian.

Malaysia's policy toward the advertising industry is interesting because it shows how religious values can influence the content of advertising and how pluralistic societies in Asia are dealing with issues of ethnicity. Although advertising censorship in Malaysia is not as strict as it is in Vietnam, all commercials nevertheless must still be reviewed and must receive a censor's certificate before they can be aired. The regulation of advertising in Malaysia demonstrates how governments resist the universal values, appeals, and strategies that multinational agencies often find most economically expedient.

## CONCLUSIONS

An advertising student applying for a copywriting job with a large New York advertising agency was given the following assignment: Write a short description of a college student in 2099. The agency was probably expecting something like this:

> Meet Sanchita McNamara Wong, who is 19 years old. She was born in 2080 in Montclair, New Jersey, and went to grammar school in Bandung, Indonesia. She spent her high school years in Florence, Italy, and will start her college courses at Princeton while she resides in Singapore (everything is offered on the Supernet now, silly). She speaks six languages (the minimum requirement for high school graduation), but she prefers to use everyday Chinglish with her friends (this is a mixture of Mandarin Chinese and English and is preferred by most young people worldwide). She loves to eat McDonald's sushi-burgers and drink papaya-Cokes.

I began this chapter by looking at the past and at how the growth of international advertising and globalization went hand in hand. I end the chapter by looking into the future. The world as we know it will dramatically change in the next 50 years. According to United Nations population estimates and projections, 97% of the world's population increase in the future will take place in the less developed regions of the globe.[55] Although the population of Europe and North America accounted for 28% of the world population in 1950, by 2050 these regions will account for only 11% of the total. Conversely, in 50 years Africa will account for almost 20% of the world's population and Asia will account for over 60%. What does this mean for advertising? It means that most of the products and services that will be sold in the future will be marketed and advertised outside the United States, or, to be more specific, that 90% of all consumer purchases will be made outside the United States by 2050. That means that billions of toothbrushes, cola drinks, and jeans will be sold to people living in what are now considered the far corners of the world. Not only will the advertising industry grow dramatically in the next 50 years, but also the need for advertising executives who understand the subtleties of communicating with other cultures will grow.

Certainly, in the future we will see global advertising campaigns. These will be aimed primarily at the young, educated segments of the world's population—consumers like Sanchita. However, most advertising will still be specialized local campaigns that are designed for local audiences. Multinational advertisers will need to become particularly sensitive to indigenous communication models, local cultural values, and new social-psychological paradigms that will redefine how consumer behavior operates outside the Western individualized framework. As we have seen in Vietnam, Malaysia, and Japan, countries will continue to regulate commercial messages to fit their political and economic frameworks. Successful global advertising agencies in the future will be those that encourage their creative staffs and research departments to study local cultures and to devise advertising styles that appeal to the universal consumption needs and the unique cultural differences of different people around the world.

## NOTES

1. Barbara Mueller, *International Advertising: Communicating Across Culture* (Belmont, CA: Wadsworth, 1996).

2. Juliann Sivulka, *Soap, Sex, and Cigarettes: A Cultural History of American Advertising* (Belmont, CA: Wadsworth, 1998).

3. John Crichton, "6 Billion Billed by 677 Agencies in 1960," *Advertising Age,* 27 February 1961, p. 1.

4. Kwangmi Ko Kim, "The Globalization of the Korean Advertising Industry: History of Early Penetration of TNAA's and Their Effects on Korean Society," Ph.D. Dissertation in Mass Communication, Pennsylvania State University, 1994.

5. Ibid.

6. Ibid., 87.

7. Ibid., 86.

8. A. Giddens, *The Consequences of Modernity* (Stanford, CA: Stanford University Press, 1990); John Tomlinson, *Cultural Imperialism: A Critical Introduction* (London: Pinter, 1991).

9. Peter Drucker, *Post-Capitalist Society* (New York: Harper Business, 1993); Joel Kotkin, *Tribes: How Race, Religion, and Identity Determine Success in the New Global Economy* (New York: Random House, 1992); John Naisbitt, *Megatrends Asia: Eight Asian Megatrends That Are Reshaping Our World* (New York: Simon & Schuster, 1996).

10. Katherine T. Frith, *Advertising in Asia: Communication, Culture, and Consumption* (Ames: Iowa State University Press, 1996).

11. Stuart Hall, "The Local and the Global: Globalization and Ethnicity," in Anne McClintock, Aamir Mufti, and Ella Shohat,

eds., *Dangerous Liaisons: Gender, Nation, and Postcolonial Perspectives* (Minneapolis: University of Minnesota Press, 1997), 173–187; Ulf Hannerz, "Scenarios for Peripheral Cultures," in Frank J. Lechner and John Boli, eds., *The Globalization Reader* (Malden, MA: Blackwell, 2000), 333–337; Roland Robertson, *Social Theory, Cultural Relativity, and the Problem of Globality* (London: Macmillan, 1991), 70–90.

12. Arthur Fatt, "The Danger of 'Local' International Advertising," *Journal of Marketing* 31 (January 1967): 61.

13. Ibid.

14. Ibid.

15. Ibid., 62.

16. Katherine Frith and Michael Frith, "Western Advertising and Eastern Culture: The Confrontation in Southeast Asia," *Current Issues and Research in Advertising,* 12 (1990): 91–93; Noreene Janus, "Transnational Advertising: Some Considerations on the Impact on Peripheral Societies," in Rita Atwood and Emile G. McAnany, *Communication and Latin American Society: Trends in Critical Research, 1960–1985* (Madison: University of Wisconsin Press, 1986), 127–141; Armand Mattelart and Hector Schmucler, *Communication and Information Technologies: Freedom of Choice for Latin America* (Norwood, NJ: Ablex, 1985); Mueller, *International Advertising.*

17. Mueller, *International Advertising;* Richard Tansey, Michael Hyman, and George Zinkhan, "Cultural Themes in Brazilian and U.S. Auto Ads: A Cross-Cultural Comparison," *Journal of Advertising,* 19 (1990): 30–39.

18. Theodore Levitt, "The Globalization of Markets," *Harvard Business Review* 61 (May–June 1983): 92–101.

19. Ibid., 92.

20. Ibid., 93.

21. Ibid.

22. Frith and Frith, "Western Advertising and Eastern Culture," 91–93.

23. Warren J. Keegan and Mark C. Green, *Principles of Global Marketing* (Saddle River, NJ: Prentice Hall, 1997).

24. Jon Sherry, "May Your Life Be Marvelous: English Language Labeling and the Semiotic of Japanese Promotion," *Journal of Consumer Research* 14 (September 1987): 174–188.

25. Katherine T. Frith and S. Sengupta, "Individualism and Advertising: A Cross-Cultural Analysis from Three Countries," *Media Asia* 18 (1991): 191–197.

26. Frith and Frith, "Western Advertising and Eastern Culture," 91–93.

27. John Merrill, *Global Journalism* (White Plains, NY: Longman, 1995).

28. Hannerz, *Scenarios for Peripheral Cultures,* 108.

29. Kenneth Thompson, *Media and Cultural Regulation* (London: Sage, 1997).

30. Thompson, *Media and Cultural Regulation,* 18.

31. Frith and Frith, "Western Advertising and Eastern Culture," 181.

32. Osamu Inoue, "Advertising in Japan: Changing Times for an Economic Giant," in Katherine T. Frith, ed., *Advertising in Asia: Communication, Culture, and Consumption* (Ames: Iowa State University Press, 1996), 11–38.

33. Ibid.

34. Ibid.

35. Ibid.

36. Ibid.

37. Ibid., 32.

38. Ibid.

39. Leo W. Jeffres, "Economic Effects of the Media," in Leo W. Jeffres, *Mass Media Effects* (Prospect Heights, IL: Waveland Press, 1997).

40. Richard Lloyd Parry, "Vietnam Insists the Future Is Red," *The Daily Yomiuri* (14 July 1996), 22.

41. Ibid., 22.

42. Seth Mydans, "Hanoi Seeks Western Cash but Not Consequences," *New York Times,* 8 April 1996, p. A3.

43. "The Bustling Market," *Saigon Times,* 12 April 1997, 13.

44. "Foreign Advertising Agencies in Vietnam," *Business Times,* 24 February 1995, p. 11.

45. Mydans, "Hanoi Seeks Western Cash but Not Consequences."

46. "Foreign Advertising Agencies in Vietnam."

47. M. Frith, *The Academic Experience in Malaysia* (Kuala Lumpur: Malaysian American Commission on Educational Exchange, 1987).

48. Katherine T. Frith, *The Advertising Code for Television and Radio Malaysia* (Kuala Lumpur: Ministry of Information, 1990).

49. Ibid., 1.

50. Katherine T. Frith, "The Social and Legal Constraints on Advertising in Malaysia," *Media Asia* 14 (1987): 100–104.

51. Frith, *Advertising Code for Television and Radio Malaysia*, 6.

52. Ibid.

53. Teck Hua Ngu, "Malaysia: Advertising in a Multiracial Society," in Katherine T. Frith, ed., *Advertising in Asia: Communication, Culture, and Consumption* (Ames: Iowa State University Press, 1996), 241–258.

54. Frith, "Social and Legal Constraints on Advertising in Malaysia."

55. United Nations, "Revision of the World Population Estimates and Projections" (New York: United Nations, 1998); available at http://www.popin.org/pop1998/1.htm.

# 12

# Globalization and Media Development in Asia's Four Tigers

## Singapore, Hong Kong, Taiwan, and South Korea

PENGHWA ANG

JOSEPH MAN CHAN

JUNHAO HONG

JAE-WON LEE

The phrase "four tigers" refers to four Far East Asian nations that experienced rapid economic growth after World War II: South Korea, the Republic of China (Taiwan), Hong Kong, and Singapore. With the exception of South Korea, ethnic Chinese are the main inhabitants of the other three countries, and hence the name "minidragons" is sometimes used (dragons are a symbol of Chinese heritage).

In this chapter four distinguished Asian media scholars provide a comparative analysis of globalization and media development in the four tigers. The scholars examine press freedom, an enduring concern among Western media scholars. They also bring a uniquely Asian perspective on the role of the media in promoting national development. The notion of the media actively participating in nation building is foreign and perhaps even outlandish to many Western media scholars. The reader must recognize that in this chapter case studies are used to examine countries that experienced poverty, even devastation, after World War II and the threat of foreign invasion. Rebuilding their war-torn societies was a national priority that involved all sectors, including the media.

The traditional Chinese belief system is rooted in Confucianism. Confucius, a philosopher who lived in 500 B.C., taught a social structure built on a patriarchal hierarchy and a moral framework based on benevolence, perseverance, hard work, loyalty, and respect for authorities, elders, and other human beings. Confucius's teachings clearly influenced the cultures of the four tigers.

Shifting to the present, although the four tigers achieved significant economic development from the ruins of World War II, their leaders put economic development before democratic development. In the devastation following World War II many citizens were willing to endure authoritarian rule for the price of survival in a dangerous and forbidding world. With the worldwide spread of democracy, however, especially after the collapse of communism in Eastern Europe and the Soviet Union, many citizens of the four tigers demanded increased freedom. One of the factors that contributed to the tigers' economic and later political development was their domestic media. Because each of the tigers has a somewhat different political system, the contributions of their mass media to their nations' economic growth and political growth vary.

Korea and China came out of World War II as divided countries. South Korea was in financial ruin and suffered poverty and starvation after the war. South Korea still faces a threat from communist North Korea (although recently relations between the two Koreas have improved), and Taiwan is still technically at war with mainland China (the People's Republic of China), but the parallel ends there. American troops in South Korea protect the nation's borders. Taiwan, however, enjoys no such guardianship. It is isolated, having lost its United Nations Security Council seat. Politically isolated, Taiwan had little external support to help develop its economy; it also has to support a large combat-ready military force (of 6–8 million troops). In this context, its high level of economic development is all the more remarkable.

Hong Kong and Singapore are both former British colonies. Singapore gained independence after World War II. Britain honored its treaty obligations and returned Hong Kong to China in 1997. Without immediate security threats, Singapore developed a benevolent and paternalistic authoritarian government, in which the government provides a stable social and economic environment for its citizens but at the cost of restrictions on individual freedoms and civil rights. Hong Kong, by contrast, benefiting from its former British rulers' socialist-capitalist system, was free to reach its economic potential. It also enjoyed a colonial-style freedom without a democratic political system.

Many factors contributed to the tigers' growth. In this chapter the focus is on the role of the mass media. Throughout the tigers' economic expansion, the press has played a role as either a government propaganda tool or a social change agent—or both—in varying degrees and in different forms. Interestingly, the political outcomes resulting from various media roles are often different among the tigers. South Korea's economic growth helps build a large, wealthy middle class, but the political system is still semi-authoritarian, and the press remains a close ally of the ruling authority and fails to call for democratic reforms. The opposite is true for Taiwan, where the wealthy middle class demanded social reform and political accountability and the press became the champion for these causes.

Singapore is a different story. The press remains heavily censored, for the ostensible goal of preserving social stability. The government treats the media as channels to educate the citizenry about what it regards as proper social behavior that preserves social harmony.

The colonial Hong Kong press was neither a watchdog nor a guard dog in a traditional sense. It assumed an active role in the political restructuring process before Hong Kong's reunification with mainland China. The future of the Hong Kong press remains somewhat uncertain in the postreunification era, although China has generally permitted press freedom thus far.

---

# Singapore: The Role of Mass Media in National Development
## PENGHWA ANG

The Singaporean government strictly controls its media.[1] The tight controls are rooted in Singapore's history and culture as a former British colony. Great Britain imposed its cultural values on the colony by several means, including the mass media.[2] For example, the major legislation that affects Singapore's media directly or indirectly is the Newspaper and Printing Presses Act. This act, derived from the 1920 British Printing Presses Act, required all printing presses and publishers to apply for an annual license.

The government has amended the act half a dozen times since the 1960s. The amendments allow for government control and prohibit foreign involvement in media without government approval. More recently, the government has begun to regulate the distribution of foreign publications. The act licenses media and permits the government to revoke the license if a publication creates communal unrest, glorifies the use of violence in politics, or causes ill will between the government and the people. Some of the rules have been adapted for other media. For example, unless approved by the government, all directors of a newspaper company must be Singaporean citizens. For broadcasting companies the majority of the board must be Singaporean citizens.

Another colonial vestige is the Singapore constitution, which allows laws to restrict the reporting of news that could affect "friendly relations with other countries." Other laws inherited from the British with some modifications to suit the local context include the laws on defamation and copyright, the Official Secrets Act, and the Internal Security Act.

## MEDIA AND NATIONAL IDENTITY

In the 1950s riots erupted between Singapore's Malay and British residents. The riots were sparked by an article in the local English daily, the *Straits Times*. The incident underscores how media can contribute to national identity. The article depicted an unretouched photograph of a Dutch girl raised as a Muslim by a Malay family praying before a statue of the Virgin Mary. Many Muslim readers believed that the British coerced the girl to adopt Christianity. The incident illustrated how the media could stir ethnic and religious emotions that, in this case, bubbled into violence.

In Singapore, as elsewhere in the region, many citizens identify themselves by racial, religious, and ethnic groups rather than by national identity. One of the obvious solutions to prevent future riots and divisions, some Third World media scholars argue, is to create a national identity. The media, they argue, can contribute to a shared national identity.

The Singaporean media have played a role in diffusing ethnic tensions and promoting national identity.[3] Western readers might disapprove of the Singaporean government's control of the media to achieve its ends, even ostensibly desirable ends, but my own surveys have found that Singaporeans generally favor the regime's policy on media control and censorship as the price for a smoothly functioning society.[4]

## STRUCTURAL CHANGES
## FOR THE MEDIA INDUSTRY

Because the Singaporean government believes that mass media contribute to national development, the government seeks to fully harness the media. Although not ordinarily expressed in this blunt manner, this sentiment is the result of a development-oriented outlook toward the media.

Singapore's laws and regulations have created monopolies or near monopolies of the major media. The government regards press concentration as necessary for healthy media growth, and concentration provides the added benefit that it is easier for a government to control and co-opt a few large media organizations rather than deal with many small media organizations. Today, the giant Singapore Press Holdings consortium publishes all the nation's daily newspapers. The consortium's eight local dailies command a combined circulation of more than 1 million. The company is a blue-chip stock and commands more than half of the $1 billion Singapore (U.S. $600 million) advertising market.[5] Singapore International Media, a government-owned corporation that commands one-third of the domestic advertising market, broadcasts all over-the-air television programs.

In recent years some noteworthy changes in domestic media have occurred, particularly in radio and television. State-run broadcasters have begun to be more commercially oriented. The changes began as early as 1980, when Radio and Television Singapore (the government department in the then Ministry of Culture in charge of both producing and regulating broadcasting) was transformed into the Singapore Broadcasting Corporation (SBC). Although the SBC was still a government entity, being a corporation provided it with greater autonomy and flexibility in personnel, financial, and production matters.[6]

The impetus that caused the SBC to become a commercial (and profitable) station came first in radio, in the form of competition from a radio station on neighboring Batam Island, only 45 minutes by boat from Singapore.[7] The popular station attracted 70% of radio listeners in Singapore. The incident underscored how commercial stations instinctively understand how to attract audiences. The Singapore government responded to the challenge by awarding more radio licenses: four to government-related agencies and about half a dozen to its state-owned Radio Corporation of Singapore. The decision to award more licenses stimulated competition among stations. The stations, in turn, produced attractive commercial programming.[8]

For television the threat of competition came from foreign satellite broadcasters. In 1994 the government restructured the SBC so that it could survive in the competitive environment. The SBC was reorganized as the Singapore International Media (SIM) and was charged with operating all broadcasting enterprises in the country, including Television Corporation Singapore (TCS), Singapore Television 12 (STV12), and Radio Corporation Singapore (RCS). Currently, TCS operates Channel 5 (an all–English language channel) and Channel 8 (an all–Chinese language channel). TCS serves as the national station. Together, the two channels command 80% of the audience share.[9]

Pay or premium television became available as cable television in 1995. The government viewed cable television as a means to compete against satellite television programs. The government hoped that viewers would be less tempted to subscribe to satellite broadcasts that provided viewers with uncensored information that could bypass the government's attempts to control the news. The potential harm, as the Singapore government saw it, of uncensored foreign programming was vividly illustrated during the Gulf War. At the time, Singapore permitted only foreign embassies to install satellite television receiving dishes. When the Gulf War broke out in 1991, Singaporean financial institutions learned of it 30 seconds after other international markets did (30 seconds was the time difference between the live CNN news broadcast and the wire service stories). The delay, although seemingly inconsequential, was important for financial traders who relied on quick access to information to make financial decisions. The delay caused significant financial losses and harm to the economy. Since then, the government has encouraged financial institutions to use satellite dishes to receive international news delivered by uncensored foreign sources, such as CNN.[10]

The government recognizes that the push to create a profitable market-based media system may come at the expense of programming aimed at minorities and educational programming. Therefore, when the government restructured its television industry, it reserved channels for minorities and for educational programming. In addition, it recently added a news channel.[11]

## CHANGING ROLES
## FOR SINGAPORE'S MEDIA

The changing role of the Singapore media reflects the government's changing national development policies. Despite the constraints placed on the media, the media have achieved some notable successes. For example, the Chinese newspaper *Lianhe Zaobao* (United Morning News) has the most visited Chinese Internet news site outside China, with a million pages viewed each day. More than 90% of the visitors are from outside Singapore.[12] The government has learned a lesson: Operating the media in a global environment requires openness and an internationally oriented mindset. Thus government censorship rules are being relaxed. On the other hand, some conservative critics decry the new openness. They fear that greater media freedom means that media will appeal to prurient values to reach audiences.[13] To counter a possible "threat" to its culture and identity, the government set rules establishing core values in media:

1. The concept of the nation before the community, the society, or the individual.
2. The family as the basic unit of society.
3. Community support and respect for the individual.
4. Consensus over conflict.
5. Racial and religious harmony.

It should be obvious that implementing these rules will be difficult. The notion of advancing such rules would seem to run counter to the desire to allow the media greater freedom to compete in the global arena. The rules underscore the contradictions and problems facing Singapore, which seeks to use the media to advance cultural harmony and to achieve economic national development. Senior Minister Lee Kuan Yew said, "Information technology, in particular the Internet, has made it impossible for inconvenient news to be suppressed for long." He said that the best that governments can do is "to require the official view to be carried in the media, along with other views over which they have no control."[14]

---

# Mass Communication and
# Development in Hong Kong
## JOSEPH MAN CHAN

China ceded the island of Hong Kong to the United Kingdom when it lost the Opium War in 1842. Since then, under British rule, Hong Kong has evolved from a small fishing village into a global metropolis. Strategically situated, Hong Kong is the gateway to China and other parts of Asia. With a population of 6 million, it boasted a per capita income of about $23,600 (U.S. dollars) in 2000.[15] When sovereignty changed hands from Great Britain to China in 1997, Hong Kong was designated a Special Administrative Region (SAR) of China. In the unusual position as an SAR, Hong Kong was allowed to engage in capitalism under the scheme of "one country, two systems." [16] With little government intervention from China thus far, Hong Kong media operate in a largely free market environment. Because of a vibrant economy, Hong Kong has a strong advertising industry that provides financial support for the media. Coupled with press freedom, this affluence helps make Hong Kong a hotbed of publications and a regional center of broadcasting and telecommunications. [17]

## NEWSPAPERS

Hong Kong's vibrant newspaper environment boasts of 14 major dailies. Media entrepreneurs operate most mainstream newspapers. Still, political parties control a few newspapers. Whether privately owned or party operated, however, many newspapers exhibit strong political views.

Ideologically, the newspapers can be classified as (1) leftist or pro−Chinese Communist Party, (2) centrist or nonpartisan, or (3) rightist or pro-Kuomingtang (KMT) (KMT is the Nationalist Party that fled to Taiwan after losing the Chinese Civil War to the Communist Party). [18]

Before the island's reunification with China, the British allowed the press to fight their ideological wars so long as these fights did not pose serious threats to social stability. Because the conservative pro-KMT newspapers folded during the political transition, the left-to-right spectrum that spanned the newspapers' political ideology lost its relevance. [19] Meanwhile, the distinction between the elite and the popular press gained importance. Since the mid-1990s, the popular press has succeeded in securing more than 70% of the market share. [20] However, the elite press continues to exert important sociopolitical influence as a source of serious political information.

## BROADCAST MEDIA

Broadcasting is subject to more government regulations than the print media, in the form of licensing, codes of practice, and other means. [21] Broadcasters enjoy press freedom and could, in theory, carry programs critical of government policies. Indeed, there is some critical political programming. Overall, however, the need for profits in the highly competitive environment forces most broadcasters to carry entertainment programs most of the time.

With a television set in almost every household, Hong Kong residents' major source of entertainment and information is television. Residents can access more than 38 channels. The Hong Kong television industry consists of two commercial broadcasters, a quasi-public broadcaster, a cable television operator, an interactive television service, and upward of a dozen regional satellite television networks. The largely locally produced Cantonese-dialect channels are particularly popular.[22]

Television stations are private enterprises in Hong Kong and are operated by entrepreneurs. There is one notable exception: Radio and Television Hong Kong (RTHK), which is nominally a government agency, but the editorial independence that it has gained since the mid-1980s qualifies it as a quasi-public broadcaster, much like public television in the United States. As for radio, Hong Kong has two commercial broadcasters and the quasi-public RTHK. The commercial stations have six channels; RTHK, seven.

Radio was the most popular medium in Hong Kong during the 1950s and 1960s. Television became the most popular medium in the 1970s. Less than half of the population listens to radio every day, whereas the typical audience member watches 3.5 hours of television every day.[23]

# MASS COMMUNICATION
# AND NATIONAL DEVELOPMENT

Hong Kong has made impressive strides in its sociopolitical, economic, and cultural development during the past 50 years. The mass media contributed to these achievements. However, unlike in Singapore, the media render their national developmental assistance not as government-controlled propaganda tools but out of a sense of duty to report government policies accurately and objectively.[24]

Many researchers regard news reporting as an act of power because events are selected for news coverage and then those events are interpreted for the public.[25] According to this view, whenever the Hong Kong government has an announcement to make, the media often faithfully report government policies, thus enabling the government to promote its policies.

# CO-OPTION

To effectively use the press for developmental purposes, the British colonial government cleverly worked with and co-opted the free press. The act of co-opting the press involves winning over the press to receive favorable coverage without use of force. Co-option often involves government tactics that confer favors on the press to gain the press's support. The SAR government inherited and used these British tactics to co-opt the press for its purposes.

The government co-opts the press through a variety of means, including granting titles or honors to media owners and journalists in recognition of their service to society.[26] Another means involves designating certain media outlets as the official venues for the publication of legal documents. This method gives these outlets visibility and helps them draw advertising revenues. Government officials can also co-opt the press by granting interviews or special briefings to favored journalists and media organizations.[27] The Hong Kong government also runs the Government Information Service to provide media outlets with free and updated information about public policies, thereby putting the government in a position to define social reality in Hong Kong.

Despite this depiction of Hong Kong media as co-opted government minions, it would be erroneous to assume universally that media lackeys do the government's bidding or are government mouthpieces. Overall, the Hong Kong media are editorially independent. Although they readily report on government initiatives, they also report views critical of government policies. Only the Communist Party−controlled newspapers go so far as to identify strongly with the SAR government.

## THE MEDIA AND STAGES OF SOCIOPOLITICAL DEVELOPMENT

Although the mass media were instrumental in facilitating economic and cultural development in Hong Kong,[28] space limitations restrict this brief review to the media's roles in hastening social and political change. These roles vary with the times and social conditions. It is worth reviewing four distinct stages in sociopolitical development.

*Stage 1.* In the first stage of sociopolitical development from 1949 to the late 1960s, the mass media served as the weak link between the people and the government.[29] In an essentially immigrant society (where most of the population came from China), the mass media were often concerned with Chinese politics rather than local affairs. Through stringent legal control and strategic co-option the British colonial government contained the undercurrents of anticolonialism and pro-Chinese nationalism. The power to define political realities about Hong Kong rested primarily in the hands of the Government Information Service, which produced news bulletins for radio broadcasters and controlled the flow of information about the government to the press. This resulted in the depoliticization of local affairs and thus the maintenance of the colonial status quo.

*Stage 2.* The second stage, dating to the 1960s, involved a demographic shift. A larger portion of society was composed of citizens born in Hong Kong, and the media responded to this shift by devoting editorial attention to Hong Kong affairs.[30] In essence, the media contributed to the creation of an emerging national identity. The growth of indigenous television programs and other forms of popular culture further enhanced this local identity. Although the British government continued to define local politics, its power began to wane when sociopolitical interest groups demanded their civil rights and economic interests in the 1970s and early 1980s. In this environment the mass media served as communication channels between the ruling elite and the public to reduce political tensions and foster social integration.

*Stage 3.* The third stage of sociopolitical development involved two factors: the gradual return of Hong Kong's sovereignty to China and increasing democratization from the early 1980s to 1997.[31] Although the mass media were instrumental in legitimizing China as the future ruler, preparing the public for impending changes, they also served as the battleground for (and as participants in) public opinion wars between China and Great Britain over transitional issues. Denied an official role in Sino-British negotiations over their future, the Hong Kong public depended on the mass media for voicing their opinions. In step with the government's democratization program, the mass media played an indispensable role in legitimizing party politics by covering the activities of political groups.[32] Since the early 1980s, Hong Kong had been in a state of protracted crisis that was dotted with large-scale controversies, such as the debate over democratization and the uproar over China's brutal Tiananmen Square crackdown on its citizens. In these uncertain times the multiple roles demanded of the mass media—as an information source and as interpreter of social and political conflicts—greatly intensified.

*Stage 4.* Hong Kong entered a final stage of sociopolitical development in 1997, when the British returned the island to China. Through the media's timely and considerable coverage of transitional issues, the SAR government, represented by its chief executive Tung Chee Hwa, was legitimized shortly after he was nominated and elected. In the past the mass media merely reported the news of various groups vying for power. In the wake of the reunification with China, the media played a role in monitoring the performance and the policies of the Chinese ruling government.

## CONCLUDING REMARKS

Hong Kong enjoys a high degree of freedom. The press is sometimes guilty of practicing sensationalism, but it generally fulfills its basic obligations to inform and entertain the public. Because the SAR government is initiating reforms in education, finance, housing, civil service, social welfare, and other sectors, it relies on the support of the public and the media to help promote and carry out these initiatives. The mass media are needed to serve not only as information channels but also as a pluralistic forum for social debates to help reach a democratic style of consensus building.

The Hong Kong media contribute to national development by responding to and reporting political events. The media need an environment that supports press freedom for them to continue this valuable function as the facilitator of development. Many commentators have noted the pressures on the mass media to self-censor since the British hand-over of the island to China.[33] Many journalists in Hong Kong are worried that the SAR government will eventually enact laws to restrict their coverage of politically sensitive issues.[34] Although it may be too early to celebrate, the state of press freedom in Hong Kong remains more or less intact at the time of this writing. This is perhaps a result of a number of factors, including the high level of social pluralism in Hong Kong, China's commitment to the concept of "one country, two systems," and China's attempt to lure Taiwan into reunification with Hong Kong by setting a good example. The challenge for

China is to continue its tolerance of dissenting voices in Hong Kong. Meanwhile, the challenge for the local media is to refrain from self-censorship and to be ready to challenge any attempt to curtail their press freedom.

---

# Press Freedom and Social Democratization in Taiwan
## JUNHAO HONG

The last few years have brought increasing press freedom to Taiwan.[35] How did Taiwan, so long a dictatorship with little press freedom, achieve greater freedom?

After several decades of phenomenal economic growth, citizens began to demand political reform. The country's rapid economic development had created a large middle class that was unwilling to tolerate the permanent state of dictatorship because of the ostensible threat from mainland China.

## THE 1950S TO THE 1980S

With the Communist Party victory in China in 1949, the Nationalist Party (the ruling party of Taiwan) retreated to the island of Taiwan. Since that time, Taiwan had been under the rule of the Nationalist Party until the Democratic Progressive Party came to power in a democratic election in 2000. The four decades from the 1950s through the 1980s saw a one-party authoritarian regime. The Nationalist Party justified its authoritarian control by asserting a need to maintain control during its cold war with mainland China. Taiwan enforced a set of martial laws until 1987. Among other restrictions these emergency laws prohibited the right of assembly and association, the formation of political parties, freedom of speech, and freedom of the press.[36] Although the constitution guaranteed those rights and freedoms, they existed only on paper.[37]

Media scholars conceive of five types of media control: (1) direct control through state monopoly stewardship of the media, (2) control by licensing and self-censorship, (3) emergency regulations and national security legislation, (4) pressure on the press, and (5) violence against journalists.[38] From the 1950s to the 1980s the Taiwan government used all these means to control the media.

The government's authoritarian control of media stunted media growth. For years the government rejected new applications for press licenses. The government assumed that the more media outlets, the greater the likelihood of dissent and the greater the difficulty controlling critical media. Until 1988 there were only 31 newspapers in Taiwan. Each was limited to 12 pages. Many cultural and media institutions were either directly owned or indirectly tied to the ruling Nationalist Party. Private and commercial media were not strong enough to exist in this environment.[39]

# MEDIA LIBERALIZATION

A number of events have brought greater democratization to Taiwan since the late 1980s, including the lifting of martial law in 1987. The impact of the political reforms caused Taiwan's media system to become more open and free.

Liberalization contributed to three significant changes. First, it brought about the swift expansion of the island's media industry. Entrepreneurs started new newspapers. Total daily circulation increased from 3.1 million in 1988 to 3.6 million in 1998, and the number of magazines increased from 3,400 in 1988 to 5,700 in 1998. More important, a few liberal or politically independent newspapers and magazines emerged and became a crucial new element of Taiwan's media system. In addition, the government lifted a long-standing ban on the establishment of new radio stations in 1993. Following this action, the number of radio stations quickly increased.[40]

In mid-1993 the government also ended a long-standing ban on the establishment of new television stations and enacted a law to legalize the booming cable television industry. Consequently, two new television networks were established; these formed a system of five islandwide television networks. The inauguration of Formosa Television (FTV) was a landmark in Taiwan's media history because FTV is associated with the major opposition political force, the Democratic Progressive Party.[41]

In Taiwan's March 2000 presidential election FTV played a vital role, along with newspapers, in helping facilitate the election of the Democratic Progressive Party presidential candidate, Chen Shui-bian. With the rapid liberalization of the media the government legalized satellite television. It was not long before Taiwan had the highest cable penetration rate in the Asian Pacific region.[42]

The second major change brought about by media liberalization was the media's role in contributing to political pluralism. As Heuvel and Dennis noted, Taiwan's media can be relied on for "impartial reporting of actions" taken by both the ruling political party and its rivals.[43]

The third major change brought about by media liberalization was the media's role in the island's communication technology revolution. The newly liberated media were financially vibrant and better equipped to adopt new technologies than they were during the days of dictatorship.

# CONCLUSION

In this liberal environment the ruling Nationalist Party realized that it had to act to maintain power. The Nationalist Party enacted a series of political reforms during the late 1980s aimed at changing the party's image. The Nationalist Party realized that only genuine political reforms would help Taiwan establish its moral superiority over mainland China and gain its political and ideological support from other countries and its own citizens.[44]

# South Korea's Society and Its Media
## JAE-WON LEE

The newspaper in Korea dates to the late nineteenth century. Until the turn of the twentieth century most of the world knew little about Korea, and Korea knew little about the rest of the world. The world regarded Korea as the "hermit kingdom" because of its isolation.[45] In this section I briefly review how Korea's media affected Korean society during its evolution from an isolated kingdom to a major economic powerhouse.

Japan, on the other hand, followed another course. Japan was modernizing during the nineteenth century, and it quickly emerged as a military power. It defeated a European nation, Russia, in two small-scale localized wars and it colonized Korea in 1910. Japanese colonial rule lasted until 1945, ending with Japan's defeat in World War II. The colonial Korean state, under Japanese occupation, produced a mixed bag of newspapers. Independence fighters founded one group of newspapers; the Japanese colonial regime founded another.[46]

## KOREA'S MODERN PRESS

The beginning of Korea's modern mass media dates to the waning days of Japanese rule in 1945. A small elite class read newspapers. During the Japanese colonial regime, the Japanese exercised rigid censorship. They suspended publications for gross violations of colonial policies and in some cases closed nationalistic Korean publications. Korea's media in this era were associated with patriotic independence fighters. They were successful in awakening the people to the need to counter Japanese colonial subjugation.

After gaining political independence in 1945, Korea experienced a surge in the number of newspapers because of the liberal political climate of the new republic. Not long after independence the Korean War (1950–1953) broke out. It ushered in an era of ideological confrontation among the Koreans. Mainland China backed North Korea, whereas the United States and the United Nations backed South Korea.

South Korea, like North Korea, was devastated by the war. Its economy was in ruins. South Korea's extraordinary economic growth today seems all the more remarkable when considered against the devastation following the Korean War. The South Korean press contributed to this rapid growth.

The South Korean press eventually became the champion of capitalist economics and democratic ideology, the backbones of the new republic. In the 1960s South Korea's military dictatorships imposed censorship and other measures to silence dissent and facilitate national development. This use of the press to facilitate development deserves attention. The dictatorships used the press by designating the media as a partner in developmental efforts.[47] As in Taiwan, the Korean government often cited the communist threat as a justification for continued restrictions on personal freedom, including press censorship. The Korean press did not experience press freedom until 1987.

## CURRENT MEDIA SYSTEM

Capitalism and democratization combined with a high literacy rate (over 95%) fostered a highly competitive media system in South Korea, especially in the print media sector. As in the West, television emerged as the primary source of information for the mass public, particularly in election campaigns. The state-run Korean Broadcasting System (KBS), a public broadcasting institution, offers two popular channels and five specialized radio outlets. KBS competes with two other commercial national channels. There is also an educational television channel. Cable became available in the early 1990s, but cable did not offer significant competition to the established television channels. The television stations, whether public or commercial, compete as if they were commercial broadcasting media.

Traditional daily newspapers, especially the national dailies, set the agenda for national news. Each of the country's nine provinces has several competing daily newspapers. There are 10 national dailies, all published in the capital city of Seoul. Three of the national dailies—*Chosun Ilbo, Joong-ang Ilbo,* and *Dong-a Ilbo*—account for about 70% of Korea's newspaper circulation. Each of these newspapers has a daily circulation of over 1 million.[48]

In addition, four national sports dailies report sports and entertainment news. There are also four national business dailies, including the English-language *Korea Times* and *Korea Herald*. Besides these mainstream publications, numerous specialized weeklies are also available, but many are small publications that play minimal roles in affecting political and social life. Some of these lesser known media often resort to unethical practices, including reporters soliciting advertising and, in some instances, soliciting bribes for either printing or not printing certain stories.

The South Korean media have been aggressive in adopting advanced communication technologies. All national dailies and national-level broadcasting channels have online news editions.[49]

## SOCIAL ROLES OF MEDIA

During the century-long history of modern mass media, Korea's newspapers have played a pivotal role in the country's economic and political transformation. In the final days of the last imperial dynasty during the early twentieth century, the nascent press advocated Korea's broader world role. During Japanese colonial rule, the domestic press championed the independence movement. After the Korean War newspapers became enthusiastic partners in the country's nation-building process. From the early 1960s to 1987 the press had to deal with the military dictatorship. It was South Korea's darkest period for press freedom.

During the civilian rule of the 1990s, the Korean media championed civil liberties and democratic rule. With democracy established, the media launched national information campaigns to help modernize the country. Examples include an antipollution campaign, a national drive for volunteerism, a clean river campaign, a respect for elders campaign, a global etiquette campaign, a "Let's Help Our Northern Brethren" campaign, a Newspaper in Education campaign, an Internet education campaign, and a love-thy-neighbor campaign.

Korea's mainstream media sponsored, initiated, or conducted additional activities to promote national development, especially activities that the government could not provide. For instance, most of the major media carry foreign-language lesson programs. They sponsor concerts, sports events, lectures, exhibitions, and various contests such as essay writing.

In these media-initiated programs the media often use the expression "we." This does not refer to the editorial "we" but rather to "we the Koreans." This expression illustrates how the Korean media identify themselves as agents of social development and reform.[50]

## INDEPENDENT AND RESPONSIBLE PRESS

Today, Korea is undergoing a massive business restructuring with an emphasis on big business's social responsibility and fair practices. The media generally applaud the business reform drive, although they do not always adhere to these free market reforms or to ethical standards. For instance, the print media continue printing excessive free distribution copies as a means to inflate their circulation figures. Similarly, broadcasters often resort to sensationalism to increase their ratings.

The Korean media decry the pervasive practice of bribery, kickbacks, and political favors in Korean politics. Yet a survey conducted in August 1999 reveals that almost two-thirds of some 700 journalists interviewed acknowledged engaging in unethical practices to enrich themselves.[51]

Because of economic advances, Korean society is becoming more diversified, sophisticated, and self-confident. As a result, various social interest groups and civic organizations, such as the Civic Alliance for Press Reform, have emerged to demand that the press make changes in its structure, management, editorial practices, and programming. These groups ask the media to do their primary job of informing the people as an independent and responsible entity.

## NOTES

1. Peng Hwa Ang and Tiong Min Yeo, *Mass Media Laws and Regulations in Singapore* (Singapore: Asian Media Information and Communication Centre, 1998); Lee Hoong Chua, "Walking the Tightrope: Press Freedom and Professional Standards—Singapore," in Asad Latif, ed., *Walking the Tightrope: Press Freedom and Professional Standards*

*in Asia* (Singapore: Asian Media Information and Communication Centre, 1998), 142–155.

2. B. Nair, *Communication in Colonial and Independent Singapore* (Singapore: Asian Mass Communication Research and Information Centre, 1980).

3. Y. S. Tan and Y. P. Oh, *The Development of Singapore's Modern Media Industry* (Singapore: Times Academic Press, 1994).

4. Ang and Yeo, *Mass Media Laws and Regulations.*

5. Eddie Kuo and Peng Hwa Ang, "The Singapore Media Scene," in Shelton Guarantee, ed., *Asian Media Handbook* (New Delhi: Sage, 2000), 402–428.

6. David Birch, "Talking Politics: Radio Singapore Continuum," *Australian Journal of Media and Culture* 6 (1992): 75–101.

7. Ibid.

8. Kuo and Ang, "The Singapore Media Scene."

9. M. Hukill, "Structures of Television in Singapore," in D. French and M. Richards, eds., *Contemporary Television: Eastern Perspective* (New Delhi: Sage, 1996), 132–156.

10. Kuo and Ang, "The Singapore Media Scene."

11. "Media's Role in Sealing Social Unity," *Straits Times,* 7 September 1998.

12. Hiang Khng Heng, "Economic Development and Political Change," in Anek Laothamatas, ed., *Democratization in Southeast Asia* (Singapore: Institute of Southeast Asian Studies, 1997), 113–140.

13. Kuo and Ang, "The Singapore Media Scene."

14. Cited in ibid.

15. "Bottom Line," *Asiaweek,* 7 July 2000, p. 59.

16. This slogan refers to China's policy of a single united Chinese nation (i.e., one country) that is ostensibly flexible enough to accommodate both communist and capitalist economic systems (i.e., two systems).

17. Joseph M. Chan, "Media Internationalization in Hong Kong: Patterns, Factors, and Tensions," in Gerald Postiglione and James Arnold, eds., *Hong Kong's Reunion with China: The Global Dimensions* (New York: M. E. Sharpe, 1997), 222–238.

18. Joseph M. Chan and Chin-Chuan Lee, *Mass Media and Political Transition: The Hong Kong Press in China's Orbit* (New York: Guilford, 1991).

19. Clement Y. K. So, "Pre-1997 Hong Kong Press: Cut-Throat Competition and the Changing Journalistic Paradigm," in M. K. Nyaw and S. M. Li, eds., *The Other Hong Kong Report 1996* (Hong Kong: Chinese University Press, 1996), 485–505.

20. Joseph M. Chan, Eric K. W. Ma, and Clement Y. K. So, "Back to the Future: A Retrospect and Prospects for the Hong Kong Mass Media," in Joseph Cheng, ed., *The Other Hong Kong Report 1997* (Hong Kong: Chinese University Press, 1997), 455–482.

21. Clement Y. K. So, Joseph M. Chan, and Chin-Chuan Lee, "Hong Kong SAR," in S. Gunaratne, ed., *Handbook of the Media in Asia* (New Delhi: Sage, 2000), 527–551.

22. Chan et al., "Back to the Future."

23. So et al., "Hong Kong SAR."

24. This should not be interpreted to mean that Hong Kong's media are necessarily of high quality. Media professionalism and objectivity represent a media ideology that prevails in Western democracies. For an analysis or demystification of media professionalism and objectivity, see, for example, Gaye Tuchman, *Making News* (New York: Free Press, 1978); and Chan and Lee, *Mass Media and Political Transition.*

25. For example, see Herbert Gans, *Deciding What's News* (New York: Pantheon, 1979); and Phillip Tichenor, George Donohue, and Clarice Olien, *Community Conflict and the Press* (Beverly Hills, CA: Sage, 1980).

26. Chan and Lee, *Mass Media and Political Transition.*

27. Chin-Chuan Lee and Joseph M. Chan, "Government Management of the Press in Hong Kong," *Gazette* 46 (1990): 125–139.

28. The mass media contribute to economic growth in Hong Kong. Although they are keen on reporting the government's economic policies, they keep a watchful eye

over any signs that may have any bearing on the health of the economy. It is difficult to imagine how Hong Kong could have developed into a global financial center without the support of its media. Cultural development in Hong Kong is tied to the rise of popular culture, which is a source of identity and national pride. Hong Kong's television programs, movies, and pop songs are popular in Chinese societies around the world, including mainland China, Taiwan, and Singapore. Chan, "Media Internationalization in Hong Kong"; Eric Ma, *Television, Politics, and Culture in Hong Kong* (London: Routledge, 1999).

29. Joseph M. Chan, "Mass Media and Sociopolitical Formation in Hong Kong, 1949–1992," *Asian Journal of Communication* 2, no. 3 (1992): 106–129.

30. Ibid.

31. Ibid.

32. Anthony Fung, "Parties, Media, and Public Opinion: A Study of Media's Legitimization of Party Politics in Hong Kong," *Asian Journal of Communication* 5, no. 2 (1995): 18–46.

33. Chin-Chuan Lee, "Press Self-Censorship and Political Transition in Hong Kong," *Harvard International Journal of Press/Politics* 3, no. 2 (1998): 55–73.

34. Hong Kong Journalists' Association and Article 19, *Patriotic Games: Hong Kong's Media Face to Face with the Taiwan Factor* (Hong Kong: Journalists' Association and Article 19, 2000).

35. This liberalization was part of a larger global trend in which media contributed to democratization elsewhere. George Gerbner, Hamid Mowlana, and Karle Nordenstreng, eds., *The Global Media Debate: Its Rise, Fall, and Renewal* (Norwood, NJ: Ablex, 1993); Cees Hamelink, *The Politics of World Communication* (Thousand Oaks, CA: Sage, 1994); J. Sinclair, E. Jacka, and S. Cunningham, eds., *New Patterns in Global Television: Peripheral Vision* (Oxford: Oxford University Press, 1996); J. Downing, *Internationalizing Media Theory* (Thousand Oaks, CA: Sage, 1996); Emile McAnany and K. Wilkinson, eds., *Mass Media and Free Trade: NAFTA and the Cultural Industries* (Austin: University of Texas Press, 1996);

Hamid Mowlana, *Global Communication in Transition* (Thousand Oaks, CA: Sage, 1996); A. Mohammadi, ed., *International Communication and Globalization* (Thousand Oaks, CA: Sage, 1997); J. Hong and Y. Hsu, "Asian NICs' Broadcast Media in the Era of Globalization," *Gazette* 61 (1999): 225–242.

36. F. Hu, "Political Democratization and Constitutional Structure," *Constitutional Reform* 2 (1999): 11–47.

37. K. Rampal, "Post–Martial Law Media Boom in Taiwan," *Gazette* 53 (1994): 73–91; *Republic of China Yearbook 1995–1996* (Taipei: Republic of China Government Information Office, 1997).

38. Brent Rubin, "New Technologies Breach the Five Barriers of Media Control," *Intermedia* 21 (1993): 22–28.

39. C. Lee, "Sparking a Fire: The Press and the Ferment of Democratic Change in Taiwan," *Journalism Monographs* 138 (1993).

40. Government Information Office, *Taiwan's Media in the Democratic Era,* Report Prepared for the International Press Institute World Congress and the 48th General Assembly (Taipei: Government Information Office, May 1999). Available at http://www .gio.gov.tw/info/ipi/index.htm.

41. S. Yu, "DDP-Backed Company Wins License for Fourth Television Station," *Free China Journal,* 23 June 1995, p. 2.

42. "Media in Taiwan Develops in Step with Free Society," *Free China Journal,* 21 May 1999, p. 7.

43. T. Metzger and R. Myers, *Understanding the Taiwan Experience: A Historical Perspective* (Taipei: Kwang Hwa Publishers, 1990).

44. Taiwan lost its diplomatic relations with most countries after it was replaced by mainland China as a United Nations member in 1972.

45. For a general introduction to the Korean media, see the Korean Press Foundation's Web site at http://www.kpf.or.kr.

46. For a general introduction to the major issues affecting Korea's mass media, see Chie-woon Kim and Jae-won Lee, eds., *Elite Media Amidst Mass Culture: A Critical*

*Look at Mass Communication in Korea* (Seoul: Nanam, 1994).

47. For an introduction to the Korean press during the military rule, see Jae-won Lee, "The Press of South Korea," in George Kurian, ed., *World Press Encyclopedia* (New York: Facts on File, 1982), 579–594.

48. These statistics must be regarded with some caution. Most major Korean press institutions refuse to join the country's Audit Bureau of Circulations. Thus there is no audit to confirm the newspapers' claimed circulation figures.

49. The Korean Press Foundation's Web site at http://www.kpf.or.kr provides links to all the major media's online versions, some of which provide truncated English versions.

50. Many media recognize that their enthusiastic support for development means that they are not objective. Some leading journalists even join various government boards as advisory members. For instance, the minister of foreign affairs and trade has a 50-member policy advisory board, of which as many as 16 are editors, editorial writers, commentators, and columnists. Furthermore, some journalists serve in the governmental units that they used to cover. Press participation in the nation-building process hence goes hand in hand with the national governing process. Given the norm and practice of the media's role in the Korean political system, there is surprisingly little professional debate over the propriety of such symbiotic press-government relationships. Publishers of several major national dailies meet with the incumbent president periodically for counseling on state affairs. These media leaders are sarcastically referred to as nighttime presidents. Sok-chun Son, "Nighttime Presidents, Daytime President" [editorial], *Hankyoreh Shinmun,* 8 September 1999.

51. Chi-song Hwang, "Ethical Views of the Korean Journalists," *Journalism and Broadcasting,* September 1999. Available at http://www.kpf.co.kr.

# PART VI

# Cultural Concerns

When a newspaper publisher named Benjamin Day sold his *New York Sun* for a penny a copy in 1833, a mass medium was born. Historically, newspapers have informed, entertained, and sometimes educated the public in more ways than one. Hence the impact of mass media on society, albeit varying across different aspects of a society, can be particularly robust in the areas of news and popular culture. As a result, concerns about the media's impact on culture exist in any modern society. However, when such concerns involve "undesirable" cultural imports, the issue of protecting the integrity of the native culture can arise.

These undesirable cultural imports are often produced by economically powerful nations, such as the United States. For instance, the U.S.-based news, entertainment, and Internet media industries have become so dominant on the world's movie, television, and computer screens that even European nations have joined developing nations in crying foul. In essence, what appears to be the most economically efficient production and distribution model for marketing cultural products has been accused of engaging in media imperialism and cultural imperialism.

The rationale behind such concerns, especially for developing nations, often originates from the fear of adding cultural dependency to the already existing political and economic dependency on a Western nation, such as the United States.

Cultural dependency refers to the process by which Third World countries depend on the industrialized world, notably the United States, for media content and other cultural goods. Although political and economic dependency may align a developing nation's geopolitics with the U.S. position, cultural dependency may gradually modify that nation's indigenous culture to conform to the Americanized ideology. Hence a classic confrontation between modernization (Westernization) and tradition flares up over what defines a nation-state's modern cultural identity.

Joseph D. Straubhaar, of the University of Texas at Austin, examines this issue from a theoretical perspective in Chapter 13. He reviews the theoretical traditions of dependency theory and explicates it further within the context of world systems models to explain how dependency is a concept arrayed along a continuum rather than being a dichotomy. This discussion is linked to a contemporary analysis of the concepts of media imperialism and cultural imperialism, which challenge the traditional wholesale notion of omnipotent media imperialists. This revisionist view of the old imperialism paradigms is elaborated on in a review of the ongoing trends in the development of local cultural industry, the dynamics of which are a product of local, regional, and world cultural (e.g., linguistic), economic (e.g., capital), and technological (e.g., satellite network) interdependence.

The next chapter, by Douglas A. Boyd of the University of Kentucky, complements Straubhaar's chapter by glancing at a culturally unique region (the Arab world) to further illustrate how media technology helps reinforce the cultural bonds in Arab societies. Because Arab nations and cultures share a common linguistic and religious bond, the media content distributed through their national media systems is often intertwined as well. Hence domestic broadcasting is usually listened to or watched by audiences across national borders. Although the media systems are generally under tight government control and are commonly used as government propaganda tools, some of these governments are now allowing limited Western news and entertainment content to be brought into the region by means of satellite networks. Because only the more elite population segment is privy to Western media programming, the much guarded negative impact of cultural or media imperialism is visibly absent.

# 13

# Globalization, Media Imperialism, and Dependency as Communications Frameworks

## JOSEPH D. STRAUBHAAR

For decades people have tried to understand the role of media in the unequal relations between countries. In the 1960s and 1970s many studies reported a one-way flow of media, particularly television programs and news, from a few First World countries to the rest of the world. For example, Herbert Schiller, a leading critical scholar, showed that 65% of all world communications originated in the United States.[1] In an international study financed by the United Nations Educational, Scientific, and Cultural Organization (UNESCO), Nordenstreng and Varis identified a strong influence of U.S. television shows on other countries[2]; other studies indicated the dominance of the four large news agencies (AP, UPI, Agence France Presse, and Reuters) around the world.[3]

Critics saw the spread of the commercial model of media, foreign investment in media, and the power of multinational advertisers as sources of both financial and commercial pressure and as threats to local development.[4] It seemed that the peoples of many nations and cultures were being assaulted by foreign media and foreign cultures, especially American media and culture. Scholars (e.g., Dorfman and Mattelart) pointed out that, although the ubiquity of such American media products as Disney Comics' Donald Duck in Chile might seem innocent, exposure to the products leads audience members to imitate the essentially middle-class American life depicted in media accounts and to become more consumer oriented.[5]

Some scholars believe that media imperialism is even more striking now. *Baywatch* was on television in about 60 countries in 1998, but the movie *Titanic* dominated video screens worldwide. Media mogul Rupert Murdoch's various companies reach about two-thirds of the globe with satellite television signals and even more countries with the corporation's movies and television programs. Global media are not just a Hollywood monopoly anymore. In fact, some major Hollywood companies are now owned by Japanese (e.g., Sony), Canadian (e.g., Seagram's), and French (e.g., Hachette and Havas) companies. Mexican and Brazilian soap operas (*telenovelas*) reach almost as many countries as *Baywatch,* and they are more popular in some places, such as Latin America and, interestingly, Eastern Europe and Central Asia.

The current international theoretical discussion tends to focus more on the globalization of cultures within a world economy,[6] although some critical writers such as Schiller insist that media and cultural imperialism are still strong.[7] In this chapter I analyze the strengths and weaknesses of media imperialism theory, globalization, and dependency theory, and reinterpret the term "asymmetric interdependence" to refer to the variety of possible unequal relationships between countries.[8]

## MEDIA AND IMPERIALISM

One dominant tendency in international television research has been to examine the global development of media, including television, as cultural aspects of U.S. and European imperialism. In this view, deriving from Marx, culture and communication are seen as the ideological superstructure of capitalist economic expansion.

Marxists view capitalist society as involving class domination; the media are seen as part of an ideological arena in which various class views are debated. The media, taken as a whole, relay interpretive frameworks consonant with the interests of the dominant classes. Average media audiences are seen as lacking ready access to alternative meaning systems that would enable them to reject the definitions offered by the media in favor of oppositional definitions.[9]

Marx and, later, Lenin extended this analysis of capitalism to the world capitalist economy as an analysis of imperialism. When they advanced their ideas, many countries, especially those in Africa, the Middle East, and Asia, were still colonies under the control of the British, French, Portuguese, Belgian, Dutch, or German empire. These empires were established over time to ensure that their colonies would be exclusive sources of raw materials, markets for the empire's manufactured goods, and political and military bases of power for the imperial countries. American students might recall that these kinds of conditions led to the American colonies' revolution against Great Britain.

Colonialism was strong and subjugated many countries and peoples. Most imperial countries had strong military power to suppress revolt; in many cases they co-opted local leaders to help them maintain the colonial status quo for their personal gains. Before 1800 only the United States and Haiti had successful revolutions against colonial powers. They were joined by most Latin American countries in the 1800s. However, even after gaining independence, most of the current nations of the world remained de facto colonies.[10] For example, Latin American countries still depend on the United States for capital, manufactured goods, and markets for raw materials.[11] The United States, like the former empires, tried to dominate trade with Latin American countries, buy raw materials at low prices, sell manufactured goods at high prices, and maintain the Latin American countries as military allies.[12] In fact, the United States militarily intervened against popular local uprisings in a number of Latin American countries, particularly in Central America and the Caribbean, to maintain economic and political control.

Lenin and other Marxist scholars, such as Baran and Sweezy, argued that this type of new postcolonial economic and political domination constituted a new form of de facto imperialism by means of concentrated or monopoly capital controlled by economically dominant industrialized countries, such as the United States, Japan, and Western Europe.[13] Two primary theoretical explanations developed for this kind of economic and political structure between a dominant core of industrial nations and a dependent periphery of developing nations: dependency theory and world systems theory.


## DEPENDENCY THEORY

With its roots in Marxist analysis, cultural dependency theory looks primarily at the ideological role of media as part of the economic relations of dependency. The peripheral or Third World countries depend on the industrialized world for capital, technology, and most manufactured goods, and they export low-cost primary products or cheap manufactured goods, which add little benefit to the local economy.[14] The reach of the industrialized nations continues to expand and draw new nations into economic dependency. Speaking primarily of Latin America, Fox observed, "Cultural dependency generally was taken to mean the domination of content, financing, and advertising of the domestic media by foreign, specifically U.S., companies."[15]

In this relationship of dependency the role of culture, including television and other media production, is both economic and ideological. Television, film, and music can be seen as another set of products sold at high prices by First World producers to Third World consumers. As we will see, however, the reality of international television, film, and music sales is considerably more complex than that. Advertising and the consumerism it promotes are seen as key vehicles of both economic and ideological expansion by the core nations.[16] In fact, many dependency theorists and researchers concentrate on advertising because it seems to have a dual role in creating dependency. Advertising directly affects consumers, drawing them into the world's capitalist economy, making them satisfied with a dependent position.[17] Advertising affects nations indirectly by drawing their media systems into the same capitalist system, making them economically dependent on major advertisers and advertising agencies from the core industrial countries.[18]

The ideological role of media in dependency can be seen as a less sophisticated form of Gramsci's concept of hegemony, in which elite groups and some others compete to use media and other cultural or informational structures to set a dominant ideology or worldview for the rest of the world.[19] Some versions of dependency are more complex, particularly those building on the idea of dependent development. This school of thought recognizes that growth and development can occur in the Third World and smaller industrialized nations, albeit in a dependent context, conditioned and restrained by the interests of the core industrial countries.[20]

Control of domestic media structures and the ideological role of advertising, imported news, and other imported media products were the primary concerns of dependency theorists. As with Marxism, this view sees structures and economic factors as determinant and does not give much attention to the interaction of the audience with the actual texts or content of the cultural products. For instance, there is conflict within the domestic elite that operates media. Media personnel can develop separate national or local agendas. Variations and differences in these tendencies accentuate the need to analyze cases separately and historically.[21] For that reason we find that even the dependent development approach is too deterministic to adequately explain current cultural dependency realities in the Third World and in smaller First and Second World nations.

Fox noted that critiques of cultural dependency theories center on three areas: (1) the failure of state-directed policy aimed at countering dependency, (2) the allure of free trade, and (3) the apparent success of some large Third World broadcasters (e.g., Mexico's Televisa and Brazil's TV Globo) and the "theoretical richness of broader areas of analysis—popular culture, post-imperialism, and world systems." I consider these areas and others later.[22]

## WORLD SYSTEMS THEORY

World systems theory seems to offer a more complex and adequate base for examining issues of world media systems, unequal media flows, and cultural interpenetration than do the more dichotomous versions of dependency theory, where nations are either dominant or dependent.[23] World systems theory recognizes that a core of industrial nations controls the essential dynamics of the world capitalist system and that a large number of developing nations are peripheral and dependent. In addition, a smaller number of nations have achieved some growth and development, which Wallerstein calls semiperipheral.[24] Semiperipheral states include the partially industrialized states of the Third World, Eastern Europe, and, at least early in the twentieth century, Russia.[25]

In this regard, world systems theory anticipated much of the economic aspect of globalization, as it is currently discussed. Capitalism spreads globally to constitute a world economic system, which strongly affects how nations structure, finance, and program their media. As more and more countries join the world capitalist economy to a more complete degree, their media audiences are cast into a primary role as consumers of advertising and advertised goods controlled by the core industrialized nations.[26] It is difficult for any nation to resist being integrated into this dominant capitalist world system. For example, Wallerstein predicted that the former Soviet Union would ultimately not be able to resist integrating itself into a role more compatible with such a powerful system.

This analysis shares a conceptual problem with Cardoso's notion of dependent development because it does not explain how the semiperipheral nations (i.e., smaller industrialized European and Eastern European countries and other nations such as Singapore, South Korea, and Taiwan) are assuming a semicore mantle.[27] For example, the World Bank has officially upgraded Singapore from the status of a developing or middle-income country to the developed or upper-income category alongside most European nations.

It seems more theoretically sensible to place nations on a continuum to depict their degree of dependency, instead of assigning them to one of the three categories (periphery, semiperiphery, or core). This continuum would then range from the poorest and most dependent countries (e.g., Mozambique), to countries that are strong on cultural production but still dependent on outside capital and technology (e.g., Brazil), to countries that are relatively developed in most respects (e.g., Singapore or Taiwan), to countries that are central to the world economic and political system (e.g., the United States).

World systems theory shares with imperialism and dependency theories an underlying economic determinism. Imperialism, dependency, and world systems theories all argue forcefully for the primacy of economics and the role of media in cultural relations between countries. Cultural issues, including the ownership, creation, and flow of media, have frequently been studied largely within a political economy framework. Many writers have argued that an understanding of political economy, which involves an analysis of who owns and controls the media, is fairly sufficient for understanding media on both the global and the national level.[28] More recent approaches recognize the complexity of forces at work and argue that political economy forces are powerful but not determinant.[29]

In general, we see a movement away from deterministic views of the political economy of television.[30] Nevertheless, these analyses correctly stress the importance of ownership, class relations, and other economic factors in the shaping of television and other media on the world, regional, and local levels.

## CULTURAL IMPERIALISM

Cultural imperialism theory generally suggests a strong connection between the concepts of economic imperialism and cultural domination as "economic power in the service of cultural domination and vice versa."[31]

Cultural imperialism usually makes strong claims about the social or behavioral effects of media, advertising, and other cultural forces. Tunstall observed: "The cultural imperialism hypothesis claims that authentic, traditional, and local culture in many parts of the world is being battered out of existence by the indiscriminate dumping of large quantities of slick commercial and media products, mainly from the United States."[32]

Cultural imperialism tends to see culture as only part of a holistic system, in which imported television programs and films, local adaptations of American entertainment media genres, and local and imported advertising and commercial media models combine to encourage increased consumption among viewers. In comparison, the theory of media imperialism focuses more on specific market phenomena, such as unbalanced television flows between countries[33] (at the expense of losing sight of large cultural issues that a cultural imperialism approach might capture).[34] As such, cultural imperialism analysis is often used to critique capitalism, both local and international. The main critiques, Tomlinson notes, are that capitalism is a homogenizing cultural force and that capitalism produces and reproduces a culture of consumerism.[35] We can consider these capitalism-induced cultural macro- or high-level effects of the globalization of television within a capitalist world system. Nevertheless, these are complex effects that operate differently among various nations and among various classes within nations.

## MEDIA IMPERIALISM

The thesis of media imperialism theory builds on holistic explanations and the degree of economic determinism implied by the dependency and cultural imperialism theories. However, media imperialism focuses primarily on unbalanced media import and export relationships between nations.[36] Lee's version of media imperialism is an attempt to define the phenomenon in terms that are more empirically measurable. Lee focused on several interrelated factors: financial or ownership involvement by First World companies in Third World media, the adoption and use of First World media models, the uneven flow of media products (particularly television from First World to Third World), and the effect of both imported models and programs on Third World cultures.[37] These factors do not tell the whole story of complex international television processes and interactions; they provide specific benchmarks to help us judge how well key aspects of media imperialism apply to specific countries, their media, and the interrelations between countries and the media.

Historical analyses of Lee's factors show that foreign ownership of media declined in the 1970s because many governments intervened to assert national control of broadcasting.[38] However, foreign ownership increased again in the 1990s, when many governments began to loosen rules on private and foreign ownership in the neoliberal climate of that decade. The end of the 1990s showed a mixed pattern in which major core country media operations invested in the media of other core countries, for example, Japanese, German, French, and Canadian purchases of U.S. media. Some other companies, such as Murdoch's News Corporation, have bought media operations, including Star TV in Asia.

The most prevalent practice during the late 1990s involved a core country's media taking a financial stake in a developing country's media through such means as minority share investments, joint ventures, coproductions, licensing deals, and purchase agreements. This practice reflects a recognition that local media companies frequently know local markets better and hence that it is better to let them take ownership risks and plan local media strategies. It illustrates the limits placed on foreign ownership of media in many countries, although the United States and other core countries work through the World Trade Organization and other trade forums to try to reduce ownership and investment restrictions.[39]

Media import models went primarily from a few First World countries to many Third World countries during the 1950s and 1960s. These media models tended to be adapted to local circumstances and suited to fit into the local culture. For instance, the American soap opera was adapted to create the Latin American prime time television serial—the *telenovela*[40]—and the kung fu historical dramas in Hong Kong. The importation of content genre models from a few primary content-producing countries to most other countries in the world continues. In fact, the United States has come to export models more directly, even to producing countries such as France. Formal licensing of television show formats illustrates how a structured, profitable trade in media formats exists.[41] Countries that license content formats include not only the United States but also Australia,[42] Great Britain, and even Brazil, which has licensed a docudrama format in which audiences choose the ending (by popular vote).

More essentially, however, as predicted by the cultural imperialism theorists,[43] there has been a tendency for commercial media operations, based in large degree on American, British, French, and Japanese prototypes, to spread globally.[44] In a more globalized economy both foreign and domestic private manufacturers and advertisers increasingly dominate most economies. This pushes media to increase advertising and to move toward private ownership and commercial operation. The model of commercial broadcasting became far more prevalent during the 1990s because of the trend toward privatizing previously government-monopolized broadcast systems in Europe, Asia, Africa, and the Middle East.

New commercial stations tend to import more, particularly from the cheapest sources, that is, those dominated by U.S. exporters. Nevertheless, Brazil, Mexico, Hong Kong, and Japan have emerged as considerable competitors to the United States. A number of regional producers now export programming within their linguistic and cultural groups.[45] In fact, imports from the United States were replaced both by national production and by imports from within their own geolinguistic regions.[46] In particular, commercial stations that became successful over time often start producing more of their own programming. By contrast, less popular stations still continue to use more imported programming.

Assessing the cultural impact of media imperialism is difficult. Little evidence has been found of effects of international media, usually television, on values such as sexual behavior or whether to emigrate or not. In-depth ethnographic studies of the television program *Dallas* (exported to over 100 countries in the 1980s) found that although people were intrigued with the program, what sense they made of it was strongly affected by their own cultures and the viewing dynamics.[47]

## CULTURAL INDUSTRY DYNAMICS

Currently, there is a worldwide tendency to create commercial cultural industries that are based on interdependence in international economic relations and adaptation of imported media forms at the national level. It is therefore important to examine the dynamics of cultural industries at various levels: local, national, regional, and world. In larger nations development of local cultural industries becomes increasingly complex and dynamic. Because technologies and economic developments permit smaller scale production, radio, newspapers or newsletters, and local video productions permit various cultural fronts or actors to produce cultural products in a commercialized format.

Improvements in industrial organization, production capacity, and genre development are associated with increased levels of television production in a variety of countries. This is reflected in the growth in number and size of networks and production companies and in an increased number of national, international, and media production exports from these countries. For example, in regions such as Latin America, Asia, or the Middle East regional cultural industries are beginning to sell to regional cultural markets, based on language, religion, ethnicity, colonial heritage, historical roots, etc. These dynamics have resulted in many types of media development, including the restructuring of the continuum of cultural relationships to include asymmetric interdependence.

Having reviewed some of the major concepts that explain the uneven flow between nations, I turn now to specific cases.

## TECHNOLOGICAL FACTORS

Another line of scholarly research related to dependency centers on the fact that the Third World still depends on imports of technology for television production, transmission, computers, etc. from First World countries.[48] This is changing slightly. Certainly there are still cycles of innovation that center on the First World. Hardware development still takes place in a few First World countries. But hardware manufacturing is diversifying. Mature technologies are moving to East Asian and Latin American newly industrializing countries for manufacturing. Brazil, South Korea, and a few other newly industrializing countries now produce VCRs, satellite dishes, microcomputers, and minor production equipment; a number of countries produce television sets.

We can conclude that increased production of media technologies in the Third World has facilitated both an increased flow of First World television programs and an increased national production of programs. Although VCRs, cable television, and direct satellite reception bring more U.S. and European television programs to elites, the decreased cost and increased flexibility in television production technology have facilitated an increase in both the numbers and the diversity of television producers in Latin America. Although we do not have equivalent information on production in the Middle East, Asia, and Africa, it seems likely that the same logic would tend to facilitate increased production.

## Movies

The media imperialism argument still fits best in the relative domination of the world film market by the United States. The United States has dominated international film production and distribution since World War I. American films filled 75% of the theater seats in Europe in 1998. It was even more dominant in Latin America.[49] American films have succeeded in a variety of markets around the world for several reasons. One set of reasons has to do with Hollywood's success as a cultural industry. No other country has a similarly large and affluent national audience or market to support the production of so many films. Hollywood benefited from the financial base and economies of scale inherent to the booming American economy. Many American films have been made with a universal human theme to capture that large, diverse audience around the world.

Another reason, however, involves how Hollywood studios, organized under the Motion Picture Export Association of America, lobbied to promote exports and control overseas distribution networks.[50] The industry's anticompetitive practice, sanctioned by the U.S. Congress under the Webb-Pomerene Act, would have violated antitrust laws domestically.

Outside the United States more films were produced in Asia than in most other regions; the most prolific of these include Hong Kong and India (which has produced more films than the United States in some years). These countries together with Egypt, the film center of the Arab world, show that, if the domestic market is large or if the countries produce for a large multinational or regional audience, their film industries could thrive under certain market protections from film imports. However, even where film industries are protected from direct foreign film inflows, Hollywood has had a substantial impact on defining film genres, which other countries then use as a basis for creating their own productions.

## Television

American television built on this base of film production and distribution controlled by Hollywood. Starting in the early 1960s, American films, sitcoms, action-adventures, and cartoons flooded into many countries. Television production was expensive and new; not many countries had the equipment, people, or money to produce enough programming to meet their needs. A few countries limited broadcast hours to what they could fill themselves, but most countries responded to audience demands for more television by importing television programs, primarily from the United States.[51]

A 1972 UNESCO study found that half of the studied countries imported over half of their television, mostly entertainment and mostly from the United States. People began to talk about cultural imperialism, or "wall-to-wall *Dallas*" all over the world through television.[52] A number of countries, from Great Britain to Taiwan to Canada, established quotas that limited the amount of television that could be imported. In response, in 1989 the European Economic Community sponsored the Europe-wide "Television without Frontiers," a Green Paper that required member nations to have at least 50% of television programming produced within Europe.[53] However, American television programs are facing increased competition on a variety of levels: regional, national, and local. More countries are competing to sell programs to others. Some, such as Brazil and Hong Kong, compete worldwide. American programs remain attractive to world audiences; this seems particularly true of better educated audiences that are likely to be more cosmopolitan in their tastes and media exposure. Still, it seems that people more frequently look for television programming that is more culturally proximate to their own languages, histories, religious values, etc.[54]

What has replaced American programming in a number of countries is the local adaptation of the American commercial model and television program formats. In the process of diffusion the American model has been generalized and adapted to a global model for commercial media. This fits the globalization model of Robertson: the deliberate adaptation of a foreign or global model to fit national circumstances.[55] Robertson observed that Japan is in some ways the prototype for this approach, and he developed the term "glocalization" to describe it. More and more nations are producing an increasing proportion of their own programming using such genres as news, talk, variety, live music, and games.[56]

## Satellite and Cable Television

Although Americans, Canadians, and some Europeans are familiar with cable television, the medium is now expanding in many countries. By contrast, Japanese and British audiences have had direct broadcast satellite (DBS) services ahead of the U.S. audience. DBS services are growing quickly in many countries, frequently spanning borders of neighboring countries. By the 1990s, however, cable systems and private satellite television channels to feed them were growing fast in Europe, Latin America, and Asia. Some of the new cable and satellite program networks are capable of making their programs simultaneously available to a world-wide audience. This group of global satellite television networks is dominated by U.S. cable channels, such as CNN, MTV, HBO, ESPN, TNT, Nickelodeon, the Cartoon Channel, Discovery, and Disney.

However, this market is more limited than some optimistic early industry estimates originally predicted. Some countries, such as China, limit the spread of satellite dishes and cable television system carriage of regional channels (such as Star TV) and global channels (such as HBO).[57] A few middle-income countries, such as Taiwan and Argentina, have a relatively high penetration of pay television (over 50% of households that own a television set) associated with cable and satellite television systems.[58] However, other major potential markets, such as Brazil, have 5% of the television audience signed up for some foreign channel pay service.[59] Audiences are limited by income and by cultural capital, because few speak foreign languages or have extensive interest in international news, sports, and documentaries.

A number of channels and DBS services have been started with a more specific language or regional focus. A number of European channels now broadcast news, music, sports, films, children's programs, etc. Satellite television services in Asia, such as Star TV, have American (e.g., CNN, ESPN, MTV, and film), European (BBC News), and Chinese-language channels. These have been the most popular with Chinese audiences in Hong Kong, Taiwan, and China. The Mexican and Saudi satellite channels are aimed at viewers in their regional markets. Increasingly, cable systems in various regions are reflecting the availability and attraction to audiences of regional and local channels. For example, the Bei-Yi Cable Network in Taipei, Taiwan, costs $12 per month for 40 channels and is one of the largest networks in the country. It features three channels from America, eight channels from Japan, two from Mainland China, two from Hong Kong, a number with programs from various countries, ten homemade cable channels, and three television channels from Taiwan.[60]

## Music

Perhaps more than other cultural industry productions, recorded music products are able to address and meet demands for national, provincial, and local cultures. A remarkable number of cultures have distinct musical traditions. Tribal, religious, and ethnic groups predate nationhood and certainly predate the globalizing impacts of current popular music culture. This is not to say that these musical traditions have not suffered foreign, even global, influences. A great deal of music is still globally exported from the United States and Europe; a great deal of it is domestically produced and exported to developing countries. In fact, music makes up most of what few media products are imported back into the United States. Consequently, many see music as the cultural product least subject to cultural imperialism.

Robertson convincingly asserts that most of the cultures we now think of as national or local have been touched and partially shaped over the centuries by contact with other cultures on national, regional, and global levels.[61] He argues that there is a certain pattern that people expect national and local cultures to follow through a reshaping process that he calls glocalization. "Much of what is declared to be local is in fact the local expressed in terms of generalized recipes of locality."[62] Because music is a tool for one of the most penetrating and accessible forms of expression for all people in the world, it is not difficult to spot how current local, subnational or regional, and national musical traditions have been shaped.

## SUMMARY AND CONCLUSION

In this review of different media we saw a continued outflow of American cultural products and "information economy."[63] Meanwhile, a number of countries have begun to produce more cultural products for themselves and even to export them. We looked at this phenomenon as a series of interdependent but asymmetric relationships from economic, technological, and cultural perspectives. Accelerating change in and diffusion of technology seems to be both driving increased world cultural flow and facilitating local productions. The flows and intermingling of local, national, regional, and international culture that most of the world's people now experience seem to become increasingly complex. We need to look critically at both the trends in media flows and the theories that try to explain them.

## Theorizing Global and Local
## Media Flow and Cultural Interaction

Media flow and cultural interaction have a common core: the interaction of cultures across national boundaries mediated by communication technologies.

To truly understand the process of global cultural interaction through media, we need to move beyond looking at world cultural and economic relations in terms of dichotomies between dependence and independence or in terms of narrow typologies, such as core, semiperipheral, and peripheral countries. It seems that there are several levels of interaction between cultures in the world: political-economic, technological, cultural production, content and content flows, and reception of culture. These are similar to the five dimensions of globalization proposed by Appadurai, who argues that globalization includes separate financial, ethnic and immigration, media, technology and cultural components.[64]

At the base, we should examine the structures and contexts for communication posed by world and national political economy. Most critical and cultural studies writers consider analysis of political economy necessary.[65] We should use it as a foundation and starting point without assuming that its factors necessarily determine others. Next, we should examine technological processes and changes. We should examine technological transfers, cycles, and effects without falling into either technological determinism or technophobia. We should examine cultural processes and actors. We start with cultural industries and institutions, then examine the actors in cultural production, flows of cultural products within and between countries, and finally those who receive and mediate the interpretation of communication media and cultural products. Although cultural imperialism sheds considerable light on this process, other theories are also useful, particularly those that encompass a more nuanced approach to asymmetric interdependence.

## NOTES

1. Herbert I. Schiller, *Communication and Cultural Domination* (White Plains, NY: International Arts and Sciences Press, 1976).

2. Karle Nordenstreng and Tapio Varis, *Television Traffic: A One-Way Street* (Paris: UNESCO, 1974).

3. Oliver Boyd-Barrett, *The International News Agencies* (Beverly Hills: Sage, 1980).

4. Chin-Chuan Lee, *Media Imperialism Reconsidered* (Beverly Hills, CA: Sage, 1980).

5. Arial Dorfman and A. Mattelart, *How to Read Donald Duck: Imperialist Ideology in the Disney Comic* (New York: International General, 1975).

6. M. Featherstone, *Global Culture: Nationalism, Globalization, and Modernity* (Newbury Park, CA: Sage, 1990); I. Wallerstein *Geopolitics and Geoculture: Essays on the Changing World System* (Cambridge: Cambridge University Press, 1991).

7. Herbert I. Schiller, "Not Yet the Post-Imperialist Era," *Critical Studies in Mass Communication* (1991): 13–28.

8. James Galtung, "A Structural Theory of Imperialism," *Journal of Peace Research* 2 (1971): 81–117.

9. James Curran, "The New Revisionism in Mass Communication Research: A Reappraisal," *European Journal of Communication* 5, nos. 2–3 (June 1990): 13–28.

10. Thomas McPhail, *Electronic Colonialism,* 5th ed. (Newbury Park, CA: Sage, 1989).

11. Frederico H. Cardoso, *Dependencia e Desenvolvimento na America Latina* [Dependency and Development in Latin America] (Rio de Janeiro: Zahar Editores, 1970).

12. Paul A. Baran, *The Political Economy of Growth* (New York: Monthly Review Press, 1957).

13. Paul A. Baran and Paul Sweezy, *Monopoly Capital: An Essay on the American Economic and Social Order* (New York: Modern Reader, 1968).

14. Cees J. Hamelink, "Cultural Autonomy Threatened," in Cees J. Hamelink, ed., *Cultural Autonomy in Global Communications* (New York: Longman, 1983), 1–25.

15. Elizabeth Fox, "Cultural Dependency Thrice Revisited," Paper delivered at International Association for Mass Communication Research Conference in Guarujá, Brazil, 1992.

16. Elizabeth Fox, "Multinational Television," *Journal of Communication* 25, no. 2 (1975): 122–127; N. Janus, "Advertising and the Mass Media in the Era of the Global Corporations," in E. McAnany and J. Schnitman, eds., *Communication and Social Structure: Critical Studies in Mass Media Research* (New York: Praeger, 1981).

17. Fred Fejes, "The Growth of Multinational Advertising Agencies in Latin America," *Journal of Communication* 30 (autumn 1980): 36–49.

18. Fox, "Multinational Television."

19. Antonio Gramsci, *Selections from the Prison Notebooks,* Q. Hoare and G. M. Smith, trans. (New York: International Publishers, 1971).

20. Fred H. Cardoso, "Associated Dependent Development: Theoretical and Practical Implications," in A. Stephan, ed., *Authoritarian Brazil* (New Haven, CT: Yale University Press, 1973), 142–178; P. Evans, *Dependent Development: The Alliance of Multinational, State, and Local Capital in Brazil* (Princeton, NJ: Princeton University Press, 1979).

21. R. Salinas and L. Paldan, "Culture in the Process of Dependent Development: Theoretical Perspectives," in K. Nordenstreng and H. I. Schiller, eds., *National Sovereignty and International Communications* (Norwood, NJ: Ablex, 1979), 82–98.

22. Fox, "Cultural Dependency Thrice Revisited."

23. I. Wallerstein, *The Modern World System* (New York: Academic Press, 1976).

24. I. Wallerstein, *The Capitalist World Economy* (Cambridge: Cambridge University Press, 1979).

25. Wallerstein, *Geopolitics and Geoculture.*

26. Ibid.

27. Cardoso, "Associated Dependent Development."

28. P. Golding and G. Murdock, "Large Corporations and the Control of the Communications Industries," in M. Gurevitch, T. Bennett, J. Curran, and J. Woollacott, eds., *Culture, Society, and the Media* (New York: Methuen, 1982); H. I. Schiller, *Mass Communication and American Empire* (Boston, MA: Beacon Press, 1971).

29. Vincent Mosco, *The Political Economy of Communication: Rethinking and Renewal* (Thousand Oaks, CA: Sage, 1996).

30. P. Audley, *Canada's Cultural Industries* (Toronto: Lorimer, 1983).

31. John Tomlinson, *Cultural Imperialism* (Baltimore: Johns Hopkins University Press, 1991).

32. Jeremy Tunstall, *The Media Are American* (New York: Columbia University Press, 1977), 45.

33. Lee, *Media Imperialism Reconsidered.*

34. Tomlinson, *Cultural Imperialism.*

35. Ibid.

36. Boyd-Barrett, *The International News Agencies.*

37. Lee, *Media Imperialism Reconsidered.*

38. Ibid.; and Tunstall, *The Media are American.*

39. E. S. Herman and Robert W. McChesney, *The Global Media: The New Missionaries of Global Capitalism* (Washington, DC: Cassell, 1997).

40. Joseph Straubhaar, "The Development of the Telenovela as the Paramount Form of Popular Culture in Brazil," *Studies in Latin American Popular Culture* 1 (1982): 138–150.

41. Albert Moran, *Copycat Television: Globalization, Program Formats, and Cultural Identity* (Luton, United Kingdom: University of Luton Press, 1998).

42. Ibid.

43. E. Fox, "Multinational Television."

44. J. Sinclair, E. Jacka, and S. Cunningham, *Peripheral Vision: New Patterns in Global Television* (New York: Oxford University Press, 1996).

45. Joseph Straubhaar, C. Campbell, S. M. Youn, K. Champagnie, M. Elasmar, and L. Castellon, "The Emergence of a Latin American Market for Television Programs," Paper presented to the International Communication Association, Miami, 1992.

46. Leslie B. Snyder, Bartjan Willenborg, and James Watt, "Advertising and Cross-Cultural Convergence in Europe," *European Journal of Communication* 6 (1991): 441–448.

47. Elihu Katz and Tamara Liebes, "Once upon a Time in Dallas," *Intermedia* 12, no. 3 (1984): 28–32.

48. A. Mattelart and H. Schmucler, *Communication and Information Technologies: Freedom of Choice for Latin America?* D. Bruxton, trans. (Norwood, NJ: Ablex, 1985).

49. *Variety,* various issues, 1998–1999.

50. *Reports and Papers on Mass Communication 92* (Paris: UNESCO, 1986).

51. Tunstall, *The Media Are American.*

52. R. Collins, "Wall-to-Wall Dallas? The US-UK Trade in Television," *Screen* 27 (May–August 1986): 66–77; Nordenstreng and Varis, *Television Traffic.*

53. "Communities: Television without Frontiers," Green Paper on the Establishment of the Common Market for Broadcasting, Especially by Satellite and Cable, No. COM 84, 300 final (Brussels: Commission of the European Communities, 1984).

54. Joseph Straubhaar, "Beyond Media Imperialism: Asymmetrical Interdependence and Cultural Proximity," *Critical Studies in Mass Communication* 8 (1991): 1–11.

55. R. Robertson, "Glocalization: Time-Space and Homogeneity-Heterogeneity," in M. Featherstone, S. Lash, and R. Robertson, eds., *Global Modernities* (Thousand Oaks, CA: Sage, 1995), 25–44.

56. Straubhaar et al., "The Emergence of a Latin American Market for Television Programs."

57. Joseph Man Chan, "Media Internationalization in China: Process and Tensions," *Journal of Communication* 44, no. 3 (1994): 70–87.

58. Gonzalo Soruco, "Argentina: Cable TV and the Renewed Fear of Cultural Synchronization," Paper presented at the Second Colloquium on Cultural Industries and Communication in NAFTA and the Mercosur, University of Texas at Austin, 1999.

59. M. Porto, "Novas Tecnologias e Política no Brasil: A Globalização em uma Sociedade Periférica e Desigual" [New Technologies and Policy in Brazil: Globalization in a Peripheral and Unequal Society], Paper presented to the Latin American Studies Association, Chicago, 1998.

60. Joseph Straubhaar and Robert LaRose, *Communications Media in the Information Society* (Belmont, CA: Wadsworth, 1996).

61. Robertson, "Glocalization."

62. Ibid.

63. John Naisbitt and Patricia Aburdene, *Megatrends 2000: The New Directions for the 1990s* (New York: Morrow, 1990).

64. A. Appadurai, *Modernity at Large: Cultural Dimensions of Globalization* (Minneapolis: University of Minnesota Press, 1996).

65. A. Mattelart and H. Schmucler, *Communication and Information Technologies.*

# 14

# Impact of the Electronic Media on the Arab World

## DOUGLAS A. BOYD

This book makes clear that electronic media cannot be studied outside the political, economic, historical, cultural, religious, and linguistic context in which they exist. Thus, before these media and their potential impact on Arab culture can be discussed, we must know something about the Arab world, which stretches from the tip of the Arabian peninsula to the eastern Mediterranean to the Atlantic Ocean.

Egypt, Sudan, Lebanon, Syria, Jordan, the West Bank and Gaza Strip, Yemen, Iraq, Kuwait, Saudi Arabia, Bahrain, Qatar, the United Arab Emirates, Oman, Algeria, Libya, Morocco, and Tunisia constitute states in the Arab Middle East (collectively known as Arabian Gulf States or just Gulf States). There are many ways to determine who is an Arab. However, the most straightforward definition is one who is a native speaker of Arabic. Not all Arabs are followers of Islam. There are identifiable indigenous Christian minorities, especially in Sudan, Egypt, Jordan, the West Bank and Gaza Strip, and Syria. There is a substantial Christian population in Lebanon, but the percentage of those professing Christian beliefs there is not known; it has been too politically sensitive to determine religious preferences since the last census in the late 1930s.

Despite the pervasiveness of Islam, some common historical background, and a common language, Arab countries are, in fact, quite different. Vastly different gross domestic products, histories, and political orientations have made it difficult for Arab states to agree on much. However, the Arabic language, despite vastly different local dialects, is the most common thread binding those in the region. Arabic is, of course, the language of the Koran, Islam's holy book.

Traditionally, there have been two types of Arabic: classical and colloquial. Classical Arabic is rich in both religious and historical connotations. The various spoken dialects are so different that North African Arabic speakers often must converse with peninsular Arabs in classical Arabic or another language, most commonly French or English. The Arabic spoken in Baghdad is different from that spoken in Cairo. The growth in Arab mass media since the 1950s, however, has enhanced the wider use of a third form: modern standard Arabic. This is the language of newspapers and the electronic media and is generally understood by the population of the Arab world.

## ARABIC RADIO BROADCASTING

Certain characteristics of Arabic speakers and of Arabic itself tend to make this language ideally suited for those who wish to make effective persuasive use of the electronic media for propaganda purposes. There is a general belief in the Arab world that the Arabic language, creatively employed and strongly delivered, has a powerful impact on the audience. Listeners to radio broadcasts from other Arab countries must be receptive to efforts to change existing attitudes, but Arabic itself is viewed as an important element in the effectiveness of a propaganda effort. The direct translation of these efforts from Arabic to English does not, of course, communicate the same meaning. Examples are Gamal Abdel Nasser's pre-1967 speeches and those of Iraqi president Saddam Hussein following the invasion of Kuwait. Laffin makes the following observations about Arabic and its use.[1]

1. To the Arab there may be several truths about the one situation, depending on the type of language used.
2. Language is not used to reason, but to persuade.
3. The Arab means what he says at the moment he is saying it. . . . The value of words is often assessed by quantity. Words can justify or rationalize anything.

Arabic is not an exact language, and much of the responsibility for interpretation is left to the listener. Sharabi observes:

> In political life Arabic is a most effective instrument of influence and persuasion. . . . In public speeches effect is created not so much by reasoning and explication as by repetition and intonation. Indeed, a speaker trying to sway an audience seldom expresses his ideas directly or succinctly; meaning is conveyed rather than directly or precisely expressed, and is always couched in terminology that evokes emotional rather than rational responses.[2]

Arabic is in several ways ideally suited to the electronic media, especially radio broadcasts specifically designed to influence others, because of its rich grammar, repetitive style, and vagueness.

## Development of Arabic Radio Services

Radio receivers are abundant in the Arab countries. Even when radio was a young medium, there was a strong desire among Arabs in this oral culture to acquire sets. During the late 1950s and early 1960s, the availability of relatively affordable transistor radios enabled lower income families to purchase them. The sets, which could be operated with batteries, became popular in villages where there was no electricity. The transistor revolution coincided with political movements in the 1950s and 1960s in North Africa, Egypt, and Iraq that overthrew ruling royal families or that were successful in gaining independence from European colonial powers.

The post–World War II Arab world leaders, such as Gamal Abdel Nasser of Egypt, were interested in rapid social and economic change and saw broadcasting, especially radio, as a means of bypassing the print media, which were primarily responsive to the literate elite who could read and afford publications. Throughout the 1980s Iraqi president Saddam Hussein used the state-run electronic media to perpetuate his carefully orchestrated personality cult. In his case television was especially important. Throughout the 1980s, 1990s and early 2000s primetime Iraqi television was for all intents and purposes wall-to-wall Saddam Hussein.

In the Arab world it is difficult to distinguish between domestic and international radio broadcasting. In the 1950s some Arab countries started building relatively powerful medium-wave (standard AM) transmitters to send a signal as far as possible. The medium-wave band at that time was not as cluttered as it is today, and these domestically targeted programs could easily be received in neighboring countries. Even now, residents of Khartoum (Sudan), Riyadh (Saudi Arabia), Amman (Jordan), and Baghdad (Iraq) can listen regularly to the domestic service of Radio Cairo and the Voice of the Arabs. These services can be heard with particular clarity at night (when medium-wave propagation permits signals to travel longer distances). In the past, these two stations were often the only service available, because the countries in which listeners resided did not have reliable national radio service coverage. The Arab culture is traditionally oral. With few competing forms of information and entertainment, radio listening was, and in some places still is, a major leisure activity. In the wealthier states and in urban areas television sets, VCRs, and, more recently, satellite television are important sources of entertainment and news. Those countries that were initially slow to develop radio services (Kuwait, Saudi Arabia, Qatar, Oman, and the United Arab Emirates) were also most vulnerable to radio propaganda from countries such as Syria, Iraq, and Egypt, which at the same time had political interests in deposing the Arabian Gulf ruling families. During the 1960s and 1970s, these more developed Arab countries rapidly developed radio broadcasting facilities because they recognized the need for reliable communication with the indigenous population and with the Arab expatriates who came to work among them. In short, they initially built radio facilities as a defensive measure. The newly oil-rich countries could afford modern high-powered transmitters and impressive radio production studios. When the price of oil quadrupled after the 1973 Middle East war, the Gulf States found themselves in potentially influential positions internationally and within the Arab world. Meanwhile, radio broadcasting became increasingly important to governments that attempted to disseminate particular political agendas.

## ARABIC TELEVISION BROADCASTING

The term "international (or transnational) broadcasting" is usually associated with radio. With the exception of FM signals, radio transmissions travel much farther than television signals, and shortwave signals can be received far from the location of the transmitter and antenna. This is due, in part, to the technical limitations of terrestrial television, a medium that is generally restricted to line-of-sight reception. However, in the Arab world television from one country frequently is viewed in other countries. Terrestrial Egyptian television can be seen during the warm summer months in Israel, Lebanon, and even Syria. It is seen regularly along the western coast of Saudi Arabia as far south as Jeddah. The tall antenna towers on apartment houses and private residences in the Red Sea city of Jeddah are not necessary to receive Saudi Arabian television; they are needed to receive Egyptian television from a well-positioned transmitter across the Red Sea.

International television viewing is pervasive in the Gulf States, where the warm, humid weather during the long summer helps transmission conditions. Indeed, in some areas of the Gulf it is possible to receive as many as 12 terrestrial television signals. The Saudi government has always had a strong desire to broadcast to others in addition to its own citizens, not only for political and security purposes but also because the kingdom is the birthplace of Islam and hosts the two most holy cities for Muslims, Makkah (Mecca) and Medina.

Television service is a reality in all Arab countries, rich and poor alike, for even the poorer countries such as Egypt, Sudan, and Yemen realize that the medium is an important political and developmental tool. Each time a poor country makes the decision to increase transmission power, buy a camera or VCR, or lease a satellite transponder, money is being diverted from developmental projects. For instance, in the large, less affluent countries such as Oman and Sudan, where it is necessary to utilize satellite ground stations and leased satellite transponders for internal distribution of television programs, the expense is considered painful but necessary. In the more affluent Arab countries in North Africa and the Arabian Gulf, television facilities are modern and extensive. Television in the Gulf region started slowly in the late 1960s but expanded rapidly in the late 1970s and throughout the 1980s and 1990s.

# DEVELOPMENT OF
# ARABIC SATELLITE SYSTEMS

Arab countries have created their own satellite system, ARABSAT. Originally suggested at a meeting of Gulf ministers of information during the oil-rich days of the 1970s as a means of linking the electronic media in the Gulf States, ARABSAT became a reality in 1985. Several satellites have been launched, including one from a U.S. space shuttle with a Saudi Arabian prince on board as astronaut. The system has had many problems, most of them financial and political. Primarily inspired and financed by Saudi Arabia, ARABSAT has its administrative headquarters in the Saudi capital, Riyadh; the technical headquarters is in Tunis, Tunisia. Interestingly, it was direct broadcast satellite (DBS) that helped ARABSAT recover from difficult financial times. There is a third-generation ARABSAT platform, 3A, in orbit that will give more transponder space to those wishing to transmit digital satellite television. Regardless, those from outside and inside the Arab world have access to a variety of satellite services, including INTELSAT and PANAMSAT, from which to select. Egypt is the first Arab country to have its own satellite, NILESAT, which was launched in 1998. NILESAT is now a multisatellite system that has established a new digital standard for satellite television from its modern headquarters in Egypt's media city of Cairo.

At first, a few Gulf States did not permit private satellite dish ownership, even though some wealthy citizens in the United Arab Emirates, Kuwait, and Saudi Arabia—usually members of the royal family or wealthy merchants—had satellite-receiving equipment. In Saudi Arabia, where dishes are officially prohibited, the ban has never been enforced because it would be almost impossible to do so. Both Western and Arab broadcasters and private corporations have a financial interest in providing Arabs with entertainment-oriented programming. The French television networks were already available in many parts of North Africa. As satellite reception dishes become smaller in size, they become not only less expensive but also less physically obvious.

Curiously, for a country initially concerned about its citizens seeing Western-oriented satellite television, Saudi Arabia has permitted—and, in fact, officially sanctioned—royal family and other ownership of satellite channels that now serve much of the globe beyond the Middle East. For example, the London-based Middle East Broadcasting Centre (MBC) is the creation of influential Saudis, most notably Sheikh Saleh Kamel. The new owner and chief operating officer of MBC is Walid bin Ibrahim al-Ibrahim, the brother-in-law of Saudi King Fahd. MBC pioneered advertising-supported, free-to-air DBS television to the world. MBC operates from the Battersea area of London from a state-of-the-art broadcasting facility inaugurated on 10 March 1995 by British prime minister John Major.[3] Programming starts in the morning and continues until after midnight.

Another satellite service, Orbit Television and Radio Network, operated by Saudi Arabia's Mawarid Investment Group, is again owned by members of the Saudi royal family.[4] Although Orbit at first provided a free-to-air preview channel, the service is subscription based because there were those in the Arab world, especially in the Gulf, with incomes sufficient to purchase the sophisticated Scientific Atlanta receiver (initially priced at $10,000, but later drastically reduced because of a lack of purchasers). This charge is in addition to monthly fees for a variety of program packages.[5] At one time, 19 programs were offered, including rebroadcasts of two Egyptian domestic channels, ESPN, the Music Channel, the Hollywood Channel, the Disney Channel, CNN International, and C-SPAN. Separate packages of Star TV film and special-interest channels are available via Orbit.

Although Orbit had what seemed to be unlimited financial resources, both Western management and Saudi owners initially misjudged the service's customer base; they made a major error in contracting with the British Broadcasting Corporation (BBC) to operate an Arabic television news service. Outwardly, the 10-year $150 million contract with the BBC to provide an Arabic television news service to Orbit was a good decision because it provided the BBC with income for its commercial venture and gave Orbit a credible independent news source. However, coverage of London-based Saudi dissident Mohammad Al-Masari's activities in late 1995 and early 1996, when he fought a successful court battle to become a political refugee in Great Britain, greatly bothered the Saudi Arabian Ministry of Interior. These concerns were passed along to Orbit's owners. The event that caused Orbit unilaterally to break its BBC contract in 1996 was a *Panorama* program on the BBC Arabic Television News showing "secretly shot [in Saudi Arabia] film of the preparations for a double execution by beheading."[6]

Finally, Arab Radio and Television (ART) is the only Saudi-owned satellite service to be operated primarily from the Middle East. ART is part of Sheikh Saleh Kamel's Jeddah-based Dallah Al-Barakah company. Although up-linked to satellites serving the Arab world, Europe, and North America from Italy, most ART postproduction is done in Cairo because of that city's vast store of film and television talent and production facilities.


## ELECTRONIC MEDIA AND ARAB SOCIETY

It is still not unusual for groups of people (mostly men) to listen to radio, watch both terrestrial and satellite television, and view videotapes in public commercial establishments or in private residences. The explanation for this is, in part, the Arab concept of friendliness and hospitality. When a person is in public, perhaps listening to music or news on a radio in the street, there is an implied invitation for others to join him. In the 1970s an American friend and I were walking in a residential area of Khartoum on a warm evening and heard the sound from an old American film on TV with Arabic subtitles being watched by a Sudanese family on their porch. Out of curiosity we peeked through the open door of the walled compound. The male head of the household saw us, came to the gate, and insisted we join them for refreshments and to watch the film. We did.

## Radio

In many of the poorer Arab countries a radio receiver remains a status symbol; the larger and more intricate the set, the higher the status. Expensive all-wave radios (shortwave, AM, and FM bands in one set) with built-in audiotape players and, more recently, CD capability are popular and have generated a pirate music industry in many Arab countries. Pirate copies of professionally recorded popular Arabic and Western music on audiotapes can be purchased in most Gulf countries for as little as $2. Although tapes are still popular, by the late 1990s pirated music CDs outnumbered tapes.

New technologies and better economic conditions have changed listening patterns since Brunner noted that a substantial amount of Arab radio listening was done by groups of people, mostly men, in village coffeehouses.[7] Egyptian Nobel Prize winner for literature Naguib Mahfouz relates both the importance of the oral culture of Egypt and the popularity of radio broadcasting in a portion of his 1966 novel *Madiq Alley*.[8] It seems that in a coffeehouse an elderly man—a poet who had managed a living from telling stories for tips and free coffee for two decades—was no longer welcome because the owner and most younger customers had grown tired of the same old stories. The owner of the establishment, dismissing the poet, reiterates the wishes of his customers and ushers in the radio era. "People today don't want a poet. They keep asking me for a radio, and there's one over there being installed now."[9]

## Television

Through individually owned sets, sets in clubs, or sets in public places, the availability of television programs in Arab countries is probably much higher than many readers may suspect, although, again, a distinction must be drawn between the affluent and the poor countries. In Kuwait, Saudi Arabia, Qatar, Bahrain, and the United Arab Emirates set ownership is high for the native-born populace. Most people can easily afford color sets. Starting in the late 1980s, large-screen projection sets were common among the wealthier families. In the mid-1990s satellite dishes often graced the tops of houses and apartment buildings.

By contrast, in countries such as Syria, Egypt, and Sudan government policy is oriented toward making television sets widely available. These governments want government programming to be seen by as many people as possible. The poor are strongly motivated to acquire television sets. For instance, in Egypt it was not unusual for a television set to be purchased by village leaders even before electricity reached their area. In a poor section of Cairo during the 1970s and 1980s, an extended family would pool resources to purchase a used set. In that crowded, polluted city it is often necessary and cheaper to be entertained in the home; and many low-income parents believe that television is a way to enhance their children's education.

## Videocassette Recorders

Until DBS became available in the Gulf States, government-run television had relatively little competition. Few cinemas and nightclubs exist (there are none in Saudi Arabia), and among those that do, few appeal to the home- and family-centered Arab culture. VCRs are therefore pervasive. Kuwait, Saudi Arabia, Bahrain, Qatar, and the United Arab Emirates were large markets for pirated videocassettes before DBS became popular. Tape libraries still do a brisk business in a few areas where satellite television reception is not allowed or where most citizens are too poor to afford a satellite receiving dish and decoder. The underground market for pirated Egyptian, American, and British television programs and feature films is still a thriving business, but not as strong as it was in the pre-DBS 1980s, when videotaped material was the only alternative to terrestrial television.

## Satellite Television

In Saudi Arabia satellite television in the late 1990s motivated the creation of an entirely new kind of coffeehouse. Any night of the week, 9:30 P.M. until 3:00 A.M., especially just outside the kingdom's large urban areas, males gather to drink coffee and tea, eat, smoke water pipes, talk, and watch satellite television. For example, a few miles outside Riyadh, just off the main highway to the oil-rich eastern province, large establishments cater to those wishing to be with friends outside the home. One such "video coffeehouse" attracts 5,000 men per night; they come to view the 146 separate color television receivers, which are rented for a few hours or for the entire evening. Arranged in cubicles of various sizes, a few completely enclosed, men are especially attracted to both Arab world and European satellite television; such fare is far more liberal with music and dramatic programs than that of Gulf television. Because some of these late-night European services are or border on being pornographic, at least in conservative Islamic terms, some Saudi Arabian religious leaders want the video coffeehouses closed; at the very least, they want to have the incoming satellite selections restricted to those that are considered suitable for viewing.

In a study of both male and female adults in Riyadh, Marghalani et al. concluded that the popularity of DBS service has been motivated by several factors, some of which helped prompt the rapid diffusion of VCRs in Saudi Arabia in the 1980s and early 1990s.[10] These include the restricted and heavily censored content on the two government-run terrestrial channels, the greatly reduced cost of DBS systems, the technological impracticality of wiring such a sparsely populated desert region with cable, and the need stimulated by the 1991 Gulf War for alternative information sources about regional and world affairs. Surveillance of the local and international environment seems to be a major force behind the rapid adoption of DBS in the kingdom.

The historical isolation of this traditional Islamic state has helped mold an audience of Saudis who want information about the cultural norms, values, and practices of other cultures and peoples, particularly where religious practices are concerned. Another symptom of the religious and cultural censorship of the government media—the rare appearance of women on these channels—is at the root of another DBS motive identified in the study: the desire among both males and females to see females on television. Marghalani et al. found that this desire is prompted among females by the need for more female role models with whom to identify and among males by sexual curiosity.[11]

## ELECTRONIC MEDIA CONTENT

### Radio Content

Arabic is second only to English as an international radio broadcasting language, with 40 international broadcasting organizations providing Arabic-language programming to the Arab world, several of them broadcasting on the standard medium-wave band. Thus people in the Arab world listen to the Voice of America, the BBC, Deutsche Welle (Germany), and Radio Monte Carlo Middle East (France). Audience surveys during the 1970s, 1980s, and 1990s indicate that these and other services are avidly listened to in the Arab world, particularly by followers of Arab and international events.[12]

One explanation for the general receptivity to such non-Arab international radio and, increasingly, satellite television broadcasts is the nature of the organization of Arab radio and television. With the exception of a few unofficial and licensed private radio and television stations in Lebanon, each Arab country has a broadcasting system that is either operated by the government or run by an organization that is funded and directly controlled by a government agency, generally a ministry of information. For example, Egypt's national radio and television organization, the Egyptian Radio-Television Union, operates directly under the Ministry of Information. Listeners understand that the government has its priorities and its points of view, and those who listen to non-Arab international broadcasts appear to be listening to gain alternative opinion about local or international events.

Listening during times of crisis is almost a standard procedure in the Middle East, particularly among the better educated. Perhaps there is no better example of such a crisis than the 2 August 1990 Iraqi invasion of Kuwait and the subsequent Operation Desert Storm and Desert Shield. BBC and Voice of America survey data show just how much Arabs rely on foreign radio broadcasting during difficult political times. For example, the BBC reported that audiences in the United Arab Emirates increased from preinvasion levels of 21 to 51% after 2 August; in Cairo and Alexandria they increased from 18 to 46%.[13] This situation has probably changed somewhat as a result of the popularity of satellite television since the mid-1990s. CNN International and BBC World are now widely available in the Arab world. For those who speak only Arabic or prefer Arabic-language news, there is, for example, some news on the London-based MBC and on the all news- and information-oriented Al Jazeera from Qatar.

## Television Content

To a great extent Arab television programming is heavily entertainment oriented. The director of Egyptian television said during a May 1980 meeting, "A television set is usually bought with the intention of entertainment. Nobody thinks of television as a means of education when they go to buy a television set."[14] However, this does not mean that educational programs do not exist. In some Arab countries a good deal of programming time is devoted to political information. In general, such educational and political programming, including news and commentary, extols the accomplishments of the political leaders, whether elected officials or members of ruling families.

Imported entertainment programs from Europe and the United States are used to some extent in all Arab television systems. The percentage of imported Western programs is higher in the Gulf States, where there is a limited artistic tradition and where, during the initial stages of television's development, emphasis was placed on construction of physical facilities for program transmission. Western programming appears to be in keeping with the beliefs of the systems' administrators (whose respective countries look to the West for political support and economic ties) and of the nations' elite (who have the funds to travel outside the Middle East and expect that Western programs will be provided as a matter of course). In multichannel Gulf States such as Kuwait, Saudi Arabia, Bahrain, and the United Arab Emirates one channel is devoted exclusively or nearly exclusively to non-Arab programming. The one entirely English-language Saudi television channel transmits both imported and locally produced material. However, the trend toward permissiveness in Western television programs has served to narrow the choices available to Arab countries. This is because Western programs have to be edited for excessive sex, violence, and, in Saudi Arabia, references to non-Islamic religions.

Television stations in the Arab Middle East have always telecast classic Egyptian cinema productions as a main category of Arabic-language programming. After the 1967 Middle East War and the end of the conflict in Yemen the Gulf States started importing new Egyptian films and videotapes. By the mid-1970s such productions were an important source of hard currency for the Egyptian Radio-Television Union, but their high prices and Egypt's signing of a peace treaty with Israel caused some states to reduce or to stop purchasing Egyptian programs. At the same time, changes in the Egyptian political and economic situation prompted some artists to work outside the country to gain more money through payment in hard currency and to avoid paying Egyptian taxes. Their new productions were essentially Egyptian written, produced, directed, and acted, but they were taped in London, Athens, Amman, or Dubai. Relatively high-quality Arabic-language programs have thus proliferated. Many programs are contemporary in that they deal with the problems of families attempting to cope with the clash of generations. Some programs are historical in nature and deal with traditional Islamic themes. These programs are particularly appropriate for sale to the Gulf States, which have attempted to make television reflect more Islamic values since, for example, the Soviet invasion of Afghanistan, the Mecca Mosque occupation, the Iranian Revolution, and the Gulf War.

As noted previously, with the possible exception of talent-rich Egypt, material for indigenous television systems has always been scarce. The exploding number of Arab world satellite channels has made the situation worse. Pierre al-Daher, chairman of the Lebanese Broadcasting Company, notes that there is especially increased competition for a limited amount of programming, particularly sports. He notes that of the 30 Arab satellite television services each is broadcasting 8,500 hours per year: 3,500 hours of local programming and 5,000 hours of imported programming.[15]

Television in the Arab Middle East has a predominantly Western style. Virtually all television stations in the Arab world were purchased from and installed by Western European, American, and Japanese equipment manufacturers; usually the installation agreement called for the buyers to receive production training from Western experts or for the buyers to receive their training in the country where the equipment was manufactured. Furthermore, various programs sponsored by both Western and Middle Eastern governments as well as by private foundations have taken experts to the Arab countries to advise them on television production or have sent Middle Eastern nationals to the United States, Great Britain, France, or West Germany to train in television production. The natural result of all this is a Western-type television program in Arabic. With regard to production techniques, there is little that is uniquely Arab in Arab world television.

## Satellite Television Content

Every Arab state has a satellite channel, if only a satellite-delivered rebroadcast of a domestic service. As noted throughout this chapter, these services are popular and are having an impact on audiences and broadcasters in the Arabian Gulf.

In 1994 ART started four free-to-air channels serving the Arabic-speaking world. ART's first four DBS channels were ART 1, a general channel showing films and television programs that appeal to a wide variety of ages and tastes; ART 2, an all sports channel; ART 3, the children's channel; and ART 4, a film channel featuring both Arab world and Western films that have been dubbed or subtitled. By mid-1995 ART added another service and had plans for more programs and a subscription service.[16] By mid-1997 ART offered six satellite program services: Variety Channel, Sports, Children's Channel, Movie Channel, Music Channel, and ART Shopping.[17] In 1999 it started an educational channel for the Arab world from its Jeddah headquarters. ART decided not to telecast any nonsports news, thus avoiding the type of problems with the Saudi government that Orbit had with its BBC Arabic Television News or criticism that MBC's news is "Saudized."

Two other news- and information-oriented satellite services deserve mention. The London-based Arab News Network (ANN) started operating in the summer of 1997. Its financial backing and political agenda are open to speculation, especially among the London-based Arabic newspapers. ANN is operated by Sawmar al-Assad, nephew of the late Syrian president Hafez al-Assad. At one point, ANN's correspondent in Syria was jailed, allegedly for anti-Syrian stories. Two general beliefs persist about the service: that it has Saudi financial backing from Crown Price Abdullah and, alternatively, that it is purely a business venture.[18]

Doha, Qatar–based Al Jazeera—essentially an outgrowth of the previously mentioned ill-fated Orbit-delivered BBC Arabic Television News—has proven to be both popular and controversial. Apparently, this news service has filled a void for CNN-type television news reporting in Arabic. Its evening call-in, interview, and commentary programs have attracted a large audience for the discussion of political, economic, and social issues seldom, if ever, aired on government-run television. *Al-Arab al-Yawm,* a daily newspaper in Amman, described the results of a poll done in 1999 by Jordan's Strategic Studies Centre indicating that Al Jazeera, with 23% of satellite viewers, was first in popularity among Jordan's satellite television audience. The newspaper suggests that the service's popularity is due to the Arab public's longing for freedom and truth and their eagerness to find out what goes on around them without falsification or distortion. "This is particularly true, since local television stations in most Arab states have turned their news bulletins into propaganda machines rather than media material."[19]

Virtually unknown outside the Arab world before September 11, 2001, Al Jazeera has become well known in the West for its coverage of the initial stages of the war in Afghanistan. The satellite television service has become a major force, as acknowledged previously by the Jordanian newspaper, because by Arab standards it provides political discussions on a variety of topics from religion to corruption that would not take place on a government-run domestic service.[20]

## SUMMARY AND CONCLUSION

Three additional aspects of Arab broadcast media deserve attention: the lack of media research, the lack of citizen input, and the lack of a broadcasting philosophy. They are related but separate problems.

First, little social scientific audience research on the impact of radio and television has been done in the Arab world. The broadcast systems in Jordan and pre–civil war Lebanon did undertake the study of listeners so that they would have information on which to base commercial rates, and some social science research has been done to determine media use in villages. However, almost no social effects research has been done even by those systems, and the social scientists have not worked in cooperation with university-based media researchers. During the 1980s and 1990s, though, some groundbreaking research was done by Arab graduate students at U.S. and European universities.

The general research void is caused by a lack of funds for an activity that is not believed to be a priority, a general misunderstanding of research methodology, and the scarcity of qualified personnel to undertake and interpret research results. Finally, at least until government terrestrial television faced serious competition from satellite television, governments were not particularly interested in knowing either audience preferences or potential impacts. Governments are inclined to give

Arab world electronic media consumers what they believe they should see and hear. The print media are still important in the Arab world as a tool for government propaganda, but in this region, where illiteracy is high, the broadcast media remain the primary channel for promoting the government's political, cultural, religious, and economic agendas.

Although not unique to the Arab world, the situation points to a second concern related to Arab broadcasting: a lack of mechanisms or structures for citizen input to the system. This does not mean that phone calls and letters from listeners and viewers are ignored. Little effort, however, is made to solicit citizen comments about radio and television programming on a regular basis. Literally no citizen advisory bodies (at least as we know them in the West) exist in the Middle East. Many media managers believe that they have the ability and knowledge to provide a well-rounded broadcast schedule that includes news, entertainment, and educational programming. For them, the statement by former French broadcast official Arthur Conte—"I am the public"—applies.[21] I once asked the Saudi Arabian minister of information why his organization did not do any audience research. He replied that the king was consulted about the programming schedule and that, as king, he knew his people.

Occasionally, the fear that citizen feedback would not be positive is voiced, and officials are not sure how to react to negative comments. To a certain extent, Arab television managers now know that some systematic citizen feedback is necessary if they are to attract viewers. Unlike the 1970s, many citizens no longer must rely on the government broadcast system for visual entertainment. Those with VCRs have become their own television station program directors. With satellite television dozens and in some cases hundreds of different Arabic and European language services are readily available for an investment of a few hundred U.S. dollars for a satellite receiving dish.

Finally, although there are exceptions in the Arab Middle East, broadcasting officials generally have neither a sound philosophy nor specific goals for radio and television that are tied to the aspirations of the country and the appropriate central planning organization. As a consequence, the inevitable interagency conflicts have not worked to the advantage of the consumer. As in many other areas of the world, television in the Arab world is increasingly dependent on commercial advertising as a source of operating capital. In this regard, satellite television channels are doing well with their pan-Arab world advertising approach. In 1997 advertising on Arab satellite channels increased 105% compared to the previous year. It is anticipated that, through 2001, the annual increase will be 35%.[22]

Despite the lack of social scientific research on the impact of the electronic media on citizens of the Arab world, it is possible to draw some conclusions about what has happened to radio and television itself and to those who view and hear these media. First, even in the less affluent countries, radio set ownership (or in some cases access to a set) is nearly universal. Second, the electronic media, following the trend in most of the world, have become popular in Arab homes, clubs, offices, and automobiles. Radio and television have been part of the fabric of daily life for over two decades. Third, these media continue to be used by those who run them—governments—to promote the prevailing government agenda.

Fourth, consumption of radio, local television, videotaped material, and satellite television programs are now a major leisure time activity. Fifth, satellite television has all but eliminated the traditional government monopoly on what citizens view in terms of entertainment and news. Sixth, although news is available on both local and satellite television, most Arab viewers see television as an entertainment rather than as an educational medium. To paraphrase the coffeehouse owner who dismissed the poet in Mahfouz's *Madiq Alley,* "People today don't want only local television. They keep asking for satellite television, and it is over there being installed now."

## NOTES

1. John Laffin, *The Arab Mind Considered* (New York: Taplinger, 1975), 81–82.

2. Hisham Sharabi, *Nationalism and Revolution in the Arab World* (Princeton, NJ: Van Nostrand, 1975).

3. "John Major Inaugurates MBC's New Headquarters," *MBC News,* issue 3 (London: Middle East Broadcasting Centre, 1995).

4. "Dispute Ends BBC's Arabic Service," *International Herald Tribune,* 22 April 1996, p. 2; "Partner Quit BBC Deal," *The Times* (London), 10 April 1996.

5. A. Zilo, CEO Orbit Television and Radio Network, personal communication, 3 January 1995, Rome, Italy.

6. Raymond Snoddy and David Gardner, "BBC-Saudi TV Row Reveals Raw Spot," *Financial Times,* 10 April 1996, p. 3.

7. Edmund Brunner, "Rural Communications Behavior and Attitudes in the Middle East," *Rural Sociology* 18 (1953): 149–155.

8. Naguib Mahfouz, *Madiq Alley* (London: Heinemann Educational Books, 1966).

9. Ibid., 5.

10. Khalid Marghalani, Phillip Palmgreen, and Douglas A. Boyd, "The Utilization of Direct Satellite Broadcasting (DBS) in Saudi Arabia," *Journal of Broadcasting and Electronic Media* 42 (summer 1998): 297–313.

11. Ibid.

12. Douglas A. Boyd, *Broadcasting in the Arab World: A Survey of the Electronic Media in the Middle East* (Ames: Iowa State University Press, 1999).

13. British Broadcasting Corporation, *Crisis Listening in the UAE* (London: International Broadcasting and Audience Research, 1990).

14. Tomaden Tawffik, "Television in Egypt," Paper presented at the Annenberg School of Communications World Communication Conference, Philadelphia, 1980.

15. "Arab Satellite World in Changes," *Sat-MidEast* (21 May 1999). Available at http://www.sat-net.com/satmideast/.

16. Douglas A. Boyd, "ART: Arab Network for All Arab Nations," *Middle East Broadcast and Satellite,* July 1995, p. 17.

17. F. Al-Amir, Training Department, Arab Radio and Television, Jeddah, Saudi Arabia, personal interview, 15 March 1999.

18. Jon Alterman, *New Media, New Politics: From Satellite Television to the Internet in the Arab World* (Washington, DC: Washington Institute for Near East Policy, 1998).

19. "Al Jazeera's Popularity Said Growing," *Al-Arab al-Yawm* (13 June 1999) (translated by the British Broadcasting Monitoring Service, Caversham Park, England).

20. Mohammed El-Nawawy and Abdel Iskandar, *Al-Jazeera: How the Free Arab New Network Scooped the World and Changed the Middle East* (Cambridge, MA: West View Press, 2002).

21. R. Thomas, *Broadcasting and Democracy in France* (London: Bradford University Press, 1972).

22. Douglas A. Boyd, *Advertising Digest Television 1998* (Dubai: Pan Arab Research Center, 1998).

# PART VII

# Diffusion

Even though technology does not always determine the outcomes of human development, technological advances aid societies and shape their social and economic infrastructures. Starting in the nineteenth century, with the advent of the telegraph and then the telephone, communication technology has been in the forefront to help modernize societies and connect people to their societies. The twentieth century witnessed technological innovations, such as communication satellites, that allow people in different regions to consume identical news, information, and entertainment broadcasts. This has the potential of turning the world into a global village of shared media experiences.

Although the social, cultural, and economic meanings of this temporal global village remain controversial, the conceptualization of what constitutes an information society is less divisive. The evolution of this information society started with computer technology. When networked computers became a medium for exchanging information and messages, they became communication media instead of mere information processors. Later, with the birth of the Internet and its related technology, anyone could communicate with anyone else anywhere by means of text, graphic, audio, and audiovisual modalities online in today's HTML and XML environments. What makes this phenomenon unique from other significant events in human history is the magnitude of the exchange of information and messages and how such exchanges came to dictate many aspects of how people live, work, and play in a society.

The chapter by Everett M. Rogers, of the University of New Mexico, addresses both issues. Rogers first traces the global village to Marshall McLuhan's belief that new media technology will shrink the physical world by connecting peoples through shared cultural experiences as expressed by the media. Rogers illustrates this concept by exploring how traditional broadcast technology brings developmental entertainment programs to the disadvantaged populations in developing nations and how satellite and video technology help broaden as well as deepen such reach. This is followed by a discussion of the role of the Internet, the newest global medium for the world's information elites, in shaping an information society. The chapter concludes with promises and potential dangers regarding the looming gap between the information haves and have-nots and with a few thoughts on the merits of a booming global media village, one that is dominated by Western cultures and ideologies.

The last chapter of this book, by Joseph N. Pelton of George Washington University, explores the political, economic, and technical aspects of technology globalization trends. Pelton explains how the technology convergence phenomenon has created dramatic shifts in international technology market dynamics and in national government regulatory philosophies and technical standards-setting policies. He also introduces those technology advances that help shape today's vibrant information technology economy. Yet, as the pace of technology advancement outgrows a national government's ability to effectively regulate its applications and global legal implications, international regulatory, trade, and technical standards-setting organizations emerge as the primary governing bodies of the global technology market. According to Pelton, the future of technology market globalization looks bright, as further technology convergence breaks down market barriers to encourage competition, deregulation, and global information technology trade.

# 15

# Technology Diffusion and the Global Village

## EVERETT M. ROGERS

My purpose in this chapter is to review the most important technological changes that have affected the nature of international communication in recent decades. A theme is that the world has recently become much more highly interconnected and thus a much smaller place as a result of advances in communication technologies, particularly in the 1990s. The most important communication technologies that have diffused in recent decades are satellite television broadcasting and, especially, the Internet.

## WELCOME TO THE GLOBAL VILLAGE

Imagine daily life in a medieval European village of 600 years ago, shortly before the Renaissance. Almost all human communication was by word of mouth through exchanges with an individual's fellow villagers. The villagers were all highly similar in their socioeconomic characteristics, ethnicity, and worldviews. The lack of diversity in the village and the absence of external contact meant that the villagers were prejudiced and ethnocentric toward out-groups.[1] In short, it was a circumscribed and somewhat brutish isolated life. The villagers had no contact with mass media, and even reading of books was rare, because few individuals were able to read and because books were not widely available.

During the Renaissance, which occurred in Western Europe and was centered in northern Italy, from 1450 to 1600, daily life in the village began to change in important ways. Gutenberg's printing press, the rise of science, and increasing trade with Asia, first overland along the Silk Route and later by ship, brought the descendants of the medieval village in contact with culturally different others. Advances in the technologies of travel and telecommunication eventually brought people into an era of global communication.

## Communication Networks

The global communication network of today is one in which Nike, *The Wall Street Journal,* and McDonald's are available in almost every country.[2] This phenomenon suggests certain economic and market connectivity in the global marketplace. A 1997 financial crisis in Asia triggers a fiscal meltdown in Brazil and Russia. The meltdown causes farm prices in the American Midwest to drop to the point that some farmers give away the pigs they have fattened for market. One might thus think of the world today as a vast web of interpersonal and organizational-commercial communication networks that link suppliers and markets, producers and consumers, communication sources and receivers. This heightened international connectivity creates a new type of global economic vulnerability, as the Asian financial crisis of the late 1990s illustrated.

Writing 40 years ago, the Canadian communication scholar Marshall McLuhan coined the term "global village."[3] He predicted that this global village would arise because of advances in communication technology. McLuhan perceived the mass media as "extensions of man,"[4] a notion that grew out of his correspondence with the anthropologist Edward T. Hall,[5] author of the influential book *The Silent Language*[6] and founder of the field of intercultural communication.[7] Both McLuhan and Hall borrowed the idea of the mass media as extensions of humans from Buckminster Fuller.[8]

The basic idea of the global village is that, because of improved communication technologies, the people of the world are becoming interconnected on a daily basis. The world is shrinking because of the new media of communication, which allow humans to see and talk with others who are far over the horizon. Our communication channels have suddenly multiplied and extended.

McLuhan was a technological determinist. He believed that technology is the main cause of social changes in society. More specifically, McLuhan believed that communication media shape society, an idea that was espoused by a fellow Canadian scholar at the University of Toronto, Harold Innis.[9] In this chapter I generally follow a technological determinist viewpoint while acknowledging that social values may shape the social construction of the technologies that, in turn, shape society. Certainly, the global village of today would not be possible had it not been for the applications of such communication technologies as satellites and the Internet.

# BROADCAST, SATELLITE, AND VIDEO TECHNOLOGY

The most important communication technologies affecting international communication are satellites, broadcasting, VCRs, and telecommunications. These new media built on the globalizing tendencies created in an earlier era by radio broadcasting.

## Expansion of Radio Audiences

The invention of the transistor radio in the 1950s started the so-called transistor radio revolution. It helped spark a rapid expansion in the size of radio audiences in the developing nations of Latin America, Africa, and Asia in the 1960s. Transistor radios were much cheaper and smaller and required less battery power than the large vacuum-tube radio receivers that they replaced. For example, most of the Colombian peasant villages that I studied in the mid-1960s were reached by radio, although not all villagers had regular exposure.[10] At that time a transistor radio cost $5. There was no frequency dial on many of the low-priced transistor models, so the radio was always tuned to one station, Radio Sutatenza, operated by the Catholic Church (priests also distributed the transistor radios, which were manufactured by the Phillips Corporation). In 1964 Radio Havana began broadcasting a stronger radio signal on the same frequency, stressing Cuban revolutionary themes.

For many of the millions of rural and urban poor people in Latin America, Africa, and Asia in the 1960s radio was their first mass media contact with the outside world. A nationwide survey conducted by the National Institute of Community Development in India in 1962 found that two-thirds of the respondents, mainly villagers, did not identify themselves as Indian citizens. Radio eventually created a national identity for these villagers by helping them understand that they belonged to a larger system beyond their immediate community; it also helped people leap the illiteracy barrier in many developing nations. Because 20% of adults in India in the early 1960s were able to read and write, radio was regarded as a magic multiplier in India's national development process.

Today, in the new millennium, radio is still the most important medium for reaching mass audiences in many poor nations, such as Tanzania, Ethiopia, Bangladesh, Pakistan, and India. Even though these nations may have well-developed television systems, radio has a better ability to reach the less educated and lower social status individuals, especially the rural and urban poor. These disadvantaged individuals often experience the most serious economic, health, and nutritional problems and thus are a priority audience for development programs.

Perhaps one might think of the total population of the poorest and most heavily populated Third World nations as a series of three concentric circles. In the center are urban educated elites, constituting perhaps 20 or 30% of a nation's total population. These people have heavy mass media exposure, high expendable incomes, and a consumer orientation, and they live much like the typical citizens of Europe and North America. In the next concentric circle are 30% of a typical developing nation's population, including many lower income urban dwellers and people living in market towns. They may have both television exposure and radio exposure, but they lack the expendable income for a modern consumer lifestyle. As a result, this audience is not targeted by commercial media. The remainder of a nation's population, composed of individuals of lower socioeconomic status, especially those living in villages and other rural areas, are reached only by radio.

Thus today radio has the ability to reach the poorest, more rural, and neediest segments of the population of developing nations. Radio has retained this important function while losing many others to such newer media as television and, in recent years, the Internet.

## Expansion of Television Audiences
## Through Satellite Technology

The 1990s saw a major shift in the distribution of television audiences worldwide, with a major expansion occurring in such developing nations as India and China. This explosion in the size of the total television audience worldwide and its increasing concentration in large-population developing nations resulted from (1) the use of satellite distribution of television signals to increase audiences and (2) research and the introduction of high-quality entertainment television programming.

Arthur C. Clarke proposed the idea of using satellites in geosynchronous orbit for broadcasting purposes in 1945. In nations with vast land areas and/or with mountainous terrains satellites have become crucial technologies for the delivery of television broadcasts (and for extending telephone and other telecommunications services). Today, many nations (or regions) either operate their own satellite systems or are served by commercial satellite systems: India (INSAT), Indonesia (PALAPA), China (ASIASAT), Africa (AFROSAT), Latin America (AsKy), the Middle East (ARABSAT), and Europe (EUROSAT). Thus satellites are important technologies in building today's global village. Here, I consider the rapid diffusion of television in the world's two most populated countries: China in the 1980s and India in the 1990s.

**China**  The rapid rate of diffusion of television in the People's Republic of China in the late 1970s and early 1980s was similar to what occurred in the United States in the 1950s. The rapid spread of television in China was all the more spectacular because the cost of a television set in the early 1980s was 400 yuan ($200), roughly equivalent to a typical factory worker's annual income at that time.[11] Consequently, a great deal of television exposure took place through group viewing, with many television sets available in public places, such as village centers, factories, and schools.

A sample of 2,430 rural and urban individuals in the Beijing metropolitan area in 1982 reported their daily exposure to radio (97%), television (92%), and newspapers (81%).[12] This level of exposure to television was particularly amazing, given that television became popular only at the end of the Cultural Revolution in 1976, six years before the 1982 Beijing Audience Survey was conducted. A process similar to this television revolution in China was happening in other developing nations, although often less rapidly and sometimes a decade or two sooner (as in Latin America) or later (as in India and Indonesia). By September 1997 an unprecedented 2 billion of the world's 6 billion people viewed live television broadcasts of Princess Diana's funeral, the largest television audience ever to gather for a single event.

**India** In India television broadcasting began in the late 1950s, but for the next three decades the only broadcaster was the government network, Doordarshan, a system originally patterned after the BBC model. In the mid-1980s, 250 satellite receiving stations were retransmitting the national television signal that they received from the Indian national satellite. This national television signal covered an area where about 75% of India's population resided. However, only 10% of the Indian population was regularly exposed to television broadcasts, in part because many of the television programs were educational development−oriented programs and hence fairly dull. There was no television advertising then.

The 1984−1985 season saw the debut of an entertainment-education television soap opera, *Hum Log,* which focused on a lower-class extended family. This extremely popular program, with audience ratings of up to 90% in Hindi-speaking North India, helped expand the size of the television audience in India.[13] Suddenly, the demand for television sets exploded. Soon more than 100 Indian companies were manufacturing sets. Further, *Hum Log,* which was broadcast on Doordarshan, carried advertising for a new food product: instant noodles. Sales of the product immediately took off.[14] Television became a profitable industry as the government television system became commercialized. Skilled talent was attracted to the television industry, and *Hum Log* was soon followed by other popular television shows.

A second major era in Indian television expansion began in late 1991, during the Persian Gulf War. Many Indians had a family member working in one of the Persian Gulf nations. At first, four-star hotels in Bombay and other metropolitan centers placed television sets in their lobbies for public viewing of CNN and the BBC broadcasts of the war. STAR-TV, a satellite system headquartered in Hong Kong, began to beam satellite signals to India. Its broadcasts featured news and entertainment programs that were much more attractive than those available on Doordarshan. Thousands of Indian entrepreneurs purchased small satellite-receiving dishes, and they strung cable connections to households in their apartment buildings or housing areas, charging each household a fee for this private cable television service. Within a year a dozen new commercial television networks sprung up in India.

Thus a television revolution was launched in India in the 1990s, featuring private commercial television networks that broadcast imported programs, including *The Bold and the Beautiful, Baywatch,* MTV programs, and Indian-produced programs that reflected strong Western influences. For example, a top-rated show in India in the late 1990s was *Tara,* based loosely on the U.S. show *Dynasty.* It depicted a slim, sexual, assertive businesswomen. This female image was in sharp contrast to the traditional perception of the Indian woman as someone who was submissive and male dominated and performed primarily housewife chores. For the first time in India, increasing rates of bulimia and anorexia were reported among young females.[15] Images such as those of Madonna in a cone-shaped bra began to replace the traditional image of the rounder female figure.

This India television revolution of the 1990s largely occurred without much influence of government policy. The private television networks produced much of their programming in India, and then they transported these programs on videotape by courier to Hong Kong or Moscow for uplinking to satellites. Thus the private networks circumscribed the Indian government's prohibition against private (nongovernment) broadcasting from Indian soil. The commercialization and privatization of Indian television in the 1990s fitted with the Indian government's new economic policy of 1991, in which foreign companies, including Coca Cola, McDonald's, and Kentucky Fried Chicken, were allowed to sell their products in India. Thus an Indian consumer (at least in urban areas) could view television advertisements for Nike shoes and then go purchase the shoes at a nearby store.[16]

Because the television audience in India grew from 10% in 1984 to 50% in 1999, the characteristics of television viewers shifted from urban elites to more middle-class individuals and people living outside metropolitan areas. In a nation with a total population of 1 billion people, this television audience (along with China's) was one of the largest of any nation in the world.

In summary, in the past 20 years the size of the worldwide television audience has expanded tremendously, with the expansion occurring mainly in developing nations. This rapid diffusion of television was facilitated by satellite technology, commercialization, privatization, and Westernized programming that conveyed a strikingly different image of women in many cultures.

## Spread of U.S. Television Programs and Films

In the early years of television broadcasting in Latin America, U.S. prime-time shows (dubbed into Spanish) dominated television program schedules. By the 1980s, however, with the rise of television production by private networks such as Televisa in Mexico and TeleGlobo in Brazil, most of the highly rated television programs were produced in Latin America.[17] Imported programming from the United States (e.g., *Dallas*) was pushed outside the prime-time evening hours and attracted smaller numbers of viewers. Television audiences in Latin America preferred local programs to those imported from the United States, Europe, or Japan. A generally similar pattern occurred in Asia in the early 1990s.[18]

Nevertheless, American films earn 80% of worldwide box office receipts, according to *Variety* (see Chapter 10). Media products are an important economic export, and they contributed $60 billion annually to the U.S. trade balance during the 1990s. Yet these Hollywood imports do not represent the extreme of cultural imperialism that had been feared in earlier decades. Although American lifestyles and cultural values conveyed in U.S. media exports are a powerful influence in the global village (for instance, basketball star Michael Jordan is the most widely recognized individual in the world today), U.S. media products have not dominated local cultures, as was once feared by many communication scholars in the 1970s.

## Entertainment-Education

One of the promising development strategies of the past several decades is entertainment-education. This involves the intentional placement of educational content in entertainment messages with the goal of changing audience members' behavior for the better.[19] Radio and television soap operas, street theater, popular music, and other forms of entertainment have been used to promote such educational themes as family planning, HIV prevention, gender equality, adult education, and environmental protection. Most of the 100 entertainment-education projects have been carried out in the developing nations of Latin America, Africa, and Asia.

The entertainment-education strategy began by accident. A Peruvian television soap opera, *Simplemente Maria,* was broadcast in 1969, first in Peru and then throughout Latin America. Wherever this soap opera was aired, the sale of Singer sewing machines and enrollment in adult literacy classes increased. These effects occurred because the plot centered around a household maid, Maria, who rose from poverty because of her sewing ability (on a Singer machine) and as a result of gaining literacy skills.

Miguel Sabido, a Mexican television executive, decoded *Simplemente Maria* to better understand how such desirable effects could occur. Sabido applied these lessons in a series of *telenovelas* (or soap operas) broadcast by Televisa, the Mexican television network, in the late 1970s and early 1980s. Sabido represented the educational idea (say, family planning) in the behavior of several positive role models in the soap opera and opposed the idea through the behavior of several negative characters. The negative characters were punished in the story line, whereas the positive role models were rewarded. Transitional role models began as negative characters, but they were later converted into positive exemplars for the educational idea.

Since the mid-1980s Sabido's entertainment-education formula has spread to India (it was used in *Hum Log*), Kenya, Tanzania, and dozens of other countries. Evaluation research on these entertainment-education programs indicates that they generally have their intended beneficial effects of changing knowledge, attitudes, and overt behaviors.[20] How do such effects occur? Research shows that entertainment-education (1) facilitates parasocial interaction, defined as the quasi-interpersonal relationship between an audience member and a media personality, (2) encourages social learning from the positive, negative, and transitional role models, and (3) stimulates peer communication among audience members as they discuss the educational issues contained in the entertainment program.[21]

## Sharing Media Products Through Videos

As discussed previously, locally produced television programs are generally more popular with audiences than are imported programs. However, several exceptions to this generalization have been studied by communication scholars, in part because they are culturally shareable. One example is *Karate Kids,* a 22-minute cartoon film/videotape produced by Street Kids International, a Canadian non-governmental organization, in collaboration with the National Film Board of Canada and the World Health Organization. The purpose of *Karate Kids* was to reduce the incidence of HIV/AIDS among street children worldwide. An experimental evaluation of *Karate Kids* with street children in Bangkok found that the video had the expected changes in audience members' knowledge, attitudes, and behaviors.[22]

*Karate Kids* has been dubbed into 25 languages and has been shown to street children in 100 countries. The main character, Karate, is based on a popular children's hero. He represents a positive role model for HIV/AIDS prevention, protecting himself and his friends. A negative character is the Bad Guy with a Smiling Face, who seduces street children by giving material rewards in exchange for sex. Street children identified the cartoon characters as like themselves in each nation in which the film/video has been shown. Further, street children viewers parasocially connected with the cartoon characters, whom they regarded as quasi-friends.[23]

Another culturally shareable media product that has proven to be popular with television audiences in the 45 countries in which it was shown from 1984 to 1995 is *Oshin,* a Japanese television soap opera. This program traces the life story of Oshin, the daughter of a poor tenant farmer in northern Japan. When she is 7 years old, Oshin's father exchanges her for a bag of rice. Eventually, she overcomes many difficulties and emerges in old age as the wealthy owner of a large chain of supermarkets. The story line was based on the real-life story of a Mrs. Wada, who founded the Yaohan Supermarket Chain.[24]

*Oshin* was very popular in Japan and set ratings records in many of the other nations in which it was broadcast. One reason for this audience popularity was that many individuals perceived a parasocial relationship with Oshin. They felt that she represented such positive cultural values as perseverance, hard work, and self-efficacy. By appealing to universal values, this Japanese television program achieved audience popularity worldwide.[25] Much more needs to be learned about why certain media products diffuse across cultures and are able to appeal widely to various audiences.

## The Internet Phenomenon

Military interest in using computers for communication began with the launch of Sputnik by the Soviet Union in 1958. Americans realized that the next world conflict would be won by the nation that was most technologically advanced. The U.S. Congress established the Advanced Research Projects Agency (ARPA) in the Pentagon to pursue research and development in computing and other technological fields. ARPA wished to interconnect these research teams, located at leading American universities (e.g., MIT, Stanford, Carnegie-Mellon, Utah, and UCLA) in a computer network so that they could exchange software programs and databases. Thus ARPANET was born in 1969. Initially, however, the main function of ARPANET became electronic mail, with the content often dealing with personal messages and jokes.

For the next 20 years computer networks grew slowly. Then, in 1989 a number of existing computer networks (e.g., ARPANET, BITNET, and NSFNET) merged to form the Internet, an international computer network. Suddenly, the rate of adoption began to take off, creating a critical mass, defined as the minimum number of adopters of an innovation needed to achieve a self-sustaining rate of further adoption.[26] The rate of Internet diffusion began to increase exponentially, creating the S-shaped curve that characterizes the rate of adoption of many innovations. However, the rate of adoption for the Internet was unusually steep, driven by technological improvements in computer networking (such as MOSAIC, the World Wide Web, and Java) and by the obvious advantages of cheap, fast transmission of e-mail messages. The rapidly increasing number of users helped the Internet have greater perceived utility for potential adopters.

Although the adoption rate of the Internet in the United States since 1989 has been extremely rapid, a somewhat similar process may be happening today in several other countries, especially in Western European countries. By early 1999, 132 million people were using the Internet in the United States, constituting two-fifths of the 327 million users worldwide. The nation with the greatest number of Internet users, after the United States, was Germany, with 23 million.[27] As the number of home pages available on the World Wide Web exploded during the 1990s, along with many commercial companies provided advertising, goods, or services on the Web, the number of individuals surfing the Web increased at a rate parallel to the rate of e-mail adoption on the Internet. The rate of adoption of the Internet during the 1990s was the most rapidly diffusing innovation in the history of humankind. Eventually, especially in the United States, this rate of adoption must begin to plateau, because many of the potential adopters will already have become users of this new medium. A leveling-off in the number of hosts (that is, computers connected to the Internet through which individuals access the Internet) has already been detected in the United States. By early 1999 there were 35 million hosts, with the number expected to increase slowly to 42 million in 2002.[28]

Perhaps 90% of the worldwide message traffic on the Internet today is in English, and most search engines operate only in English. American dominance of the Internet has led to concern that this new medium may become another means of American cultural invasion. For example, the French are concerned about the lack of French language use of the Internet, one reason for the relatively low rate of adoption of the Internet in France.[29]

## Censorship and Control of the Internet

I begin the discussion of censorship and control of the Internet with three examples: Singapore, South Korea, and China.

Singapore is an island nation of 3 million people in which almost every household is connected to the Internet. Singaporeans are predominantly English speaking, and their government is committed to their nation becoming an "intelligent island." However, the government seeks to protect Singaporean citizens from pornographic materials on the Web by blocking access to certain home pages. The

Singaporean government is known for its authoritarian governing style, one that censors many aspects of its national life, including the press.

Another attempt at Internet censorship occurred in the Republic of Korea. This event suggests that such gatekeeping is usually only partially successful because of the decentralized nature of the Internet (which can be traced to the fact that ARPANET was designed in the cold war era to be difficult to destroy in a nuclear attack). This story involves Sung Hi Lee, a Korean American woman who was born in Pusan and migrated with her parents to the United States at the age of 8. After studying at Ohio State University for three years, the 27-year-old Lee worked as a model for the New York Big Apple Company, and her nude photographs appeared in U.S. adult magazines.

Although local online sites with adult content are banned by the Korean government, young Korean Internet surfers soon found Lee's nude photos on the Internet (accessible because they were not programmed or presented on the Web in Korea). Soon Lee came to be regarded by young Koreans as a superstar, representing a symbolic protest against traditional Korean values. In 1997 she earned half a million dollars in a 12-day visit to South Korea.[30]

The government of the People's Republic of China in 1999 sentenced Lin Hai, a Shanghai computer engineer, to two years in jail for sending 30,000 Chinese e-mail addresses to an electronic publication in the United States. Although the Chinese government encourages use of the Internet by its citizens as one means of modernization, the Chinese people are forbidden to convey any political content online. Further, certain Web sites are blocked because they carry information that Beijing considers politically unfriendly. Lin Hai was accused of providing the e-mail addresses to a U.S. organization that would use them to send information to the overseas Chinese democracy movement.

These three examples suggest the difficulties that national governments face in trying to regulate message content on the Internet. When one individual sends an electronic message on the Internet, it may follow any one of millions of possible pathways to reach its destination. Each computer in the sequence passes the message along to another computer, routed by available telephone lines connected to any number of telephone networks around the world. Such a decentralized system, resulting from the Internet's roots as ARPANET in the cold war days of 1969, make the Internet almost uncontrollable by censors or gatekeepers. Moreover, the system is designed to prevent computer hackers or enemy states from infiltrating military intelligence and defense technology secrets. This type of military defense-minded structural design inadvertently helped create the freewheeling Internet that we access today.

## CONCLUSIONS

All parts of the world are increasingly linked by trade, news flows, entertainment, etc. into the global village with the help of various communication technologies. Will nation-states disappear or at least become relatively less important as the world increasingly becomes an economic, information, and entertainment global village? Will the English language and American cultural values become even more dominant because of the near ubiquitous distribution of English media products, primarily produced by Hollywood and the U.S. online industry?

We have seen that the global village may have both advantages and disadvantages. For example, a small but increasing number of people experience information overload, defined as the degree to which an individual receives more information than he or she can process. Today, populations residing in developing countries are advancing their social and economic development more rapidly because of their access to communication technology. However, the existing information and knowledge gap between developed (or industrialized) and developing nations is widening instead of narrowing, as a result of the inability of developing nations to keep pace with accelerating technology advances in developed nations.

The global village as it exists today contains the poor, the middle class, and the wealthy, just as any village or city around the world. Communication technologies have helped link many citizens of these different sections of the global village so that they can share certain economic and social growth opportunities. Nevertheless, the uneven growth rates between the poorer and the wealthier sections in this global village will not quickly even out. How citizens in the global village communicate with each other and utilize their communication technologies will ultimately determine their quality of life.

## NOTES

1. Everett M. Rogers and Thomas M. Steinfatt, *Intercultural Communication* (Prospect Heights, IL: Waveland Press, 1999).

2. James L. Watson, *Golden Arches East: McDonald's in East Asia* (Stanford, CA: Stanford University Press, 1997).

3. Marshall McLuhan, *The Gutenberg Galaxy: The Making of Typographic Man* (Toronto: University of Toronto Press, 1962).

4. Marshall McLuhan, *Understanding Media: The Extensions of Man* (New York: McGraw-Hill, 1964), 31.

5. Edward T. Hall, *Beyond Culture* (New York: Doubleday, 1976).

6. Edward T. Hall, *The Silent Language* (New York: Doubleday, 1959).

7. Rogers and Steinfatt, *Intercultural Communication*.

8. Matie Molinaro, Corinne McLuhan, and William Toye, *Letters of Marshall McLuhan* (New York: Oxford University Press, 1987); Everett M. Rogers, "The Extensions of Men: Correspondence of Marshall McLuhan and Edward T. Hall—Letters and Mass Communication Research," *Mass Communication and Society* 3, no. 1 (2000): 117–135.

9. Harold A. Innis, *Empire and Communication* (New York: Oxford University Press, 1950). Harold A. Innis, *The Bias of Communication* (Toronto: University of Toronto Press, 1951).

10. Everett M. Rogers with Lynne Svenning, *Modernization among Peasants* (New York: Holt, Rinehart and Winston, 1969).

11. Everett M. Rogers, Xiaoyan Zhou, Xhongdang Pan, Milton Chen, and the Beijing Journalism Association, "The Beijing Audience Study," *Communication Research* 1, no. 2 (1985): 179–208.

12. Ibid.

13. Arvind Singhal and Everett M. Rogers, *Entertainment-Education: A Communication Strategy for Social Change* (Mahwah, NJ: Lawrence Earlbaum Associates, 1999).

14.  Ibid.

15.  Sheena Malhotra, "The Privatization of Television in India: Implications of New Technologies for Gender, Nation, and Culture," Ph.D. dissertation, University of New Mexico, Albuquerque, 1999.

16.  Sheena Malhotra and Everett M. Rogers, "Satellite Television and the New India Woman," *Gazette* 62, no. 4 (2000): 407–429.

17.  Everett M. Rogers and Livia Antola, "Telenovelas: A Latin America Success Story," *Journal of Communication* 35 (1986): 24–35.

18.  David Waterman and Everett M. Rogers, "The Economy of Television Program Trade in Far East Asia," *Journal of Communication* 44, no. 3 (1994): 89–111.

19.  Singhal and Rogers, *Entertainment-Education.*

20.  Ibid.

21.  Ibid.

22.  Parichart Sthapitanonda Sarobol and Arvind Singhal, "Cultural Shareability, Role Modeling, and Para-Social Interaction in an Entertainment-Education Film: The Effects of *Karate Kids* on Thai Street Children," in S. Ralph, J. L. Brown, and T. Lees, eds., *Youth and the Global Media* (Luton, England: University of Luton Press, 1999), 178–179.

23.  Ibid.

24.  Corinne L. Shefner-Rogers, Everett M. Rogers, and Arvind Singhal, "Parasocial Interaction with the Television Soap Operas 'Simplemente Maria' and 'Oshin,'" *Keio Communication Review* 20 (1998): 3–18.

25.  Peer Svenkerud, Rital Rahoi, and Arvind Singhal, "Incorporating Ambiguity and Archetypes in Entertainment-Education Programming: Lessons Learned from 'Oshin,'" *Gazette* 55 (1985): 147–168.

26.  Everett M. Rogers, *Diffusion of Innovations* (New York: Free Press, 1995).

27.  Arvind Singhal and Everett M. Rogers, *India's Communication Revolution* (New Delhi: Sage, 2000).

28.  Ibid.

29.  Ibid.

30.  Seongcheol Kim, "Cultural Imperialism on the Internet," *The Edge: The E-Journal of Intercultural Relations* 1, no. 4 (1998): 1–11.

# 16

# The Changing Shape of Global Telecommunications

## JOSEPH N. PELTON

Global telecommunications changed more radically in the past 30 years than it had over the previous century. In the past three decades the size and scope of international communications has increased 500 times. Telephones, television receivers, personal computers, faxes, radios, CDs, and electronic switches have increased in number and performance—exponentially so. Totally new on the global telecommunications horizon are the Internet, electronic data interchange, the nonstop global corporation, and international electronic commuting. Likewise, we have seen the successful arrival of fax, global television (11,000 satellite television channels worldwide), and surging numbers of personal communications service and cell phones. The rate of innovation continues to increase. Transmission speeds for fiber optic systems are doubling every 12 months. This is even faster than the 18-month doubling of computer speeds predicted by Moore's law, which has held true for the past two decades.

In the satellite arena alone we have seen the emergence of direct-to-the-home and mobile satellite systems, broadband and low earth orbit satellites plus satellite messaging and the Global Positioning System (GPS) space navigation systems. Third-generation personal communications services (PCS), increasingly smart and functional Palm Pilot units, and new stratospheric platforms promise a decade of expansion in broadband multimedia wireless services. In fact, telecommunications

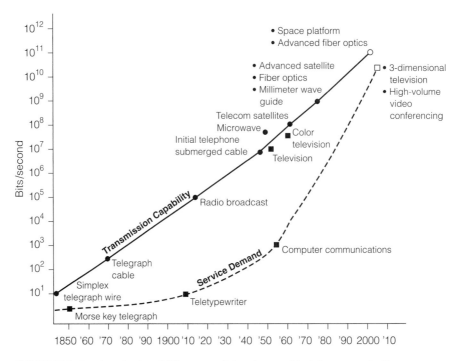

**FIGURE 16.1** One hundred and fifty years of development in telecommunications transmission systems and applications

and systems applications have been increasing exponentially for 150 years, and, if anything, the future shows even faster rates of innovation (Figure 16.1).

These changes and more are serving to combine (by means of integrated digital networking and processing) all forms of information services and systems. Thus we see the telecommunications industry merging with the newspaper, book publishing, entertainment, computer, cable television, and software industries. Some are referring to this process as the ICE Age, where ICE stands for information, communications, and entertainment. The ICE industry is now becoming a digitally integrated $4 trillion dollar a year colossus.[1]

Accompanying this trend and partially causing it are deregulation and competition, the emergence of such entities as the World Trade Organization, the European Telecommunications Standards Institute, the Asia-Pacific Telecommunity, and the demise of telecommunications monopolies in most of the economically advanced nations. In short, the entire landscape of global telecommunications has shifted in terms of technology, digital standards, regulatory environment, available services, cost, and general changes in perspective on the pivotal role of telecommunications in the twenty-first century. Figure 16.2 shows the six major interrelated forces of change in international information and communication systems and how they relate to the global marketplace.

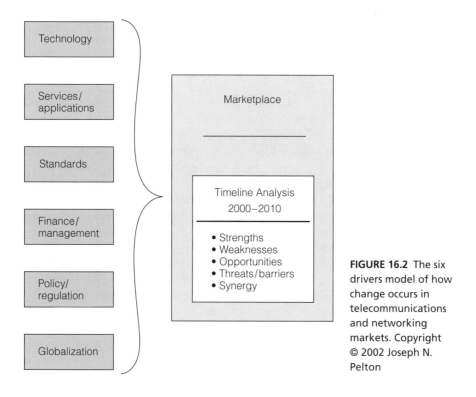

**FIGURE 16.2** The six drivers model of how change occurs in telecommunications and networking markets. Copyright © 2002 Joseph N. Pelton

At the end of the 1960s telecommunications was focused on communities and countries. Today, in the age of the World Wide Web, the predominant paradigm in telecommunications is that of planetary and low-cost connectivity that supports global commerce, entertainment, and science. Here are six ways that the world of telecommunications has changed: (1) globalization, (2) convergence, (3) the changeover from analog to digital, (4) advanced multiplexing, (5) signaling and switching, and (6) fiber optics, coaxial cable, and cable television modems. These six ways are discussed in the following sections.

## Globalization

At the end of World War II there were fewer than 50 nations in the world. With the end of colonialism, the new balkanization of Eastern Europe, the end of the USSR, and the consequent spin-off of more than a dozen new republics, we have seen the creation of many new nation-states around the world (especially among island territories). The number of nation-states has now surged past 200. A number of these countries, such as Tuvalu, with a total population of 7,000 and a territory that includes a number of islands distributed over 500,000 square miles of ocean, are greatly challenged for survival. Clearly, such countries are heavily dependent on effective telecommunications.

Only in the last few years have many new countries been able to establish independent telecommunications systems nationally and internationally. The number of telephones worldwide has expanded from 150 million in 1970 to 900 million telephone handsets in operation globally today. As of 1970 only a few thousand intercontinental telephone circuits were in operation; today there are more than 1 million operational satellites, fiber optic, and tropo-scatter telephone circuits—a 300-fold increase in less than 30 years.[2]

As of 1970 the so-called industrializing and developing countries represented less than 15% of the total global trade in products and services; today that number has risen to 24%. Indeed, a number of developing countries have moved to the status of either industrializing or even developed economies, for example, Taiwan, South Korea, and Singapore. There can be no doubt that modern telecommunications is an important aspect of the trend toward globalism and that international trade in services is rapidly growing. Indeed, services are now as important as international trade in products in terms of economic output.[3] Tariffs on international telecommunications can take on enormous importance, especially in developing countries. In countries such as Jamaica, Senegal, and Sri Lanka as much as 30% of the hard currency influx into the national treasury can come from international telecommunications.[4]

## Convergence: The Five C's of Communications

In the past communications, computers, cable television, computer software and entertainment, and consumer electronics were totally separate industries. Today, the technology of digital encoding and transmission has integrated these industries in new and powerful ways. In a world where a "bit is a bit is a bit" the separation among publishing, electronic marketing, cable television, entertainment, telecommunications, computers, television production, etc. is quickly disappearing. The power of digital convergence is reshaping markets, consumption patterns, and industries around the world. This phenomenon has been characterized in a number of different ways. There is the concept of the five C's (communications, computers, cable television, content, and consumer electronics) and of the so-called ICE Age.

As of 2000 the information products and services market will generate $2 trillion per year in revenues, communications related revenues will be $1 trillion per year, and entertainment will be another $1 trillion per year. Altogether, this mega-industry is worth $4 trillion per year, representing about $1 in every $12 spent in the global economy. Furthermore, smart energy and smart transportation will increasingly be included as an additional segment in this giant digitally based enterprise. Today, one only has to look to the digitally based high-tech enterprises (e.g., GM/Hughes, Microsoft, Mitsubishi, Motorola, Intel, Toyota, AOL, AT&T, and Alcatel) to appreciate how extensive and fast moving digital convergence already is—the boundaries that separated traditional markets from one another are now virtually gone.[5]

## From Analog to Digital

One of the biggest changes in all of telecommunications has been the shift from analog to digital communication systems. The advantages of digital communication include the ability to provide a higher quality of service while offering increased throughput efficiencies (through a variety of processing techniques). These techniques include increased use of frequencies through multiple cellular beams, digital compression and speech interpolation, and digital signal processing. In general, myriad digital protocols have resulted in progress that allows data to be sent more efficiently for framing, synchronization, and error control. The new protocols allow all types of services and applications to be transmitted and to support voice, data, video, imaging, and multimedia services. In parallel with these developments that support the transmission of digital services over the public switched telephone networks has been the evolution of the Internet, which is supported by the Transmission Control Protocol/Internet Protocol (TCP/IP). Today, the merging of Internet and public switched telecommunications systems is being actively promoted to transmit data streams at an incredibly high speed. Furthermore, TCP/IP is being updated and improved to support near real time services such as voice and video services.

## Advanced Multiplexing

Multiplexing involves a way of sending more concentrated information through a fixed communication channel. The most common systems now being deployed are time division multiple access (TDMA) and code division multiple access (CDMA), as used in satellite systems. TDMA divides information into packets that are sent in sequential time slots and uses all the bandwidth available in the carrier for a limited increment of time. CDMA codes the information in packets and sends the coded information packets across a wide-spectrum range; thus CDMA is sometimes called spread spectrum. This coding allows signals to be sent over the same spectrum over and over again. This and similar encoding techniques will probably become increasingly important as the problem of radio frequency signal interference escalates over time as more and more telecommunications systems are created.

The most recent multiplexing scheme of global importance is the optical spectrum. This process, called wave division multiplexing, exploits the fact that multiplexed signals can be sent again and again on a closely packed basis within the optical spectrum. The key is to shift each carrier wave apart from another within a fiber optic cable by shifting the wavelength of the carrier wave by an infinitesimal amount (now as small as 0.25 nanometer). Once the multiplexed signal or carrier wave has been shifted to another light wavelength, an entirely new burst of information can be sent through the same optical light pipe. In theory, this process of sending multiple carrier waves, or multiplexing, can be done thousands of times. The efficiency of dense wave division multiplexing technology unlocks virtually unlimited information-carrying capacity in the new low-loss monomode fiber optic cable systems.

## Switching and Signaling

The rapid development of global communications has been spurred by new high-throughput digital transmissions systems such as coaxial and fiber optic cable, satellites of various types, and cellular wireless systems. The other key has been the rapid evolution of new electronic switching systems with advanced signaling capabilities that add new "intelligence" to telecommunications and data networks. The earliest switching and signaling systems simply delivered calls to the correct exchange and number of the subscriber. Today, signaling systems help to route calls more efficiently, provide specialized ringing, indicate caller identity, create conference calls, etc. These signaling systems also help to seamlessly interconnect mobile, wire, fiber optic, and satellite networks.

One of the most important innovations that draws on computer processing power and advanced software is the so-called seven-layer model developed by the International Standards Organization (ISO). The model establishes a hierarchy of protocol interconnection. This seven-layer model begins with the physical interconnection level and builds to the applications layer. This ISO model is a key element in allowing telecommunications and computer networking equipment around the world to interconnect without major interruption. It is as key to satellite, wireless, and fiber optic systems working together as it was to the seamless linking of telephone, fax, multimedia, television, and computer networks.

## Fiber Optics, Coaxial Cable, and Cable Television Modems

The terrestrial telecommunications environment has grown in the competitive telecommunications markets. The economic incentives to add new fiber optic networks and to employ hybrid fiber optic/coaxial cable networks to serve urban areas and large countries have continued to improve. However, these impressive new networks, which are tens of thousands of miles in length, connect only major cities and the various continents together; they do not provide links directly to the consumer. Urban networks that serve businesses and the home consumer use a combination of fiber optic trunks, copper wire (enhanced with digital transmission technology such as DSL), and coaxial connections to the home. These networks can also use cable modems to provide home broadband telecommunications and entertainment or high-speed Internet access.

Modern fiber optic networks can provide 1 megabit/second of information services to the consumer for under $0.01 per minute, and hybrid fiber optic/coaxial cable networks can be installed in the home at a net cost of under $900. The so-called X-DSL or ADSL technology—a form of digital transmission system that compresses the signal to squeeze in more transmission capacity—can be added to copper wire networks at a cost of $300 per home. The seamless interconnection of these expanded capacity wire, coaxial cable, and fiber optic networks will allow consumers in many countries belonging to the Organization for Economic Cooperation and Development (OECD) to rely on wire-based communications networks for much of their telecommunications services in the twenty-first century.[6]

Development of fiber optic and hybrid fiber optic/coaxial cable networks is not yet a reality in developing countries. Other types of communication networks are needed to meet all forms of telecommunications needs, especially in developing countries that have distributed populations. Wireless local loop and satellite technology must be a part of the integrated telecommunications solution in, for example, Indonesia, with 18,000 islands, in Brazil with its vast tract of tropical rainforest, and in Chile with the Andes mountain range splitting the country into two parts. Further, as noted earlier, wireless technologies and satellites are also needed to provide mobile services.[7]

## WIRELESS TECHNOLOGIES

The most surprising aspect of global telecommunications in the past 15 years has been the dramatic surge in wireless telecommunications that has risen from the success of cellular technology. Wireless technology has allowed the reuse of available frequencies through the creation of small cells. This in turn has set the stage for the deployment of digital cellular technology, known as personal communications service (PCS). Initially, PCS was a product for business people so that they could have access to mobile telephone and data services. In a short time the technology became popular with average consumers, who enjoy the convenience and emergency communications capability that cell phones offer.

In developing and industrializing countries the cell phone revolution took hold quickly. These wireless systems could be deployed quickly to augment aging and out-of-date terrestrial wire systems. In many cases overseas investors with capital to invest were allowed to supplement conventional telephone systems that were unable to meet emerging demand. The technology constituted an easy way to allow competition with the established monopoly carrier. Over 300 million wireless telephone and data units will be in service on a worldwide basis by the end of 2002. By the end of 2003 the new broadband PCS, known as the third-generation PCS system, will also be increasingly deployed globally in developed countries.

In addition to analog cell phones and PCS or digital cell phones, other wireless services can be offered; these include multimegabit multipoint distribution service (MMDS), which is sometimes known as wireless cable television, and the local multipoint distribution service (LMDS), often deployed in group living quarters such as hotels and apartment buildings in both remote and urban areas. These services, which are cheaper to launch than a wired network today, have made limited impact on U.S. markets and even less around the world, but there can be no doubt that there will be a growing demand for broadband mobile services in the decades ahead.[8]

## SATELLITES

When satellite service began with the Early Bird satellite of INTELSAT in April 1965, the service was seen as largely international in scope and was to serve only limited trunking pathways, where heavy streams of traffic justified the building of a large and expensive earth receiving station facility. Today, satellites are used to provide direct-to-the-home entertainment services (e.g., DirecTV) and direct mobile services (e.g., mobile phone services), and they are now providing direct broadband services to microterminals (e.g., satellite and mobile telephones) as well. The key in this regard has been the advent of higher-powered satellites with multiple beams that can reuse frequencies and the consequent use of so-called very small aperture terminals (i.e., a satellite terminal that is 1–3 meters in size). Soon, satellites with higher power that use higher frequencies will begin to operate ultrasmall aperture terminals or microterminals (i.e., a small satellite antenna 35–65 centimeters in size).

Today, 300 commercial communications satellites are in orbit. Within the decade that number will probably exceed 1,000; we will also see the evolution of a number of stratospheric platforms or high-altitude platform systems that can operate directly with the smallest and the most economical user terminal receivers. This growth in the number of satellites will occur because of a combination of new market demand, falling prices for many new types of satellite services (particularly those going directly to end-users, such as mobile personal communications and direct-to-the-home entertainment), and the need to deploy many more satellites in low earth orbit systems (rather than higher orbits) to achieve global coverage.[9]

## TRENDS IN TECHNOLOGY

Probably none of the key changes in global telecommunications would have occurred without the dynamic force of technological change. Fundamental changes at all levels have occurred. The most important of these changes include telecommunication network architecture and bypass technologies.

### Telecommunications Network Architecture

The basic architecture of telecommunications networks has escaped from the one-dimensional aspect of hierarchically switched and rigidly concentrated networks. Today there are much more flexible options for traffic interconnection. The traditional approach of terrestrial wire, cable, and concentrating switches is essentially a vertical or hierarchical network, as shown in Figure 16.3. In contrast, wireless and satellite networks can connect consumer users together without elaborate layered traffic concentration networks (i.e., horizontal networks), as shown in Figure 16.4.

### Bypass Technologies

When applied to new satellite and wireless networks, the new digital technology will also facilitate the establishment of more flexible and responsive meshlike networks that can establish needed links flexibly and on demand. All these technical achievements move telecommunications closer to the consumer and allow

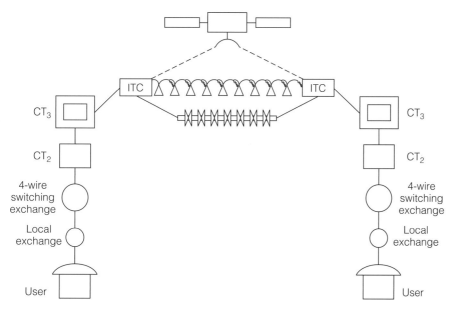

**FIGURE 16.3** Traditional or vertical model of long-distance and international communications. Copyright © 2002 Joseph N. Pelton.

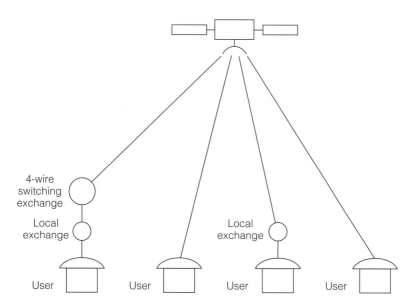

**FIGURE 16.4** New nonconcentrated or horizontal model of how traffic will flow in advanced satellite telecommunications networks. Copyright © 2002 Joseph N. Pelton.

traditional wire and coaxial cable networks to be bypassed. These breakthroughs provide new start-up firms with a greater ability to compete with traditional and dominant carriers and to establish new direct links to customers.[10] The phenomenon of bypassing in the delivery of telecommunications and data services has given rise to new types of companies. These include:

- Internet service providers (ISPs) (e.g., AOL, MSN, PSI).

- Direct-to-the-home satellite entertainment systems or direct broadcast satellite systems (e.g., DirecTV, Echostar, Eutelsat's Hot Bird, Astra, and Asiastar).

- Mobile voice and data communications satellite systems (e.g., ACeS, Globalstar, and Thuraya).

- Cable television and competitive local exchange carriers that offer more than entertainment (e.g., cable television service and hybrid fiber optic/coaxial cable systems).

- All types of broadband telecommunications services, including Internet connections through very fast digital subscriber loop (DSL) offered by traditional carriers, LMDS and MMDS, and new third-generation PCS.

These new industries, which have opened up new digital pathways to businesses and the home, have also helped to stimulate so-called e-commerce, or businesses that sell their services and products directly to the consumer. By offering new and low-cost connection by means of the Internet to consumers, many traditional retailers are directly threatened. Despite these many changes in technology and the new, more openly competitive regulatory environment, many constraints remain, and new telecommunications systems remain in conflict with more traditional telecommunications networks.[11]

## TRENDS IN APPLICATIONS

Clearly, most of the rules in modern telecommunications have changed. The biggest change is that a competitive marketplace and consumer demand for applications rather than monopoly carriers have assumed the primary role in deciding what services will be provided. Almost everyone underestimated consumer demand for mobile telephone service, fax services, and especially Internet-based services. It is a mistake to assume that this diversity of choice among a highly competitive market brings only advantages. In fact, there are problems with consumer confusion and frustration and the lack of an effective safety net for poor and rural customers. Certainly, open competitive markets and the elimination of subsidies can limit or even eliminate special telecommunications and information services that respond to special needs, such as those of the blind, the hearing impaired, the elderly, and the handicapped or bedridden.

This new environment has given new primacy to ISPs such as AOL, MSN, and PSI. These changes have lessened the market strength of traditional telecommunications carriers such as AT&T, increased the size and importance of wireless and satellite services, and created instability in telecommunications markets around the world. The future will be defined by demand for broadband (i.e., broad bandwidth services that can accommodate multiple communication services requiring different frequencies and bandwidths), multimedia services, response to new demands from telecommuters and small or home offices (the so-called Soho market), and innovations in rural and remote telecommunications services. The altered status of large telecommunications carriers has led to mergers among the larger international carriers and acquisition of ISPs, cable television systems, and carriers seeking to cross over into Internet markets.

## TRENDS IN STANDARDS MAKING
## AND KEY INTERNATIONAL INSTITUTIONS

Thirty years ago the world within which telecommunications services were provided was dramatically different. Most nations had state-owned monopolies, and standards were agreed on by a small club of scientists and engineers from a select group of committees under the guidance of the International Telecommunication Union (ITU). The ITU, located in Geneva, Switzerland, is the most important international organization devoted to the regulation of telecommunications technology and services. It is a specialized agency of the United Nations and has nearly 200 members today; its Standardization Bureau handles technical standards issues of telecommunications technology and services for radio and terrestrial communications.

Today, the number of national and regional organizations engaged in standards making has increased greatly. This has resulted in a proliferation of global standards, because each region has lobbied for its own standard to become globally accepted. In general, there is the vertical, structured, and controlled philosophy of telecommunications carriers on the one hand and the nonhierarchical approach and philosophy of ISPs on the other.

The last decade has seen the greater empowerment of national and regional standards bodies, such as the Telecommunications Technology Committee of Japan, the American National Standards Institute of the United States, and especially the European Telecommunications Standards Institute and Asia-Pacific Telecommuting. The movement to create strong national and regional technical standards has made it increasingly difficult for single global standards to be created. For instance, in areas such as PCS we see that several regional standards are being accepted as part of a global standardization process.

The Internet and the World Wide Web, consisting of over 50,000 loosely linked computer networks, is more of a highly creative, fluid, and nonstructured process than a unified system. No single entity is responsible for the content or the accuracy or currency of information on the Internet—at once its greatest asset and its most difficult problem. This stands in stark contrast to the heavily segmented world of telecommunications, which includes strict standards for such services as integrated services digital network (ISDN) and broadband ISDN by means of asymmetrical transfer mode (ATM) telecommunications systems. In short, this loosely knit worldwide Internet Society is almost the antithesis of the ITU.[12] It is not surprising that there is a dispersion of authority from the ITU to groups such as the worldwide Internet Society, the Society for Worldwide Interbank Financial Transactions, the ISO, the International Electro-Technical Committee (IEC), and the Institute of Electrical and Electronics Engineers (IEEE).

## OTHER INTERNATIONAL INSTITUTIONS IN TELECOMMUNICATIONS

The expanding world of telecommunications and information continues to become more complex and to affect more aspects of our global society. Today, the linkages between telecommunications branches can influence virtually anyplace and can involve more that just international financing of telecommunications projects. Table 16.1 describes the international institutions that have a key relationship to international telecommunications and information technology.

In addition to the agencies listed in Table 16.1, a growing number of nongovernmental and governmental international and regional organizations coordinate, plan, or help standardize telecommunications. The most important of these were noted in the previous section, but there are hundreds more of these organizations, many of which are listed in the *Yearbook of International Organizations* and other similar reference works.

## COMPETITION AND REGULATORY RESTRUCTURING OF GLOBAL MARKETS

Since the 1984 divestiture of AT&T into the seven regional Bell Operating Companies (Ameritech, Bell Atlantic, Southwestern Bell, Pacific Bell, U.S. West, NYNEX, and Bell South), there have been sweeping changes in the world of global telecommunications services. The initial actions in the United States and the avalanche of change that followed in Japan, Europe, and other parts of the world triggered a major global trend toward deregulation, competition, liberalization, and significant internationalization of the telecommunications industry. These changes greatly increased the importance of free and open trade in telecommunications and international data networking.

Throughout the developed countries of the OECD over the past 18 years, the parallel processes of deregulation, liberalization, and competition have been occurring apace. New Zealand, the United States, Japan, and Europe have moved to eliminate monopolies, open telecommunications markets to competition, and streamline regulatory processes as market conditions have taken hold. Some countries, such as Australia and the United Kingdom, revamped their regulatory processes to create a small and streamlined unit that hands out stiff fines when they

**Table 16.1 International Institutions in Telecommunications**

| Organization | Field of Interest |
| --- | --- |
| World Intellectual Property Organization (WIPO) | Copyright, patents, and intellectual property |
| United Nations Educational, Scientific, and Cultural Organization (UNESCO) | Education, communications development, press, and culture |
| United Nations Development Program (UNDP) | Financing for communications and information development |
| World Maritime Organization (WMO) | Maritime communications and safety |
| World Health Organization (WHO) | Telehealth, telemedicine |
| International Civil Aviation Organization (ICAO) | Aviation safety and regulation |
| International Standards Organization (ISO) | Telecommunications, electronics, and information standards |
| International Telecommunications Union (ITU) | Regulation and standards for telecommunications, frequency allocation and registration, telecommunications development |
| Economic committees for Europe, Asia and the Pacific, and Latin America | Information, telecommunications, and intellectual services |

find dominant carriers trying to suppress competition in the marketplace but otherwise leave the running of telecommunications to the service providers. The aggressive support of procompetitive policies by the European commissions and their willingness to support new start-up telecommunications ventures against national carriers has fueled rapid telecommunications growth in Europe.

Perhaps the most important aspect of this transition in terms of open telecommunications trade was the agreement in the General Agreement on Trade and Tariffs to extend this international process from goods to services. Most profound of all was the agreement to create a United Nations agency called the World Trade Organization (WTO). The WTO, a specialized agency of the United Nations, was established to widen the patterns of competition and to broaden open access to national markets, but this is still an evolving and longer-term process.[13] The WTO created the new General Agreement on Telecommunications Services (GATS). The GATS has championed the cause of open and fully competitive international and national telecommunications markets. Participating countries have volunteered their individual plans to open their markets to competition and to allow foreign telecommunications services either to compete in local markets or to form partnerships with local firms.[14]

## NEGROPONTE FLIP VERSUS PELTON MERGE

There are two dramatically different views of the future of telecommunications: one shaped by technological constraints and the other formed by the market needs of the public. It has been suggested that increasingly narrow band services be placed on wireless media to support mobile voice and data service and that all

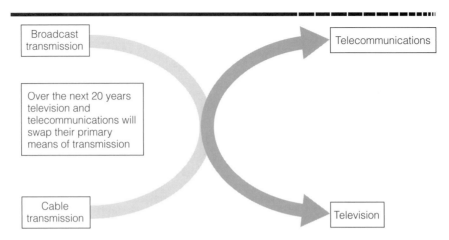

**FIGURE 16.5** Technology- or spectrum-driven forecast for the future of telecommunications and networking: Negroponte flip. Copyright © 2002 Joseph N. Pelton.

broadband services (especially television) be taken off the air and placed on cable systems because of the lack of spectrum. In light of the dramatic gains achieved in fiber optic–based transmission speeds as a result of monomode fiber optic systems and dense wave division multiplexing, the primacy of terrestrial cable for heavy route communications is certainly not in doubt. This conception that there will be limited broadband service available through wireless technology has become known as the Negroponte flip.

There is an alternative view of the future, however. This is that we will see a merger of wireless, satellite, and cable systems to handle all types of telecommunications demand, including broadband. Known as the Pelton merge, this view suggests that the marketplace is not neat or orderly and that the public will want broadband mobile services through satellite and wireless systems. These two views are shown in Figures 16.5 and 16.6. To date, the Pelton merge seems to predict actual marketplace behavior more accurately than the Negroponte flip. This is to say that wireless revenues are outstripping the growth of terrestrial cable revenues and that broadband wireless services, such as direct broadcast satellite services, are growing rapidly.

## SUMMARY AND CONCLUSIONS

Today, information is expanding 300,000 times faster than the world's population. Innovations such as the Internet, global satellite and fiber optic networks, artificial intelligence and expert systems, and large research institutes have increased exponentially. The speed and global scope of telecommunications development have in turn spurred the rate of world economic development, especially in the services industries. Of the many relationships that can be charted between economic

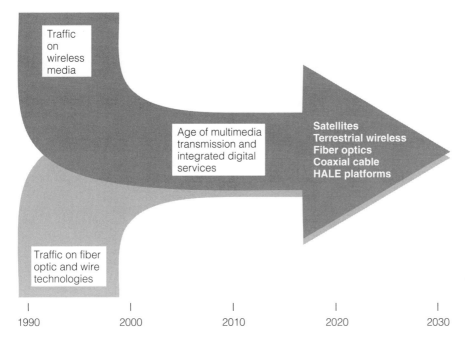

**FIGURE 16.6** Market- and standards-driven forecast for the future of telecommunications and networking: Pelton merge. Copyright © 2002 Joseph N. Pelton.

growth and development, the most consistent and proven one is the correlation between telephones per capita and gross domestic product per capita. In future years the correlation around the world between income per capita and personal computers, Internet access, and PCS units will chart the global conversion to an ever-wealthier information economy.

At the start of the twenty-first century telecommunications revenues are growing at record levels of more than 9% in many industrializing countries and 6–7% in developed countries. In contrast, the parallel growth of Internet and Intranet (localized Internet service that serves a corporation or an institution internally) traffic continues to increase at phenomenally high rates, with the usage increase exceeding 30% per year. Furthermore, the volume of traffic on private Intranets is approximately 10 times the volume sent on the global Internet system.

Further, the share of the global telecommunications pie being claimed by developing and industrializing countries is growing, whereas the share claimed by North American and European countries is actually shrinking. It is likewise true that Internet traffic is now growing considerably faster in the developed countries of the OECD.

Although telephone-related revenues continue to grow, it is the new data, video, multimedia, and other enhanced information services that are dominating new patterns of growth. Satellite and wireless local network technologies are allowing new and more cost effective solutions for rural and remote communications. The largest challenge of the next decade will be to develop effective and seamless global standards that will allow all types of transmission systems—fiber optic, coaxial cable, wireless, satellite, and even newer high-speed data transmission and networking platforms—to interconnect on a global basis and to respond to the dramatic new consumer and business demands of an information economy.[15]

These new demands will include widespread telecommuting, interactive entertainment, around-the-clock global business services, multimedia e-commerce support, intelligent information highways, enhanced tele-education and tele-health networks, automated air and sea navigation, enhanced surveillance and reconnaissance for military and civil justice applications, offshore business, automated and robotic manufacturing operations, universal personal telecommunications services (which will initially be known as IMT-2000), and much, much more. As the spread of broadband services and applications continues, several key trends will continue:

- The price of telecommunications and information access will continue to fall.

- Convergence will break down the market barriers between communications, cable television, consumer electronics, computer and information services, and content (i.e., entertainment, publishing, and software).

- Competition and deregulation will continue and thus will allow market economies to drive the economic and technological future of telecommunications. Meanwhile, there will be a return to certain types of governmental oversight in terms of control of radio and optical frequencies, the development of controls on e-commerce, increased attention to global technical and service standards, support for universal service funds, and new protections for personal privacy.

- Global trade will increase under new WTO guidelines and incentives and will, among other factors, aid rural and remote telecommunications and information development. If, as a part of this process, the North American Free Trade Agreement free trade group in the Americas and the Asia Pacific Economic Community should merge, this will particularly help telecommunications development in these regions of the world.

## NOTES

1. Joseph N. Pelton, *Wireless and Satellite Telecommunications* (Upper Saddle River, NJ: Prentice-Hall, 1996).

2. Yoshio Tusumi, "Keeping in Touch Internationally," *Communications Technology Decisions* 8 (autumn 1999): 10–14.

3. Samuel Pitroda, "Keeping the World in Touch," *Communications Technology Decisions* 12 (autumn 1999): 50–52.

4. Gregory Staple, *TeleGeography 1999* (Washington, DC: TeleGeography Inc., 1999).

5. Pelton, *Wireless and Satellite Telecommunications*.

6. Subcommittee on Computing, Information, and Communications Research and Development, *Information Technology Frontiers for a New Millennium* (Washington,

DC: National Science Foundation, 1999), 1–105.

7. Joseph N. Pelton, *The Wireless Industry and the Coming Personal Communications Service Revolution* (Chicago: International Engineering Consortium, 1997).

8. Stephen Morgan, "The Future of Wireless," *Intermedia* 28 (February 2000): 16–20.

9. Joseph N. Pelton and Alfred U. Mac-Rae, eds., *Global Satellite Communications Technology and Systems* (Baltimore: International Technology Research Institute, 1998).

10. Kevin Kelly, *New Rules for the New Economy* (New York: Viking Press, 1998).

11. Staple, *TeleGeography 1999.*

12. Stanley Besen and Joseph Farrell, "Choosing How to Compete: Strategies and Tactics in Standardization," *Journal of Economic Perspectives* 8 (1994): 117–131. Also see Pelton and MacRae, *Global Satellite Communications Technology and Systems.*

13. G. Wakefield, *The General Agreement on Trade in Services: The Telecommunications Pact* (London: Wilde Sapte, 1997).

14. Ibid.

15. Pelton, *The Wireless Industry and the Coming Personal Communications Service Revolution.*

# Index